The Creation of
NIKOLAI GOGOL

The Creation of
NIKOLAI GOGOL

—

Donald Fanger

THE BELKNAP PRESS
OF
HARVARD UNIVERSITY PRESS
Cambridge, Massachusetts, and London, England
— 1979 —

Library of Congress Cataloging in Publication Data

Fanger, Donald.
   The creation of Nikolai Gogol.

   Includes bibliographical references and index.
   1. Gogol', Nikolaï Vasil'evich, 1809–1852—Criticism
and interpretation.   I. Title.
PG3335.Z8F3   891.7'8'309   79-14135
ISBN 0-674-17565-4

To the memory
of
Frank I. Fanger

Preface

Nikolai Gogol is Russia's greatest comic writer. He is arguably Russia's greatest creator of prose. He inaugurated the so-called Golden Age of fiction in the nineteenth century and after that had run its course began a second life, re-viewed, as a crucial influence on the modernists of the twentieth. His genius was recognized early, and the recognition has been unwavering.

Under the circumstances, there are probably few descriptive observations to make about his writing that have not appeared somewhere in print. Yet large problems of interpretation remain, and they begin, I would suggest, at the level of formulation: we are still searching for the appropriate questions to ask of Gogol's refractory text, along with appropriate contexts in which to set it.

By and large Gogol studies, like their subject, tend to excess in the direction either of conventionality or of eccentricity, and so tend to leave some large portion of the singular phenomenon that goes by his name unaccounted for. The eccentric view is especially prevalent in American and European criticism today—an understandable reaction against the civic-pietistic view traditional in Russia. But its legitimate work has now been done. Surely we need no longer be ironizing over the formulations of Belinsky and his heirs, which so often treat the texts cavalierly (when they treat them at all); better by far to try to understand such reactions as historical facts. Nor does anyone need to prove again that Gogol was—among other things—queer, crafty, and devious both as man and as writer. What seems in order, rather, is a study of the function *and the limits* of those qualities in his work, an attempt at comprehension rather than further exercises in casual, exclamatory, categorical, hyperbolic, or paronomastic criticism.

For these reasons I have tried consistently to avoid the terminology that informs most Gogol studies to date—"realist," "romantic," "tragic," "grotesque," and so on. Like Major Kovalyov's nose, such terms have tended to take on an autonomous life of their own and to become part of the problem they purport to be confronting. It seemed more promising to start from an observation made by the poet Nekrasov three years after the publication of *Dead Souls.* Gogol, he found, "unquestionably represents something utterly new among creatively gifted personalities"; therefore "the bases of our judgments about him must be new ones." Nekrasov hoped that a new generation of writers would take up and extend the pioneering work of Gogol and, in the view of most observers of Russian fiction less than ten years later, they had done just that. But the bases of judgment which *their* productions required proved inapplicable to the achievement of their putative father without the most painful kind of forcing, and Gogol's work accordingly remained respected and read but unexamined for most of the rest of the century. As late as 1909 Andrei Biely, who was to produce one of the most brilliant book-length studies of the writer, could declare with reason: "We still do not know what Gogol is." Gogol, he recognized, "is a genius who cannot be approached with schoolboy definitions." Stressing the elusive nature of that genius, he added: "I have a tendency toward symbolism; consequently, it is easiest for me to see the traits of symbolism in Gogol; a romantic will see the romantic in him; a realist will see the realist."

What calls for explanation here is the nature of a body of work that can so easily accommodate—and escape—such differing labels. For the case is less one of rich complexity than of what we might call complex primitivism. We still do not know what Gogol is; he seems, in Max Hayward's phrase, "protected by an indeterminacy principle which excludes or frustrates any single approach." It is clear, however, that any effort to answer the question while respecting the intricacies of the phenomenon under observation must avoid terms that might prejudge it—must become, in some sense, an exercise in applied phenomenology, where the interaction itself is constantly scrutinized, examined, and justified.

So the book falls into four parts, the first of which attempts to characterize the uniqueness of what I have called the Gogol problem, and then to sketch the specifically Russian cultural context, all too often neglected, in and against which the Gogolian oeuvre evolved. The second and third parts trace the exfoliation of that oeuvre, Gogol's step-by-step self-improvisation as a writer. Individual texts are considered chiefly with a view to defining their distinctive contributions to this process—those unique elements or emphases they add to the developing body of his work. In no case is the aim to give a complete critical account; rather it is to characterize each as succinctly as possible in terms of artistic function, so that the main lines of an emerging pattern may stand out the more clearly. This needs particularly to be borne in mind in connection with the discussions of *The Inspector General,* "The Overcoat," and *Dead Souls,* his supreme masterpieces, whose comic texture is at once their most prominent feature and the one least dwelt on in these pages. A number of critics (among them Slonimsky, Eikhenbaum, Chizhevsky, Gippius, and Nabokov) have made the most important points in this respect; my relative silence on these matters should be construed as a sign of respect for what they have accomplished and a desire to complement their findings through other interrogations.

The historical approach essayed here, mixing broadly sociological concerns with literary concerns proper, can, I believe, help fix the Gogolian phenomenon in a pragmatic way and illuminate both the nature and the extent of the achievement it represents. But that achievement clearly transcends its historical context. Gogol is as immediate a contemporary presence today as he was in his lifetime—and an international one, despite the fact that he may lose more in translation than any other Russian prose writer. So in Part Four of this book ("The Surviving Presence") I attempt to confront directly the irreducible core of art which survives the world from which it drew its materials—to account for the peculiarities of the medium that carries (and largely constitutes) Gogol's enduring poetic message. Originally conceived as an independent inquiry whose congruity with the first was far from certain, this turned out to reveal a pattern of thematic concentricities which appeared, quite unbidden, to suggest an image of wholeness. In pursuing these matters I have made no effort to be exhaustive, but have tried rather to find the simplest minimally adequate formulation in the most generally valid terms—because the nature of Gogol's writing, to the (large) extent that it resists such an effort, only underlines thereby the need for it. Under sustained scrutiny his best works often show a trompe-l'oeil effect: what seemed background a moment before can appear suddenly as foreground, stable masses turn fluid, vaguenesses crystallize momentarily into clarity, and perspectives that seemed to be receding evince a disconcerting salience. The result is that Gogol's reader is constantly invited to descry larger meanings and the outlines of different, more cogent artistic messages than a particular text can be shown to sanction. When the invitation is textually explicit, it must be accepted—but accepted for what it is: the sign of no more and no less than an eternal virtuality. I have tried throughout to distinguish the responses Gogol's text seems clearly to authorize from those it seems to authorize unclearly—and to give primacy to the first. Observing the distinction can explain why so much Gogolian interpretation has an arbitrary ring, by showing how regularly these texts tempt the interpreter to make unwarranted assumptions, extrapolating from ambiguous cues.

Given the nature of the task and of the material in question, a certain circularity is inevitable in its working out. What Ortega said of the *Quixote* applies equally to the Gogol problem: it will not yield to frontal assault, but must be taken like Jericho. Repetitions in the pages that follow are thus likely to be deliberate; what look like discrete points in the smaller circles reappear as segments of the larger ones and disclose different meanings in different contexts. The purpose of these maneuvers—reflected also in the organization of the book—is to preserve as far as possible the *dimensionality* of the Gogol phenomenon. Viktor Frankl explains the methodological concept in question:

A phenomenon, say, a cylinder, projected out of its own dimension— *i.e.,* three-dimensional space—down into different dimensions lower than its own, for example into horizontal and vertical planes, yields pictures that are *contradictory* to one another. Here we get a circle and here a rectangle . . . What is more, if you imagine this cylinder to represent a tumbler, an open vessel, the openness of this vessel completely disappears in the projections into lower dimensions. The circle as well as the rectangle are closed figures rather than open vessels. ("Nothing But—: On Reductionism and Nihilism," *Encounter,* November 1969, pp. 54–55.)

Any kind of analysis involves such projections, but the risk of falling into reductionism—taking a single aspect as the chief or only important one, assuming finally that a thing is *nothing but* something else—becomes particularly acute when dealing with a career and work as irregular as Gogol's. Some valuable studies have been written of Gogol as rectangle, others of Gogol as circle. My aim has been, by a plural approach, to respect the singleness of the phenomenon. Thus the successive projections in the pages that follow. The object—the Gogolian text—I have construed broadly to include not only the projects he published (articles, fiction, drama) or began with a view to publishing (drafts and variants), but the voluminous correspondence as well. Taken together, they represent the evidence of his continuous self-creation—and, as he claimed more than once, the only life he had.

In the tracing of that self-creation certain large questions are implicated: Gogol and the rise of Russian fiction; Gogol and the model of the nineteenth-century Russian writer; the function of literature in society (so much more interesting than the reverse); modal and generic problems of comedy, satire, and irony; and ultimately the theory of fiction itself. All come in for recurrent attention; each might organize a different book; none has been allowed to dominate here. To echo Ortega once more: *Doy lo que tengo; que otros capaces de hacer más hagan su más, como yo hago mi menos.*

D. F.

Acknowledgments

THE PREPARATION of this book has involved a great many occasions for gratitude—

To institutions: The Inter-University Committee on Travel Grants, Stanford University Center for International Studies, Howard Foundation, American Council of Learned Societies, Russian Research Center at Harvard University, Guggenheim Foundation, Christian Gauss Seminars at Princeton University.

To expert helpers: Sergei Belov, Phyllis Reed, Joseph Brenckle, Joan Murach, Alison Arsht, Laszlo Dienes, David Sloane, Betty Forman, Beth Holmgren, Jan Nattier-Barbaro, Judy Hitchcox.

To generous colleagues and patient friends, whose reading, writing, and conversation contributed crucially: Bayara Aroutunova, Edward J. Brown, Vera S. Dunham, Victor Erlich, Efim Etkind, Joseph Frank, Henry Gifford, Stephen Gilman, Max Hayward, Michael Holquist, Roman Jakobson, Simon Karlinsky, Ivo J. Lederer, Harry Levin, Stephen Lottridge, Hugh McLean, Georges Nivat, Krystyna Pomorska, Laurence Senelick, Vsevolod Setchkarev, Harry Shukman, Andrei Sinyavsky, Jurij Striedter, Kiril Taranovsky, Andrzej Wirth.

To Saul Steinberg for quite exceptional kindness.

And to Margot, Steffen, Ross, Kate, who bore the daily brunt.

SEGMENTS of the text have appeared under the imprint of Mouton ("The Gogol Problem," in Michael S. Flier, ed., *Slavic Forum,* 1974); University of California Press ("Dead Souls: The Mirror and the Road," *Nineteenth-Century Fiction,* June 1978); Stanford University Press ("Gogol and His Reader," in William M. Todd, ed., *Literature and Society in Imperial Russia, 1800–1914,* 1978).

Contents

PART I
Approaches

1 The Gogol Problem: Perspectives from Absence   3
2 The Sense of Absence: Immediate Contexts   24

PART II
Improvising a Vocation

3 Beginnings: Miscellaneous Writings   47
4 Beginnings: Fiction   85
5 Confronting a Public, I   125

PART III
Embracing a Calling

6 Epic Intentions   145
7 Dead Souls: The Mirror and the Road   164
8 Confronting a Public, II   192

PART IV
The Surviving Presence

9 The Gogolian Universe: Notes Toward a Theory   229
10 Sense, Shape, End   257

Notes   267
Index   297

Подколесин: Но признайтесь: верно, вам покажется странным то, что я вам скажу?

Агафья Тихоновна: Помилуйте, как можно, чтобы было странно,—от вас все приятно слышать.

Подколесин: Но этого вы никогда не слышали.

Женитьба

Podkolyosin: Tell the truth: what I'm about to tell you will seem strange, won't it?

Agafya Tikhonovna: Don't be silly, how could it be strange? Everything you say is pleasant to hear.

Podkolyosin: But you've never heard anything like this.

Getting Married

On Transliteration

Since a knowledge of Russian is not prerequisite to the reading of these pages, the text presents Russian names and terms in their most phonetically accessible or most familiar guise.

Documentation is a different matter. There the aim is to allow unambiguous reconstruction of the Cyrillic original, and for that the international scholarly system of transliteration is clearly preferable.

I have tried to follow this double standard consistently.

PART I
———

Approaches

———

Ou l'écrivain existe-t-il en effet avec le plus de vérité,
sinon dans la somme concrète de ses livres?

Jean-Pierre Richard

1

The Gogol Problem:
Perspectives from Absence

The Gogol problem is coterminous with the whole complex phenomenon that goes by the name of Gogol—the life, public and private; the mind and temperament; literary views and filiations; the sense of separate writings no less than of the whole they comprise. It already baffles approach on the simple descriptive level, where even the attempt to marshal pragmatic evidence of the usual sort quickly founders on dubieties or incompletenesses, reinforcing that air of enigma which has surrounded Gogol and his work from the beginning.

"Truly," the future author wrote shortly before his nineteenth birthday, "I am considered a riddle by everyone . . . At home they consider me capricious, some kind of unbearable pedant who thinks he is smarter than anyone, that he has been created differently from other people . . . Here [at school] they call me humble, the ideal of meekness and patience. In one place I am the most quiet, modest, courteous; in another, melancholy, pensive, uncouth, etc.; in a third, garrulous . . . with some clever, with others stupid . . . Consider me what you will, *but only once I have embarked on my real career will you come to know my true character.*"[1]

Fourteen years later, he had more than embarked on his real career; he was celebrated as the creator of *Dead Souls, The Inspector General,* and all the artistic work he would publish in his lifetime. He had avoided or renounced all commitments save the commitment to his art—that is, to a continual self-improvisation, of which he eventually wearied but which he could not escape. In his last difficult decade he was to exclaim more than once that he had "no life outside literature," thereby stressing the extent to which his identity itself was a work in progress, indistinguishable from the

3

continuation of *Dead Souls*. Only the fulfillment of that project, he insisted, would finally solve the riddle of his existence (XII, 58). Ten years later, most of the long-promised, once- (perhaps twice-) burned manuscript of Volume Two was burned again (by mistake, he said); ten years of the life (excepting one fiasco, *Selected Passages from Correspondence with Friends,* which needed to be redeemed by the progress of his novel) were canceled; and his death, clearly not without suicidal intent, followed quickly, turning the riddle permanent.*

What made the fact momentous was its extraordinary social resonance. Gogol's drawn-out identity crisis as an author runs parallel to a cultural identity crisis in Russia (and one that carried, inevitably, political implications). He quickly became a cynosure, crystallizing an unprecedentedly broad public. So, when he died in 1852, there was a general sense that a greatness had passed from the scene whose explanation lay in the future. Ivan Aksakov said as much in an obituary notice that alarmed the Minister of National Education: "A great deal of time must still pass," he wrote, "before all the deep and weighty significance of Gogol is fully understood—Gogol, that artist-monk, Christian-satirist, ascetic and humorist, that martyr of the exalted ideal and the unsolved riddle." Why, the Minister inquired nervously in a secret letter, should so much time be necessary to grasp Gogol's significance fully? "Can the writer of this article really think that this significance is so unfathomable that none of our contemporaries is in a position to form a clear understanding of Gogol from his works?

---

* He did, it is true, hint at least at a partial solution which he said he had prepared as a posthumous gift to his fellow-countrymen. *Selected Passages* opens with a testament, and there he wills them "the best of all the things that my pen has produced . . . my composition entitled 'A Farewell Tale' (*Prošćal'naja povest'*)." It would reveal to them "if only in part the strict secret of life and the most sacred heavenly music of that secret." He was reserving publication, he explained in a footnote, because what could have significance after the writer's death has no sense during his lifetime (VIII, 220–222). "A Farewell Tale" was apparently never written—and Dostoevsky did not hesitate to brand Gogol's references to it as *vran'yo* (prevarication). Gogol, he suggested, here and elsewhere, was an early version of his own "underground man." It was "that same underground nature, which made Gogol, in a solemn testament, speak of a final tale which had sung itself out of his soul—and which in reality did not exist at all." Dostoevsky goes on to suggest that when Gogol began writing his testament he may not even have known that he was about to mention a "final tale." See V. V. Vinogradov, *O jazyke xudožestvennoj literatury* (Moscow, 1959), pp. 398–399.

And why is such a deep and weighty significance attributed primarily to Gogol?"[2] The grounds for official nervousness here
came alike from the potency of Gogol's work and from its unclear
purport—from the fact, as Prince Vyazemsky noted at the time,
that "everyone saw in him what he wanted to see, and not what
was really there."[3]

Several factors combined to make this possible. There was the
enigmatic nature of many of the works themselves—and in the
work as a whole the unreconciled presence of contradictory elements, any one of which might plausibly be emphasized at the expense of the others and so proclaimed the key. There was the
awareness of a continuing development, bound in its unpredict-
ability to contain surprises—but, as it turned out, deprived of a
terminus by which to measure and assess the journey. There were
the passionate preoccupations of ideological parties, each anxious
to claim Gogol as example and ornament, if not as spokesman.
There was, abetted by the mystifications of the writer and man, a
sense of fundamental mystery. And yet the most sensitive literary
minds had agreed, from the mid-thirties on, that Gogol was a phenomenon of the first importance.

Pushkin himself had greeted Gogol's first collection of stories
(in 1831, when Gogol was twenty-two) as something so uncommon as to constitute an event in Russian literature.[4] Belinsky went
even further four years later, claiming the young Gogol as a literary and social phenomenon of the first order, and naming him heir
to the place Pushkin had allegedly vacated, not only the hope but
the *head* of Russian literature.[5] *Dead Souls,* while still an unknown
quantity, was nevertheless awaited with impatience by the literate
Russian public. The same air of expectation, progressively more
burdensome to its author, was to hang undissipated over the
promised Volume Two of *Dead Souls* throughout the 1840s; and
Gogol's strangest book, *Selected Passages from Correspondence with
Friends,* which appeared in 1846 to appease that expectation,
proved an event of a kind unprecedented even in its author's career.

What sympathetic contemporaries consistently agreed on, in
short, was the novelty and importance of what Gogol was doing;
the particular nature of his achievement, though quarreled over,
tended to go unanalyzed. This is not surprising: it is the usual contemporary response to writers, and in Gogol's case it took added

force from the fact that a widespread cultural demand found in his work a single source of supply. The process of satisfying a need does not—for a society any more than for an individual—tend to be accompanied by a passion for analysis.

The nature of that need is the subject of the next chapter; but it is important to note here the inevitably limiting effect it had on the way contemporaries received Gogol's work. Put most simply, Russia was awaiting an artist who would, through the creation of new prose forms, provide works in which a broad public could find the basis for a sense of collective cultural identity. Supplying that need meant inaugurating a new phase in the cultural and literary life of the nation—but that development, once it had been successfully initiated by Gogol, doomed him to speedy supersession. When *Dead Souls* appeared in 1842, Pushkin and Lermontov were dead, and Gogol seemed more than ever the sole hope of Russian literature;[6] yet just four years later, two collections, *The Physiology of Petersburg* and *The Petersburg Miscellany,* had assembled early works by Dostoevsky, Turgenev, Nekrasov, Herzen, Grigorovich, and others; Belinsky was acknowledged to have "erected a new journalistic university" to help form and educate a public for these writers."[7] By the end of 1852, the year of Gogol's death, Goncharov, Tolstoy, Pisemsky, and Saltykov had made their appearance in print, completing the roster of names associated with the so-called golden age of Russian fiction and forcing even an unsympathetic critic to recognize that a new realistic literature, "philanthropic," "social," and "civilizing" in tendency, was beginning to flower.[8]

So rapid a development only intensified the tendency to label the Gogol phenomenon instead of examining it. The endless citation of Dostoevsky's apocryphal statement, "We all came out of Gogol's 'Overcoat'," typifies this tendency—particularly considering that the story in question was scarcely noticed by reviewers when it appeared in 1843 and occasioned little serious critical discussion throughout the rest of the nineteenth century. Instead, the Gogol label was made a banner in the 1850s, by a group of critics whom Gogol would assuredly have deplored and who cited Belinsky on Gogol much more than they ever cited Gogol himself. Under this banner they waged a successful cultural battle against a more esthetically oriented party whose banner carried the name of Pushkin. The result was to install in a position of cultural dominance a politically radical and philosophically utilitarian criticism that proved enormously influential in the development of the Russian intelligentsia, despite the fact that it was basically indifferent to literature, taking the texts of the latter as pretexts for preparing social change. Thus one image of Gogol was enshrined: Gogol the realist, fighter for freedom, progressive unmasker of autocracy and the serf-owning system, compassionate spokesman for the little man. It can be seen in the statue Stalin had erected in Moscow on the centenary of the writer's death: tall, serene, and smiling, "the great Russian artist of the word" stands with a book in his hand, as if welcoming the bright dawn of a better day.

This view of the citizen-writer remained dominant in Russia until the end of the century, when the symbolist revaluation of the literary past led to a fresh look at Gogol's writing. Annensky, Merezhkovsky, Bryusov, Biely, Blok, and Rozanov among others tended to bypass the whole debate over Citizen Gogol and deny the primacy of conventional, material "reality" in his work. Instead they stressed its extreme peculiarities. These had been noted before, but only incidentally. Where the civic tradition had followed Belinsky in seeing Gogol's art as rendering reality with absolute and faithful fullness, Bryusov in a famous lecture of 1909 (to scandalized cries of "Enough!" "Shame!") elaborated on the constant hyperbolic tendency that permeated both the life and the work, so that the man emerged as a mass of quirks and the work as a long exercise in artistic deformation.[9] Annensky explored the nature and results of that deformation, and even its afterlife in Russian literature; Merezhkovsky in his book *Gogol and the Devil* portrayed him as the artist of one constant tragic theme. And Biely, who was later to give Gogol's texts their most sustained scrutiny to date, (*Gogol's Artistry*, 1934), observed the centenary of the artist's birth by sketching a new view of him as visionary, insisting on the unique and historically precocious nature of the Gogolian genius. It is this symbolist image of Gogol that inspired the other Moscow statue, unveiled in 1909, discarded by Stalin and restored after his death, if not to pride of place at least to coexistence with the one he favored. Designed by the sculptor Andreyev, it depicts the writer seated, an enormous traveling coat like a shawl or loose winding sheet over his hunched shoulders, his head inclined. Every detail suggests a passionate inwardness, the invincible sadness of a man who contemplates the life passing before and beneath him—while around the pedestal, in a symbolically appropriate bas-relief, the grotesque characters of his creation reenact the routines that define them.

These two—the civic-realist and the visionary-symbolist— are the chief critical "icons" in the history of Gogol's reputation in Russia. To them must be added some memorable interpretations from the point of view of Orthodox religious thought, Freudian psychology, and Formalist criticism, most of which incline to tendentiousness as well, achieving their best results by excluding large aspects of the Gogolian text and thus avoiding the need for crippling qualification. This is not the place to attempt an interpretive survey of Gogol criticism in Russia, but any listing of the problems of approaching him must include, on the extrinsic side, the continuing absence of such work.[10] The successive views of Gogol as put forth by his more articulate readers—even today—constitute a process of reaction and counter-reaction, often unacknowledged, which has a momentum all its own, at times relegating the ostensible object to a quite secondary role. This process continues to keep Gogol criticism off balance. In some sense the victim of history during his lifetime, he has remained a victim of history ever since.

THE "GOGOL" signaled here is a hybrid abstraction, biographical-textual, in the same way that generalizations about "Tolstoy," for example, are likely to involve an image of the sage of Yasnaya Polyana in peasant blouse and boots, the qualities of the man merging with those of the works—and legitimately, since a continuing relation between the two can easily be demonstrated. The thematics of any single Tolstoyan work relate it not only to other Tolstoyan works but to the same themes in the diaries and letters, and in a whole library of memoirs. The illumination is reciprocal in the deepest sense, the drama of a life taking on deeper interest because of the stature of the writings that arose from it, the writings achieving added resonance from our awareness of their genesis in that uncommon corner of the world of common experience. The creation of major art, particularly since the advent of romanticism, confers a significance on the person of the creator, invests him with an exemplary quality of vision and thought if not of wisdom, stimulates a curiosity about the transmutations of consciousness and experience from life into art.

Here too, however, Gogol's case proves anomalous, and if there is a lesson to be drawn from the consideration of life-and-works, it comes from the impossibility of performing the usual critical operations. Both terms reflect the qualities of his genius in their gravitation to the fragmentary, the grotesquely proportioned, and the unresolved. This can be seen in particular writings no less than in the work as a whole. One can hardly speak fruitfully of periods in his work, for example, or hope to clarify much by approaching him in terms of creative development.

To be sure, his first published work and his last, separated by eighteen years, are as different from each other as they could be—but they also stand radically apart from the bulk of his central achievement. *Hanz Kuechelgarten,* published in 1829, is a long, jejune poem subtitled "An Idyll in Pictures"; *Selected Passages* (1847) is a patchwork of moral, social, and literary essays, couched in epistolary form and offered after five years of silence to a public clamorous for the second volume of *Dead Souls. Selected Passages* is rather more complex than the view of it that became traditional after Belinsky's impassioned rebuttal. But the point here is that each of these works in its own way represented a blind alley for Gogol, a mistaking of his essential talent.

Leaving them aside, then, we find that all the rest of Gogol's writings were published in an intensely productive eleven-year period, from 1831 to 1842. Of these, the years 1831–1836 (up to his departure from Russia) are those of the greatest variety; here he tries his hand at all the forms of prose then being practiced: short stories from an operatic Ukrainian past (*Evenings on a Farm near Dikanka,* 1831–32) ostensibly continued in *Mirgorod* (1835); essays —lyrical, historical, esthetic, pedagogical—most of them collected in *Arabesques* (1835); stories from contemporary Russian life (some in *Arabesques,* some in periodicals); book reviews and literary journalism of a very high order; stage comedies (*The Inspector General,* early drafts of *Getting Married,* several fragments); not to mention weighty works on history (Ukrainian and universal) and geography.* From 1836 to 1842, he eschews journalism and concen-

---

* None of the latter seems actually to have been undertaken. But his announced interest in this kind of writing was more than grandiloquence. He did produce the draft of a textbook of literary forms in 1845 (see *PSS,* VIII, 468–488), and was still collecting materials for works on geography and lexicography late in his life.

trates almost exclusively on *Dead Souls* (together with reworking some of his earlier pieces for the *Collected Works* of 1842–43); his novel and "The Overcoat" are the masterpieces of these years and quite overshadow the few narrative and dramatic efforts, most of them fragmentary, to which he also turned. He was twenty-two when the first volume of *Evenings* came out and made his reputation as a writer; he was thirty-three when *Dead Souls* and the *Collected Works* were published, and his slow, silent, self-inflicted martyrdom began.

Clearly he did develop, but the *process* of that development (as opposed to the direction) is not clear because of his working habits. "He did not move," as one of his critics observes, "from one work to another but rather, as it were, in a single drawn-out moment embraced at once the whole sum of his artistic ideas—and then, fitfully turning now to one project, now to another, returning again to the early ones and at the same time polishing the new ones, suddenly appeared to history entire, in all his greatness." [11]

Other conventional lines of approach are hardly more fruitful. The vexed question of his literary filiations, for example, is the subject of an enormous monograph by a man whose surname—Chudakov—seems to vouch for his qualifications in something like the way the name of a student of Dickens' style—Randolph Quirk—does for his. [12] (Chudakov might be Englished as Quirk.) Despite all the painstaking scholarship that has gone into the question, the fact remains that there are few clear facts. We know that Gogol was familiar with the work of the Russian poets of his time —but he wrote in prose. We know that he read Richardson's *Clarissa,* because he says so in a letter; we know that he read a novel by Dickens in 1840 or 1841, because a Moscow professor caught him in the act in a Roman café. But we have no reactions to either of these—and, with respect to the foreigners from whom he said he drew inspiration, no evidence of first-hand knowledge at all.* His 1500-odd letters have much to say about his moods, am-

* In a characteristic passage from a draft of *Dead Souls,* Chapter XI, he mentions looking up from his desk occasionally, to regard the portraits hanging on his wall—"of Shakespeare, Ariosto, Fielding, Cervantes, Pushkin, who reflected nature as it was, and not as someone or other may have wished it to be" (*PSS,* VI, 533). Save for Pushkin, neither the letters nor the essays betray signs of direct acquaintance with works by any of them. This, of course, does not settle the question but only shows its intractability.

bitions, and fluctuating creativity—but almost nothing about literature itself, Russian or foreign, in practice or in theory. Despite the similarities Helen Muchnic has noted, then,[13] he is no Flaubert with respect to the articulations of artistic consciousness. His correspondence gives us little notion of his reading, knowledge, tastes, or even specific awareness of literature in the forms he himself cultivated. As a result, these areas remain all but empty categories, among so many others in the Gogol phenomenon.

As FOR the temperament and the life, the more scrupulous the attempt to deal descriptively with them, the likelier it is to be studded with question marks, pockmarked with perhaps, and all but vitiated by conscience-induced gaps. The man was secretive, and though alarmed at what he took to be misinterpretations of his work, he did little to help his contemporaries understand its novelty or what he took to be his intentions.[14] Those whom he did admit to a kind of intimacy found themselves, so to speak, in small rooms that did not communicate; thus the most useful memoirs—Aksakov's, Annenkov's, Smirnova's—give convincing but often contrasting pictures, and the key that would reconcile them is missing. One side of this problem may be illuminated by two categorical statements Gogol made on the subject of sincerity, together with one probable example of it. "You will believe my sincere feelings, won't you?" he writes to Rayevskaya on 25 June 1840: "I do not know how to lie" (XI, 190). On 14 December 1844, however, he confesses to Shevyryov: "I have absolutely never been able to speak frankly about myself" (XII, 394)—a frank generalization that contains the grounds of its own Gogolian undoing. It may well be that both statements are true in this sense: in speaking of himself Gogol could never be sure whether he was lying or telling the truth. He "confessed" to Smirnova that his relations with literary friends and confrères had always been based on his calculation about how each of them could be useful to him, from which he divined "just what could and could not be said to each"; for a variety of somewhat contradictory reasons, he said he had never spoken of his personal plans or of what related personally to his fate (XII, 433).

In short, Gogol's few attempts to speak frankly in his letters were all attempts to speak *about* frankness, and one feels in them the anguished desire of a man bewildered by his own chronic evasions and mimicry to find his "real" voice and discover what it might have to say.[15] Beginning already with the later drafts of *Dead Souls,* Volume One, he assumes the authoritative tones of the prophet; his last book, *Selected Passages,* is written entirely in that vein with few conscious concessions to the perspectives of artistry. This voice, he thought, was that of his very soul, expressing its noblest concerns, inspired by God. But in the fiasco that followed publication Gogol was forced ruefully to recognize that the devil had tricked him; that he had chosen only the least effective of that "orchestra of voices"[16] which had produced his best narratives; that indirection and implication were his only effective tools; that he was, however drawn to stable identity and single truth, condemned to approximations.

"I never created anything through imagination," he said (VIII, 446). But he also complained that Pushkin had failed to perceive that the characters which so depressed him in the first draft of *Dead Souls* were all "caricature and my own invention" (VIII, 294). "I cannot say categorically," he wrote late in his career, "whether the writer's field is my field" (VIII, 438), but he also protested that it was as necessary for him to write as to breathe. One could make a long list of such contradictions, and see precisely their presence as signaling the Gogolian authenticity. It seems likely, in other words, that elusiveness was more than a deliberate tactic with him, that it was also an essential trait of his being. The motif of evasion, after all, is central in both the life and the work—and Gogol seems to have failed only when he canceled out the grounds of his genius by trying to evade that fact. Such a perspective from absence, indeed, may allow the most fruitful connection of the life to the work, and of both to the cultural situation in which they took their course.

For the life itself is scarcely tractable in biographical terms, showing as it does an astonishing paucity of experience. This must be understood in a special sense. The period from roughly 1830 to 1836 was not only the time when most of his works were written or conceived; it was the time, as well, of his maximal engagement in the life of Petersburg. He was, often simultaneously, writing stories, plays, lectures, essays, and reviews. He worked as private tutor and lecturer (later professor) in history; he took lessons in painting at the Academy; he visited theaters and followed the magazines; he cultivated the acquaintance of Pushkin, Zhukovsky, and other leading figures in the literary world. In short, the life (like the works) of these years show all the signs of having been a sustained series of energetic tentatives in several directions at once —an affair in which constant motion took the place of any of the usual continuities in a man's life, and tended to mask their absence. This is no more than appropriate when a young man is finding himself; what makes the case "Gogolian" is that the conflicting tentatives were not resolved but simply abandoned for a dozen years of European expatriation (punctuated by two disturbing returns to Russia, in 1839–40 and again in 1841–42). Since the causes of his decision to flee Russia are unclear, that decision itself cannot offer a perspective on the events that preceded it—and if we seek illumination of the works from the record of the life, the best we can do is to register the frequency with which the works show a similar abruptness and apparent discontinuity, taxing our sense of adequate form and clarity of viewpoint.

In any case, from this point on, dedication to the work in progress largely drains the biography (as opposed to the career) of visible content, manifesting something like that "trope of fictiveness" which Andrei Biely saw as underlying *Dead Souls:* the specification of featurelessness, the bodying forth of an absence. In all those years, as before, no scandals, no duels, no arrests; no wife, no mistresses, no sex—"no first-hand knowledge of all those involuntary relationships created by social, economic and political necessity . . . Some writers have spent their lives in the same place and social milieu; [he] kept constantly moving from one place and one country to another. Some have been extroverts who entered fully into whatever society happened to be available; [his] nature made him avoid human contacts as much as possible. Most writers have at least had the experience of parenthood and its responsibilities; this experience was denied [him]." The words are Auden's, describing D. H. Lawrence, and the conclusion he draws can apply to Gogol's case, in the late letters and *Selected Passages:* "It was inevitable, therefore, that when he tried to lay down the law about social and political matters . . . he could only be negative [or naive—D. F.] and moralistic because, since his youth, he had had no firsthand experiences upon which concrete and positive suggestions could have been based."[17]

Even financial necessity could not bind him. His income came only from being a writer, but not exclusively from writing itself. He mentions money fairly frequently in the letters and makes it

clear that sales of his works brought in amounts that were insufficient. He was often nearly penniless and made to realize, as he
wrote in a letter of the late thirties, that a writer actually could die
of hunger. Yet he never became a proletarian, never was forced to
those desperate expedients that left so deep a mark on Dostoevsky's life and art. He was guarded from this by a series of subventions from the Tsar and "loans" from admirers of his talent—a
situation made possible on the historical side by the fact that the
professionalization of letters was only beginning in his time and,
on the personal, by the fact that he had nothing beyond his talent
and a frail body to support.

His only needs were for writing and travel, but even the record of his travels cannot be very usefully related to the writings.
He did not visit new places to observe, to describe, or to learn, as
Tolstoy was to do; his journeys through Europe were neither a
cultural pilgrimage nor a flight from creditors, as they were to be
for Dostoevsky; nor was Turgenev's mixed political and sentimental motivation for expatriation in any way paralleled in his
own. Gogol seems to have chosen new places to visit for their cli-
mate or the presence of well-recommended doctors and well-born
compatriots. The journey itself often counted more than the desti-
nation, change of place being a spiritual tonic for him, so that
when he left Rome or Naples, Paris or Vienna, Ostend or Baden-
Baden, he was not so much abandoning a place as resuming a condition.

Evasion being so prominent a feature of the life as of the
works, both must appear hermetic, unapproachable except in their
own enigmatic terms, closed to the application of external norms
or data. Most of his voluntary relationships were guarded and calculated; the crucial involuntary ones—and they are astonishingly
few—seem all to have been with his own divided psyche. He did
not come to define himself through being bound in some continuing experiential way to class or politics or place, and if he was a
slave to his body, he contrived to be that in the one way that could
not further his self-knowledge through experience of another: hy-
pochondria, centering on the digestive system.

There is, in short, no record of meaningful personal experience either as material for the art or as alternative to it, so that the
only clear relation of the biography to the works becomes paradoxical, resting on shared motifs of absence, ambiguity, and lack

of resolution. Gogol did, to be sure, speak of his works in their succession as representing the history of his soul, but it is hard to find two separately discussable entities in that formula; and neither in his retrospective tracings nor in his fiction itself is there much to suggest that he saw individual experience as a progress or a process. Change he recognized and portrayed, but most often as abrupt metamorphosis, carrying overtones of the uncanny and hinting at some radical instability in the order of things. Only in *Dead Souls* did he undertake to show a life changing through time; the part containing the attempt is the part he never considered satisfactory enough to give to the world.

Gogol's last and highest aspiration was to wisdom, but even here he could see no necessary connection with experience:

He who already possesses intelligence and reason cannot receive wisdom except by praying for it both night and day, entreating it of God day and night, elevating his soul to the mildness of a dove and ordering everything within himself to the utmost purity in order to receive that heavenly guest who shuns dwellings where the spiritual household has not been put in order and where there is not full harmony in everything. (VIII, 265)

Not Blake's road of excess—and not any road at all—will lead to the palace of wisdom; one receives wisdom as a gift. There seems to be a suggestion that one must desire it, but there is no question of earning it actively through engagement with circumstance and one's fellows.

In light of all this, it is not surprising that the major biographical works in Russian seem to confess defeat by the very qualifications of their titles: two years after Gogol's death, P. A. Kulish published "An Attempt at a Biography of Gogol"; revised and expanded, it was published as "Notes on Gogol's Life." The most ambitious work, in four volumes, is Shenrok's no less tellingly entitled "Materials Toward a Biography of Gogol"; and the most influential in this century (serving as chief source for Nabokov's work, among others) has been V. V. Veresayev's "Gogol in Life" —a massive dossier (or "montage," as the form was called in the twenties and thirties) of uncommented and unreconciled documentary excerpts. One may fill in the gaps with supposition—the most serious such attempts are Konstantin Mochulsky's "Gogol's Spiritual Path" (*Duxovnyj put' Gogolja*) and Simon Karlinsky's *The Sexual Labyrinth of Nikolai Gogol*—or one can take the documen-

tary collections as a kind of do-it-yourself kit for the construction
not of a biography, but of a *context* for the eternally absent life. For
a positive center we must turn to that life which Gogol proclaimed
from the late thirties on to be his only one: his writing. In that area
and that area only will we find sufficient material for a study of this
elusive pilgrim's progress: a study of a *career* and the pursuit of a
vocation. History, moreover, lends such an inquiry a particular
sanction, for in working out a model of the writer's calling, quite
as much as in the fiction he produced, Gogol turned out to be a
pioneer, his improvisations the starting point of a tradition.

THE ABSENCE that recurs on so many levels of the Gogol problem,
then, is a given. But even as it closes off conventional avenues of
approach, it opens others—in the first place, that of a nontradi-
tional kind of literary history which avoids the usual rubrics and
catalogues of names to investigate the literary function as it existed
in a given time. Boris Eikhenbaum provided the key here nearly
half a century ago when he observed that "the question which
troubled Gogol all his life was . . . *how to be a writer and what it
meant to be a writer.*"[18] This must be understood as referring to
something beyond the personal discovery of vocation that faces
every writer; for Gogol, the question was nothing less than the *invention* of a vocation. "I have had no other guides than myself, and
can one alone, without the help of others, perfect oneself?" (X,
122). Gogol asked the question with regard to the lyceum education he was just completing at nineteen in 1828—but he might
well have repeated it twenty years later, when his artistic career
was effectively over. Others, in fact, repeated it for him, among
them Belinsky, who noted in 1848 that "Gogol had no model and
no precursors, either in Russian or in foreign literature."[19]
     One tends so readily to associate Gogol with the great age of
prose he introduced that it can come as something of a shock to
consider the nature of the cultural situation he entered, characterized as it was by a sense of absence and concern with the radical
possibility of literature. Yet this situation not only had practical
consequences of a fundamental sort for Gogol's work; it may well
have been the making of him as an artist. For if his genius lay in the
way he managed to turn lack of experience and relationship into
the positive center of his art, it was nonetheless his historical fortune to have done so at a time when absence and stasis could be

taken, by those preoccupied with them in other forms, as social and cultural commentary of the profoundest and most necessary sort.

"The more ordinary an object is," he wrote in an early essay, "the greater a poet one must be to draw what is extraordinary from it" (VIII, 54). In most of the fiction and drama he subsequently produced he showed the truth of this observation. Small wonder, then, that in surveying his completed career he would cite with pride Pushkin's comment that "not a single writer had had the gift of exhibiting so clearly the *poshlost'* of life, had known how to sketch with such skill the *poshlost'* of the *poshlyj* person. There you have my chief quality, belonging to me alone" (VIII, 292). This Russian word has been so memorably and lengthily elucidated by Nabokov ("the obviously trashy," "the falsely important, the falsely beautiful, the falsely clever, the falsely attractive") that we may do well to recall that *poshlost'* was only beginning its career of semantic and morphological proliferation in Gogol's time. The Dictionary of the Russian Academy in 1822 omitted it, and the Academy dictionary of 1847 offers these two contemporary meanings (along with two archaic ones): "1) Low in quality, quite ordinary, of little significance. *The* poshlyj *painting in the picture betrays the youth of the art.* 2) Low, simple (*prostovatyj*). Poshlye *speeches.*"[20] Without disputing the more elaborate connotations later found in Gogolian *poshlost',* we may best interpret the term as locating Gogol's main talent in the vivid exhibition of the ordinary in characters and their life styles, an ordinariness which, being low in quality, common, and of little significance in life, constitutes a special challenge to the artist who would endow its representation with high poetic value.

In fact, it was his concentration on *poshlost'* that led contemporaries to dub Gogol a realist, by which they meant a poet of unvarnished and neglected "reality." However misleading the terms, the designation clearly had a basis in his art. We may prefer to speak, with Gogol himself, of caricatures, and we may prefer to emphasize the imperishable poetry over the vanished "reality." Still, the fact remains that in his most original works—"Ivan Fyodorovich Shponka and His Auntie," "Old-World Landowners," the story of the two Ivans, most of the Petersburg Tales, *Getting Married,* "The Carriage," *The Inspector General, Dead Souls*—the caricatures are of recognizable types and milieux, treated *as objects worth attention in their own right* and not simply assigned an ancillary role in some more conventional scheme of values. Never had they been contemplated with such thoroughness; never had character and milieu been so intimately and totally expressive of each other. (Here, too, the simplifying approach of the caricaturist was likely to be confused with the social-organic awareness of the "realist.")

It would be misleading to speak of themes in this connection. What is in question is a certain intensity of attention to a certain "low" level of life as material for art. "Only that came out well," he wrote retrospectively in "An Author's Confession," "which I had taken from reality, from data known to me. I could only divine the man when the smallest details of his exterior were present to me" (VIII, 446); the process is described at length in the opening of Chapter 6 of *Dead Souls,* where the author describes how he used to drive through provincial towns, scrutinizing things and people and "following them in thought, into their poor life" (VI, 110). The common forms of this poor life (the adjective in the first draft is *poshlyj*) attracted Gogol's relentless attention, and a large share of his best work is a demonstration of the artistry that could "draw the unusual from it." This operation can be called a matter of vision only if we agree with Malraux that the style precedes and creates the vision. "I never *drew* a portrait," Gogol wrote, "in the sense of a simple copy; I *created* a portrait" (VIII, 446). But he insisted that this was only possible when he had seen the original in nature. Creation was thus a kind of alchemy whereby the base stuff of the world that met his gaze was transmuted into something precious. The word was "God's highest gift to man." And not only the word: "One marvels at how precious our language is: every sound is a gift; everything is grainy, tangible (*krupno*), like the pearl itself, and indeed it may happen that the name is even more precious than the thing itself." (VIII, 231, 279).

Dostoevsky would fill his notebooks with psychological observations and ideas for his novels, Tolstoy with what had filled his days, Chekhov with situations. Gogol—who seriously considered compiling a dictionary—filled his with lists of words: names for objects or activities or people whose attraction lay in precision, or sonority, or both. Combining them, he exploited these gifts of sound, and not infrequently he drew the unusual out of everyday, conversational words by the unexpectedness of his juxtapositions. If his characters are seldom lifelike in the sense that they resemble people one might meet in life, they are both vital and memorable in their speech. Indeed, many of the Gogolian vulgarians are, as George Ivask has noted, "great wordsmiths" whose human insignificance is redeemed by the verbal artistry they deploy and incarnate.[21] The reader who looks to the content of Gogol's fictions for experiential value of any kind, for lessons learned or illustrated, is bound to come away disappointed: Gogol's most successful characters seldom aspire, achieve, change, or learn. But such a reader is looking in the wrong place. The stories are, in Gogol's own word, exhibitions; they are also, as Eikhenbaum pointed out, performances. And it is in the brilliance of the narrative performance, in the management of those grainy words, that a peculiar and dynamic play of experience can in fact be found. The significant relations in a story like "The Overcoat" are less between Akaky Akakievich and his tailor, or his fellow clerks, or the Important Personage himself, than they are between the author and his story, on the one hand, and between the author and the reader on the other. The problematics of the story of Akaky Akakievich (himself so little capable of being problematic) lie in the fluctuations of tone and point of view, in the shifting mix of mockery and pity, by which he is presented.

"But what is strangest, what is most incomprehensible of all, is how authors can choose such subjects. I confess, that is utterly baffling, that is as if . . . no, I don't understand at all . . . And yet, when you think it over a bit, there is after all something in all this." That is the narrator at the end of "The Nose," questioning his own narrative, forcing the conclusion that irony is at work here —but witholding the key, the norm that underlies it. "Why Major Kovalyov?" Why, for that matter, Shponka or Chertokutsky, the "hero" of that monument to emptiness, "The Carriage," or so many others?

The answer is: as pretexts, as grounds for a performance that would turn common materials into the stuff of art. Gogol asserts in Chapter 7 of *Dead Souls* that "a great deal of spiritual depth is required to throw light upon a picture taken from a despised stratum of life, and to exalt it into a pearl of creation." He uses the image more than once—and he could hardly have found a more apt one for his own practice.* Like pearls, his works were produced and polished by a process of gradual accretion and embel-

---

* Cf. Flaubert: "Rien ne s'obtient qu'avec effort; tout a son sacrifice. La perle est une maladie de l'huître et le style, peut-être, l'écoulement d'une douleur plus profonde." *Correspondance*, III (Paris: Conard, 1927), 342.

lishment, their starting point one or another detail from a despised stratum of life. His characters and their situations are progressively revealed through the addition of another and yet another translucent, nacreous verbal layer, rather than by linear development.

Sergei Aksakov reports in his memoirs how in 1850 Gogol read the first chapter of *Dead Souls,* which the Aksakov family had heard many times before but which now seemed even better, as if totally rewritten. Pleased with this impression, Gogol told them: "That is what is meant by a painter's putting the finishing touch to his picture. The corrections appear to be absolutely minor—here a little word removed, there added, in another place transposed—and the whole thing turns out different. The time to publish is when all the chapters have been so touched up." Vasily Rozanov, who cites this passage, goes on to suggest that Gogol's literal uniqueness lies precisely in this genius for combining words. The figure of Plyushkin he calls astonishing, not because the conception is in any way original but because the artistic execution so patently is. *Dead Souls* appears to be made up of "pages like other pages," Rozanov notes, "only the words are somehow set up in a special way. How they are set up is a secret known to Gogol alone. For him words were some sort of immortal spirits; somehow each little word knew how to say what it had to, and to do what it had to. And once it's gotten inside the reader's skull, you can't get that word out with steel pincers."[22] Biely's analytic studies bring him to the same conclusion and his subject's own metaphor: Gogol, he finds, "opens up techniques of writing undiscovered by anyone else, saturating the verbal texture with a rain of popular, colloquial, occupational, and local words, polished into pearls of language. People had spoken like that here and there, but no one had written that way."[23]

Gogol's material, then, was of secondary importance in the generation of his art; the important thing was that it should lend itself to elaboration. He frequently used incidents from life as starting points, and what he made of them was inversely proportional to their intrinsic interest ("The Carriage," "The Overcoat"). He badgered his literary acquaintances for anecdotes that he might elaborate into stories, plays, or episodes for his novel—something to wrap his creative energy around. "Do me a favor," he writes Pushkin, "give me a subject, if only some anecdote, funny or unfunny, but purely Russian. My hand is itching to write a comedy the while" (X, 375). *The Inspector General* came from one such favor, *Dead Souls* from another.

It was not knowledge *of* but knowledge *how to* that produced the results—a point Russian readers were slow to grasp. Indeed, a prominent academician created something of a scandal in 1913 by publishing an article entitled, "Gogol Absolutely Did Not Know Real Russian Life," in which he demonstrated that the author of *Dead Souls* had spent a total of no more than forty-nine days in the Russian provinces, most of them inside a carriage.[24] This was scandalous because Gogol continued to be revered for having given a faithful depiction of provincial life in his novel—when in fact what he had done there was to evade lifelike proportions and clarity of statement to body forth an emptiness, a collection of illusions, at best a virtuality. His ignorance of rural Russia, his lack of personal experience, and his avoidance of the unsolved problems of fictional form were all enabling factors in the bodying forth, whose very existence turned out to have the greatest possible public validity. The brilliance of his linguistic performance and the sureness of the symbolic intuitions that guided it made manifest and palpable the absences so many Russians had been deploring, and turned them into a presence capable of provoking further developments.

Gogol's achievement was as nearly as possible to demonstrate the power of a medium without a message: to offer a literary prose as pure potential and to bring together in the process a new audience for it. His best works are all self-reflexive and ultimately "about" the nature of their own literary being. That is the great Gogolian theme—the possibility of literature, the freedom and power of writing to affirm its own material existence in the very registering of absences. In that sense Gogol's work positively invites the formula Shestov misapplied to Chekhov's: "creation out of nothing."

2

The Sense of Absence:
Immediate Contexts

Gogol left Russian literature on the brink of that golden age of fiction which many deemed him to have originated, and to which he did, clearly, open the way.* The literary situation he entered, however, was very different, and one cannot understand the shape and sense of Gogol's career—the peripeties of his lifelong devotion to being a Russian writer, the singularity and depth of his achievement—without knowing something of that situation. In an important sense it defined his opportunities and set their limits; it provided specific terms for his ambitions as well as obstacles to their working out; it influenced his own view of his work no less than the views of his readers. (His paralyzing notion, to take one example among many, that all of Russia was hanging on his words in 1842 has a considerable basis in fact: there was simply no serious competition, and Belinsky spoke for more than his ideological party when he told Gogol in that same year, "You are now *the only one* among us."[1]) Aspects of that situation, moreover, inform the very structure and themes of his art, most radically in the way the latter takes on existence by teasing the question of its own possibility, nature, and purport.

---

* Not single-handedly, of course. It has been convincingly argued that the foundation on which the fiction of the Russian golden age was built is tripartite, consisting of Pushkin's *Eugene Onegin* (1823–1831) and Lermontov's *Hero of Our Time* (1840), as well as *Dead Souls* (1842). Gogol's contribution, however, coming last, completed the foundation; it was also most directly connected with the incipient realism of the late 1840s, the work of the so-called natural school. See Waclaw Lednicki, "The Prose of Pushkin," in his *Bits of Table Talk on Pushkin, Mickiewicz, Goethe, Turgenev and Sienkiewicz* (The Hague: Martinus Nijhoff, 1956); A. G. Cejtlin, "Russkij obščestvenno-psixologičeskij roman," in his *Masterstvo Turgeneva-romanista* (Moscow, 1958), pp. 5–60.

For this ramifying question dominated the intellectual life of the 1820s and 1830s in Russia. Throughout the period it was alternately being posed rhetorically and answered by events; the 1820s show, roughly speaking, a predomination of rhetoric over events, and the 1830s the reverse. When conventional literary history deals with this period, it tends to concentrate rather on the esthetic theories, mostly of German origin, that exercised serious minds in Petersburg and Moscow. Gogol himself imbibed many of their tenets—about the sublimity of art, its ennobling of nature, the rights of genius, and so on;[2] they were in the air. But far more significant than what he (or any of his contemporaries) thought they thought about such matters were their concerns as expressed on a more pragmatic level, by word and deed.

THE SWELLING chorus of complaint begins to be heard in the early 1820s. "We have neither literature nor books," Pushkin writes in 1824 in a note entitled "On the Causes Impeding the Development of Our Literature." The following year Polevoy, in the first issue of the *Moscow Telegraph,* refers to the Russians as "barely having begun to write and study, children in literature."* In 1825, Bestuzhev concludes from his "Glance at Russian Literature During 1824 and the Beginning of 1825" that the general law of cultural (he calls it natural) development does not apply in Russia: "We have criticism but no literature." Vyazemsky, who had written in 1822 that "we are rich in the names of poets, but poor in creations," added a year later that "judging by the books that are printed in Russia, one might conclude either that we have no literature, or that we have neither opinions nor character." And Venevitinov, about the same time, was calling the edifice of Russian literature "illusory," and the situation in the literary world "completely neg-

---

* For this reason he went on to question the possibility of filling a journal exclusively with Russian works: "Would it not be better, instead of proposing to publish only Russian works and filling it for the most part with schoolboy prose and poetry, to widen the framework and give the readers not Russian work alone but simply everything of an elegant, pleasing and useful nature that can be found in the domestic, as well as in all the ancient and modern literatures? How much there is of interest that is still unknown to us—the sort of thing that a European absolutely has to know!" *Moscow Telegraph,* 1825, no. 1, "Letter to N. N."; quoted in N. K. Kozmin, *Očerki iz istorii russkogo romantizma* (Saint Petersburg, 1903), p. 23.

ative." In a letter to the editor of the *Moscow Herald* (1828) Pushkin refers to "our infantile literature, which offers no models in any genre," and two years later the fifteen-year-old Lermontov indicates in his notebook what this can mean for a beginning writer: "Our literature is so poor, that there is nothing I can appropriate from it." In 1832 Kireyevsky declares Russian literature "still a baby which is only beginning to speak purely," while the critic Nadezhdin, with grateful wonder, acknowledges a few poetic blooms "amid the general void and barrenness." In 1834 Pushkin returns to his theme, now ten years old, projecting an article under the title: "On the Insignificance of Russian Literature." Belinsky begins his career as a critic in the same year by sounding the same note.[3]

The list of such complaints could be easily extended. Despite variations in emphasis, most observers of the literary scene in this period agreed that they were contemplating, if not an absolute void, then at least a general absence of criticism as well as literary production. "Do we have any criticism?" Pushkin asked rhetorically in 1825. "Where is it, then? Where are our Addisons, La Harpes, Schlegels, Sismondis? What have we discussed? Whose literary opinions have become part of the Russian consciousness? Whose criticism can we refer to, or base ourselves on?"[4] The best that could be said of the literary situation near the end of the 1820s was that it showed signs of an activity that might take a promising direction. Thus Odoyevsky in a letter of 1828: "Some sort of frenzy has possessed our journalism. You [Polevoy] will sneer at this, for the new journals promise little that is good . . . but I view all this with delight. I forget about who is writing and what is being written; I see only that ink is being expended, paper is being used up, compositors' benches are groaning, and in the best circles of society there is an interest in Russian literature and people are reading at least the announcements of Russian journals. I see that schools are proliferating, a Pedagogical Institute is arising with a department of philosophy in it . . . and I repeat with enthusiasm that all this, taken together, is what is called activity!"[5]

Odoyevsky's optimism is exceptional for its time, and revealing in its implications: how small and few are the blessings that suffice to stir his gratitude. What is most striking in his view is the sense of awakened expectation—and that, of course, is the burden of all those sad discussions in the twenties and thirties of the lack of a Russian literature to discuss.[6]

Put most simply, what observers missed was a collective national *voice*. What it might utter, no one could guess; the stress was on instrumentality. The voice, once discovered, would find its roles—would learn how, in Gogol's phrase, to "give us our very selves" (VIII, 186). Indeed, its authenticity would be proved by its ability to do just that. So long as journals (whose number began to increase dramatically in the mid–1820s) had to rely willy-nilly on translations or on native works that were clearly derivative and inferior, there could be no visible basis for cultural pride or a sense of national identity that went beyond the formal, governmental one. And the voice that educated Russians were listening for had little to do with official nationality (*nacional'nost'*); it would rather be the organic expression of intrinsic nationality (*narodnost'*)—a quality deemed to be outwardly expressible only through art, and through the art of the word first of all. People had finally become convinced, Pletnyov wrote in a dreary but representative piece called "On National Character in Literature," "that the true and real history of a people is its literature, all of it, studied in all its epochs."[6] Pletnyov, who in 1833 can name as contemporary spokesmen for the Russian national spirit in literature only Krylov and Karamzin, betrays no uneasiness over this state of affairs; but his smug conservatism does lend his testimony a particular ironic value.[7]

More forward-looking in his development of this question was Ivan Kireyevsky, who devoted to it two manifesto articles in the first number of his brilliant but ill-starred journal, *The European* (whose title is as significant as that of Pushkin's *The Contemporary*) for 1832. Combining desciption and prescription, Kireyevsky sees the tendency of recent literature as being "to accommodate imagination to reality," "the finish of artistry to the depth of naturalness." "The taste of our time," he concludes, "demands something new, something lacking in previous writers, something for which a true poet has still not appeared." The majority of the reading public is "a half-educated crowd," for whom beauty is a secondary value even in poetry; the first thing that crowd demands is "relevance to the current moment."[8]

This sense of a novel and more popular art about to be born is not unique to Kireyevsky; where he is most original and prescient, however, is in the specification (through careful Aesopian language) of the particular social role reserved for the new Russian literature. He is, I think, the first to formulate it—but, as modern Russian literature took shape, some such consciousness must have weighed on all the serious writers who contributed to it; and none could have been more vulnerable to the implied responsibility than Gogol, in his role of lonely pioneer.

In no other country, Kireyevsky writes, does current literature have the importance it does in Russia. Elsewhere, he goes on to explain, "matters of state, absorbing all minds, serve as the chief measure of their enlightenment"; in Russia, by contrast, "the indefatigable solicitude of a far-seeing Government frees private individuals from the necessity of concerning themselves with politics, and thus the sole index of our intellectual development remains literature.* That is the reason why in Russia not only literary men but every citizen of his fatherland must follow the progress of literature."[9]

THE ABSENCE of Russian literature was the absence of an institution; the absence of the institution argued an incompleteness in society, of which that institution was to be an expression. Yet the very complaint was itself a beginning and, taken up by more and more voices, turned finally into a Kulturkampf on whose battleground the institution came eventually to be erected. By about 1830, it was becoming clear that the battleground would be one of prose. This was the medium of competition for a broader reading public; it was also the medium for the principled criticism that might aid in the formation of writer and audience alike. The frequent complaints about the lack of a Russian prose in this period thus referred, not always clearly, to a range of interconnected problems: lack of a mature and flexible instrument, of a normative native style, of examplary genres and techniques in fiction—this

---

* Here, incidentally, is one important key to that peculiar triangle of misunderstanding involving Gogol, his works, and his readers. Profoundly unpolitical, Gogol tended to act in conformity with the literal meaning of Kireyevsky's proposition—that is, to concern himself increasingly with the moral and spiritual state of Russia. Many of his readers, however—among them Herzen and Belinsky— saw his work in the light of Kireyevsky's *coded* message and applied to it the same decoding technique, transposing from the level of literature to the level of potential sociopolitical comment, while the censorship, representing the "indefatigable solicitude of a far-seeing Government," kept them company.

last finally subsuming the others because of its almost unlimited elasticity, European achievements having already legitimized a view of the novel as incorporating "epic and drama, lyricism and philosophy, all of poetry in its thousand facets, all one's age from cover to cover."[10]

For such tasks the language of the salons on which Karamzin had based his stylistic reform at the end of the previous century was clearly too constricting. The majority of Russian writers, Orest Somov declared in 1828, "either wander off the road into the rough fields of the archaic Slavonic-Russian language, or slip and fall on the ruins once heaped together from alien stocks (Gallicisms, Germanisms and so on), or else sink in the base and swampy ground of the coarse, unrefined language of the simple folk."[11] Pushkin had put it plainly: "scholarship, politics and philosophy have still not found an expression in Russian; a metaphysical language is absolutely nonexistent among us. Our prose is still so little developed that even in simple correspondence we are obliged to *invent* turns of phrase to convey the most ordinary concepts."[12] The point was echoed repeatedly. "We need," wrote academician Sokolov, "not poets but people who can manage to write correctly and clearly in prose: we have neither an epistolary nor a business style."[13]

One of the chief reasons for this situation clearly had to do with the cosmopolitanism of the educated classes—with the fact, as Marlinsky noted, that "we have been brought up by foreigners, and have drunk in with our mothers' milk non-Russianness [*beznarodnost'*] and admiration only for what is foreign."* The result is derivativeness: "There was a time when we were misguidedly wont to sigh in the manner of Sterne; then we took to being amiable in French; now we have flown off into Never-Never land in the German manner. When will we find our proper sphere? When will we write straightforwardly in Russian? God knows!"[14] By 1832, when the early fiction of Pushkin and Gogol had already been

---

* Uvarov, author of the notorious formula, "Autocracy, Orthodoxy, Nationality" (*Samoderžavie, pravoslavie, narodnost'*), himself spoke Russian with difficulty, that language being in disfavor at the court and not very popular in high-society conversation. It was the linguistic purist Admiral Shishkov who translated into Russian the proclamations that had been offered to the Tsar for his signature in French! A. Koyré, *La Philosophie et le problème national en Russie au début du XIXe siècle* (Paris, 1929), p. 11n1.

published, Belinsky's first mentor, Professor Nadezhdin, could still depict Russian prose as a tower of Babel, "a confusion of all the European idioms that have overgrown in successive layers the wild mass of the undeveloped Russian word."[15] The general condition of Russian prose, described by Marlinsky in 1825 as a "steppe, occasionally enlivened by the swift passage of journalistic Bedouins or ponderously moving caravans of translations," was to persist for two decades before a major wave of settlement began.[16] In the late twenties and early thirties this steppe was, to be sure, visited by flashy and eccentric soldiers of fortune like Marlinsky himself; patent-medicine men like Bulgarin and Senkovsky; sympathetic reporters like Pavlov, Pogodin, and Polevoy (who wrote short stories informed by pity for victims of social injustice); ethnographers like Dahl; prospectors in search of the philosopher's stone like Odoyevsky. Some of them even prospered—Marlinsky was by all accounts the most popular practitioner of fiction in the thirties—but their tracks were soon covered by dust. Significantly enough, the most popular among them proved precisely those who cultivated stylistic innovation and experiment. Thus Dahl wrote of his own work: "It was not the stories themselves that were important . . . but the Russian word, which is so hemmed in by us that it could not appear in public without a special pretext and occasion—and the story provided the pretext." This lexical foregrounding, which later led Dahl to compile a great dictionary of popular speech, was shared in his own way by Osip Senkovsky, whose puns and word-play did much to make him the most widely read journalist of the 1830s. As for Marlinsky, his garrulous and mannered prose found this justification: "I want to and do find the Russian language ready for anything, able to express anything. If this is a fault in me, it is also my merit. I am convinced that no one before me gave Russian phrases such variety."[17]

The first to survey this landscape with an eye to permanent building was Pushkin, and he did it as a conscious response to his perception of the Zeitgeist. From 1830 until his death in 1837, he wrote increasingly in prose, trying his hand at practically every form then extant—the essay, critical and familiar, travel notes, history, biography, parody, historical novel, short story; he even set up as editor of a journal, *The Contemporary*. Historically considered, the virtues and limitations of Pushkin's prose style derive from its being a poet's (*not* a poetic) style; the economy of form and purity of diction and guiding intelligence—all signs of its masterful *intentionality*—are enlisted to do the work that verse could not.[18] Russian prose, like all modern prose, was later to prove imperialist; Pushkin kept it on the drill ground. The nature of that drill, the *strategy* of that training, is what concerns us in this contextual sketch—and of this, two projected works may offer the handiest example.

Both were conceived as responses to Faddei Bulgarin's enormous success with his didactic-satirical-picaresque novel, *Ivan Vyzhigin*—which was announced and excerpted in the periodical press of 1829 under the title, *A Russian Gil Blas, or the Adventures of Ivan Vyzhigin.* More important than the fact that Bulgarin was appropriating the title of an earlier "Russian Gil Blas," written by Narezhny, is the attempt in both cases to appropriate the prestige of Le Sage's work, to suggest that the achievement of a major French writer had been duplicated in Russia and that the muse of fiction (if one had existed) now qualified for Russian residence.[19]

Pushkin's response was double. On the one hand, he announced a lampoon of his own entitled, "The Real Vyzhigin: A Historico-Didactic-Satiric Novel of the Nineteenth Century"—making fun not only of Bulgarin's form, but also identifying the central rogue with the creator of Vyzhigin. Here with particular clarity we see one of Pushkin's main fictional tactics: the deflation, via parody, of an established convention. "Vyzhigin" is false coin, though current; Pushkin will literally debase it by offering his "real" Vyzhigin. (The same sort of play with conventions of plot and language is evident in more than one of the stories of the Belkin cycle; it is a ground–clearing operation in the domain of Russian prose.)

The other form of Pushkin's response was to project a long novel under the title of "A Russian Pelham." The reference here is to a novel of Bulwer-Lytton's—*Pelham, or The Adventures of a Gentleman* (1828)—seen as a *roman de moeurs,* depicting the life of just that sort of aristocractic circle to which Pushkin himself belonged. In this case, the strategy is plainly one of adaptation, of Russianizing (and perhaps deepening) a foreign model, foreign types, foreign conventions.[20]

What makes Pushkin's plans typical should be obvious even from this very sketchy exposition. A poor "Russian Gil Blas" provokes a parody—a literary work about a literary work based on literary work; it also provokes the plan for a counter-example—

the real thing, after the false thing: but even the real thing must point in its title to another literary work. To Bulgarin's Russified Blas, Pushkin plans a salvo from behind his own Russified Bulwer. The point is that Pushkin's experiments with prose were highly conscious and principled ones, conducted by a professional on literary materials, and (as his finished prose makes clear) informed with an awareness that a whole range of problems (from formal and generic to syntactic and lexical) remained to be worked out before the instrument might be applied as the times seemed increasingly to require.[21] The result was to invest much of his fiction with an aura of stylization, other literary presences tending to loom more or less distinctly through the translucent character of his writing. So those who were scanning the horizon for a "prose-poet of Life" continued to do so—until they found him in Gogol. Like Pushkin, but free from the distractions of erudite literary awareness, Gogol saw the need for experiment and improvisation (thus his reference in 1836 to "all the present-day *attempts* at novels and stories"); like Pushkin he was concerned with the problematic *possibility* of an artistically serious Russian fiction. But where Pushkin's pursuit of this problem was mediated by existing literature, Gogol's turned out to be unmediated and radical: he borrowed freely, but only to assimilate and transform past recognition.[22]

BY THE early thirties the absence of a Russian literature was generally construed as a qualitative absence—in the first place of novels and stories, which Belinsky had by now identified as the dominant forms of poetry, seconding Ivan Kireyevsky's opinion that the age of verse had passed, and that the spirit of the times was marked by "a prosaic quality, empiricism (*položitel'nost'*), and a general . . . aspiration to practical activity."[23] Quite disparately inclined observers concurred, finding fiction "the signboard of contemporary literature," abundant enough to provoke a fear of perishing from a flood of stories and "narrating ourselves and our contemporaries to death."[24] Fiction of a sort, then, was flourishing —but for reasons too little removed from those that had made it popular around the turn of the century, when Karamzin had found novels "captivating for the large part of the public, engaging its heart and imagination . . . Not everyone can engage in philosophy or put himself in the place of the heroes of history, but everyone loves, has loved or wants to love, and so identifies with a romantic hero."[25]

Gogol himself reviewed such a novel, published in 1836 by one M. Voskresensky and entitled *He and She.* There are now three kinds of novels established in Russian literature, Gogol begins,

fifteen-ruble novels, almost always thick, long, solid, in four parts of about 300 pages each; other novels of the middling sort, eight- or six-ruble novels, also on occasion in four parts, though they may also come in two . . .

The novel under consideration belongs to the first sort; that is, to fifteen-ruble novels, although the author—as is evident from the opening pages—is often impatient and cannot sit still or occupy himself for long with a single character. Nothing has remained in my head from a reading of half of the first part. There is only a recollection that some count and some student or other roam around the streets of some city, perhaps Moscow, get Katya and carry her off, then again get Katya and again, it seems, carry her off. For the rest, whoever wants can read it himself and find out what happens after that. (VIII, 199–200)

An alternative to *He and She,* reflecting the themes made popular by Scott and Vigny, is *The Founding of Moscow, or The Death of the Boyar Stepan Ivanovich Kuchka, A Historical Novel Taken from the Times of the Princedom of Izyaslav Mstislavovich,* by one I . . . K . . . v, also published in 1836 and reviewed by Gogol:

One of those novels of a kind of which very many are being published, especially in Moscow. Their plot is usually taken from the history of the fatherland. They are usually skinny, thin little things, but divided into four parts, and sold very cheaply . . . The author usually makes his heroes speak in the style of Russian muzhiks and merchants, because over the last ten years . . . the thought has arisen that our historical figures and, in general, all the heroes of the past must without fail speak the language of present-day simple folk and emit as many proverbs as possible. In the last two or three years, the new French school . . . has exerted its perceptible influence even on them, occasioning some exceptionally strange phenomena in our novels. Sometimes a Russian muzhik will come out with such a theatrical piece of business as even a Roman wouldn't venture. He will arise from his pallet or from his stove and set out with the tread of a Napoleon; some Vasily, Ulita, or Stepan Ivanovich Kuchka will, after demonstrating some Russian gesture or emitting a folk saying, suddenly bellow, "Death and damnation!" In another place the reader is prepared for two muzhiks to roll up their sleeves and start punching each other, but instead he sees that they have cast dark glances at one another and !! here the author usually places a few dots, adding: "and they understood each other." Or sometimes he will even add: and in that silence there took place a terrible drama and that sort of

thing . . . The general character of these little novels, which are multi-
plying so quickly and so abundantly in Russia, is utter childishness. It
would be most unfair for us to say that they display only stupidity, as our
journalists often reproach them for doing. Not at all, not stupidity, but
the creation of the most immature child, who is engrossed now by one
thing and now another, who wants both this and that: no constancy.
(VIII, 201–202)

It may seem unfair to cite such pitiful specimens with the implication that they are in any sense typical of the level Russian fiction had achieved; the unfairness is a relative matter. The best
novels of the period—those of Marlinsky, Veltman, and Zagoskin
—could only be praised with faint damns. Thus Pushkin's reply to
his friend Vyazemsky, who had criticized a novel of Zagoskin's for
lacking truth in thought, feeling, and situation: Pushkin agreed but
felt obliged to emphasize "that the situations, although strained,
are interesting; that the conversations, although false, are lively;
and that the whole thing can be read with pleasure."[26] Readers of
Russian fiction had, at least until the forties, to be grateful for small
blessings.

Unsolved technical problems were manifold. Boris Eikhenbaum has shown how, aside from the enormous problem of language itself, writers in the 1830s were beset with questions about
how to handle exposition, how to manage transitions between
scenes, and so on.[27] The utter childishness which Gogol found in
simplistic historical fictions had its counterpart even among more
serious writers in the form of a widespread and naive primitivism,
alike of construction and of the narrator's relation with the reader.
This is the burden of an article published by Odoyevsky in *The
Contemporary* for 1836. Entitled "How Novels Are Written
Among Us," it observes how "A diffuse muttering has turned into
a general cry, 'prose, prose,' because, despite all the multiplicity of
novels, 'we are poor, all but paupers, in original works of this
genre.'" What is the sense of this poverty amid apparent plenty?
Odoyevsky explains:

Many among us think that one can write a good novel without the poetic
vocation. An honest, honorable man has lived long enough in society; he
has seen much of good and bad; his heart has been shaken at the spectacle
of injustice, his mind has been horrified by the spectacle of absurdities; he
has stored away in his head a multitude of experiences, of observations,
of anecdotes: how good it would be to communicate all this to other
people! *But how can he connect the materials he has collected, one to the other?*

It is hard, Odoyevsky says, even for a clever man to write a moral treatise. So what does he do?

He takes the first event that smacks of fiction to come into his head, and pastes all his thoughts and observations, like patches, onto it; he foists his thoughts on the characters he has introduced; whether to the point or not, he tells the little stories he knows.

Such people seek "not words for their characters, but characters for [their] words." As for readers, the majority skim over the author's most prized thoughts, experiences, and observations, seeking precisely what the author began by considering secondary, the romance. Better, the article concludes, to write in one's own person, as essayist, autobiographer, or chronicler, for an authentic novel is "a living, organic work" and requires "a little poetry."[28]

It is striking that Odoyevsky names Cervantes but cites no Russian examples of such a novel. He could not; there were none —though it was precisely about that time that Pushkin was urging Gogol to undertake a large work on the pattern of Cervantes, and giving him the basic situation from which *Dead Souls* was to grow. We are reminded once more of what alternately exhilarated and paralyzed Gogol himself: Russia was awaiting the advent of a work of prose art in which it might at length recognize its own features and its own voice—a work that, in Pushkin's terms (he is defining the novel) could body forth "a historical period, developed through an invented narration."[29]

THE EVIDENCE so far cited shows a familiar Russian pattern, in which one group presumes to speak in the name of another: the reader's putative needs are articulated in print, by writers. Throughout the 1820s, however, this had a particular legitimacy, for, as one of the best twentieth-century scholars of Russian literature reminds us, "the differentiation of the intelligentsia into 'writers' and 'readers' was then only beginning." Those outside the small circle of the elite were contemptuously dismissed as "rabble," literature being "largely a 'domestic' matter, a diversion for the leisured who were capable of combining *otium cum dignitate.*"[30] The 1830s broke this class monopoly, broadening both categories and rendering the terms newly and disconcertingly problematic.

Judging from the title of an essay of 1808 by the poet Zhukovsky, "The Writer in Society," the unwary historian might be tempted to trace a concern with that problem to the early years of the century. In fact, neither of those promising nouns is construed as it would be three decades later. The opening sentence makes this clear: "The position of the writer in society seems difficult to you; you say that he must not hope for success there." Society thus turns out to be a narrow concept, comprising the restricted circle of people with breeding and taste, whose elegant manners and conversation may lend polish to the expression of those deep thoughts which the writer must nourish in romantic isolation. "Just because the writer is a writer," Zhukovsky asks, "does this mean he is devoid of the qualities of an amiable man?"[31] The problem of the writer's vocation here—as of his audience—seems not to exist.

By the late 1820s it is beginning to be recognized. Prince Vyazemsky, consciously distinguishing the different terms for "society" as it had not occurred to Zhukovsky to do, writes in 1827: "According to the social [*svetskoe*] code of our society, [*obščestvo*], authorship is not a calling whose representatives have their voice and legitimate share in Society's council of ranks. The writer in Russia, when he is not with pen in hand, when he is not engrossed in his book, is an abstract, metaphysical entity. If he wishes to lead an actual existence, then he had better have in reserve some supplementary calling—and this episodic role will eclipse and outweigh the main one."[32]

Pushkin himself gives evidence of such an attitude more than once. In an essay on Baratynsky of 1830, he describes what was still a common attitude among serious writers (by which he could only mean poets). Service to the Muse is associated with isolation, aloofness, almost secrecy. Literature being "a refined and aristocratic pursuit," the mature poet "finds an echo of his poetry only in the hearts of a few admirers of the art, isolated like him, and scattered in society."[33] Like Charsky, the hero of Pushkin's story "Egyptian Nights," such serious writers assiduously cultivated the role of amateur, and the greater their feeling for art, the more insistent their attempts at dissimulation once their notebooks were laid by. Charsky, who knew true happiness only in moments of solitary creation, "was in despair if any of his society friends happened to find him with pen in hand." This is because "the bitterest, most intolerable evil for a poet is the name of his calling—and the nickname with which he is branded . . . The public looks upon him as its own property; in its opinion, he was born for its *use and pleasure*."[34]

Of the whole network of relations involved in this view of the writer, only his relation to his art is exempt from criticism. The trouble begins as soon as his social position and function come into question. The writer becomes a problematic being, in other words, as soon as his reader—or, more properly, reading public—enters the picture. For the relationship with a reading public presupposes in its turn adequate media of dissemination (journals, books) and involves the question of compensation, the basis of the writer's professionalism.

Before the 1830s, the poet confronted his audience as social equals in a handful of noble salons. A memoirist of the twenties, mentioning the houses where the cultural elite gathered regularly, noted: "In these houses scholars and thinkers, poets and artists were not visitors, but as if at home . . . And one must say that they were not many: one roof, one family was enough for them." By 1869, he goes on, "such concentrations are perhaps no longer needful. The representatives of the movement in learning and art have multiplied; now they form not 'circles,' but an element."[35] By the middle of the century, in other words, direct meeting of writer and reader was no longer either necessary or possible; their meeting place was in the pages of the famous "thick journals."

Meanwhile, so long as the writer was primarily a poet affecting the role of dilettante, so long as he tended to rely on the security of his noble status and could address a good part of his audience by name, publication was bound to be a casual thing.[36] To be sure, it was acceptable in the twenties to publish in book form—because books were expensive and almost always unprofitable; but publication in journals ran the constant risk of being demeaning. Though magazines rarely paid their contributors, there were many who shied away even from unpaid contributions. The poet Yazykov, for example, responding in 1827 to Pushkin's invitation to send verses to the *Moscow Telegraph,* observed with all due respect that "collaborating in a journal is not a poetic thing." "A journal," he explained, "is in the literary world what a post carriage is in the material world: It is sometimes pleasant, even useful, for a robust man to go riding in one, but it's an entirely different thing to drive it."[37] The alternative to this was publication in an almanac or miscellany, which became the favored form of the late twenties.[38] Elegant and closely, they graced the tables of the aristocracy to enliven their idle moments.

Pushkin's attitude toward these matters was anomalous. The

chief poet of his time, he shared the aristocratic pride of most of his fellows; but he was at the same time seeking to work out a position as professional man of letters. Beginning in 1830 he broadened his activity to include work as editor, critic, short-story writer, and novelist. No less striking than the brilliance of his gifts is the way they evolved in deliberate response to the changing literary situation and the needs of the time. For this reason—as well as because Gogol took him as literary mentor and model in the early years of his own career—his case has a particular illustrative value.

Pushkin's departure from standard practice may be seen as early as 1824, when he startled the literary world by selling his Byronic poem, *The Fountain of Bakhchisarai,* for 3000 rubles (two years before, his *Prisoner of the Caucasus* had brought him only 500). The accepted pattern at the time was for a poet to print a work at his own expense, distributing copies to booksellers for sale on a commission basis and receiving money only for copies actually sold. But poetry for Pushkin was more than a gift or a calling: it was, he wrote in a letter of 1824, "my trade, a branch of honest industry, which provides me with food and domestic independence." That last word is the crucial one in his thinking; fiercely aware of his own noble status, Pushkin had to reject the notion of patronage as unthinkable, demeaning in a fundamental sense. The only answer for aristocrats such as he, unable to live on revenues from their estates, reluctant to serve in the bureaucracy, prizing literature as a vocation, was to make it a respectable and paying profession. So he was drawn to declare the very "spirit of our literature" contingent on the "status of the writer."[39]

These concerns led to another: the question of an audience sufficient to reward the independent and uncompromising writer. Pushkin did, to be sure, repeatedly proclaim the poet's necessary independence of the "crowd""—but he also confessed that he was "brought up in terror of the most esteemed public, and [saw] nothing shameful in seeking to gratify it and follow the spirit of the time."[40] An indication of his imminent turn to journalism and prose may be seen in a remark of 1829 about how the fables of Krylov—"in all respects our most popular poet (*le plus national et le plus populaire*)"—share one thing with novels: "the literary man, and the merchant, and the man of fashion, and the lady, and the maid, and children all read them. But a lyrical poem is read only by lovers of poetry—and are there many of them?"[41]

This question of a broad readership took on special point that year when Pushkin published his narrative poem *Poltava,* only to find its failure with the public as resounding as the success of Faddei Bulgarin's potboiling novel *Ivan Vyzhigin,* which appeared about the same time, sold out in seven days and immediately went into a second printing.* The experience must have been sobering for Pushkin. Bulgarin was unquestionably a hack and his belief (reported by Pogodin in a letter) that Pushkin remained his only rival was laughable judged by literary standards. Nonetheless, judged by commercial standards, Bulgarin deserved the public congratulations he received "on his general victory."[42] In this sense, the rivalry did indeed exist, and its seriousness was underlined when, in the same year, the Society of Devotees of Russian Literature announced the election of two new members—Pushkin and Bulgarin, "these two leading lights of our literature."[43] The fatuous phrase contained its share of truth, in that two *kinds* of writer were, for the first time, being drawn into competition for the attention of an indistinct but powerful new entity: the Russian reading public. Bulgarin and, soon after, Senkovsky were already developing a form of literary professionalism, serving not the Muse or any rigorous conception of what literature should be, but openly catering to the appetites of that "crowd" to which they themselves belonged.[44] If a serious Russian literature was ever to exist, public tastes would have to be educated.

The first attempt at deliberate competition came within a year, with the founding by Pushkin and his friends of their short-lived *Literary Gazette.* This was a challenge to *The Northern Bee,* a Petersburg periodical with a monopoly on government announcements, through which Bulgarin and his associates waged a vigorous and unscrupulous campaign to promote their own works and denigrate those of rivals. The *Literary Gazette* failed within a year; it had scarcely a hundred subscribers, a lazy editor in Delvig, and a motley group of ill-wishers who resented the aristocratic manners

---

* An article by Nikolai Polevoy testifies, even by its undertone of sarcasm, to the extent of Bulgarin's success: "In studies, drawing rooms, stock exchanges, in cities, in villages, in all of Russia the compositions of Mr. Bulgarin, and especially *Ivan Vyzhigin,* constitute the object of conversations. The educated and the ignorant, the wise and the unreasonable, ladies, old men, officers, merchants, civil servants, even girls and children exchange opinions about Bulgarin . . . The compositions of Bulgarin are being read in all of Russian Russia . . ." N. A. Engel'gardt, "Gogol' i Bulgarin," *Istoričeskij vestnik,* 1904, VII, 164.

even more than the opinions of its contributors. But at least battle had been joined against those who were, in Vyazemsky's words, "corrupting the reading public, both morally and intellectually."[45]

The corruption in question took the form primarily of flattery. Shevyryov may have been right to observe in a review of Bulgarin's four-volume *Works* that "the warmth of feeling or thought which unites the souls of reader and writer is completely absent," and that the chief characteristic of Bulgarin's works was "lifelessness." Nonetheless, Bulgarin knew what he was doing when he dedicated these volumes "To the Russian reading public, as a sign of respect and appreciation"—and signed himself humbly "The Writer" (*sočinitel'*: a self-deprecating word suggesting an unpretentious craftsman or purveyor).[46] The point was not lost on Shevyryov, who could only observe somewhat helplessly that "the number of subscribers does not always reflect the worth of the works."[47]

The problem was to persist through the thirties and well into the forties, for a time involving the young Gogol, whose theoretical proposals for meeting it were sound and original, if doomed. It was not simply, as Nadezhdin complained in 1832, that "writers do not understand each other; society does not understand the writers; the rabble rises up against the scholars; and the scholars contemptuously crush the rabble with their heavy phrases."[48] This ignores the crucial class coefficient in the social equation. The spirit of the salons continued to dominate—and so to limit—most of the defenders of literary values. Panayev, himself an outsider, recalls in his memoirs how influential even in the 1830s was the salon of Madame Karamzin, the widow of the writer and historian. "It was there that diplomas were awarded to literary talents," and reputation among the arbiters of taste depended on admission to these select gatherings, where "the aristocratic writers paraded their aloofness, and only occasionally recognized their confrères on the outside, referring to them with noble condescension."[49]

The sadness of a doomed conservatism pervades such common complaints as Odoyevsky's that "our ears have been coarsened from the clatter of the steam engine, our fingers are calloused from banknotes, shares and other such paper." Benthamite philosophers, he said, had given high-sounding names—industry, enrichment, business—to a phenomenon that in the end resolved itself "into something much simpler and truer: the *stomach*." Even the more detached and ironic view of Vyazemsky turned out in practice to be a confession of impotence:

Examine the institutions of our book trade and you will see that if one side of our literature knows how to write, then the other side knows how to publish with the aim of selling what is printed as quickly as possible. And this skill amounts to something like primogeniture, without which no aristocracy can be powerful. We live in an age of industry: theories are yielding place to practice, hopes to cash totals . . . Thus the literary industry, which is the essential aristocracy of our age, has no reason to shout about the so-called aristocracy which is alien to the operations of industry.[50]

The defenders of literary value deplored more than they actually wrote; and their judgments often betrayed an obfuscating class bias. This can be seen in Shevyryov's astonishing advice to Gogol that he raise the tone of his writing by taking his readers into genteel society. It can also be seen in the self-vitiating terms of Vyazemsky's defense of Gogol's language in *The Inspector General,* against those who found it *mauvais genre:*

Affectation, prudishness, squeamishness, circumlocutions—these are the distinguishing features of people who do not live in good society, but who wish to ape good society. A man born in the sphere of the drawing room is at home in the drawing room. Does he want to sit down in an easy chair? He sits down in his easy chair. Does he want to speak? He is not afraid to speak out. Look at the provincial, at the upstart: he doesn't dare to sit otherwise than on the edge of the chair; he moves the edges of his lips, holds himself unnaturally, excuses himself with the pompous phrases of our didactic novels and won't say a word without qualifying it. This is why many of our critics, rallying voluntarily to the defense of good society and the inviolability of its laws, commit such ludicrous blunders when they say that such-and-such a word is indecent, such-and-such an expression impolite . . . Your ears may be offended by the language of *The Inspector General:* but the best society sits in the loges and boxes when it is played; and the printed text lies on fashionable Hambs tea tables.[51]

What has all this to do with the status of the Russian writer in the 1830s? A great deal. For the division of labor Vyazemsky had suggested—between the custodians of taste and those who know how to publish successfully—was unrealistic. The existence of successful publishers brought with it the need for professional writers who could supply a demand and write simply to be writing. One such was Bulgarin, who defined the activity of the professional writer precisely in these terms.[52] And in a feuilleton called "The Russian Writer" he mocked those who, out of devotion to an ideal, persisted in trying to ignore his existence. "Do you know," he begins, "what is the most peculiar creature not only in Russia but in all of Europe, and perhaps even in the whole world? You couldn't guess. It is the Russian writer, or, as we like to say, *sočinitel'*—in general European parlance, author . . . The Russian writer exists, speaks, sees, hears, and even writes, but . . . no one hears him—or, what is almost the same thing, no one listens to him, and scarcely anyone reads him."

In Europe, he says, a man will identify his vocation as *littérateur* or *homme de lettres*. But, if one were to range the whole of Russia in a single rank and proceed to a vocational inquiry, he would find "nobles, honored citizens, merchants, bourgeois, peasants, petty squires, cossacks, *raznochintsy,* clerks, military men—but not writers," though among them all "there are people who *write* both in verse and prose, who write and even *publish;* that is, who do everything that is done by people who sign themselves on official papers and on visiting cards as *literary men.*" The latter are, socially speaking, "impalpable, invisible, inaudible." His conclusion: "Literature has been adopted; but those who produce it have remained orphans."[53]

Bulgarin's irony here is crude and sometimes obscure, but his main point is clear enough. He is reminding the aristocrats, whose claims he parodies, that the literary vacuum they found deplorable was worse than that so far as nature was concerned: it was abhorrent, and it was being filled. "Literary activity," the poet Kuechelbecker lamented, "is ceasing to be considered a calling (*vocation*), a priesthood, a disinterested and pure, great and exalted labor." Recently enough, a literary novice would have been glad to have his work published in a journal and would hardly have thought of accepting payment. By the mid-thirties, the situation had been reversed and, what was worse, some people wished to turn literary men "not simply into artisans (that would still be tolerable)—no, into clowns, cavorting to satisfy and entertain the senseless crowd."[54]

To the new period that Bulgarin welcomed and Kuechelbecker deplored, Belinsky gave a name: the ages of Lomonosov, Karamzin, and Pushkin had now been succeeded by that of Smirdin, the Petersburg bookseller. "A. F. Smirdin," he wrote, "is the head and manager of this period. Everything flows from him and to him . . . He has concentrated our whole literature in his massive journal."[55] Reference is to the *Library for Reading,* founded in 1834. Subtitled "A Journal of Literature, Sciences, Arts, Industry, News, and Fashions," the *Library* was the first of the thick journals which were to remain a feature of the Russian cultural scene up to the present day. Conservative in outlook, it was nevertheless revolutionary by virtue of its very existence. The initial subscription list ran to 5000, an unheard-of figure for the time. In this sense, it was not simply a journal, but the discovery of a readership,[56] and it signaled the establishment in Russia of what Balzac called "la littérature marchande," Sainte-Beuve "la littérature industrielle."

The moving spirit behind the enterprise was its editor, Osip Senkovsky, a complex figure of practical genius. He instituted prompt and generous payment to all contributors and saw to it that each monthly issue appeared on schedule, an astonishing innovation for the time. Conservative in outlook, he nonetheless was deemed by Herzen to have exerted a progressive influence by the compulsive (and often groundless) irony that filled his innumerable pseudonymous articles, reviews, and causeries. The journal itself was autotelic. The best—and worst—that could be said of it amounted to pointing to its thriving existence. Absence of principle seemed its only literary principle. Thus Senkovsky on criticism:

My idea of impartial criticism is when, with a clear conscience, I tell those who wish to hear me what personal impression a given book has made upon me . . . Consequently, there can be no room for argument after one has read a critique.[57]

As for literature, Senkovsky's conception of it was set forth with unusual directness in an article of 1834:

The name of belles-lettres, in the strict sense of the word, belongs alone to the fruits of the imagination, or, more simply, to works that serve as light and pleasant reading. Poems, that is, poems in verse—and poems in prose, that is, novels, stories, and tales, all sorts of satiric and descriptive creations, intended for the transitory delectation of the educated man: these comprise the area of literature and its present boundaries. Imagination is the guiding spirit and sovereign in this area. The charm of clever society talk and of friendly conversation, without witnesses, in privacy— these things, transferred to paper and accessible at any time, constitute the first idea of Literature.

Seldom has literature been so complacently proclaimed a commodity. Its language, Senkovsky says, should be that used by "decent people"; its true audience is a class "terrified of boredom, avid for novelties, sensations, playthings, events, glitter, prefabricated enjoyments and prefabricated thoughts, absorbing all concepts like a sponge, from light reading." Literature thus amounts to "the Philosophy of the public." And "if [it] is in any way necessary to society, then its first obligation, in the present situation, is by all means to strengthen the social and familial ties, to pacify minds, to inculcate trust in one's own strength and in the holiness of our nature, not to aid political delirium", etc.[58] Here is a view of the writer as more than tradesman—as popular entertainer and purveyor of tranquilizers. By the same token it implicitly degrades criticism to the level of advertising (which in fact it became in the hands of Senkovsky and his colleagues). Cynical and reactionary, it operates on a level where none of the problems facing serious literary artists exists as such.

SUCH, in broad outline, was the scene on which Gogol was fated to assume a role. Drawn at once to the ideals of poetry and the practice of prose, he remained outside both parties—the aristocratic party of great expectations, to which he inclined by conviction, and the party that was industriously creating the first mass audience in Russia by pandering to it. Compelled to make an independent way, in improvising a heterogeneous body of work he was, more consistently and consciously than is usually assumed, essaying original responses to all the problems that the times made implicit in the twin challenges of "how to be a writer" and "what it means to be a writer." Insofar as these questions can be separated, they dominate, respectively, the two main periods of Gogol's activity, the Petersburg years (1829–1836) and the years that led through *Dead Souls* to the impasse of his final book (1836–1847).

PART II

Improvising a Vocation

I continue to hold the opinion—not without cause—that in the first period of his development Gogol was a completely free man, carving a way for himself with exceptional skill.

P. V. Annenkov

At first he was inclined to go into the civil service, but a passion for pedagogy led him to my camp: he has gone into teaching as well. Zhukovsky is enthusiastic about him. I am impatient to bring him around for your blessing. He loves the sciences for themselves alone, and like an artist is ready to submit to any privations for their sake. This touches and delights me.

Pletnyov to Pushkin, 1831

Les autres nouvelles du volume . . . montrent la variété du talent de M. Gogol, mais je regrette que, pour un premier recueil, on n'ait pu choisir une suite plus homogène et plus capable de fixer tout d'abord sur les caractères généraux de l'auteur: le critique se trouve un peu en peine devant cette diversité de sujets et d'applications.

Sainte-Beuve

3

Beginnings: Miscellaneous Writings

"I cannot say categorically," Gogol wrote near the end of his career, "whether in fact the writer's calling is my calling." The statement occurs in what he referred to as "the tale of my authorship" (1847), published posthumously as "An Author's Confession." Shortly before, however, he assured the poet Zhukovsky that he had been following "a single road"—the writer's way—all his life. There is no contradiction here, for the doubts he began to voice in the 1840s arose directly from his literary achievement to date and signaled a new stage in its unfolding. His repeated insistence that his life was indistinguishable from his writing—that his selfhood was ultimately a textual matter*—deserves to be taken at face value, and it is in that light that any apparently biographical references should be understood in the pages that follow. Gogol's literary invention was at the same time an evolving self-invention, and it is fruitless to look for privileged statements (whether of intention or interpretation), because all are alike elements of a work in progress, a *single text*—comprised of artistic works, letters, journalism, notes, and drafts—in which the phenomenon called Gogol ultimately has its only important existence.

The rest is suppositious or incidental. Though his schoolboy letters mention a career in law; though at nineteen, about to leave for Petersburg, he lists some fallback positions ("I am a good tai-

---

* See his letter to Danilevsky of 26/14 February 1843: "You ask why I don't write you about my life, about all the trifles, about dinners, etc., etc. But my whole life, for a long time now, has been proceeding within me, and internal life . . . is not easy to convey. Volumes are needed for it. Moreover, its result will appear later, all in printed form" (XII, 139). Elsewhere he speaks of "living and breathing through my works" (XI, 325).

lor, can decorate walls with *al fresco* painting not badly, work in the kitchen and know a good deal already about the art of the cook"; I, 133); though he apparently sought a position as an actor and did work briefly in a government office, he had indeed embarked on the writer's way by the time he was twenty.

The work of his Petersburg period shows him essaying, through an astonishing variety of tentatives, all the current forms of authorship—poet, essayist, historian, journalist, short story writer, playwright, novelist—seeking to form a self and establish it in the cultural life of the capital. Though the note of simultaneous experimentation on many fronts never quite disappears, it is particularly strong in these years, making a strictly chronological tracing mercifully impossible. Since some schematization is inevitable, I have chosen to consider his nonfiction first because it is too easily neglected. Little as it may have contributed to Gogol's immortality, the light it sheds on the process of his self-creation is of capital importance.

The basic ingredients—which is to say the basic contradictions—of the Gogol problem are present in his text from the beginning, reflecting that naive stock of impulses, beliefs, and aspirations which the adolescent Gogol nourished in school and brought to Petersburg with him in 1829, at the age of nineteen. They are by no means all specifically Ukrainian; but it is fair to say that they are innocent of any sense of the Petersburg cultural scene, which Gogol was subsequently so quick to acquire and put to use. The text at this stage consists of letters and an "idyll in scenes," *Hanz Kuechelgarten,* published pseudonymously soon after his arrival and only posthumously attributed.

The letters Gogol wrote as a schoolboy in Nezhin show the early stirrings of a sense of vocation; they make clear as well the guiding impulses and the strong sense of self that shaped them. "As for me," he writes at sixteen, "I shall make my way in this world, and if not in the manner in which most men are destined to do so, at least I shall try as far as possible to be such [*sic*]" (X, 59–60). Gogol's desire to believe himself enigmatically but absolutely different recurs constantly in these letters, and would not be worth remarking if it had not continued throughout his life. Much of the impulse was negative, a recoiling against what was to become the most "Gogolian" of his mature themes: mere existence. "How miserable to be buried with creatures of base obscurity in dead silence!" he exclaims. The creatures in question are the citizens of Nezhin, who "have smothered the lofty calling of man with the crust of their earthliness and trivial self-satisfaction. And it is among these merely existent beings that I must drag out my days" (X, 98). The key charge against the self-satisfied herd is not ethical but metaphysical; their lives are insignificant. So the future writer's dream of fame and glory is tantamount to a saving quest for meaning: "A cold sweat breaks out on my face at the thought that I may be fated to perish in the dust without having marked my name with a single beautiful deed; to be in the world and not to mark my existence—that would be terrible for me" (X, 111). The interest here is not in life itself—Gogol's bias against external experience is already evident—but in the value that may attach to a life. What conferred meaning as well as glory was art. "I deny even my most extreme needs," he wrote his mother at eighteen, "to be able to satisfy my thirst to see and feel *the beautiful*." So he has set aside forty rubles—"no small sum for one in my condition"—and bought a set of Schiller. "I also do not neglect the Russians, and order whatever comes out that is first-rate [at the rate of one book every six months] . . . It is astonishing how strong the urge to the good can be. Sometimes I read an announcement of the appearance of a beautiful work; my heart beats fast—and with heavy heart I drop the newspaper, recalling the impossibility of having it. The dream of acquiring it agitates my sleep . . . I don't know what would become of me if I could not feel this joy; I would die of yearning and boredom" (X, 91–92).

Beauty was self-justifying. In Tolstoy's ungenerous summary: "Unfortunately, at the time Gogol entered the literary world . . . there reigned with respect to art what I can only call that incredibly stupid teaching of Hegel's, according to which it transpired that building houses, singing songs, painting pictures and writing stories, comedies and verses represented some sacred activity, a 'service to beauty,' which stood only a step lower than religion."[1] Hegel or not, the 1820s were certainly a time when art and the artist were being exalted. So at the end of the decade Gogol realized the first of his dreams (and found his first disillusion) by moving to Petersburg, where he promptly courted poetic glory by publishing a short lyric ("Italy") and, at his own expense, *Hanz Kuechelgarten*.

Advertised as the work of one "V. Alov," *Hanz Kuechelgarten* is alleged on the title page to have been written in 1827. This may or may not have been a self-protective mystification, but the unsigned prefatory note certainly was that. "Circumstances important only to the author," we are told, account for the appearance of "this product of his eighteen-year-old youth." Parts of the manuscript were, regrettably, missing: "They probably gave more connection to the now-uncoordinated excerpts and fleshed out the portrayal of the chief character" (I, 60). *Hanz Kuechelgarten* more than justifies this uneasiness; it is the kind of preromanticism fashionable a few years before, borrowing from Voss's sentimental *Luise, a Rustic Poem in Three Idylls,* as well as from Byron, Chateaubriand, Zhukovsky, Pushkin, Kuechelbecker, and Thomas Moore.[2] Virtually all of Gogol's works show such borrowing, though most often transformed beyond recognition in the crucible of his genius. Here there is no such transformation and the poem's residual interest—aside from occasional passages that seem to anticipate traits of twentieth-century poetry, much as his best prose would do[3]—lies in the evidence it affords of the terms in which the young Gogol regarded the artist's vocation.

Hanz, like his creator, is a young man, moved by vague but powerful emotion as he contemplates "the great, unbounded world" and "his own unknowable lot." "A child of the earthly world," he has not yet known "destructive earthly passions" (I, 66). He lives amid quiet routine and material abundance, described in the same affectionate detail that would go into Gogol's early masterpiece, "Old-World Landowners." But as in "Old-World Landowners," the cosy comforts of domestic snugness border on the mortal dangers of provincial smugness; the here-and-now offers no nourishment to the soul and is but a fallen version of the there-and-then. Positive value for Gogol was always to be associated with an absence, with the temporally or geographically remote; here its locus is classical Greece. "Oh! how wonderfully you, Greeks,/ Populated your world with dreams!/ How you enchanted it!/ But ours—it is poor and orphaned,/ All plotted out in measured miles" (I, 70). So Hanz's impulse is to flight: "Everything in this godforsaken country/ Struck him as stifling, dusty, and/ His heart beat strongly, strongly/ For a distant, distant land" (I, 71–72). The helpless repetitions show the strength of the impulse—in Gogol, if not in his creation—and a later passage makes clear what is involved: "Am I now to perish spiritually here?/ To

know no other goal?/ To find no better goal?/ To doom myself a
victim to ingloriousness?/ While still alive be dead to the world?/
With a soul in love with glory,/ Am I to love insignificance in the
world? . . ./ And not encounter beauty there?/ Not mark my existence?" (I, 78–79).

Hanz's journey to Greece, of course, ends in disillusion: "Sad
are the antiquities of Athens./ Cloudy is the row of pictures of the
past./ Leaning upon the marble cold,/ In vain the avid traveler
thirsts/ To resurrect the past within his soul,/ Vainly endeavors to
unroll/ The scroll all tattered of past deeds . . ./ The troubled gaze
on every hand/ Reads shame and ruin side by side." Better to have
let "these ethereal dreams live in thoughts!" (I, 89).

Gogol seems to endorse the preference for dream over reality
—but, as in "Nevsky Prospect," with one condition: The dreamer
must have rare strength of character, an "iron will"; he must be an
artist not only in temperament, but in monklike practical devotion, justifying his apartness by a kind of puritanical dedication.
This the weak (read: ordinary) Hanz is made to realize in a passage
which strikingly summarizes the young Gogol's aspirations and
makes clear how little the late Gogol departed from them:

> Blessed is that wondrous moment
> When in the time of self-discovery,
> The time of one's powerful energies,
> He who is chosen by heaven grasps
> The highest aim of existence;
> When not the empty shadow of daydreams,
> Not the tinsel glitter of fame
> Disturb him night and day,
> Drawing him to the noisy, stormy world,
> But thought alone, both strong and hale,
> Enfolds him and torments him with desire
> For happiness and good,
> And schools him for great works.
> For these he does not spare his life.
> In vain the mob cries mindlessly:
> He's firm amid this live debris,
> And only hears the sounding of
> The blessings of posterity.
>
> For when one's prey to artful dreams
> That bring the thirst for some bright lot,
> If iron will steel not the soul

To stand steadfast amid the hurly-burly,
Were it not better, sheltered and in peace
To flow along the fields of life,
To find in modest family life content,
And pay the noisy world no heed? (I, 95)

The poem ends with Hanz "reborn" through that recognition. Now "a devotee of earthly beauty," he bids his "perfidious dreams" farewell, amid a welter of emotions which Gogol in his concluding lines likens to those a schoolboy feels as his schooling ends.

While there is obvious autobiographical content in *Hanz Kuechelgarten,* care must be taken in drawing conclusions from it. Gogol himself was indeed to embrace the role of artist as ascetic — but only some years later. In the meantime, when the first of three devastating reviews confirmed his own misgivings about the poem, he collected all the copies he could find and burned them; then he fled abroad to Germany for six weeks, "fleeing from myself . . . and trying to forget everything that surrounded me" (X, 151). The remarkable letters he wrote his mother on this occasion show him, as Nabokov comments, "at his best, that is, using his imagination for the purpose of complex and unnecessary deception."[4] Literary in that sense, heavily rhetorical and informed by a wild and fictive self-characterization, the first of them (24 July 1829) also mentions his own prospective literary work for the first time.[5] If the fiasco with his poem was traumatic, it had a salutary side as well. Convinced that poetic glory was not his to seek, he put aside high seriousness to explore the Petersburg cultural scene and his own possibilities as a writer of prose.

TWO YEARS before he had envied a school friend already serving in Petersburg "the sweet assurance that your existence is not without significance, that you will be noticed and appreciated" (X, 80). The equation here is revealing. Indeed, it may not be too much to say that Gogol's subsequent experiments had in view, beyond providing needed income, a *relationship.* Seeking to fashion a publicly presentable self, he sought at the same time to discover a public that might value and so validate the presentation. As in a courtship, preoccupation with the self and the other alternated.

For nearly two years—from late 1829 to the fall of 1831*— Gogol devoted himself to the most varied preparatory work. Already in February 1830 he reported to his mother that his main revenue now came from writing, an exaggeration evidently meant to underline the importance of his renewed requests for information about Ukrainian customs, anecdotes, and the like. In fact he had only one publication to send her, the story "St. John's Eve," which appeared anonymously under the title "Basavrjuk" in the February 1830 issue of *Notes of the Fatherland*. (A translation he had made of a French article on Russian trade in the sixteenth and seventeenth centuries was accepted a month before but never published.) In December he expressed high hopes for 1831, based in good part on continuing literary acceptances of highly disparate material: "Hetman," a chapter from a historical novel, appeared in *Northern Flowers* that month (signed "0000"[6]); the following month the *Literary Gazette* printed a chapter from "The Terrible Boar" (signed "P. Glechik"), "Some Thoughts on Teaching Geography to Children" (signed "G. Yanov"), and the effusive sketch, "Woman"—the first publication to be signed with Gogol's name. By that time he had completed the stories that would make up Volume One of *Evenings on a Farm near Dikanka*. Published in September 1831, their reception must have gone far toward erasing the shame of *Hanz Kuechelgarten*. Pushkin himself welcomed the collection as an event in Russian literature.

Such recognition, together with good sales, obviously encouraged Gogol to continue writing fiction, but it did not impinge on the variety of his vocational tentatives. The record of these years contains no indication that Gogol took much pride or invested much ambition in the writing of stories. Like everyone else

---

* It was precisely in this period that he worked as a government clerk, but only to secure "the accursed, vile money" he needed to live (X, 138). The bureaucratic side of Petersburg he quickly recognized as a variant of that soulless routine he had despised in Nezhin: "no spirit glitters in the people, all of whom are employees and office-holders; everybody talks about his department and colleagues; all are weighed down, mired in the trivial, insignificant labors on which their life is fruitlessly expended" (X, 139). The milieu was hateful, but its demands on his time were light enough to let the pursuit of a vocation go on outside it. Gogol's letters of this period contain abundant evidence of his attitudes toward government employment; the facts of that employment are set forth in V. V. Gippius, ed., *N. V. Gogol': Materialy i issledovanija,* I (Moscow-Leningrad, 1936), 288–306.

in Russia at the time, he was prepared to regard them as amusements. There was still no warrant for believing that Russian prose might vie with poetry as a vehicle of serious artistic expression; only Gogol's own progress in this line would eventually provide it. Meanwhile, throughout the first half of the 1830s, he devoted himself to a more or less simultaneous exploration of the remaining varieties of being a prose writer, producing learned essays and journalism as well as imaginative works. However confusing their sequential logic, they show strong patterns of internal relation. These involve most obviously the expression of views and values; they involve also the young writer's sense of the current cultural situation and its possibilities. But Gogol's texts may have their greatest significance beyond what they say—in what they *do* (or seek to do) as part of his ongoing discovery of a literary identity vis-à-vis a clearly implied reader.

This can be seen even in the bizarre fruits of his work as a teacher of history. It was his publication of a chapter from a historical novel that led to acquaintance with Pletnyov, a critic and professor; and that acquaintance in its turn led to a teaching post, first at the Patriotic Institute in 1831 and then, three years later, to a short-lived professorship at Petersburg University (obtained through the good offices of Zhukovsky). Literary auspices thus surround this episode, and the only historical writing that seems unrelated to some literary interest is the writing he promised but never produced—a world history and geography ("Land and People") in two or three volumes, announced early in February 1833 and abandoned in the same month with a confession that the book was to consist of his students' papers (X, 256, 262); "a history of the Ukraine and the south of Russia and a world history" of a kind unexampled in Russia or Europe (December 1833; X, 290); "a history of the Ukraine from beginning to end . . . in six small or four large volumes" (January 1834; X, 297); and "a history of the Middle Ages in eight or nine volumes" (January 1835; X, 349). The quantitative specification here is evidently a sign of an ambition that proved as misdirected as it was intense. Some 150 pages of closely printed notes have survived from the period in question (IX, 29–172), along with a greater number from the 1840s on related matters of geography and ethnography; but what actually got written amounts only to a handful of essays, five of them published in the *Journal of the Ministry of National Education* over the course of 1834. These are "A Plan for the Teaching of World History," "A Glance at the Composition of Little Russia," "On Little-Russian Songs," "On the Middle Ages," and "Al-Mamoun." All of them reappear in his volume called *Arabesques* at the beginning of 1835, where, in the company of other essays and three short stories, they can most clearly be seen to serve a fundamentally literary strategy.

Taken in isolation, the pedagogical work looks simply like a blind alley, and it is hard at first glance not to share Hugh McLean's contention that, "in view of the severe limitations of his educational background and general culture, one can only say that Gogol exhibited astounding arrogance—or an equally astounding lack of realism in his self-estimation—in undertaking . . . to become a professor of universal history at Petersburg University. One's amazement at Gogol's bravado, his *khlestakovshchina,* in accepting such a post is equaled only by one's astonishment at the irresponsibility and folly of those who appointed him to it."[7] The judgment, however, is too vehement. The letters of this period make clear, in Vasily Gippius' phrase, that Gogol "was dreaming of some grand personal exploit" quite independent of its particular content.[8] History, which did not then require original research, might well have seemed a promising field for innovation: "In the 1830s the great majority of historians approached their task exclusively from the external and anecdotal side. Campaigns, diplomatic parleys, court intrigues, the personalities of the sovereigns and their retainers—such were regarded as the central manifestations of historical life at the time."[9] In such circumstances even Gogol's delight with an early sixteenth-century history because it speaks about the extermination of lice and the introduction of Indian bedbugs into Germany takes on point, especially if one notes that the letter expressing this delight goes on to praise Pushkin's nearly completed *History of Pugachev* as a uniquely interesting work, "a veritable novel" (X, 269). To be sure, Pushkin's historical works were incomparably more focused, more original, more mature. But Pushkin's very interest in writing them—which embraced at one point a history of the Ukraine[10]—licensed the young Gogol's extending his *literary* ambitions in a comparable way, that of the popularizer.

Tempting as it is to consider his pedagogical efforts a fiasco analogous to his poetic efforts in *Hanz Kuechelgarten,* one has in justice to see them as more complex. Gogol was genuinely drawn to historical materials (especially to chronicles and folksongs evocative of the Ukrainian past). From the beginning, however, there was a conflict between his independent interests and the ends he tried to make them serve. In the contemplation of "alas, vanished life and, alas, vanished people" (X, 284), he finds those positive characteristics—drama, color, harmony—which he was never able to discern or portray in the present; here is history feeding the writer's imaginative faculty. But the demands of pedagogical commitment posed the question not of what study could contribute to the unformed writer, but its opposite: what might an unformed writer contribute to the study of history? Gogol, already known as an original writer of fiction, had to become a student again. Cribbing and cramming, he tried to demonstrate how an intelligent and impatient reader might deal with a series of set examination questions. (The questions were always broad, his responses always general.) All this he did successfully, but just barely, and it is no wonder that the strain showed. He was providing quasi-literary performances that purported to be something else. Evidence of his success, along with the grounds of his failure, may be seen in the account left by one of his students of the introductory lecture in Gogol's course on the Middle Ages, delivered at Petersburg University in September 1834:

I don't know whether even five minutes had passed before Gogol had completely absorbed the attention of his listeners. It was impossible passively to follow his thought, which streaked and branched like lightning, continually illuminating picture after picture in the murk of medieval history. However, the whole of that lecture is published in *Arabesques* . . . Not trusting himself, Gogol had committed the already written lecture to memory, and although he spoke animatedly and quite freely while delivering it, he could not depart from the memorized phrases and so added not a single word to it.

The lecture lasted three quarters of an hour. When Gogol had left the auditorium, we crowded round him . . . and asked him to give us the lecture in manuscript. Gogol said that he had only a rough outline, but that he would work it over and give it to us; and then he added: "This first time, gentlemen, I have tried to show you only the general character of medieval history; next time we shall take up the facts themselves, and for that we shall have to equip ourselves with the anatomist's scalpel." [11]

For such surgical attention Gogol's reserves of preparation proved inadequate. In any case, the conclusion seems plain that the pedagogical episode was fundamentally another exercise in writing and that it had negative value in proving that he could not for long write to order, on subjects that constricted his freedom to embellish, digress, extrapolate. "Examine more closely and attentively," he had written in the lecture on the Middle Ages, "and you will find connection, aim, and direction; but I would not deny that for the very ability to find all this one must be gifted from above with that olfaction (*čut'e*) which few historians possess." His editor bridled at the word "olfaction," but Gogol insisted on it ("There is no equivalent . . . we have to appropriate certain virtues from the quadrupeds"; X, 340–341, 485). The quality in question is the one he relied on above all in this work, and the word itself reflects a cardinal aspect of his aspiration: "They reproach me, claiming that my style . . . is too flashy, that it is unhistorically fiery and alive; but what is history if it is dull!" (X, 294).

To Pogodin, an established historian and editor, Gogol was meanwhile sending self-confident advice on journalism and sharply contrasting, confused, and apologetic comments on his own performance as historian. "Don't look at my historical excerpts," he writes in December 1834, "they are youthful; they were written long ago. Also don't look at the article on the Middle Ages . . . It was done only in order to say something, and only to stir up my audience's desire to find out what kinds of things still need to be talked about." From exculpation he moves to complaint: "Do you know what it means not to find sympathy, what it means to meet no response? I am lecturing in solitude, in utter solitude, in this university. No one listens to me; not once have I found a single person to be struck by the vivid truth. And so I am now utterly abandoning any artistic polish, and even more any desire to stir my sleepy auditors . . . If even one creature among the students understood me. They are a people colorless as Petersburg" (X, 344).

After this acknowledgment of failure, he goes on to speak of the textual residue: "You ask what I am publishing. I am publishing a grab bag. All those compositions and fragments and thoughts which have at times engaged me. Among them are historical pieces, some already known, some not. I only ask you to look on them as charitably as possible. There is much that is young in them" (X, 344–345). The reference is to *Arabesques*. A month later, Gogol sent Pogodin a copy of the book. He speaks of having erudite enemies, but his attitude is now crude and categorical: "Screw them!" The book was published hastily, he explains, "to clear all the old material off my desk, so that I might give myself a shake and begin a new life" (X, 348). These fragments that Gogol shored against the ruins of his scholarly dreams are by and large of little intrinsic interest today. Their extrinsic importance, in the exfoliating Gogolian text, is quite another matter.

Arabesques, subtitled "Sundry Writings of N. Gogol," is a miscellany but not a catchall. The author's description of it (in a letter to his friend Maksimovich) as "a chaos, a mixture of everything" (X, 349) indicates its organizing principle but fails to suggest the care he took to select the contents and provide a semblance of symmetry. He made two provisional lists of contents before settling on the final one, in which each of two parts consists of nine items, some of them essays, some fiction. The essays are esthetic, pedagogical, and historical; the fiction consists of two chapters from an unfinished historical novel and three of his Petersburg tales: "The Portrait" and "Nevsky Prospect"—both about artists—together with "Diary of a Madman," originally conceived as the "Diary of a Mad Musician" and vestigially related to the other two even in its finished form. If there is theoretical warrant for such a "mixture of everything," it is probably to be found in the romantic exaltation of art's power to reveal "the primordial connection of nature and history, life and activity, the real and the ideal," as a Russian popularizer of Schelling put it in the 1820s.[12] Gogol's book was not art, of course, but it discussed art and it employed art, consistently seeking not merely to proclaim but to demonstrate the range and penetration of a uniquely endowed nature, one that might yet prove "in his free individual creation" to be one of the elect, "a priest and guardian of the holy flame."[13] To put the matter this way is to ascribe to Gogol an intention he never articulated, but such ideas were in the air during Gogol's formative years and find their reflection in almost everything he wrote up to and including *Arabesques.*[14] His debts to Wackenroder, Schelling, Novalis, and their early Russian interpreters have long since been noted by scholars, and it is clear that his view of the artist's nature takes its sanction and its terms from the romantic commonplaces of the time.* His consistent emphases, however, suggest a personal and strategic concern as well. These pieces may appear risible as history, ethnography, or esthetics; they are rather less so if regarded in the light of Gogol's ongoing experiments with the ways of being a writer.

In *Arabesques* we find him essaying the role of polymath, confidently and prescriptively, as the liberal censor Nikitenko noted in his diary, writing "all sorts of things about all sorts of things"—planting his flag in every area of cultural activity and "aspiring directly to the ranks of genius."[15] Nikitenko's statement requires only a slight readjustment. What Gogol appears to be doing here is establishing his right *to be associated with* a varied assortment of geniuses. He uses the latter word frequently, connecting it with a broad notion of the poet as one particularly able to perceive and render the lofty—thereby implying certain claims about his own percipience and, through his concern with conveying lively impressions, about his own quasi-poetic and quasi-pedagogical gift. Thus in the opening essay, "Sculpture, Painting, and Music," sculpture is seen as "the clear specter of that bright Greek world which has receded from us into the depths of the centuries, vanished like mist, and become reachable only by the thought of a poet" (VIII, 9)—which Gogol goes on to provide. By the same token, he asserts in "On the Middle Ages" that to see through the chaotic surface of history to its underlying order one must be among the few to whom is vouchsafed "the enviable gift of seeing and presenting everything with astonishing clarity and shapeliness. After their magic touch an event comes to life and takes on its quiddity [*sobstvennost'*], its capacity to interest; without them, it will appear dry and senseless to anyone for a long time" (VIII, 16). Even the nineteenth-century architect, if he is to be a genuine, cos-

---

* There is confirmation in a letter of 1839 when, recalling his earlier years, he writes: "That was the time of the freshness of my young powers and of a pure effusion, like the sound produced by a sure [violin] bow. These were years of poetry; at that time I loved the Germans without knowing them, or maybe I confounded German scholarship, German philosophy and literature with Germans. Whatever the case, German poetry at that time carried me far off into the distance, and I was pleased at that time by its utter remoteness from life and reality. And I regarded everything that was ordinary and everyday then much more contemptuously. To this day I love those Germans whom my imagination created . . . " (XI, 244–245).

mopolitan creator, "needs to be a genius and a poet" ("On the Architecture of the Present Time," VIII, 72). The terms so overlap as to be virtually interchangeable—the notion of the poet is more than simply literary and the notion of the genius involves gifts of expression as well as grasp. Thus the essay on Al-Mamoun, ninth-century Caliph of Baghdad, distinguishes common poets from great ones, the latter being those "who unite in themselves the philosopher, and the poet, and the historian; who have plumbed nature and man, penetrated the past and seen into the future; whose word is heard by the whole people. They are the high priests" (VIII, 78).

The article "Schloezer, Mueller, and Herder" presents these three leaders of the eighteenth-century school of world history in the same terms. Schloezer, "being one of the first to be excited by the thought of the majesty and true aim of world history, had inevitably to be an opposition genius" (VIII, 87). The statement is supported almost entirely with reference to style—and it is noteworthy that Gogol's very praise seeks to function in the same way, exemplifying what it points to ("Everything of his glitters with such sharp features, the powerful stroke of his eye is so true, that reading this concise sketch of the world one notices with astonishment that one's own imagination is aflame, expanding and supplementing everything in accordance with that very law which Schloezer defined by a single all-powerful word, [the reader's] imagination sometimes charging on still farther, because the bold road has been pointed out"; VIII, 86). The contrasting characterization of Mueller is similarly stylistic in emphasis, and when Gogol awards Herder pride of place, it is not because of his ideas (none is mentioned), but because "as a poet he stands higher" than the others (VIII, 88): "Like a poet he creates and digests everything in himself, in his isolated study, filled with a higher revelation, selecting only the beautiful and lofty, because this is already the property of his pure and elevated soul. But the lofty and beautiful are often extracted from a base and despised [plane of] life, or else are evoked by the pressure of those innumerable and multifarious phenomena which constantly variegate human life and of which the sage, abstracted from life, rarely succeeds in taking cognizance. His style more than anyone else's is full of vivid pictures on a large scale, because he is a poet" (VIII, 88–89). The ideal universal historian, Gogol concludes, would join to these gifts the dramatic and narrative art of a Walter Scott or a Shakespeare (VIII, 89).*

This essay is worth pausing over. Like the majority of its companion pieces, it is at once vivid and hollow. Style in both the subject and the object overwhelms content; everywhere it is literary concerns that predominate. Here as throughout the collection, we find Gogol assembling an eclectic company of geniuses (real and hypothetical), citing the examples of excellence familiar to him in a whole range of fields to model an ideal, cosmopolitan intelligentsia. And—by his manner and the evidence he provides of understanding what is not accessible to everyone—he is at the same time claiming a place alongside that company. Better, the *Library for Reading* sneered in a review, if these articles had "demanded expression" not from the soul, as Gogol averred in his preface, but out of some prior learning.[16] For all their callowness, however, the fact is that they retain a posthumous interest precisely because of what they tell us about the tendencies of that "soul," whose history all his writings comprised.

The concept of style is the key element here. Style is the animating force of all Gogol's texts, the sign of his profoundest originality; in masterpieces like "The Overcoat" and *Dead Souls* it is clearly primary, outweighing plot and character, constituting the one unambiguous value. In *Arabesques,* however, it is—or was meant to be—ancillary. The pedagogical pieces repeatedly stress the importance of presentation: "The professor's style should be fascinating and fiery" (VIII, 28), to attract and hold the attention of his auditors. The art critic Stasov, a pupil at the School of Jurisprudence when Gogol's book appeared, recalls how welcome Gogol's book was to him and his classmates, contrasting as it did with the lethal boredom engendered by the more conventional presentations of their teachers, who seemed "not to suspect that we had imagination, vital drives and a craving for elegance of form."[17] One of the pieces Stasov singles out for praise is "On the Middle Ages," whose concluding paragraph offers a fair example of Gogol's precepts in practice:

---

* Compare Frank Kermode's observation: "World history, the imposition of a plot on time, is a substitute for myth." *The Sense of an Ending* (New York: Oxford University Press, 1967), p. 43.

See now between what colossal events the time of the Middle Ages is enclosed! A great empire, which had ruled the world, a nation twelve centuries old, decrepit and exhausted, falls; with it sinks half the world— all of the ancient world with its half-pagan manner of thought, its taste- less writers, gladiators, statues, with the weight of its luxury and the re- finement of its depravity. That is their beginning; the Middle Ages also end with a most enormous event: a universal explosion which sends everything into the air and turns to nothingness all the fearsome author- ities who had so despotically embraced them. The power of the popes is undermined and falls; the power of ignorance is undermined; the trea- sures and worldwide trade of Venice are undermined; and when the uni- versal chaos is cleansed and clarified, there appear to our astonished eyes monarchs who hold their sceptres with a mighty hand, ships that with broadened stroke fare through the waves of the boundless ocean past the Mediterranean Sea; in the hands of the Europeans instead of a powerless weapon there is fire; printed pages fly to all the corners of the world; and all this is the result of the Middle Ages. The strong pressure and intensi- fied oppression of the powers seemed only to have come into being the more strongly to produce a universal explosion. The mind of man, closed in by a strong thickness, could not break through otherwise than by mustering all its efforts, its entire self. And for that reason, perhaps, no century shows such gigantic discoveries as the fifteenth, the century which so brilliantly ends the Middle Ages, majestic as a colossal Gothic cathedral, dark and gloomy as its intersecting vaults, variegated as its particolored windows and the heap of omnipatterning decorations; ex- alted, upsurging like its columns and walls that fly toward heaven; and terminating in a spire that is glimpsed fleetingly among the clouds.[18]

Stasov recalls that he and his fellow pupils tried to write like this themselves. One can understand, though not without wincing. Senkovsky's *Library for Reading* was also impressed and repro- duced the passage above, underlining and interpolating exclama- tion points. "It takes a strange notion of the knowledge and ear of Russian readers in 1835 to write thus about History," the reviewer concluded, "and to write thus in Russian! The strong pressure and intensified oppression of the powers, please observe, squeezed the mind of man which was closed in by a strong thickness so power- fully that the unfortunate mind, mustering all its efforts, flared up horribly enough out of despair to discover gunpowder, printing, and America!"[19] This, too, may occasion a certain wincing sym- pathy.

　　If, however, instead of judging Gogol as historial essayist we seek to judge the essays as Gogolian instances, the results are more interesting. Even the passage quoted takes on a somewhat redeeming significance in light of the lines that precede it, which give evidence of a deeply personal, almost confessional subtext: "If one can compare the life a single individual with the life of all mankind, then the Middle Ages will be tantamount to the individual's education in school. His days flow along imperceptibly to the world, his acts are not so strong and ripe as they must be for the world: no one knows about them, yet they are all the result of impulse and disclose in a single flash all that individual's inner movements, without which his future activity in the social sphere could not take place" (VIII, 24). A similarly personal quality informs the whole collection, sometimes openly, as in the essay "On the Architecture of the Present":

I always grow sad when I look at the new buildings constantly being constructed, on which millions have been spent but of which few arrest one's astonished eye by any majesty of outline, willful daring of imagination, or even luxury and dazzling mixture of colors in the decorations. Unbidden the thought intrudes: "Can it really be that the age of architecture has passed irrevocably? Can it be that majesty and genius will no longer visit us . . . ?" (VIII, 56)

But even where the text eschews the first person, the marks of an individual temperament are constantly present. Favored adjectives appear on almost every page: wondrous, fantastic, gigantic, colossal, mighty, bright, dazzling, original, uncommon, unequaled, boundless, horrible, implacable, poetic, astonishing, incomprehensible. They are clearly intended to show the writer's percipience,[20] his ability to find high drama and deep significance where others have not; what they show in fact is a passionately projected craving for the prodigious. The purported descriptions that are really ascriptions, the hyperbole that is meant to vivify but ends by eclipsing its object, all tend to show the writer as no less interesting than his theme. "But one may say that vividness is only an external sign of the events of the Middle Ages; their internal merit is a gigantic colossalness, almost miraculous; a courage that belongs only to the age of youth; and an originality that makes them unique, unmatched, and unrepeated either in ancient or in modern times" (VIII, 17). Gogol's style here is all aspiration, resolving discourse into performance.

The aspiration itself is hyperbolic, universalistic, global. Whether the subject be Ukrainian songs, history, or architecture, the quest is for "one beautiful whole" (VIII, 99). Thus the historian should present "a sketch of *the whole history of mankind*" (VIII, 30); the creative architect should be *"all-embracing,* should study and contain in himself *all the innumerable variations"* of the taste of all the world's peoples—"on the level of idea, and not in trivial external form and particularities" (VIII, 71–72). *"Everything* [in the Middle Ages] was poetry and instinctiveness" (VIII, 24). Schloezer sought "with a single glance to embrace *the whole world, everything that lives"* (VIII, 85). Folk songs "reveal *the whole life* of the people"; in the case of the Ukraine, they are "everything: poetry, and history, and forefathers' graves" (VIII, 90–91).

Often this global aspiration takes panoramic form, as in "On the Architecture of the Present," where the reader is treated to a critical survey of world architecture as a step toward suggesting new possibilities for the genuine "creator" in this field. Elsewhere the panorama turns literal as the writer scans eons to observe momentous allegorical entrances and exits on the stage of human experience. Thus "Life," an adolescent prose-poem about the supersession of Egyptian, Greek, and Roman views of life with the birth of Christ, opens with a dream vision of the vast Mediterranean, watched from three sides by "the burning shores of Africa with its thin palm trees, the bare Syrian deserts, and the populous, jagged shore of Europe" (VIII, 82). Repeatedly in this collection Gogol gives evidence of what might be called a wide-screen mentality— as he did most memorably in his Cossack epic *Taras Bulba,* published about the same time. This tendency was certainly encouraged by the several romanticisms abroad in Russia at the time, but its lyrical excess suggests a more specifically Gogolian provenience. He was, as Valery Bryusov belatedly observed, a chronic hyperbolist; his skill as a writer rested on energetic imputation. These early essays show the impulse not yet under control. In an odd way they are both insufficiently personal (in their standardized vocabulary) and too personal (in their earnest refusal of ambiguity and indirection). Like *Selected Passages* a decade later, *Arabesques* shows Gogol's vision, only tenuously anchored to real knowledge or concrete objects, in an almost free state that regularly risks unintended comedy. If only these inflated statements could be attributed to fictional characters—or to a fictional narrator—many would appear brilliant. Gogol himself seems to have sensed his strategic mistake in electing to be earnest. He deliberately misdated a number of articles to bear out the prefatory claim that they had been written "at various epochs of my life" and that even a year earlier, "when I was more strict with regard to old works of mine," some of them might not have been included (VIII, 7). As for his explanation that he had chosen to write only about "what struck me forcibly," the matter might be put more accurately by saying that in each of these self-advertising essays he concentrated on whatever touched his esthetic preoccupations.

There are in *Arabesques* two pieces—on Bryulov and Pushkin —which stand out as major exceptions to what has just been said. Both support the claims of Gogol's preface without stretching, and it is significant that both have a concrete contemporary focus, suggesting that he was at his most soundly original in dealing with what was undoubtedly closest to his heart: the situation of the Russian artist in his time.

That time itself receives passing characterization in many of the other essays, usually to invidious effect. "Never have we so thirsted for bursts of feeling that lift the spirit as at the present time, when we are inundated and oppressed by all that miscellany (*drob'*) of caprices and enjoyments which our nineteenth century keeps racking its brains to invent" (VIII, 12). This characterization in the opening essay sets the theme. The nineteenth century is an age of "coldly dreadful egoism" and "mercantile souls" (VIII, 12), a debased successor to the remote ages when, in Gogol's mythical view, harmony and unity prevailed. Time and again he recurs to variations on the word *drob'*—fraction or fragment—to describe the modern condition. Thus, speaking of architecture: "As soon as the enthusiasm of the Middle Ages died down and man's thought was fragmented, pursuing a multitude of various aims, as soon as unity and the integrity of the whole disappeared—greatness disappeared with them. Fragmented, his powers became small ones; suddenly and in all genres he produced a multitude of amazing things, but there was no longer anything truly great, gigantic" (VIII, 58). These ideas are more than romantic commonplaces. They seem to have had the deepest meaning for Gogol, as if modernity, variety, and pluralism were a personal burden and a personal threat from which he dreamed of escape into an ideal society where membership already conferred dignity, morality became a simple matter of loyalty, individualism was punished as treason, the earth gave abundant nourishment without labor, and divine order manifested itself through the colossal harmonies of a public art that sustained man even as it dwarfed him. Indeed, these themes—all but the last, which had as yet no embodiment in Russia—can be found in Gogol's literary work of the period: "A Terrible Vengeance," "Old-World Landowners," *Taras Bulba,* "Viy," and others. Escape from solitary selfhood, as George Ivask has claimed, may well be the fundamental pathos and impulse of Gogol's imaginative life[21]; if so, it operated in a variety of ways and on a series of levels. The multifarious and the superficial are negative; as opposed to God's ideal harmony, they represent the work of the devil. (Compare, for example, "Nevsky Prospect": "The extraordinary diversity of faces utterly bewildered [the young artist Piskaryov]: it seemed as though some demon had chopped up the whole world into a multitude of different pieces and mixed them all senselessly and indiscriminately together [III, 23–24].) The ramifications of this theme must be reserved for a later chapter. The point here is that Gogol's intimate imaginative economy so marks his text as to suggest a personal reference even in ostensibly objective observations. Thus a certain, perhaps subliminal uneasiness with the miscellaneous nature of his own work to date surfaces with unusual clarity in this crucial remark from the piece on architecture:

Our century is so shallow, its desires scattered so widely, our knowledge so encyclopedic, that we are absolutely unable to focus our designs on any single object and hence, willy-nilly, we fragment all our works into trivia and charming toys. We have the marvelous gift of making everything insignificant (VIII, 66)

Bryulov and Pushkin, however, represent for Gogol two cases where the challenge of the age has been met:

If the truly striking has by and large shown up only in the trivial, the fault lies in the paucity of major geniuses and not in the enormous fragmentation of life and knowledge to which it is usually ascribed. I don't remember who it was said that in the nineteenth century the appearance of a universal genius who might comprehend in himself the whole life of the nineteenth century was impossible. This is absolutely untrue; such a thought testifies to hopelessness and smacks of faint-heartedness. On the contrary: never will the flight of genius be so brilliant as in our times. Never have the materials for it been so well prepared as in the nineteenth century. And its steps will surely be gigantic, and seen by all and sundry. (VIII, 109)

Bryulov's gigantic painting, "The Last Day of Pompeii," marks nothing less than the resurrection of pictorial art. After a period of the atomistic refining of technical skills, it is a "universal creation" because "it contains everything"—or "at least comprehends more disparate material than anyone had managed to do before him," and subordinates all to "the spiritual eye" of authentic talent, thereby justifying striking effects in a time when everybody, from the poet to the pastry cook, is avid to produce them.

The nature of this justification is the important thing: "His are the first works which can be understood (albeit differently) by the artist with the most highly developed taste and by the man who doesn't know what art is" (VIII, 113). The problem of the artist vis-à-vis a mass public was paramount for Gogol, who had already confessed a year before, "I don't know why I thirst so for contemporary fame" (X, 262); spoke of being haunted by visions of a large audience (X, 263), but felt repulsion for those who commanded one. (Thus his annoyance at his mother's misattribution of something of Senkovsky's to him: "His filthy writings please only the lower class" [X, 314].) Bryulov offered proof that this need not be so, that it was possible to keep faith with one's art and at the same time appeal to those who were not equipped to appreciate such fidelity.

I HAVE saved the essay "A Few Words About Pushkin" for last, though it was one of the earliest written and served apparently as the nucleus around which *Arabesques* took shape. Before considering it, however, a few further words are in order to about the effects of art as Gogol seems to have envisaged them in this period. If false art can have harmful consequences on the crowd that accepts it, then genuine art must have beneficial consequences—but of what kind? The answer cuts across the usual distinctions between "elitist" or "popular" conceptions, as it does between "esthetic" and "moral." Genuine art, as Gogol invokes it, has the same effect on connoisseurs and laymen: it exercises the soul. Even "people who seem to have fled forever from their own world of the soul—which is hidden in themselves and inscrutable to them —[even they] are forcibly returned within its borders."[22] Art, in other words, can redeem dead or deadened souls. This last word, one of the commonest in his lexicon, is not always or necessarily religious in connotation. Broadly speaking, it designates that faculty by which man transcends his merely physical or social self, the ground of an authentic, vital selfhood. The merely physical or social selves that dominate Gogol's comic writing do so as a negative ideal, and that writing serves less to ridicule foibles or expose vices than to exhibit radical insufficiencies, even as it supplies them through an almost magically vital and authentic language. Virginia Woolf, like the Vicomte de Vogüé before her and D. H. Lawrence after, saw the soul as chief character in Russian fiction of the nineteenth century. Gogol in his paradoxical way stands at the head of that tradition.

This is so despite the deplorable vagueness with which such terms as art and soul are left to function in Gogol's writing. He is uninterested in refining and clarifying his ideas; rather, he builds into their expression a contradiction by which striking and categorical statement, suggesting firmness of belief, is wedded to a covert insistence that all this is *provisional,* that final clarification is not part of his responsibility, at least at the moment. Only a tendency is clear—and that is lyrical, more a matter of demonstration than of argument. Esthetic propositions—to the extent that they remain vague or contradictory—testify to the sensitivity of the soul that enunciates them, become credentials: "Great one!" his porte-parole declares of the poet in an early sketch, "when I unroll your wondrous creation . . . a holy chill courses through my veins and my soul trembles in horror, having summoned the Deity from its boundless bosom . . . If heaven, the sun's rays, the sea, the fires that devour the interior of our earth, the infinite air that embraces the worlds, angels, the flaming planets, all were turned into words and letters, even then I could not express with them one tenth of the heavenly phenomena that take place at that time in the breast of my invisible self." Only corresponding emotion in the presence of art, a later passage explains, constitutes communication; words are powerless or worse, a sacrilege.[23]

The principle of art, then, is clearly a quasi-religious one for Gogol, invested for the time being with the solemnity of a Christless Christianity. By emphasizing this, the writer seems to relegate all subsidiary questions to the status of quibbles and frees himself from any obligation to be consistent, since the mystery of the inexpressible can only be approached approximately. It was not so much his views that changed later; it was his emphases. And what prompted the change was his experience as a writer, that unfolding

process of trial and error by which his own soul—his creative urge
—found changing expression and elicited changing justification.

"A Few Words About Pushkin" exemplifies this relation, applying the concerns of the Bryulov piece (contemporary Russian
art and its audience) to the area of Gogol's most immediate preoccupation: It is the only essay in the collection to concentrate on literary art. As if in compensation, Gogol put into it all that concerned him most about the possibilities of literature in his own
time and place, surveying the field that lay open to the ambition he
would later avow only at Pushkin's urging.

Pushkin was the one major Russian writer in the early 1830s,
unique in uniting what Gogol called a sense of "holy vocation"
with a consistent professionalism. Hailed here as a unique embodiment of "Russian nature, the Russian soul, Russian character, Russian language," he is said to have extended the borders of the latter
and shown "all its spaciousness" (VIII, 50). Writing romantically
of the exotic Caucasus and Crimea, he astonished "even those who
lacked the taste and mental development to be able to understand
him"; his fame spread with unprecedented and enviable rapidity.
And this, Gogol insists, was legitimate because the bond between
poet and reader was authentic: "A poet can even be national when
he is describing a quite alien world but regarding it with the eyes
of his national element, with the eyes of the whole people, when
he feels and speaks in such a way that it seems to his compatriots
that they themselves are doing the feeling and speaking" (VIII, 51).
But the closer to home the poet's subjects, the less able his audience may be to follow him. When Pushkin transferred his attention to the heart of Russia, seeking to be "a fully national poet," his
broad appeal began to wane—a phenomenon Gogol finds "not so
hard to explain." Once accustomed to "the boldness of his brush
and the magic of his scenes," his readers "incessantly demanded
that he take patriotic and historical events as subjects for his poetry, forgetting that one cannot portray the quieter and much less
passion-filled Russian way of life with the same colors [that are appropriate to] the Caucasus mountains and their free inhabitants."
The mass of the public is "most strange in its desires": it asks for a
truthful portrayal but will not accept one because it is not prepared
to appreciate an appropriately lowered subject matter and style as
literary (VIII, 52).

The poet's dilemma in the face of this situation constitutes the heart of the essay. So long as he confines himself to objects that justify a vivid style, the public—and its money—will be on his side. But if he chooses to be loyal to truth alone, then he must bid farewell to a readership unable to see that "a wild mountaineer in his warrior's costume, free as the wind, his own judge and master," and "our [Russian] judge in his threadbare, tobacco-stained frock coat . . . are both phenomena that belong to our world [and] must both have a claim on our attention." The more ordinary the object, Gogol insists, the more one must be a poet in order to draw the unusual out of it without violating truth in the process. But the more one is a poet in this way, the greater is his miscalculation—"not with respect to himself, but with respect to his multitudinous public" (VIII, 53–54). Pushkin's unnamed "smaller works" (*melkie sočinenija*) illustrate, "alas, the irrefutable truth that the more a poet becomes a poet—the more he renders feelings familiar to poets alone—the more markedly the crowd around him will dwindle," becoming finally so sparse "that he can count on his fingers all his true judges" (VIII, 55).

"A Few Words About Pushkin" thus shares the outward characteristics of most of the essays in *Arabesques*. It is categorical in tone, vivid in expression, and relentlessly unspecific, disdaining example and analysis. More than the others, however, it does seem to have been prompted by an inner need. Its designs are broader, its self-revelation more deliberate and controlled, and its strategic focus sharper.

By praising high artistry where others—"reputed connoisseurs and literary men" among them—had failed to discern it, Gogol vaunts his own familiarity with "feelings known to poets alone" and validates his right to stand in the company of the greatest poet of his time, the incarnation of Russianness. Here is the tactic of self-advertisement that underlies many of the other pieces as well: eminence by association. ("Criticism based on deep intelligence," he was to write soon afterward, "possesses a worth equal to that of any individual creation" and may make the critic "even more prominent" than the writer under discussion [VIII, 175].) Gogol, however—with Pushkin's help and encouragement —had been consolidating an eminence of his own as a writer of stories. As a result, the implicit association is both more plausible and more significant, and it turns this essay into a kind of literary manifesto, where praise for Pushkin's evolving poetics functions at the same time as advocacy for Gogol's own. His remarks about "extracting the extraordinary from the ordinary" offer an important key to the rationale of such Gogolian works as "Shponka" or "The Carriage"—and to his subsequent conception of *Dead Souls* as a *poema*. Indeed, signs of a veiled apology can be seen throughout the essay, in his praise of works "quiet and undramatic as Russian nature," and of "minor compositions [which] one rereads several times" in contrast to works "where a principal idea shows through too plainly."

Thus Gogol links his own name with Pushkin's in propagandizing for a particular esthetic program[24]—and implicitly broaches the possibility that prose works (as a whole and not simply in lyric passages) may perform the functions hitherto ascribed only to poetry. He, of course, was soon to be praised for providing proofs of this proposition. Belinsky, writing some years later, endorsed the propriety of citing Pushkin's example by noting how the latter showed "that the difference between verse and prose lies not merely in rhyme and meter, but that verse [itself] . . . can be both poetic and prosaic. This meant understanding poetry in its inner essence, and no longer as something external."[25]

Gogol takes his stand with Pushkin against the uncomprehending reading public. But when he deplores the paucity of "true judges" ("In all Petersburg there are perhaps only some five individuals who understand [literary] art deeply and truly" [X, 362]), he is engaging in more than self-congratulation or elitism. For he is deploring the state of the reading public *to* the reading public, a fact that makes this the boldest pedagogical essay in the book. The pessimism of his conclusion is not absolute; it adds force to the challenge contained in such statements as that Pushkin's words "can only be understood completely by one . . . whose motherland is Russia, whose soul is so delicately organized and developed in feeling that it can comprehend Russian songs and the Russian spirit, devoid though they be of surface brilliance" (VIII, 54). The ideal reader adumbrated here is not so much an esthete as a cultural patriot; he requires not so much rare gifts as "a taste higher than one that can understand only excessively sharp and large-scale features." What he needs chiefly is an orientation—and Gogol, in preferring the "internal brilliance" that does not leap to the eye over "cascades of eloquence," puts all his effort into elucidating one. His essay promotes a new scale of literary values and a newly sensitized public taste. The hope that this bespeaks is reflected even more energetically in the journalism to which he turned soon after the publication of *Arabesques*.

GOGOL's brief foray into journalism follows directly on the publication of *Arabesques* and comes as the culmination of his most intense engagement in the literary life of the capital. This is the time of his most active production—clearly the moment when his talents were reaching maturity but had yet to be committed in any single direction. Aside from his ill-fated professorship, which continued throughout 1835, in that year he published two volumes (*Arabesques* in January, *Mirgorod* in March), completed two of his best stories ("The Nose" and "The Carriage"), began three plays (*Vladimir of the Third Class, Getting Married, Alfred*), finished the draft of a fourth (*The Inspector General*), and started *Dead Souls*. In the first half of 1836, involved in the preparations for staging *The Inspector General*, he gave himself over to editorial work and reviewing for *The Contemporary*, the first volume of which, in April, carried a story, a dramatic excerpt, and reviews by him, along with his capital article "On the Development of Periodical Literature in 1834 and 1835."

Only three years before he had dismissed journalism categorically, observing with relief that Pushkin had abandoned his plan to publish a newspaper: "To take up the discredited trade of a journalist at this time hardly reflects well even on someone who is unknown; but for a genius to engage in this means to sully the purity and chastity of his soul and to become an ordinary man" (X, 247). In the meantime, however, the *Library for Reading* had appeared, had assembled the largest readership to date in Russia, and was complacently monopolizing it. Some worried about the commercialism of the enterprise: the high salaries paid to Krylov and Senkovsky as nominal and effective editors, respectively; the generous remuneration offered to contributors (and even noncontributors, so long as they would consent to having their names listed on the cover); the willingness to buy out prospective competitors.[26] Gogol's concern lay elsewhere. Signs of it appear already in his reaction to the first number of the new journal. Senkovsky, he writes in a letter, is like

an old drunkard and debauchee whom even the publican himself has long tried to keep out of the tavern, but who nonetheless has burst in and is heedlessly, drunkenly, smashing flasks, bottles, goblets, and all . . .

The class standing above Brambeus' [Senkovsky's] is indignant at [his] shamelessness and insolence . . . Being a class that loves propriety, it disdains but reads him. Heads of sections and directors of departments read him and split their sides with laughter. Officers read him and say, "The son of a bitch, how well he writes!" Provincial land- owners . . . subscribe and, doubtless, will read him. Only we sinners keep [the magazine] in reserve for household use . . .

The worst of it is that we've all been made fools of! Our literary big- wigs have suddenly caught on to this—but too late. The esteemed edi- tors have been making hay with our names, have collected subscribers, made the people gape, and are now traveling on our backs. They have laid a new cornerstone for their power. This is another [*Northern*] *Bee!* Behold our literature without a voice! And all the while these raiders are acting on the whole of Russia.

The last point is crucial, for Gogol is aware that Moscow and Pe- tersburg are not to be confused with the real Russia. That, he knew, was only to be sought in the heart of the country (X, 293– 294).

The *Library for Reading* with its all-inclusive list of contribu- tors promised to be a kind of "storage room for all the wares pro- duced by writers, a periodical exhibition of contemporary Russian literature." In the vaunted absence of a guiding editorial policy, the journal could be characterless at best. The first two numbers al- ready showed something else: that libraries were not, in the words of one observer, for reading alone, but for "the literary auction of reputations, for the monthly provisioning of friends with praise, for Bedouin raids on enemies."[27] In the hands of Senkovsky, criti- cism in the *Library* was self-willed and capricious; above all it was fatuous: "In our criticism" he declared, "you will not find a drop of criticism; what you'll find is . . . —just so!—something or other!—a sort-of criticism!—what all people write, imagining to themselves that they are writing criticism."[28] One looks for a re- deeming irony behind this kind of silliness, but in vain. Nor is it hard, in view of the journal's power, to see why such emptiness could appear grotesque and even ominous to those who believed with Gogol that the reading public needed to be addressed respon- sibly so that it might become more discriminating. The attacks in his stories on self-satisfaction, vulgarity, emptiness, vanity, inau- thenticity—all take on a new point in light of the writing of Senkovsky and his friend Bulgarin. Those incarnations of the void that appear so often in his artistic work are not merely the products of imagination; they are symbolic counterparts of the vacuity that appeared to be dominating the literary scene at the time.

Hence Gogol's interest in a journalistic competition for the new audience. This manifested itself first in energetic (if pessimistic) efforts on behalf of the *Moscow Observer,* which was founded precisely for that purpose. In November 1834 he writes Pogodin of his gladness that some of the more serious Moscow writers have planned a journal and promises to help as much as he can. His advice is eminently practical:

Our journal must be sold at as low a price as possible. Better for the first year to refuse any remuneration for articles . . . Only in this way can one take the upper hand and to some degree stem the tide of the rabble flocking to the stupid *Library,* which has too fast a hold on its readers by virtue of its thickness. Further: as much variety as possible! . . . People are impressed most of all by quantity and mass. And let there be laughter, laughter, especially at the end. For that matter, it wouldn't be bad to lard the pages with it throughout. And the main thing: give it to them without pulling punches. (X, 341)

Within three months he is already in despair. "All you Moscow literary men are scoundrels," he writes Pogodin:

No good will ever come of you. It's all words with you. You say you've undertaken a journal and nobody wants to work?! But how can you rely on outside contributors when you're not in a position to rely on your own people? Shame, shame, shame! Take a look at how the Petersburg journals manage their affairs. Where can you show that kind of constancy and labor, and agility, and wisdom? . . . And you don't have articles yet for the first issue . . . If even a common cause can't get you moving . . . together, then what good is there in you, what can come of you? I confess, I can't believe in your journal's existing for more than one year . . . My God! so many minds and all of them original: you, Shevyryov, Kireyevsky. Damn it, and they complain of poverty! Baratynsky, Yazykov—ai, ai, ai! . . . Tell me, please, how I am supposed to work and labor for you when I know that none of you is willing to work. Mustn't my ardor naturally cool? I'll hurry as fast as I can to finish the story I'm preparing for you. (X, 353–354)

The story in question was "The Nose." Quite without any of the pathetic undertones of the three published in *Arabesques,* it would have been out of place in that collection. On the other hand, it accords particularly well with Gogol's new views of what is needed in the current literary situation, and with the energetic high spirits that accompanied his efforts to realize them.

All the more disillusioning was the journal's rejection of his story as "filthy," and its laudatory but obtuse and patronizing review of his *Mirgorod,* in which he found himself urged to turn his attention to educated society, "us ourselves."[29] The *Moscow Observer* could neither compete effectively in the marketplace nor sympathize intelligently with Gogol's own artistic practice. As a result, by the end of the year he had transferred his hopes and support to Pushkin's newly undertaken *Contemporary.* It printed "The Nose" and "The Carriage," commissioned a series of book reviews, and carried in its inaugural issue Gogol's long and shrewd survey of the current literary-journalistic scene, in which he elaborated nothing less than a program for the deliberate creation of a contemporary literary culture.[30]

"On the Movement of Periodical Literature in 1834 and 1835" opens by insisting on the cultural importance of his subject, which is

as necessary in the area of sciences and arts as communications are for the state, or as fairs and exchanges are for merchants and trade. It controls the taste of the crowd, circulates and sets in motion everything that comes to light in the world of books and would otherwise remain, in both senses, dead capital . . . Its voice is the true representative of the opinions of the whole age and century, of opinions that would disappear without trace but for it. Willy-nilly it catches and carries into its sphere nine tenths of everything that appertains to literature. How many people there are who judge, speak and interpret [only] because all their judgments are handed them almost ready-made—and who would not, of themselves, interpret or judge or speak. (VIII, 156)

Noting evidence over the past two years of "a general need for intellectual food," the result of a significant increase in the number of readers, he goes on to consider the response to that demand, chiefly as offered in the *Library for Reading.*

Unique Gogol grants the *Library* to be, but hardly all-inclusive: "With the publication of the first issue the public saw clearly that the tone, opinions and ideas of *one person* clearly dominated in the journal, and that the names of writers whose brilliant column filled half the title page had only been rented for the occasion to attract a greater number of subscribers" (VIII, 157). So he proceeds to consider Senkovsky's practice, discovering in him a kind of literary Nozdryov:

After reading everything he has put in this journal, following all his words, we cannot but pause in astonishment: What is all this? What has made this man write? We see a man who certainly does not take money for nothing, who works in the sweat of his brow, not only lavishing concern on his own articles but even reworking other people's—in short, a man who is inexhaustible. What is all this activity for? (VIII, 158–159)

Reading his criticism, it is impossible to determine what he likes and what he doesn't: "In his reviews there is *neither positive nor negative taste—there is none at all*" (VIII, 160). Yet this same man unabashedly "corrects" articles on every conceivable subject—"and all without any evil intent, even without any clear realization, without being guided by any feeling of need or propriety. He even tacked his own ending onto a [classic] comedy of Fonvizin's, failing to notice that it already had an ending" (VIII, 166). What is more, he confesses the practice openly: "In the *Library for Reading* things are not set up as they are in other journals: We do not leave any story in its original form, we rework every one: Sometimes we make one out of two, sometimes out of three, and the piece is significantly improved by our revisions!" (VIII, 162).

These last words are quotation, not invention—suggesting again how the emptiness, vulgarity, and mindlessness that fill Gogol's fictions may have had unsuspected sources in current literary practice. Instances have been identified in *The Inspector General* (Khlestakov and the mayor alike) and are surely present in *Dead Souls* (whence his insistence on the serious national import of trivial characters and empty speech).[31]

Gogol goes on to survey the ineffective competition, dwarfed by the *Library*, which stands among them "like an elephant among the minor quadrupeds":

Their battle was too uneven, and it seems they failed to take into account that the *Library for Reading* had some five thousand subscribers, that the opinions of the *Library for Reading* were spread in layers of society where people had not even heard of [their] existence . . . that the opinions and works published in the *Library for Reading* were praised by the editors of that very *Library for Reading*, hiding under different names—and praised with enthusiasm, which always has an influence on the larger part of the public; for what is ludicrous to educated readers is believed in all their simpleheartedness by more limited readers of the kind one must assume the *Library*'s readers to be, judging by the number of subscribers—the majority of whom besides were new people who had not hitherto been familiar with magazines and consequently inclined to take everything as gospel truth. (VIII, 165)

Finally, he notes, the *Library* had reinforcement in the 4000-strong circulation of *The Northern Bee*.

The attempt to break "such an unprecedented monopoly" by setting up a new rival in the *Moscow Observer* he brands as misguided throughout. For one thing, the new journal arose to meet the needs of writers uncomfortable with the *Library*'s whimsical tyranny, more than it did to meet the needs of the reading public. This was reflected in the first issue, where Shevyryov's blast at the new commercialism ("Literature and Commerce") quite missed the point: "This article was comprehensible only to literary men; it vexed the *Library for Reading,* but brought no message to the public, which didn't even understand what the problem was." Moreover, these attacks were unwarranted: "Literature was bound to turn into commerce, because the number of readers and the demand for reading had increased. It was natural in view of this that enterprising people without much talent should profit most, because in any trade where the consumers are still unsophisticated the more adroit and pushy merchants profit most . . . That a literary man has bought himself a building that brings in income or a pair of horses is not such a catastrophe; what is bad is that some poor people have bought low-grade merchandise and are still boasting of their purchase. Mr. Shevyryov should have paid attention to the poor customers, rather than to the sellers" (VIII, 169). Gogol's central concern is with these customers, particularly those in the provinces who may seldom have held a book in their hands before. He seems to have wavered in his estimate of their present state of development. Thus in an excised passage from his first draft he speaks of Senkovsky's having "considered his public as rabble, forgetting, perhaps, that a good half of the readers of Russia were already on a higher level than that of the language in which he addressed them" (VIII, 526).

In any case, Gogol's notion of the reader here is clearly a composite one, combining the actual with the "implied" reader and favoring the kind of criticism that cultivates discrimination by supposing its possibility. (A journal exists, he wrote in his draft, only by virtue of its criticism, "only here can its aim be seen" [VIII, 542].) Having surveyed what Russian journals contained over the past two years—"You would think that not a single important event had occurred in the literary world"—he turns to what they failed to register: the death of Walter Scott, the rise of the *école frénétique* in France, the spread of novels and stories at the expense of poetry, the publication in new editions of such major writers as Derzhavin and Karamzin—all demanding evaluation or reevaluation and posing questions for which readers looked in vain. What was Walter Scott and how is his influence to be understood? What is contemporary French literature, whence did it arise, and what accounts for its aberrant taste? Even more importantly: "Why has poetry been replaced by prose compositions? How relatively educated is the Russian public, and what is the Russian public? What constitutes the originality and the distinctive quality of our writers?" (VIII, 172).

Instead of confronting such questions, Russian journalists preferred to speak about what was nearest and dearest to them—about themselves, manifesting the unconscious principles of their writing as: (1) "a disregard for their own opinions"; (2) "literary unbelief and literary ignorance"; (3) "a lack of purely esthetic enjoyment and taste"; and (4) "triviality in ideas," together with a "trivial foppishness" (VIII, 173–175). These observations pave the way for a concluding exhortation considerably harsher in draft than in the published version:

During this time neither Zhukovsky nor Krylov nor Prince Vyazemsky expressed his opinions—not even those who had recently been publishing journals and who had voices of their own and had demonstrated taste and knowledge in their articles: Can one wonder under the circumstances at the state our literature is in?

Why did these writers, who had shown such deep esthetic feeling in their works, not speak out? Did they consider it demeaning to descend to the sphere of journalism . . . ? We do not have the right to answer. We must only observe that criticism based on profound taste and intelligence, the criticism of a high talent, possesses a value equal to any original creation: in it one sees the writer being analysed; in it one sees still more the writer who is performing the analysis. A criticism informed with talent outlives the ephemeral existence of a journal. For the history of literature it is priceless. Our literature is young; its leaders are few; but for a thoughtful critic it offers a whole field, work for years. (VIII, 175)

To the still common view of the young Gogol as no more than an esthete lost in rapturous abstraction, this article offers a vigorous corrective. He may have been vague and overblown in writing about art as an ideal, but his writing about literature, motivated by a shrewd professionalism, is generally clearsighted and pragmatic. So here he calls in the most practical terms for what amounts to the deliberate fostering of a literary culture—the marshaling of a usable past, the illuminating of present tendencies at home and abroad—by writers turned critics. In his draft he acknowledges that it may seem strange "to demand that writers of large talent . . . sully themselves in the base area of journalism," but justifies the demand on grounds of practical necessity and self-interest alike. The corrupt opinions currently circulating are "creating and forming the majority of the reading public"; failure to offer a corrective must "weigh on the souls of great writers"— who, he adds prophetically, should see in the "inaccurate, ignorant, nonsensical" things that keep being repeated about their predecessors the fate that also threatens them (VIII, 536–538).

"On the Movement of Periodical Literature" marks the high point of Gogol's active optimism with respect to *la chose littéraire* in his time—an optimism that attached as well to his *Inspector General,* then being readied for performance. "The theater is a great school," he had written, "profound is its allotted task. To a whole crowd, to a thousand people at once, it reads a vivid, useful lesson" (VIII, 562). When the crowd failed to take that lesson by evidencing signs of moral regeneration on the spot, Gogol, a disappointed maximalist, fled abroad, breaking the promise he had made to be "a faithful contributor" to *The Contemporary*. Pushkin evidently foresaw the possibility of this defection; in any case, it was clear that Gogol's exhortations were not likely to stir his associates to action, and that of them the only one who might be counted on to pursue the course he had advocated in his article was Gogol himself. Hence Pushkin's editorial disclaimer in the third issue: "The article, 'On the Movement of Periodical Literature,' was printed in my journal, but it does not follow from this that all the opinions expressed there with such youthful high spirits and forthrightness fully coincide with my own. In any case it is not and could not have been the program of *The Contemporary*."[32]

GOGOL's association with *The Contemporary* entailed book and theatrical reviewing as well. His performance in the former category was somewhat capricious; the form of a theatrical survey, by contrast, allowed his analytic bent to operate on a more general level and, at the same time, accommodated more easily his prescriptive tendencies. "The Petersburg Stage" was written in the early months of 1836, shortly before the premiere of his *Inspector General*. Subsequently revised and amalgamated with another article, "Petersburg and Moscow (From the Notes of a Traveler)," it appeared only the following year as "Petersburg Notes for 1836."

In it he continues his exploration of the artist's place in Russia, but with new emphases. A draft defines romanticism as "nothing more than an attempt to move closer to our society, from which we have been utterly removed by the imitation of society and people to be found in the creations of ancient writers"; thus "present-day drama has shown an attempt to deduce the laws of action from our own society," the perception of which, however, requires "a great talent" (VIII, 553, 555). As before he is concerned with the writer and his public, but the third term—society—adds a new and overarching element.

He begins by contrasting Moscow and Petersburg—Moscow being necessary to Russia as its heart, Petersburg representing something like the wave of the future. "It is difficult to seize the expression of Petersburg," that is, to characterize it as a social entity. Likened to "a European-American colony," with its unassimilated mixture of foreign settlers and indigenous population, the capital consists of sundry nations and social strata—"aristocrats, government workers, artisans, Englishmen, Germans, merchants—[which] constitute absolutely separate circles, rarely coming together, for the most part living and making merry invisibly to each other" (VIII, 179–180). Each of these classes, moreover, threatens to dissolve into quite separate subclasses. "Even the literary man, up to now an ambiguous and dubious figure, stands utterly apart." This state of social atomization (which he had already sketched in "Nevsky Prospect," "Diary of a Madman," and "The Nose") explains the unique value Gogol assigns to the theater— and the hyperbolic hopes he attached to it in connection with his own play. The theater is the one potential locus of that Petersburg society which is still only virtual. In the theater and only there can it discover itself and so come into being.

Gogol stresses the love of all classes for theater, and the way currently available fare cheats them, providing not comedy or tragedy but only their debased and alien forms: vaudeville and melodrama. "Where is our life? Where are we with all our contemporary passions and peculiarities? If only we could find some reflection [of all this] in our melodrama! But our melodrama lies in the most shameless fashion . . . The whole trick is to relate some happening, which must be new and must be strange, something never yet seen or heard of: a murder, conflagrations, the wildest passions—things of which not a trace is to be found in our present-day societies! . . . A spectator has never yet come out of the theater moved to tears; on the contrary, with a certain uneasiness he has hastened to enter his carriage and for a long time been unable to order his thoughts" (VIII, 182).

Returning to a theme first broached in the Pushkin essay, he emphasizes the paradox that "what surrounds us daily, what is inseparable from us, what is ordinary, only a deep, great, extraordinary talent can notice." But a new connection—with comedy and laughter—gives the observation a new point. Where Pushkin's talent for rendering the ordinary restricted his audience to a handful of esthetes, an infinitely broader field lies open to the comparably gifted comic playwright. He can, in a double sense, "give us ourselves" (VIII, 186) and, by holding up a mirror to society, produce a purgative recognition in the microcosm of that society which is the theater audience.

There is some confusion in Gogol's argument—a sign, probably, of the momentousness of his intuition here, for he is struggling to articulate the assumptions on which the next half dozen years of his quasi-monastic literary work would rest. The intuition in question centers on the esthetic seriousness and social value of comedy. Laughter is discovered to be "a great thing" and the theater "a pulpit from which a lively lesson is read at once to a whole crowd, where, in the solemn glitter of the lights, to the thunder of music, in the presence of general laughter, a familiar vice that has been trying to hide is exposed and, with the secret voice of universal sympathy, a familiar, timidly revealed, lofty feeling comes to the fore" (VIII, 186–187).

The audience in this ideal prescription is united by deep esthetic feeling—which it owes to and shares with the rare writer whose "lofty mind" can create "a rigorously thought-out comedy," one that "by the profundity of its irony" produces a kind of laughter Gogol is at pains to distinguish from "laughter born of superficial impressions, a passing witticism or word play" and from "that laughter which moves the coarse crowd of society with its need for convulsions and caricature grimaces." What he cele-

brates is "an electric, vivifying laughter born of tranquil enjoyment which breaks forth unbidden, freely and unexpectedly,
straight from the soul . . . (VIII, 181).

Two lines of connection, then: Comedy, defined as "a true
copy of society," mirrors the audience at the same time that it
makes of them in their shared reaction a newly authenticated entity, a society in microcosm. Recognizing themselves in what is
exposed on stage, moreover, the spectators thereby transcend the
exposure through a kind of comic catharsis, and emerge emotion-
ally and morally elevated. This is plainly naive because anachronistic, harking back (as Gogol always did for examples of the positive) to a model in the remote past—that of Aristophanic "Old
Comedy." Gogol's own *Inspector General,* as Vyacheslav Ivanov
has shown, conforms to the model not only in its social emphases
but in its designs on the audience; and it is *The Inspector General,*
mentioned in passing in "Petersburg Notes," that fills those notes
with its virtual and exemplary presence.[33]

If Gogol's comedy aspired to be Aristophanic, however, his
audience was hardly Athenian. Even the actors were nonplussed
by the novelty of his conception and proved unequal to its demands.[34] All the more so, Gogol found, was the larger audience,
which in its simplicity was inclined to take everything personally:

If we are shown some lifelike character on the stage, we are already
thinking, Isn't this some personal attack? . . . If it is said, for instance,
that in some city one court counselor is of inebriate behavior, then all
court counselors will take offense, and some counselor of a completely
different sort will even say: "What's all this about? I have a relative who
is a court counselor, and an excellent man! How can anyone say that
there is a court counselor of inebriate behavior!" . . . And such touchi-
ness in Russia extends to absolutely all classes. (VIII, 186)

In "On the Movement of Periodical Literature" Gogol had
advocated collective action to supply the defects of what he had
surveyed; here, against the absence of a serious theatrical culture,
he sets only his own views and, by implication, his own work. The
closing pages show a turning inward and a new perspective, colored by more than simply the solemnity of the Easter season,
when "all the vapid and insignificant people will probably lie
sleepy and exhausted and forget to come around to bother me
with their vulgar conversation about whist, literature, awards, the
theater" (VIII, 187). Though the crowd in the market may look

the same as ever, it and the author are changed. Each individual is filled with "feelings different [from those of] a year before; his thoughts are already more severe; his soul smiles less on his lips, and with each day something of his former liveliness falls away" (VIII, 188). The writer dreams "of a distant road under other skies" (VIII, 190). In the draft of *After the Play,* written about the same time, the thought is even clearer: "I shall go away: I need a wilderness . . . I shall follow my wandering fate into other, distant regions . . . The temporary and turbid darkness will lift from my eyes, and clothed only in her splendour and profound purity, Russia shall appear before me" (V, 390).

The letters of this period sum up the experience of six years of searching for self-definition as a writer and for an audience that would confirm the results of that search. Both had been successful, the first in a positive, the second in a negative sense. The theory of comedy enunciated in "Petersburg Notes" offered a rationale for the newly articulated ambitions he attached to his future writing. The reactions to his play led to an abandonment not of those ambitions, but only of hopes for their immediate vindication: "Contemporary fame," which he had thirsted for, courted, and found, proved to be illusive. "Now I see," he writes ten days after the premiere of his play, "what it means to be a comic writer. The least shadow of truth—and not one man but whole classes rise up against you" (XI, 38). "The contemporary writer, the comic writer, the writer of manners should be as far as possible from his country. The prophet is without honor in his homeland" (XI, 41). "We should have posterity in view, and not base contemporaneity" (XI, 77).

In his first letter from abroad (to Zhukovsky, from Hamburg) he recognizes that his practical pursuit of a vocation has reached "a great turning point":

In fact, strictly and fairly considered, what is everything I have written up to now? It seems to me as if I am leafing through the old notebook of a student, in which carelessness and laziness are visible on one page, impatience and haste on another, [everywhere] the timid, trembling hand of the beginner and some bold doodling . . . From time to time, perhaps, a page will be found that might be praised, [but] only by a teacher who saw in it the germ of the future. (XI, 48–49)

From the first, Gogol had been disposed to dismiss each successive piece of writing in this way. What he was now dismissing, however, was a body of artistic work which had already caused the young Belinsky to speak of his occupying the throne of poetry allegedly vacated by Pushkin. Of his masterpieces, only two—"The Overcoat" and *Dead Souls*—lay in the future. The rest were by now in print. Differently and more centrally, they too show Gogol's evolving response to the question of how to be a writer.

4

Beginnings: Fiction

Gogol's first, pseudonymous volume of stories, *Evenings on a Farm Near Dikanka,* opens disarmingly with an act of double ventriloquism: the voice of a hypothetical reader filtered through the voice of a fictive narrator, Rudy Panko, the garrulous old provincial beekeeper. Only two years before, *Hanz Kuechelgarten* had been offered to an "enlightened public" that was less a figment of the author's imagination than the poem's German hero. Now, rather more enlightened about that public, Gogal can flaunt his awareness of what it means "for a rustic like me to poke his nose out of the backwoods into the great world"—and turn that awareness to creative account, realizing his gift for mimicry as the ground for stylistic experiment. The very compositors who set these stories in type chuckled at them, he reported to Pushkin, from which he concluded "that I am a writer quite to the taste of the rabble (*čern*)" (X, 203). Pushkin, publishing this anecdote, noted that the scene would have gratified a Molière or a Fielding. Successful prose, he had once written, required "chatter." Gogol's stories provided this with unprecedented success and variety, offering a range of speech forms from country-colloquial to conventionally literary, in tones from farcical to lyrical.

The enabling device was indirection. The stories in the first volume are ascribed to separate narrators with distinct leanings—the aged sexton of the Dikanka church, Foma Grigorievich, who is responsible for "St. John's Eve" and "The Lost Letter," and the "fine young gentleman with his bookish phrases," who provides "The Fair at Sorochintsy" and "A May Night." Two others—an anonymous teller of frightening stories and Rudy Panko himself—are held in reserve for the second volume. Thus Gogol justifies a play with contrasting styles and narrative attitudes while escaping identification with any one of them.

For this freedom he is significantly indebted to his friend and early mentor, Pletnyov, who for reasons of literary politics suggested that the stories be published anonymously and offered the title. That brought with it the personage of Panko, which, once created, could serve as a prism, refracting Gogol's own assaying of contemporary literary styles.[1] The value of this framing presence can be seen if we compare the opening of "St. John's Eve" as published before the invention of Panko with the version that appeared in Volume One:

My grandfather had a wonderful skill in storytelling. It used to be that you'd stand an hour or two before him without lifting your eyes, as if rooted to the spot: so engrossing was his way of speaking—there's no comparison with the fancy-talking jokers of today who, God forgive them, make you yawn till you're ready to climb the walls. I remember well how it used to be in the long winter evenings, when my mother would be spinning in the dim candlelight, rocking the cradle with one foot and humming some mournful song whose sounds I seem to hear even now, and we children would gather around our old grandfather, who in his feebleness hadn't crawled off the stove ledge for more than ten years. You should have seen how raptly we listened to his wonderful accounts—of bygone years full of merrymaking, of the days of the hetmans, of the wild raids of the Cossacks . . . But most of all we liked the stories that were based on some ancient supernatural legend, which the know-it-alls of today would not hesitate . . . to call a fabrication; but I'd stake my life that grandfather never lied so much as once. To convince you that this is true, let me tell you right now one of those tales that pleased us so much in those days, hoping that you, too, will like it. (I, 349–350)

That is from Gogol's first, unsigned appearance as a prose writer; the tale is identified as being told by the nameless sexton of the Pokrov Church. The revised opening presents a dramatized scene in place of this dull cliché:

Foma Grigorievich had one special peculiarity, a mortal dislike of telling the same story over again. You might occasionally persuade him to repeat one, but then he'd either throw in something new or change things around so that there was no recognizing it. Once one of those gentlemen —it's hard for us simple folk to know what to call them: they're not exactly scribblers, more like the horse traders at our fairs; they pick up or beg or steal all sorts of things, and then bring out little books no thicker than a primer every month or week—one of those gentlemen, I say, wheedled this very story out of Foma Grigorievich, who promptly forgot all about it. Well, no sooner does that same young gentleman in the pea-green coat—I've spoken about him before and I think you've read one story of his—no sooner does he arrive bringing a little book than he opens it in the middle and shows it to us. Foma Grigorievich was already about to settle his spectacles astride his nose when he remembered that he'd forgotten to fix them with thread and wax, and so he handed the book to me. Since I know more or less how to read and don't wear glasses, I started aloud. But I hadn't got past two pages before he stopped me with his hand: "Wait a minute! Tell me first what that is you're reading." I must admit such a question nonplussed me a little. "What do you mean, what am I reading, Foma Grigorievich? It's your story, your own words."

"Who told you they were my words?

"It's here in black and white: 'told by the sexton of such-and-such.'"

"To hell with the fellow who printed that. He's lying, the damned Russky! Is that the way I told it? The damn fool must have slats in his head! Just listen, I'll tell it to you now."

We moved up to the table and he began. (I, 137–138)

Neither Rudy Panko nor Foma Grigorievich is what could be called a developed character, but both are vivid and effective presences as voices, and Gogol manages their interplay here in a quasi-Cervantine way to set off their existence from the "lifeless" pages of inauthentic "literature." Faddei Bulgarin himself succumbed to the effect, praising "the unshakable internal belief in the marvelous stamped on each word of [Foma Grigorievich's] story, giving it the kind of ancient simplicity from which we have deviated so far, led astray by the mannered forms of our life and attuned to the counterfeit—even in the use of language."[2]

This tribute from a leading literary enemy points to another aspect of Gogol's achievement with his first collection. Though from our vantage point the chief interest of *Evenings* lies in technique and style (and in the quasi-autonomous thematic value they always carry in his writing), Gogol's contemporary success rested to a large extent on his subject matter.

His very first letter to betray a literary intention (30 April 1829) had described Petersburg as lacking the impress of national character (X, 139) and noted at the same time how "everything Ukrainian so interests everybody here" (X, 142). Romantic theory exalted ethnography and folk poetry as expressions of the Volksgeist, and the Ukraine was particularly appealing to a Russian audience in this respect, being, as Gippius observes, a country both "'ours' and 'not ours,' neighboring, related, and yet lending itself to presentation in the light of a semi-realistic romanticism, a sort of Slavic Ausonia."[3] Gogol capitalized on this appeal as a mediator; by embracing his Ukrainian heritage, he became a Russian writer.[4]

Much has been made of the question of authenticity in these and other stories with a Ukrainian setting, but the debate—conducted by Russian and Ukrainian scholars from Gogol's time to our own—is kept alive by tacit value judgments that may have more to do with national pride than with literature as such. The letter to his mother (30 April 1829) reporting the general interest in things Ukrainian in Petersburg contains urgent requests for details:

In your next letter I expect descriptions of the full costume of a village deacon, from outer clothing to the very boots, along with the names by which everything used to be called by the most traditional, the oldest, the least changed of Little Russians; similarly, the name of the dress worn by peasant girls right up to the last ribbon, and also [what is worn] by married women and the peasant men today . . . Also a few words about caroling, about St. John the Baptist, about water nymphs. If there are, besides, any spirits or house goblins, then about them, as precisely as possible, with their names and what they do; among the simple people there are a great many beliefs, terrifying legends, traditions, various anecdotes, and so on. (X, 141)

In the same letter he asks for copies of his father's Ukrainian comedies—and in the next (which informs his mother of his flight to Luebeck) he confesses that he is preparing a store of Ukrainian fictions which he may, with time, publish. Amid the surrounding mystifications, his passing remark that this book will be "in a foreign language" has been taken simply as another—though in a broader context it may suggest no more than that correctness of Ukrainian reference is particularly important in a work written in Russian. (His preface to the first volume of *Evenings* bears this out by containing a glossary of words "that may not be comprehensible to everyone.")

Related to the question of authenticity is that of derivation. Much of the novelty of these stories for Russian readers has been shown to have identifiable precedents in Ukrainian writing and folk traditions. Indeed, some of these are indicated in the epigraphs to each of the thirteen chapters of the opening piece, "The Fair at Sorochintsy." To argue whether Gogol is faithfully extending or willfully ransacking a tradition is to quibble; to find precedents for most of his narrative tones and devices is only to show what can be shown of his later, non-Ukrainian works as well: he was a literary magpie, taking traits for his own creation wherever he could find them, from published and unpublished sources, much more often than from observation or direct personal experience. From all such demonstrations—and the recond contains some substantial ones—the sense in which Gogol was writing "in a foreign language" only becomes clearer. The comic narrative stance, the lively colloquialisms, blurring the boundaries between popular speech and literary language—the whole stylistic spectrum employed in his stories—may well have seemed familiar to those who knew the Ukrainian tales (in verse and prose) of Kotlyarevsky and Gulak-Artemovsky, not to mention Tsertelev's collection of songs, just as situations and incidents from his stories might appear familiar to those who had read the fictions of Narezhny and Somov and seen Ukrainian puppet shows. Nonetheless, for the Russian public in 1831 these stories in their totality and variety represented something qualitatively new.

That is the burden of Pushkin's first response: "I have just read *Evenings near Dikanka*. They have astonished me. Here is genuine gaiety, sincere and unforced, without affectation, without primness. And in places what poetry! What sensitivity! All this is so unusual in our current literature that I haven't yet come to my senses."[5]

The assessment is unspecific, but as Victor Erlich has observed, it may well refer beyond particular felicities to the magical sense of contingency that can be seen already in the first volume—and even more clearly in the collection as a whole.[6] That whole was itself a product of contingency, the result of a series of experiments* with stories disparate in kind and quality, ranging

---

* There is no record of Gogol's intentions or attitudes in undertaking these experiments, but V. A. Sollogub, a minor writer of the time, reports having asked him how he learned to write so well and freely. Practice, Gogol is reported as replying: "Set yourself the rule that you will write every day for two or three hours. Lay out the paper and pens in front of you, set up the ink bottle, note the hour, and write." But what if nothing comes to mind, Sollogub objects. "Write 'Nothing comes to mind.' Tomorrow you'll add something, the day after you'll add something more, and your hand will become practiced. And you'll be a writer. That's the way I did it" (V. A. Sollogub, *Vospominanija* [Moscow-Leningrad, 1931], p. 378, n. 2). Gogol's advice in a letter to his friend Prokopovich (25 January 1837) bears this out: "Don't try to undertake a big thing, but start with something small; write stories, anything you like, only write without fail, contract with all the magazines, place your things and accept money. You have a tongue but you haven't loosened it up yet." A year or two of such practice and then, "it goes without saying, you yourself will have learned and comprehended your mission and will decide how and what to take up" (XI, 85).

from the slapstick of "The Fair at Sorochintsy" to the somber opera of "A Terrible Vengeance." With these eight stories Gogol created the first sketch of a world of his own, and he did it by fashioning a kind of overlay that matched reality in enough places to make many contemporaries believe they were experiencing only an account of the latter—a paradoxical tribute to the force of his creative intuition and the effectiveness of its verbal embodiment.[7]

The coherence of this world can be variously approached, first and most obviously through the poetic geography already referred to. The stories all contribute to the depiction of a culturally integral community, united by language, custom, and religion; it has little contact with any other community, offering a corporate version of the solipsism Gogol later embodied in individual characters. Anything that does not belong to the community is assumed or discovered to be hostile, of the devil's party. In thematic terms, Gippius finds this last feature central, uniting all but the first story and the last: "the irruption of the demonic principle into people's lives and their struggle with it."[8] But the struggle may be comic or dramatic, as may the demons themselves. And the supernatural may be presented as being "real" or fictive, serious or entertaining, the agency of tragedy or of farce.

A variant of this approach that carries far-reaching implications is Bakhtin's emphasis on the holiday atmosphere already indicated in some of the titles ("The Fair at Sorochintsy," "Christmas Eve," "St. John's Eve"): "The holiday and the beliefs connected with it," he writes, "the special atmosphere of license and gaiety, remove life from its usual rut and make the impossible possible (including the conclusion of previously impossible marriages) . . . Food, drink and sexual activity in these stories bear a holiday, Lenten–carnival character"—as does the comic *diablerie* and, ultimately, the characteristically Gogolian laughter, which Bakhtin relates to the Rabelaisian tradition.[9]

Most pervasive of all the identifying features of this first Gogolian world—and its chief link with what came after—lies in its resemblance to that of the *Kunstmärchen,* the sophisticated literary fairytale, as exemplified in the stories of Tieck and Hoffmann. What is at issue, as James M. Holquist has argued, is not the one-to-one influence of particular texts, but rather the sanction Gogol found in the Germans for mixing supernatural elements of a folk tradition with the elements of modern, individual narrative consciousness. This, of course, amounts to a yoking of two irreconcilable poetics, and it produces a constant interference of systems—the timeless world of legend with what looks like historical specificity, the conventions of comedy with those of horror stories—by which not only the identity of people and things but the identity of narrative perspective on them is subject to change as sudden as it may be unmotivated.[10]

What emerges as dominant is precisely the author's freedom from a single perspective. This can be seen in the first piece, "The Fair at Sorochintsy," with its lyrical introduction, its broadly comic intrigue, followed abruptly by a personal conclusion that introduces new tonalities and hints at issues unbroached in the story —as if the author were reconsidering what he had just done. Nor is it simply the shift of tone that is problematic; oddities of expression creep in, as portentously suggestive as they are baffling. Here is the passage in full:

A strange feeling, impossible to put into words, would have overcome any spectator seeing how, at one bow stroke of the fiddler with the twisted mustaches and the homespun jacket, everything was turned willy-nilly into unity and harmony. People on whose sullen faces it seemed that a smile had not gleamed for years were tapping their feet and wriggling their shoulders. Everything was in motion; everything was dancing. But an even stranger and more perplexing feeling would have awakened in the soul of an onlooker at the sight of old women, whose ancient faces breathed the indifference of the grave, shoving their way amidst new, laughing humanity. Carefree! without even childlike joy, without a spark of sympathy, moved only by drink as a puppeteer moves his lifeless puppet in the semblance of human action, they soundlessly wagged their drunken heads as they danced after the rejoicing crowd and cast not a single glance at the young couple.

The uproar, laughter, and songs grew fainter and fainter. The strains of the fiddle fell away and died out, indistinct notes lost in the emptiness of the air. The sound of dancing feet could still be heard somewhere, along with something like the murmur of a distant sea, and soon all was emptiness and stillness again.

Is it not thus that joy, a lovely and fleeting guest, flies from us, and the lonely sound seeks vainly to express gaiety? In its own echo it already hears melancholy and emptiness and heeds it, bewildered. Is it not thus that the playful friends of a stormy and unconstrained youth stray off, first one and then another, about the world, leaving their one old brother alone at the end? It is dreary for the one left behind! Heavy and sorrowful is his heart and there is nothing to help him. (I, 135–136)

To view the wedding feast as a dance of death might be to enrich a perspective by emphasizing mortality. But this is more than a reprise in a new key. The transformation of the crowd by a single stroke of the fiddler's bow has sinister overtones, and the unity and harmony it creates are in fact called quickly into question by the image of a sinister puppeteer (one that Dostoevsky would apply to Gogol himself). Finally, as the point of view recedes from the noisy scene, the reader finds that he has backed into the presence of an unidentified voice, lamenting an incomprehensible solitude.

The problematic is thus removed from its usual locus in narrated event or psychology and made to function on the level of the narration itself. Bewilderment, a constant theme, is not confined to the experience of Gogol's characters but comes to color *the reader's* experience of Gogol's protean narration. Perceiving the collection as a play of contrasts, the reader is compelled to recognize the primacy of play,[11] which is to say, the writer's sovereign independence in addressing both his material and his audience. To find unclarities in the "message," then, is to acknowledge not so much the faults as the qualities of the medium Gogol has used for his literary self-creation. That particular instrumentality is stressed in a fragment from this period, which begins: "It's been a long time since I told you any stories. I confess it's very pleasant if somebody sets about telling something . . . If he speaks not too loud, not too soft, but just so, like a cat purring next to your ear, then it's a pleasure that no pen can describe and nothing else can produce" (I, 318). Here, through one of those masks that freed his talent by rescuing him from a poetry of clear statement, Gogol stresses the pure pleasure of narration. The most astute anatomist of Gogol's texts, Andrei Biely, elaborates the point, analyzing "the melody that filled his consciousness" and finding the Ukraine that serves him as an image of the world to be "an exhalation of semi-mythical images over a song without words. All the rest is 'literature,' which for the time being Gogol does not need; the litterateur in him is still only potential. His plots are literarily contradictory; his colors are motley . . . Gogol [at this point] is still the verbal musician, chanting out and drumming out his rhythms . . . Literarily he is not convincing. But his images are all the more convincing for that—in rhythmic composition."[12]

Images, passages, rhythms—these are forms of Gogol's principal achievement in *Evenings*. In their quality and orchestration they sustain the collection. No single story is without its felicitous contribution to this achievement, but it must be said that none quite comes up to it either—with the possible exception of "A Terrible Vengeance." The only story quite without humor, written in the most sustainedly rhythmic prose, permeated with dread, it shows Gogol's quasi-folkloric imagination at its most intense and offers fertile ground for psychological analysis, exemplifying the dictum it contains, that the conscious mind does not know a tenth of what the unconscious does.[13] For all its extraordinary passages, however, even this story has its lapses and is set finally in a frame that weakens the intensity it is supposed to justify. The other anomaly in the second volume, "Ivan Fyodorovich Shponka and His Auntie," unites a Sternean mockery of plot with the kind of deadpan dwelling on insignificant detail and character that was shortly to become a Gogolian hallmark. Its manner has almost nothing in common with that of the other tales; and its best claim for inclusion may lie in the way it symbolizes the incompleteness with which that collection supports any analytic generalizations, showing how quickly Gogol's talent outgrew the format in which it first manifested itself.

WITH THE publication of *Evenings,* Gogol was launched as a writer. Reviews were largely laudatory, if frequently off the mark in treating him exclusively as entertainer or ethnographer, and the volumes sold briskly. The usual printing of 1200 copies seems to have been exhausted by July 1832, four months after the appearance of the second volume, moving Gogol to complain of the booksellers' indifference to "universal demand" and to raise the question of a second edition. Pride in this success, however, quickly turned into impatience with what he had done, and by early 1833 he was resisting talk about a new edition. Unwilling to add new stories, indifferent to financial reward, he claims to have forgotten even that he was the creator of these stories: "To hell with them! . . . May they be doomed to obscurity until something weighty, great, artistic comes out of me" (X, 256–257).[14]

What that might be he himself seems not to have known. "I have a hundred different beginnings," he writes in November 1833, "and not a single story, not even one full excerpt" to submit for publication (X, 283–284). Between *Evenings* in 1831–32 and the stories published in *Mirgorod* and *Arabesques* in early 1835 he experiments broadly—with a historical novel, *The Hetman;* with stage comedy (*Vladimir of the Third Class,* abandoned in anticipation of censorship troubles, and *The Gamblers*); and *Alfred,* a tragedy based on English history. The residue of this and other experimentation—carried out alongside his teaching and historical work—consists of two major cycles, to be followed shortly by two major plays (*The Inspector General* and *Getting Married*) and the inception of the novel that would consume the rest of his creative energies.

The customary Russian view divides this work according to setting and sees an implied progression from the Ukraine to Petersburg to the Russian provinces as being one from romanticism toward realism, the latter two milieux representing "the contemporary." The view is not without a certain plausibility, but it simplifies, slighting the variety of his approaches to each of these social areas—a variety dictated by his pursuit of an audience he was coming to conceive more clearly, and with which he was fashioning a more subtle, complex and serious relationship.

That process is hardly sequential. Work in several genres and on the several milieux either alternates or goes on simultaneously, suggesting a lack of single or sustained intention—which may help to explain the fact that in the later "Story of My Authorship" he treats the fictions in question summarily, without naming any of them, as spontaneous, *ad hoc* productions.

The subtitle of *Mirgorod* announces the collection as "Stories Serving as a Continuation of *Evenings on a Farm near Dikanka.*" "Serving as": the reviewer for *The Northern Bee* missed the hint, rhapsodizing over the presence in both books of the "the Ukraine, the whole Ukraine, with its clear sky, its cherry orchards, its black-eyed Cossack maidens, vodka, seminarians; with its superstitions, laws and customs, with the distinctive way of life of its inhabitants, present and past."[15] In fact, the title is arbitrary. The city of Mirgorod figures in only one of four stories, and the epigraphs describing it (from a geography and the notes of an unnamed traveler) have no relation at all to anything in the book—a clue, as F. C. Driessen observes, of some importance, suggesting that Mirgorod serves Gogol as a symbol of "that Ukrainian world which is the home of all his dreams, be they grandiose or tender, cruel or happy," and indicating the irrelevance of anything that mere outsiders might perceive.[16]

The Ukrainian setting, then, is put to new use, made the carrier of themes at once more personal and more general. Different and broader perspectives are brought to bear on the closed and parochial community represented in *Evenings*. Portrayed in the earlier books entirely from within, it is now seen from outside as well, in all its spatial and temporal limitation. Gone are Rudy Panko and all the other identified storytellers from the earlier collection, to be replaced by *a writer* whose single temperament more obviously informs all the narrations. Indeed, three of the stories employ a conventionally reliable narrator; and even in the highly mannered story of the Ivans, the ironic mask is lowered just before the end. The first word of the collection is "I," the last an apostrophic "ladies and gentlemen"—and neither the opening confession nor the closing address to the reader is to be taken ironically: the new goal is complicity.

Mirgorod, a pivotal work in Gogol's development and his most personally revealing book,[17] shows him bringing to consciousness and seeking perspective on the kind of self-expression that went more directly into the earlier tales (and fragments like "Woman"). Thus the importance of his new orientation toward the Russian reader, who is now invited to take the author as *semblable* if not as *frère.* In "Old-World Landowners," the title characters are recalled "from here," a point outside and above their little world, by a narrator devoid of idiosyncrasy who explains local usages in literary Russian. In the opening pages of *Taras Bulba,* the old Cossack leads his sons into a parlor "decorated in the taste of that time, of which hints have survived only in songs, and in folk poems that are no longer sung in the Ukraine" (II, 43). "Viy" is equipped with a footnote explaining the Ukrainian nomenclature and informing the reader that "this whole tale is a folk legend" which "I have not wanted to change in any way and tell almost as simply as I heard it told." Even the story of the two Ivans—published previously as another of Rudy Panko's—appears here without his name, equipped with an ironic preface: "I consider it my duty to state in advance that the occurrence described in this story relates to a very distant past. Moreover, it is a complete invention. Mirgorod is now quite different. The buildings are different; the puddle in the middle of town has long since dried up; and all the dignitaries—the judge, the clerk and the mayor—are respected and loyal people" (II, 221).[18]

These brief examples may suffice as indications of Gogol's shift of position: *with his reader* he looks down and in on the world portrayed, its very presence colored by the framing acknowledgment of its absence. Whatever else they may be, the stories themselves are essays in evaluation; and to the extent that one may speak of problematics in them, one must speak of an attitudinal problematics. This is most obvious in the keynote story, "Old-World Landowners," where Gogol presents his ambivalence so artfully that generations of readers, forced to share both his affection and his uneasiness over it, have debated the relative worthiness of these good-natured cretins to provoke such feeling.

This, I think, is to miss the point. Gogol's concern is not with the value of *living* such a life; it is rather with the value of a certain way of life in the spiritual economy of *an occasional visitor.* "I very much love the modest life of those isolated owners of remote villages . . . I sometimes like to descend for a minute into the sphere of that unusually isolated life, where not a single desire strays beyond the palisade surrounding the little yard . . . The life of their modest owners is so tranquil, so tranquil, that for a minute you forget yourself and are ready to believe that the passions, desires, and those restless inventions of the evil spirit that trouble the world do not exist at all, and that you have seen them only in some brilliant and garish dream" (II, 13). The value is that of a daydream: Recalling this "lowly bucolic life" amid "noise and crowds and modish dress coats" brings respite—a reverie in which "you renounce, at least for a short time, all your ambitious dreams" (II, 14). The old couple thus stands at the center of a reciprocating series of dream symbols, they and their estate (almost a single entity) being conjured up in the mind of the writer as a dream potent enough to displace "real" life, the life of active desire, making *it* appear the less authentic.

So the narrator, for all his shadowiness, must be seen as the main character. It is he who sets the terms of presentation with their arbitrary limits. It is he who supplies the associations and who ratifies the sense of the uncanny in the story of Afanasy Ivanovich's death by citing analogous experiences from the days of his own childhood (II, 37). Finally, it is he who introduces the central issue—habit versus passion—an issue quite absent from the lives of his characters.

The story, then, conforms to Gogol's later notion of the idyll, which "may embrace the routine life of many people [other than shepherds and farmers], if only simplicity and a humble lot" characterize it. The idyll "paints this life in the finest detail, and however trivial its sphere may appear to be, containing neither a lofty lyrical mood nor dramatic interest nor yet any strong or striking event—however much it may appear to be no more than what first strikes our eye in ordinary life, he who takes it only in that sense will be mistaken. [For] it is almost always dominated by some inner idea particularly close to the poet's soul, and he has used routine life and the idyll itself as only the most convenient forms" (VIII, 480–481). "Old-World Landowners" uses character and detail precisely in this way, as material for a rumination on the idyllic, on its value and fate—an orchestration of themes that anticipates in its elusive subtlety the supreme achievement of "The Overcoat," which is no more the story of a poor clerk than this is the story of Afanasy Ivanovich and Pulkheria Ivanovna. Here as in the later work time is alternately absent and present, bringing sharply contrasting perspectives on characters too simplified even to be called humors. In both, perspective is further varied problematically by juxtaposing the central characters with others. Both ultimately dramatize an unresolved ambivalence in which the concepts of significance and value are put in question.

In "Old-World Landowners" Gogol produces his first "pearl of creation"—not a story but an original kind of narrative discourse, the play of a partially individualized consciousness with two congenial caricatures in a sharply observed physical setting, amid a pattern of reflections and asides. The import of the piece is coextensive with a text which itself *constitutes* more than renders significant experience. By eschewing plot (as he was to do in all his best works), Gogol alters the code of Russian fiction, producing something midway between a story and a performance—a verbal artifact whose charm lies entirely in the modulations of its unfolding (to the confusion of readers who, judging it from memory, find that they are dealing with an artifact of their own creation, as different from Gogol's text as that text is from life).

Taras Bulba is, by contrast, a weaker, more conventional work—particularly in the *Mirgorod* version, before revision in 1839–40 had nearly doubled its bulk, intensifying the Homeric reminiscences, adding descriptive touches from chronicles and folklore, smoothing excesses, and shifting the patriotic burden from Ukrainian to proto-Russian. Of Gogol's several experiments in historical fiction, this is the only finished one, and it grows directly out of his historical work as reflected in *Arabesques*. Written at almost the same time as the essay "On Ukrainian Songs," it develops many of the motifs cited there and seeks to prove his claims for these songs as the record of "a vanished way of life." They may, Gogol writes, disappoint the reader in search of specific fact. "But if he wants to know the true way of life, the elements of character, all the convolutions and nuances of the feelings, joys, sufferings, merrymakings of the people represented; if he wants to sample the spirit of a bygone age, the general character of the whole and of its separate constituent parts, then he will be fully satisfied" (VIII, 91).

The interests of the intuitive historian dominate this first version and keep the balance between historical fiction and epic on the side of the former; the "Shakespearean exuberance" that Mirsky remarks, like the "merry heroism" and elements of a "Ukrainian saturnalia" detected by Bakhtin, belong rather to the second version's reversal of this emphasis. Set in an aoristic past, *Taras Bulba* depicts the Cossack military encampment, the Sech, as "a sort of constant feast, a ball which had begun noisily and lost its end," a "wild orgy of gaiety," where every new arrival "forgot and abandoned all that had hitherto concerned him. One may say that he spit on his whole past and with the enthusiasm of a fanatic gave himself over to freedom and the companionship of those who, like himself, had neither dear ones, nor a corner of their own, nor family except for the free sky and the eternal feast of their souls" (II, 301).

Gogol's language strains to embody a point which, too often, it can only assert; the imagination that creates these feasting souls is unabashedly adolescent—"This was a close circle of school chums" (II, 302)—and nowhere more so than in describing female beauty and its consequences. The Polish girl who moves Bulba's esthete son to treason has "eyelashes long as daydreams" that stand out "like dark thin needles against her heavenly face," which has taken on "an infinity" of new features, "beautiful as the heavens":

He threw himself at her feet, pressed close, and gazed into her mighty eyes. A smile betokening a certain joy sparkled on her lips, while a tear hung on her lash like a diamond.

"My queen!" he said, "What shall I do for you? What do you wish?"

She looked fixedly at him and laid her wonderful hand on his shoulder. With the devouring flame of passion he covered it with kisses . . .

"And your comrades? your father?—You must go to them," she said softly . . .

"What are you saying!" declared Andriy . . . "What would my love be if I abandoned for you only what is easy to abandon! . . . That is not how I love: father, brother, mother, homeland, everything on earth, I give it all up for your sake. Farewell all! I'm on your side now! I am yours! What more do you wish?"

She inclined her head to him. He felt her electrically ardent cheek touch his, and a kiss—ooh, what a kiss!—glued their mouths together. (II, 317–318)

One need only recall Gogol's comment that Byron is "too heated," speaking about love "too much and almost always with frenzy" (X, 252), to realize how far his impulses eluded his better judgment here.

The problem is not simply psychological[19]; it attaches more generally to his uneasiness with omniscient narration. Alternating with such excesses is a banal flatness of statement ("On the pale and bandaged faced of Bulba could be seen an effort to recall the circumstances"), which suggests that Gogol was cramping his gifts by adopting (rather than adapting) a currently popular form —and being tempted thereby into cliché. How much he borrowed may be inferred from an ironic recipe for historical fictions that appeared in the *Moscow Herald* in 1828:

Our writers favor *the fall and destruction of castles and cities* as their subjects . . . The choice has many advantages: in the first place, there can be a lot of clatter and thunder in the description of the siege; secondly, this permits the introduction of *two lovers, of whom one should belong to the besiegers, the other to the besieged,* for greater interest . . . *Jews* [as ancillary characters] *are in great fashion* . . . As for the form of the story, it is best of all to divide it arbitrarily into chapters, and *begin each chapter with a description* of either morning or night or a storm. In style, the more *ornate* the expressions, the better.[20]

Enlivening a familiar form with touches that had the ring of poetic and historical authenticity, *Taras Bulba* not surprisingly appealed most to those readers who were most baffled by Gogol's originality. Thus the conservative reviewer for *The Northern Bee* praised it as the best of the collection: "The character of the Cossack colonel and his two sons, the military encampment, the battles, the raids, the Jews, Lithuania, and the Ukraine are described in a lively and original way; the story is absorbing; the local colors gleam with an astonishing freshness."[21]

AT THE END of *Taras Bulba* all the principals are dead, and the Cossack warriors in retreat talk of their lost leader, thus suggesting the origin of the legend Gogol purports to be retelling. "Viy" even more openly claims a connection with folk tradition, by way of the footnote cited earlier. This is undoubtedly a mystification, but a more complex one than may appear. The Viy is apparently not "the Ukrainian name for the chief of the gnomes"; there seem in fact to be no gnomes in Ukrainian folklore.[22] On the other hand, the motifs of the death-dealing glance and the eyes that must be opened with some instrument do appear in Russian, Siberian, and even American Indian myths. If Gogol's assertion that "this whole story is a popular legend" cannot be accepted, its basis in folk imagination can.[23] The particular affinity of Gogol's own imagination with popular myth has often been remarked. In Sinyavsky's recent formulation, Gogol draws patterns of experience from his own psyche that are identical to those of folklore and corroborate the latter "from below, from within, like an original text or a literal translation."[24] The introductory footnote thus does signal a kind of authenticity but seeks transparently to disown its intimate provenience by passing off as an impersonal product what is actually the objectification of a personal psychological state.

That state is fear, as powerful as it is vague—and specifically associated with erotic experience. Throughout Gogol's work the erotic threatens the sensitive male with annihilation. In *Taras Bulba* where it moves Andriy to treason, his doom receives an external, social explanation; here the terms are less distinct. Amid a prosaic world, ironically and "realistically" presented by an impersonal, thoroughly written narration, a latter-day Cossack, the seminarian Khoma Brut, blunders into an adventure with an old witch, who takes him on a magical skyride to the accompaniment of orgasmic sensations. Eventually recalling his prayers, he gains the upper hand and rides *her* until, finding a log, he begins to belabor her with it:

She emitted wild howls; at first they were angry and threatening, then they became weaker, more pleasant, purer, and then quiet, scarcely audible, like fine silver bells, sinking into his soul; and inadvertently the thought flashed in his head: Is this in fact an old woman? "Oh, I can't any more!" she exclaimed in exhaustion, and fell to the earth . . . Before him lay a beautiful girl, her luxuriant plait of hair disordered, her eyelashes long as arrows. Unconsciously she had thrown wide her bare white arms and was moaning, her eyes staring upward and filled with tears. Khoma began to tremble like a leaf on a tree: he was overcome with pity, together with some strange excitement and timidity he had not known before. He began to run as fast as his legs would carry him. On the way his heart pounded uneasily, and try as he might he could not account for the strange new feeling that possessed him. (II, 187–188)

Soon after, he learns that the daughter of a wealthy Cossack chieftain has returned home badly beaten and dying; her last request is that Khoma read the prayers for the dead over her coffin for three nights. Once again he shudders "from some instinctive feeling which he himself could not account for." Forced to comply, he finds himself praying over a corpse whose beauty strikes him with "panic terror." First the corpse threatens him, then an assemblage of spirits and monsters, and finally the Viy himself, who alone can see Khoma, on condition that Khoma look at him—as he does, despite an inner voice that whispers not to, and promptly dies of terror on the spot. Here as before, what is most effective is not the claptrap machinery but the evocation of Khoma's sensations. They convey that "breathless and unexplainable dread of outer, unknown forces" which Lovecraft specified as essential to supernatural horror in literature.[25]

Unknown they clearly are—but how clearly "outer"? The story's chief failing, for all the effectiveness of its sensational scenes (and the humorously prosaic ones they alternate with), lies in the inconsistency of the psychological and supernatural explanations, both of which the text insists on. The climactic scene—capped by the first mention and only appearance of the Viy—does have a dramatic intensity that appears to justify the story's title. It is pervaded, moreover, by a strong sense of inevitability (the fatal temptation to know death? the fear of being seen for what one is?). But these qualities are nearly autonomous; if they derive necessarily from the narrative that precedes them, it is only in the implication that the "strange new feeling" aroused by a surrender to lust predisposes Khoma to death as well. There are, however, missing links in this line of interpretation, just as in the one that sees

Khoma as a failed Cossack because he yielded to the fear against which the genuine Cossack is proof. Why, in this case, should he be punished with death? The evidence of the text finally leaves him guiltily guiltless.* It invokes several systems of meaning—psychological, moral, ontological, social—without quite anchoring Khoma's fate in any of them as the objective narration implicitly promises to do.

Still, the story is undeniably powerful and Tolstoy, who listed it as one of a handful of works producing "an enormous impression" between the ages of fourteen and twenty, was closer to the mark than Nabokov, who dismisses it as "a gooseflesh story, not very effective."[26] Compelling in a way reminiscent of "A Terrible Vengeance," "Viy" marks an advance on that story by the uncanny authority with which it unites apparently incompatible qualities—""laughter and terror, everyday life and miracle, beauty and ugliness, the phlegmatic simplicity and banal unseriousness of the whole figure of Khoma Brut and his improbable, wild and fatal end."[27] To the discovery of Gogol's mature manner, as to the thematics of his total created world, "Viy" makes a central contribution. Among the stories of *Mirgorod,* it points at once back to the demon-infested Dikanka stories and forward to the Petersburg Tales in its concentration on one individual, supremely ordinary, solitary, kinless, and doomed.

"The Story of How Ivan Ivanovich Quarreled with Ivan Nikiforovich," which closes the *Mirgorod* cycle, is the only one to have been published earlier and attributed to Rudy Panko. Its narration is a development of the Panko manner: "Ivan Ivanovich has the unusual gift of talking in an extraordinarily pleasant way. Lord, how he can talk! The only sensation that can be compared with it is when someone is hunting lice on your scalp or running a finger lightly over your heel. You listen and listen—and you hang your head. It's pleasant! Exceptionally pleasant! Like a nap after bathing" (II, 226). What this underlines is the self-sufficient, almost sensual esthetic value of skillful discourse, quite independent of its content: the principal value of the story itself. Here, to use the Russian Formalist term, is a masterpiece of *skaz*—a monologue in

---

* The phrase is Gogol's, from *Selected Passages:* "There are guiltlessly guilty people and guiltily guiltless ones" (VIII, 351).

the guise of a narration: colloquial, individuated, free from the constraints of consistency in point of view, permeated with a paradoxical lyricism and an irony that ranges from blatant to enigmatic —but *written,* and serving literary ends.

The primacy of language as such is indicated not only in the power of a single word, "gander" (*gusak*), to turn friends into enemies when uttered as an insult, but in its power to foil a reconciliation when uttered inadvertently without hostile intent. Even earlier, at the beginning of Chapter 2, a stubborn literalness turns a rhetorical question into a real one and satiation into acquisitiveness, preparing the catastrophe by a logic as much linguistic as psychological. Ivan Ivanovich, recumbent,

surveyed his storehouses, yard, barns, the hens running around the yard, and thought to himself: "My Lord, what a good farmer I am! What haven't I got? Birds, outbuildings, barns, hens, anything I fancy; distilled vodka with herb and fruit infusions; in the orchard pears and plums; in the garden poppies, cabbages, peas . . . What haven't I got? . . . I'd like to know, what haven't I got?" Having posed such a profound question to himself, Ivan Ivanovich fell to musing; meanwhile, his eyes found new objects, crossed the fence into Ivan Nikiforovich's yard. (II, 228)

This linguistic playing with absence, creating a presence in the very act of denying it, recurs continually: "O, if I were a painter, how wonderfully I would depict all the charm of that night!" A long and splendidly lyrical depiction follows, each sentence beginning, "I would depict," only to conclude with an ironic gesture toward the limits of possibility: "But I would scarcely be able to depict Ivan Ivanovich as he emerged into this night" (II, 242). In Chapter 7: "I am not going to describe the sorts of dishes that were at the table! I shall mention nothing, either about the *mnishki* in sour cream, or about the *utribka* they served with the borsch, or about the turkey with plums and raisins, or about that dish which looked a lot like a pair of boots soaked in *kvas,* or about that sauce which is the swansong of an old cook—that sauce which was served in flaming spirits to the amusement and terror of the ladies" (II, 271).

Artifice is underlined constantly in the narrator's remarks about the inadequacy of his brushes and colors and the bluntness of his pen. This, of course, fosters the illusion that the events and characters exist apart from the rendering, validating it with reference to some extraliterary reality. But it also points to the esthetic goal of this experiment, which is to find comic prose equivalents for the effects of other media and genres. Alongside references to the painter's art is a significant invocation of puppet theater in Chapter 2, as Ivan Ivanovich contemplates the uniform airing in his neighbor's yard: "Everything, blending together, constituted for Ivan Ivanovich a very engrossing spectacle, while the rays of the sun, catching here and there a blue or green sleeve, a red cuff or a piece of gold brocade, or playing on the spire of a sword, turned it all into something unusual, resembling those puppet shows that strolling entrepreneurs bring to the villages" (II, 229). In this key passage, Gogol sets forth one of the principles of the deformation he effects—and the explicit license for the dumb scenes that punctuate the story (Chapters 2 and 7). Parody—of legal documents (Chapters 4 and 5), of epic description (Chapter 6), or military exploits (Chapter 3)—is another instrument of stylization in this unflaggingly resourceful narration.

The reviewer for *The Northern Bee* recognized the art in all this but was nonplussed at his inability to reconcile it with what he expected of Art:

[This story] describes the prosaic life of two neighbors in a poor provincial town, with all its uninteresting details, and describes it with astonishing fidelity and liveliness of colors. But what is the aim of these scenes, which arouse nothing in the soul of the reader except pity and disgust? They contain nothing amusing, or touching or funny. Why, then, are we shown these tatters, these dirty rags—however artfully they may be presented? Why draw an unpleasant picture of the backyard of life and humanity, without any apparent aim?[28]

As Gogol continued to explore this original vein of what we now call "Gogolian" writing, such complaints continued to be voiced; indeed, he parodies them at the end of "The Nose." They are symptomatic of the unpreparedness of readers for the novel poetics he was fashioning. These readers sought character and story, fidelity to the "reality" of the world they took for granted—and found only a semblance of those things. They expected to be touched or amused unambiguously but found themselves confronted by a radical denial of the code that guaranteed some final resolution of attitude in one of these keys. They expected the reinforcement of "normality" as they conceived it—in artistic decorum and in the experience conveyed—and found that expectation mocked.

Gogol himself was to join his critics all too soon, conceding that he had laughed in his first works "gratuitously," without a clear aim. This was when he had already formed his talent—when the energy that had been absorbed in fashioning an original medium was freed by the success of that effort to substitute a "why" for the "how" that had hitherto preoccupied him. The story of the two Ivans, however, all is "how"—a triumph of sustained narrative self-invention, and so a kind of tour de force. Gogol has taken the slenderest of events, the most minimally drawn of characters, as the basis for a narration abounding in subtleties of tone and expression, which teases the reader with abortive hints of undeveloped themes. One of these is sexual. There is an ambiguous suggestiveness about Ivan Ivanovich's first sight of his neighbor's rifle—the object he decides he must have, thus preparing the famous quarrel. That object makes its appearance in the yard alongside Ivan Nikiforovich's enormous trousers, moving his friend to reflect: "What does this mean! I never saw Ivan Nikiforovich with a rifle! What does he need it for? He doesn't shoot with it, and yet he keeps a rifle! What does he need it for? And the thing is a beauty! I've wanted to get such a one for a long time. I'd really love to have that little rifle; I love to play around with a little rifle."

The innuendo is reinforced in Ivan Ivanovich's conversation with the woman who has put the object out to air:

"What's that you've got there, granny?"
"You can see for yourself: a rifle."
"What kind of a rifle?"
"Who knows what kind it is? If it was mine, maybe I'd know what it's made of. But it's the master's."

And when Ivan Ivanovich goes to pursue the matter with his friend (who apologizes for being "in a state of nature"), he argues that "God hasn't set up your nature for shooting," adding, "You have such a dignified bearing and figure" (II, 230–233). The overtones—especially amid all the physical description and the hints about Ivan Ivanovich's mistress and bastards—are unmistakable, but they are too transient to support an interpretation of the story as a whole. Something similar applies to the recurrent mentions of the devil, all of them jocular, but acquiring, in the course of this prolonged immersion in triviality, a faint air of plausibility, so that when the carefully planned reconciliation miscarries, the ghost of literalness may appear in the narrator's summary comment: "Everything went to the devil!" (II, 273).

All that remains as a certain value is the energetic authority of the text itself. This is a matter of style, movement, and passing suggestion, and it is what makes Gogol's best works so resistant to summary discussion. As an example we might take the bravado piece of burlesque "description" that introduces the mayor's ball in Chapter 6. My bracketed comments are meant to indicate something of how the passage works.

The mayor was giving a ball! [*Metaphorical digression:*] Where shall I find brushes and colors to portray the variety of the assembly and all this magnificent feast? [*Further metaphorical digression:*] Take a watch, open it, and look at what is going on there! Awful rubbish, isn't it? [*Comic abdication, but also an ironic characterization of the very narration of all these imbecilities.*] Well, just imagine almost as many, if not more, wheels standing in the mayor's yard. [*Not a digression after all. A simile, but just barely.*] What carriages and carts were not there! [*Faint suggestion of literalness, as in Ivan Ivanovich's question earlier.*] One with a broad rear and a narrow front; another with a narrow rear and a broad front. [*Mechanical contrast, reminiscent of the contrast between the two Ivans.*] One was a carriage and a cart at the same time; another was neither a carriage nor a cart [*two varieties of nondescription, with ontological overtones*]; another was like an enormous haystack, or a fat merchant's wife; another resembled a disheveled Jew, or a skeleton not quite freed from its skin; still another was in profile a perfect pipe with its stem; another [*a final "baring the device"*] was like nothing at all, representing some strange entity, utterly ugly and extremely fantastic. From the midst of this chaos of wheels and driver's seats towered the semblance of a carriage with a window like that of a room, intersected by a thick sash. Coachmen in grey jackets, coats and jerkins, in sheepskin hats and caps of various caliber, pipes in mouth, were leading the unharnessed horses through the courtyard. What a ball the mayor gave! Allow me to name all those who were there: Taras Tarasovich, Yevpl Ankifovich, Yevtikhy Yetikhievich, Ivan Ivanovich—not *the* Ivan Ivanovich but a different one, Savva Gavrilovich, our Ivan Ivanovich, Yelevfery Yelevferievich, Makar Nazarievich, Foma Grigorievich . . . I can't go on! It's too much for me! My hand is weary of writing! And how many ladies there were!—dark ones and fair ones, tall ones and short ones, ladies as fat as Ivan Nikiforovich and others so thin that it seemed you might hide them in the scabbard of the mayor's sword. How many caps! How many dresses!—red, yellow, coffee-colored, green, blue, new, turned, re-tailored; kerchiefs, ribbons, reticules! Farewell, poor eyes, you'll never be good for anything after this spectacle! And what a long table was stretched out! And how everyone talked, what a noise they raised! A mill with all its millstones, wheels, gears, and mortars couldn't compete with it! I can't tell you for certain what they talked about, but one must suppose it was about many pleasant and useful things, such as: the weather, dogs, wheat, bonnets, ponies. (II, 264–265)

A chaos of things—some "present," some invoked by analogy or association—overshadows and threatens to absorb the identifiably human; miscellaneousness swamps significance; sound threatens meaning. The passage is ironic, of course, but normlessly so: what is being branded as insignificant is never presented to us apart from such playful irony, so that ascription hangs in the air, as it were, without an object. Still, a certain value beyond the linguistic does inhere in such passages and in the work as a whole, since there can be no such thing as pure performance. Nekrasov defined it as "poetry and lyricism," finding it not only in the two Ivans themselves, but even in "the wet jackdaws sitting on the fence."[29] Kuechelbecker may have come even closer in his observation that "in the foolish and stupid, when carried to the highest degree, there is a sort of loftiness—*le sublime de la bêtise* . . . 'pure joy'."[30]

This purely esthetic effect goes beyond satire—and is in fact incompatible with it. Gogol is creating, rather than unmasking. There is no one and nothing to unmask; even litigiousness, a familiar target for satire, serves only as a ground for parody and new forays into absurdity. The story of the two Ivans is an exercise in generating and sustaining comic narrative—by a sheer creative energy that exceeds the needs of objective observation or objective statement so far as to make them irrelevant. Gogol does not evoke vitality, he *confers* it. Since the interest of reading lies there, rather than in plot or character, it is appropriate that the work should end not with an emphasis on character or plot, but with a withdrawal of that conferring energy. Gogol's famous closing line—"It's dreary in this world, ladies and gentlemen!"—has been too easily interpreted out of context, and taken at face value as the expression of a new voice introducing a moral perspective.[31] Rather, it is a comment on this kind of comic narrative, consonant with everything that has preceded it. There is no new narrator, only a voice newly aware of time and distance, depressed by the weather, as he had formerly been inspired by the play of sunlight. He is hardly more sensible (or less ironic) than before: "As I began to approach Mirgorod, I felt my heart beating hard. Good Lord, how many memories! For twelve years I hadn't seen Mirgorod. At that time two unique men, two unique friends lived here in touching friendship. And how many famous men had died! The judge, Demian Demianovich was already deceased" (II, 275).

The theme introduced by the closing line is the instability of the comic attitude. The narrator's cry is a reaction to a particular kind of writing which constitutes experience instead of dealing with it—and which, like many pleasures, exists only in process and leaves behind only a sense of absence. The theme will recur later, notably in Chapters 3 and 6 of *Dead Souls,* for Gogol's progress as an artist is accompanied by a progressively greater share of reflection on art, within his works as well as outside them. The fact that *Mirgorod* concludes with such a reflection is one sign of its crucial role in Gogol's self-creation as a writer.

THOUGH none of Gogol's collections lends itself easily to generalization, a few summary remarks may be made about the tendency of *Mirgorod* as a whole. The four stories, taken together, represent a lost world. The road—that central image in Gogol—appears in each, connecting the several closed milieux with what in the earlier stories had been simply "not ours": a world of difference. Conflicting perspectives come into play, abetted by the introduction of historical time. *Mirgorod* is a book of residues, built on a pattern of stressed disappearances: in "Old-World Landowners" of the cat, Pulkheria Ivanovna, Afanasy Ivanovich, and finally the very idyllic existence they represent, leaving nostalgia; in *Taras Bulba* of all the principals, along with their Cossack world, leaving legend; in "Viy," of Khoma Brut and the scene of his trial, leaving legend; and in the two Ivans, of the comic élan that brought an idyll of banality into temporary existence, leaving nostalgia for that élan and the illusion of timelessness it created.

    Mirgorod, then, is elegiac overall. Each of its stories represents a new experiment in using some earlier literary source as starting point for a markedly original narrative embodying some intimate Gogolian concerns. The basic thematic complex in this respect—subsuming the patriarchal and libidinal themes, Cossack virtue, passion and stasis—might be extrapolated from such passages as these in his early text:

(1) "What is love?—the fatherland of the soul, the beautiful striving of man toward the past, where the immaculate beginning of his life took place, where everything bears the inexpressible, ineffaceable trace of innocent infancy, where everything is *patria* (*rodina*). ("Woman," 1831; VIII, 146)

(2) "Who said that my homeland was the Ukraine? Who gave it to me as a homeland? A homeland is whatever our soul seeks, what is dearer than all to it." (*Taras Bulba,* Ch. 6; II, 106)

(3) What a terrible, glittering beauty! [Khoma] turned away and tried to step back; but out of some strange curiosity, out of that strange self-contradictory feeling that will not leave a person, especially at times of terror, he could not refrain from looking at her as he went, and then, as he felt that familiar trembling, looked again. The striking beauty of the deceased girl seemed terrible indeed. Perhaps she would not have inspired such panic fear if she had been a little less beautiful. ("Viy"; II, 206)

(4) Full of feelings not to be tasted on this earth, Andriy kissed those fragrant lips . . . and in that mutually joined kiss was experienced what man is given to feel only once in a lifetime. (*Taras Bulba,* II, 107)[32]

(5) Good Lord!, I thought, looking at him: five years of all-destroying time and already an insensible old man, an old man whose life seemed never once to have been troubled by a single strong sensation of the soul, whose whole life seemed to have consisted only of sitting on a tall chair and eating dried fishes and pears—that and the telling of good-natured stories. Yet such a long and fervent sadness! What in fact has more power over us: passion or habit? ("Old-World Landowners," II, 36)

(6) It seems to me that in the country, in that domestic sphere, one can find so many pleasures and so much cheerfulness of the kind no great city can offer; one need only know how to find them . . . I don't know how people can complain of boredom! Such people are always unworthy of being called people. (Letter to M. I. Gogol, 16 April 1831; X, 194)

Originality enters by way of the shifting, peculiarly personal connections among these themes—and the frequent ambivalence those connections reveal. This is seen on the level of individual statement, and even more in the broader patterning within and among the stories. In varying proportions, comic and serious perspectives illuminate the same material; where their relation is least problematic, as in *Taras Bulba,* the narrative is weakest, because it solicits more conventional expectations from the reader and saddles the narrator with responsibilities of objectivity he cannot meet fully enough. But when Gogol subordinates the experience of his characters to that of an individualized (though unspecified) narrator, he virtually disarms criticism because every contradiction and peculiarity may be justified by its contribution to the reader's sense of that shadowy and brilliant persona. In all his best narratives Gogol was to insist on this primacy of an unidentified protean voice over the elements of story. In *Mirgorod* the voice is no longer simply that of a mediator or entertainer; it insinuates the problem of ethical valuation even as it broaches the thematics of individuation.

Gogol's major achievement here is the discovery of a kind of narrative discourse whose liveliness, sophistication, and seriousness are inversely proportional to those of its objects. Informed by deeply personal themes, this brilliant discourse revealed a new artistic gravity, and even more strikingly when the locus shifted to contemporary Russia.

GOGOL's last cycle of stories comprises the so-called Petersburg Tales, three of which appeared in *Arabesques* in the same month that *Mirgorod* was published ("Nevsky Prospect," "The Portrait," and "Diary of a Madman"). "The Nose" was printed the following year in Pushkin's *Contemporary,* and the cycle as such brought together—with the significant addition of "The Overcoat"—only in 1843.[33] As the chronology of their publication suggests, most of the stories were written alongside the fictions of *Mirgorod.* They show Gogol forgoing the charm of the exotic and the vanished to deal with a setting his readers would find at once familiar and present—not only literally but literarily. More even than in the Ukrainian stories he was capitalizing on a current vogue—in this case for rendering aspects of urban experience.[34] Once more the response is experimental; each of the stories presents a different formal model, though they show a new thematic cohesion in the way each contributes to characterizing the milieu they share.

Gogol's first impressions of the capital, recorded in the letter to his mother of 30 April 1829, were to remain unchanged: no stamp of individuality or national character, an atomistic collection of foreigners and Russians, sharing little, locked into meaningless bureaucratic rituals, obsessed with rank and appearance—stunted selves imprisoned in predefined social identities. Here was "fragmentation" with a vengeance—and a new rationale for narrative deformation, which now became symbolic. This can be seen already in the dramatic essay on Pushkin's *Boris Godunov,* written in 1829 though unpublished in Gogol's lifetime. Set in a Petersburg bookstore where the thunder of street traffic lends a singular vibration to the scene, the anonymous speakers are identified as "a coffee-colored overcoat," a "senatorial hazel-grouse," "a fat little cube"; outside, the city "roars and glitters," "crowds of people and shadows are glimpsed on the streets and on the straw-colored walls of giant buildings, whose windows, like countless fiery eyes, cast flaming paths on the snowy pavement" (VIII, 148-149). A later fragment, "A Streetlamp Was Dying," shows a heavenly young woman attended by a strange two-dimensional figure: "The forehead did not descend straight to the nose, but was absolutely slanted . . . The nose was a continuation of it—large and blunt. Only the upper lip protruded . . . There was no chin at all. A diagonal line ran from the nose to the very neck. This was a triangle, the apex of which was at the nose: the sort of face that most of all expresses stupidity" (III, 331). Such visions fill the finished stories well, synedoche and absurdity serving to reinforce the suggestion of a world out of joint, "some madness of nature."

"Nevsky Prospect," praised by Pushkin as Gogol's fullest work to date, takes the principal avenue of the capital as characterological key. It is, as a draft explains, "the only street in Petersburg where our mysterious society," so colorless as to "make one doubt its existence," shows itself. "The painter of characters, the sharp observer of distinctions, will burst with vexation if he tries to portray it in lively, fiery features. No sharp particularity! No sign of individuality!" (III, 339). Petersburg appears in the first place as a challenge to the artist in this most direct of his fictional attempts at a statement about the city. The passage was excised, one supposes, as being extraneous to the matter of the story, for none of Gogol's characters, here or elsewhere, shows any curiosity about the city itself or any inclination to reflect on it as an entity. All are quasi-solipsists, pieces in a puzzle which only the author perceives as such. Thus the artist within this story, the young dreamer Piskaryov, is introduced as belonging to "a class that constitutes a rather strange phenomenon among us and belongs among the citizens of Petersburg just as much as a face we see in dreams belongs to the world of reality" (III, 16). He is essentially a temperament—naive, idealistic, virginal—and when he finds reality mocking his dreams of what it should be, he can only respond by fleeing reality: "Finally, dreams became his life and from that time on his whole life took a strange turn: he slept, one might say, waking, and had his waking life in dreams" (III, 28). When at length a beautiful prostitute spurns his desperate offer of a life of honest love and labor ("How dare you! . . . I am not a laundress or a seamstress that I should take up work"), he goes mad and cuts his throat. "So perished the victim of a mad passion, the poor Piskaryov, gentle, timid, modest, simplehearted as a child, bearing within him the spark of a talent" (III, 33). The implication is clear that were it not for this mad passion, Piskaryov would most likely have lived out the life of an artist manqué, doomed by the allied antagonism of Petersburg nature and Petersburg society to his calling.

His friend and quasi-double, Lieutenant Pirogov, is similarly proof against experience, his confident "realism" no less a matter of deception than Piskaryov's visions of harmony and goodness. "We know you all!" he mutters, setting off in pursuit of the wife of a German tinsmith who eventually gives him his comeuppance in the form of a sound thrashing. Thus his comic misadventure complements the pathetic one of his artist-friend; the satire of empty vanity complements the melodrama of weak idealism. The stories of both these pre-individuals, however, are exempla, suggesting not only something about the scale of survival values in Petersburg* but taking their significance from the framing layers of Gogol's narration.

"Nevsky Prospect" is the key to the Petersburg cycle because it is the most explicitly and successfully intentional of the stories. Surrounding the twin episodes (with their reminiscences of Janin and Hoffmann) is a stratum of generalization reminiscent of Balzac. The artist represents a class in Petersburg; and that class is described not only in terms of its marginality, but in concrete images of its daily life and behavior. Similarly, Pirogov's adventure is preceded by a sketch of the society to which he belongs, more satiric in tone but no less broadly descriptive. And these passages take their place as a part of the generalizing introduction, in which the Nevsky Prospect is seen as the preserve of particular groups at particular times of the day, beginning with honest workmen and ending with crowds of disembodied vanities. In this Gogol follows the format of the "physiological" urban sketches so popular in France and adapted by such now-forgotten contemporaries as Bashutsky (with whose *Panorama of St. Petersburg* in three volumes [1833] this aspect of his story shares a good deal).

Finally, enclosing and permeating all this is the voice of the narrator, by turns choral, mimetic, ironic, and idiosyncratically personal. So skillful are Gogol's modulations here that one scarcely notices how tenuously the parts are connected to give the illusion of unity. Thus the full extent of his opening ironies ("There is nothing better than the Nevsky Prospect, at least in Petersburg . . . No reference book or information bureau will give such reliable information") becomes evident only at the end, when a meditation on the paradoxical workings of fate turns local and

---

* They also show how survival in Petersburg amounts to a prolongation of anonymity and disappearance to a confirmation of it.

monitory: "Oh, do not trust that Nevsky Prospect! . . . All is deception, all is dream, all is not what it seems!" (III, 45). The theme of misleading appearances developed here through a series of whimsical examples is more properly a matter of the difficulty of judging by *any* appearances. The turn is neat but arbitrary. Though the two anecdotes scarcely support it, the rhetorical build-up screens that fact and the piece ends with a prestidigitator's flourish: "It lies at all times, that Nevsky Prospect, but most of all when night covers it with a thick mass and sets off the white and straw-colored walls of the buildings, when the whole city turns into thunder and glitter, myriads of carriages pour off the bridges, outriders shout and bounce on their horses, and when the demon himself lights the lamps only to show everything in an unreal guise."

This casual invocation of the devil adds a hint of supernatural malevolence, a suggestion that Piskaryov and Pirogov are victims not of their own illusions but of a trap. It is no more than a hint, but it suffices to color the vision of disorder—the parade of costumes and features, Piskaryov's visual sense of a world topsy-turvy and his conviction that the beautiful prostitute represents a diabolical perversion of "the harmony of nature." Out of this hint will grow the story of "The Portrait," where an artist does fall victim to the devil's temptations; so too the implied doubling of the artist and the officer, victim and "successful" survivor, will be travestied in "Diary of a Madman," and the ironic autonomy of mustaches and smiles be extended to the adventures of "The Nose."

"Nevsky Prospect," in short, is an effective essay in assimilating the urban setting to fiction. The two young men are not really characters but mentalities, set up to represent social groups that are better individuated in the story than they. Elements of the currently popular urban sketch, romantic artist story, and satirical-burlesque anecdote have been added to those of puppet theater and that free narrative performance which Gogol developed in *Mirgorod*—all of them linked by association to body forth an image of the indifferent and faintly sinister city, where Schiller is a tinsmith, Hoffmann a cobbler, and absurdity need never lack for an implicit rationale.

"THE PORTRAIT" extends the theme of the artist's fate in Petersburg, making literal the presence of the devil and sharpening the question of the moral ambiguity of esthetic values. In part a disquisition on esthetics, in part an exploration of romantic demonology, it draws on motifs, ideas, and structures to be found in Wackenroder, Hoffmann, Maturin (whose *Melmoth the Wanderer* appeared in Russian in 1833), and Balzac—and shows analogies with a number of other works popular at the time.[35] As usual, Gogol's debts are difficult to pinpoint as such, but the loss is not great. What is most important is the fact that he is accepting a series of already fading conventions here, rather than turning them to fresh use. In "The Portrait" he forgoes the comic along with narrative polyphony in the interests of a high seriousness which he would only later recognize might be available without such crippling sacrifice. The result is an allegorical fable, rendered in terms of apocalyptic earnestness—a mixture that Russian critics have insisted on calling tragic.

Subsequently revised and considerably expanded, the story as it appeared in *Arabesques* tells of a poor young painter, Chertkov, who is mysteriously drawn to a portrait with uncanny living eyes, buys it, finds money in the frame and customers for his own work suddenly at his door. Under the baneful influence of his acquisition, he becomes facile and fashionable, dooms his own talent, turns maniacally jealous of real creations (which he buys up only to destroy), and ends in madness, quickly followed by death. All this comprises only the first half of the story; the second (like the ending of "A Terrible Vengeance") provides the *Vorgeschichte* that explains his fate by telling how a Petersburg moneylender, possessed by the Antichrist, had persuaded a painter to prolong his evil existence by incarnating it on canvas. The painter, later repentant, redeems his compliance by becoming a hermit and icon painter; and his son—who tells the story at an auction where the portrait is for sale—completes the redemption, as his father has charged him to do, by telling the story during the first full moon exactly fifty years after the portrait was made. The portrait metamorphoses into an innocuous landscape, and the story ends.

Demonism and moralizing aside, Gogol's passionate estheticism produces a cloudy message about the "horrible reality" art can reveal when it pursues nature too slavishly.[36] The suggestion seems to be that God and the Devil are copresent in the world and that any representation of phenomena must serve one side or the other. The artist who succumbs to vanity and courts social acceptance—or even the artist who allows himself to pursue the phantom of truth unguided by a vision of beauty—does the Devil's work. Here is adumbrated a defense of Gogol's own concern with the banal and the trivial. For the artist, nothing in nature has fixed value; everything depends upon the quality and intention of the imagination behind each concrete rendering. But there is another inference to be drawn from "The Portrait": the world as such needs to be redeemed by art. Redemption lies in the conferring of value and meaning on what is otherwise a void, a "horrible reality"—ordinary human experience, which is for Gogol increasingly the realm of dead souls.

"DIARY OF A MADMAN" is an original if masked variation on this theme. Unique among all Gogol's tales in being a first-person narrative by the central character—to whom all the narrative oddity attaches—the story at the same time manages to be subtly and quintessentially Gogolian, a masterpiece on several planes. Originally conceived as "The Diary of a Mad Musician," in sympathetic response to Prince V. F. Odoyevsky's story-cycle, "The Madhouse," itself one of many Russian developments of Hoffmann's *Kunstlernovellen,* Gogol's story as it evolved in his mind incorporated other sources—with the result that a low-level civil servant came to be the central figure. This was a transposition of genius, broadening the import of the story. One stimulus to the change may have come from the flood of newspaper stories about insane asylums and their inmates (particularly in *The Northern Bee*) which reached its apogee about a year before "Diary of a Madman" appeared. From one such report, Gogol might have learned that the majority of patients in at least one Petersburg asylum were civil servants, the most common pathological symptoms being pride and ambition, followed by fear and timidity. Alongside details of their treatment, he might have found reports of the French shop assistant who added to his passport, "King of France and Navarre"; of the Parisian convinced that he had inadvertently swallowed a captain of the Hussars at dinner when the latter fell into his wineglass; of the rabbit who grew feathers instead of fur, the girl with two noses, the astronomer who predicted in 1833 that the universe would be destroyed by a passing comet in 1832.[37] Gogol's madman, Aksenty Poprishchin, reads *The Northern Bee,* and his lumpen-intelligentsia language shows him to be at once its ideal reader and—in Gogol's artful handling—its satirical scourge.

Finally, the story clearly draws on Gogol's own brief experi-

ence as a government clerk, "copying the stale fantasies of department heads and others" (X, 143). The civil service that dominated
Petersburg was a machine, its workers interchangeable cogs. Its
very mindless routines differed qualitatively from the mindless
routines of "Old-World Landowners" or the two Ivans, for the
latter had at least an indisputably if deplorably human source and
rootedness, whereas in Petersburg the semblance of worth attached rather to the office than to the individual who filled it and
was defined by it. (Poprishchin, secretly enamored of his director's
daughter, finds her hand, in Alex de Jonge's happy translation,
"fragrant with the rank of general.") Gogol's oft-repeated fears of
burial alive thus found a new variant in the bureaucratic world of
the capital: involuntary routine would either stifle consciousness or
alienate it. All this gives "Diary of a Madman" its particular psychological subtlety (and may account as well for the submerged
persistence of the theme of the artist).

As a result, this story is his "fullest" to date—in depth, as
"Nevsky Prospect" was alleged to be in breadth. Utilizing the elements of *skaz* hitherto reserved to his nameless narrator, it subordinates them to a single objectified psyche. Dealing as before with
routine and the quasi-individual who represents it, Gogol adds a
pattern of significant experience—but without recourse to plot.
Instead, the twenty diary entries enact a process, each of them representing a stage of Poprishchin's dementia.[38] This new form
newly rationalizes both the devices and the themes Gogol has been
perfecting. There is stylization of language and discourse—to
express the poor clerk in his envious discontent and complacency,
and to show his excessive aspiration in all its unconscious limitation. There is the familiar riddle of identity, compounded by sudden metamorphosis. There are the Petersburg themes of vanity
and sensitivity (Poprishchin being, as it were, an unexampled
combination of the careerist and dreamer)—and there is a nuanced
travesty of the recognition theme, the awful power of the *regard
d'autrui*. Finally, there is a new complexity in the theme of deception and illusion. Poprishchin, like Don Quixote, is deceived in his
madness—but he is deceived as well in the escape that madness
seems to promise, for he finds in it neither freedom nor nobility.
Thus his story ends not with a reconciliation but with a new and
no less doomed impulse to flight, outward ("Drive, coachman,
ring, little bell, soar, steeds, and carry me out of this world!")—

and backward ("Mama, save your poor son! . . . There is no place for him in the world!").

The Cervantine parallels here are striking. Not only does this Gogolian "exemplary tale" exploit "El coloquio de los perros"; it combines that dog's-eye satire with the Quixotic principle itself. The unusual adventure of the opening entry is Poprishchin's hearing the conversation of two dogs, one of them the pet of his director's daughter, Sophie. Pruriently curious about the life of the aristocrats he so envies, he decides to learn about it by seizing the letters the dogs have spoken of exchanging. "These letters will reveal everything to me" (III, 201). They are, of course, a figment of his imagination. The very form of the diary entry in which they are quoted makes this clear. All the other entries are conventionally retrospective, summarizing the day's happenings and reflecting on them; this one alone is in the present tense, suggesting not recollection, but composition: "Well, let's have a look: The writing is clear enough. Just the same, there is something sort of doglike in the handwriting. Let's read it" (III, 201). What follows is an extraordinarily delicate—and extraordinarily inventive—inching toward a truth that cannot be faced without such indirection. The letters veer from domestic details to dog food as Poprishchin, carried away by imagination, temporizes. ("An exceptionally uneven style," he observes. "It's evident from the start that a human being didn't write it. It begins properly enough, but ends in dogginess.")But at the end he confronts, through the lapdog's assurance, the fact that Sophie will marry "either a general, or a Gentleman of the Bedchamber, or a colonel of the army," and that "Sophie just can't keep from laughing when she looks at him," Poprishchin. This prompts rebellion against a world where the best of everything goes to Gentlemen of the Bedchamber or to generals (III, 205). "Why am I a Titular Councillor and for what reason am I a Titular Councillor? Maybe I'm some count or general, and only seem to be a Titular Councillor? Maybe I myself don't know who I am" (III, 206). The way is now open to the discovery of a more exalted identity; the newspapers have been reporting struggles over the Spanish throne, and in the entry headed "April 43rd of the year 2000," Poprishchin announces in triumph: "There is a king in Spain. He has been found. I am that king." From this point on, the Quixotic principle dominates. The resources of crazy imagination, which had created the dogs' correspondence and led him to a truth he could no longer either deny or accept, now go to reinterpreting Petersburg as Spain and the insane asylum to which he is committed as the Spanish court. Poprishchin's resourcefulness increases with the actual hopelessness of his situation, comedy with pain. What Gogol referred to as "freshness" is what animates his protagonist here, and provokes admiration in the double sense. Like his creator, Poprishchin seems endlessly fertile in ascription—until, like his creator at the end of "The Fair at Sorochintsy" or the story of the two Ivans, he registers a sudden loss of creative energy and reveals the subsistent world in all its melancholy and bleakness.

The "Diary," like all of Gogol's best writing, is an improvised discourse, a performance sustained by verbal felicity, shot through with ambivalence, haunted by the near presence of conventional significance. Gogol's madman is unquestionably a victim of the Petersburg bureaucracy and the Petersburg press; but he is a victim because he is the quintessential government clerk and the ideal reader of Bulgarin and Senkovsky.[39] He rebels not against a world of rank but against his lowly place within it, and he can find no more effective target for rebellion than his own self. So he elicits a real but equivocal sympathy—real because of his human unhappiness, equivocal because of the banality of his aspirations. To see this is to realize the originality of Gogol's achievement in this story. In place of an unrecognized genius (the "mad musician" of the original project), he gives us an unrecognized malcontent and vulgarian who cannot discriminate between Pushkin and his fourth-rate rivals, lends him his own lively gifts of expression—and grants him in writing the recognition that he is denied in his fictive "life."

To Poprishchin's own double perspective, veering between sanity and madness, Gogol adds another: that of the outsider who reads and responds to what Poprishchin can only experience and record. In this perspective "Diary of a Madman" takes its place among the Petersburg Tales as another indictment of the city's baneful effect on human aspiration. At the same time, it shows the startling congruence between the madman's vision of Petersburg and the vision that informs the other stories.

THAT CONGRUENCE is underlined in the parallel opening of "The Nose": "On March 25 an unusually strange occurrence took place in Petersburg." The occurrence in question is the unaccountable disappearance of the nose of another ambitious civil servant, its metamorphic adventures while independent, and his frantic pursuit of it until it reappears mysteriously in place—a happy ending for a character who doesn't deserve one. The narration is by Gogol's elusive *skaz* narrator—ostensibly omniscient, but full of gaps, irrelevancies and non-sequiturs—ready to acknowledge oddity but only with a disconcerting fitfulness. The first draft of the story had ended by explaining that "everything described here was a dream" of Major Kovalyov, the bereaved bureaucrat (III, 399), thereby rationalizing bewilderment and illustrating Gogol's own definition of a dream as "simply incoherent excerpts, which have no sense, taken from what we have thought and then pasted together to make up a kind of salad" (X, 376–377).

Removing this rationale in the published version, Gogol turned his story into an experiment in absurdity—a puzzle without a key and a provocation to his readers: "An exceedingly strange story!" he exclaims at the conclusion of the first published version:

I absolutely can't understand anything in it. And what is all this for? What is its relevance? I'm sure that more than half of it is implausible . . . I confess I can't understand how I could write this! And it's incomprehensible to me in general how authors can take up that kind of subject! Where does all this tend? What is its aim? What does this story prove? . . . Even supposing that there are no rules for the fancy, and granting that many absolutely inexplicable things do really happen in the world; still, what have we here? . . . Why Kovalyov's nose? . . . And why Kovalyov himself? . . . No, I don't understand, I don't understand at all. (III, 400).

Further refining his text for the collected works of 1842, Gogol subtly adjusts this closing emphasis; the authorial voice no longer articulates the reader's rational objections but plays with them, unreliably, and ends by pointing not to the creative but to the ontological mystery: "And nonetheless, despite everything, although, of course, one may grant this and that and the other, may even—well, but where are there not absurdities?—All the same, when you think it over there really is something in all this. Whatever anyone may say, things like that do happen in the world— rarely, but they do happen" (III, 75).

The censor charged with passing the story for its third publication—in 1854, two years after Gogol's death—proved an ideal reader. "The aim of the author is obscure and capable of being interpreted in various ways," he observed, "and so approval of this story requires the permission of the chief censorship authority."[40] The point is an unwitting tribute to a quintessentially Gogolian masterpiece, in which the quest for significance is displaced from the experience related in the work to the reader's experience of the text. Rejected by the *Moscow Observer* as being vulgar and trivial, "The Nose" is obviously neither. Pushkin was closer to the mark when, publishing it in *The Contemporary,* he praised it as an inspired joke. The inspiration is in the artistry, which not only sustains the comic effect but compels assent to the author's insistence that "all the same, when you think it over, there really is something in all this." Readers in search of profundity have found it there by following their own noses, seeing the story as an indictment of physicality, an orthodox Freudian castration fantasy, a sermon against godlessness, a symbolic comment on the drift away from Orthodox observance, and so on.[41] Most of these interpretations are plausible, and justified to a point, but each is unconvincing because too much of the text escapes it. Gogol has created a puzzle that many keys may fit, but none open. A trap for the unwary, it represents his most original achievement to date in confronting the question of how to be a writer.

As usual, he bases his work on an original recombination of familiar motifs—from Sterne, Hoffmann, Tieck, Veltman, Zschokke, all of them current in Russian, many of them forming part of what was a large literature on noses in the 1820s and 1830s. Viktor Vinogradov, who first unearthed much of this material in the 1920s, draws from it the important conclusion that, to contemporary readers, there was nothing strange or unusual in the subject matter of Gogol's story. Noses were fashionable; so were stories about usurping or absconding shadows, reflections, parts of the body.[42] What Gogol did was to supply a new justification for such whimsical or supernatural accounts. Encouraged perhaps by Pushkin's *Little House in Kolomna,* a playful and provocative exercise in self-regarding verse narrative, he confronted, in Setchkarev's words, the task "of writing a tale capable, merely by the form in which it is told, of making downright nonsense credible, suspenseful, and equal to all the demands that one places on a work of art."[43]

But there is more than downright nonsense here. The temptation to read meanings into the story arises from the fact that fragments of meaning can be read out of it. When Major Kovalyov confronts his runaway Nose dressed in the uniform of a State Councillor, he reproaches him (or it): "This is strange, sir . . . It seems to me . . . you should know your place" (III, 55)—a comic restatement of the theme that runs through all the Petersburg Tales, the theme of the place in this world obsessed with appearances of the artist, the dreamer, the bureaucrat, the vulgarian. Kovalyov clearly subordinates self to rank, and all but equates his nose with his selfhood: the physical, the spiritual, and the social are satirically juxtaposed—the unavoidable implication being that this parody of a supernatural adventure set in a prosaic Petersburg exists also (but not primarily: no theme is primary here) to exhibit the central character as a type whose very insignificance must somehow be significant.

Irony, Roland Barthes has written, "is nothing but the question posed to language by language," and he has suggested that, in contrast with "the poor Voltairean irony, narcissistic product of a language too self-confident, one can imagine another irony which for lack of a better term one might call baroque, because . . . it expands the language rather than narrowing it."[44] Such expansion is the principal achievement of "The Nose," which forces the reader to contemplate nothing less than the autonomy of the word (as he tries to picture the nose frowning, praying, hurrying, decked out in a resplendent uniform.) The counterpart on the formal level is the arbitrariness of transitions, the narrator's refusal to explain the connections between his chapters. Both are extensions involving a qualitative difference from the simpler kind of illogic found in the speeches, behavior, and description of characters, all of which attach to the world of the puppet show or satire.

In the consistency of its provocation, "The Nose" may finally be read as a manifesto. By contrast to such programmatic statements as are found in both versions of "The Portrait," this one arises from the nature not of the art he was planning but of the art he found himself producing, whose radical originality amounted to a generic mutation. The parallel with Pushkin's assertion of the poet's sovereign freedom to shape his material has been noted by scholars, and legitimately; but Pushkin's subtlety is always decipherable, his poetic logic apprehensible. Gogol, lacking a tradition and a readership ready to see art in prose, had to create his forms—

and this he did by an unprecedented combination of motifs and conventional cues, all of them familiar when taken separately but finally transformed by the new context in which he set them to functioning. "The Nose" may be called a manifesto because the story as a whole mocks a serious attitude toward plot (the accepted notion of significant form), mocks ordinary assumptions about intentionality (the very notion of language as the carrier of messages), insists openly on this mockery, and at the end encourages the beleaguered reader's assumption that "all the same, when you think it over, there really is something in all this." And there is: only not within the story, but in the very fact of its existence. Misled by fragments of meaning and the semblance of an adventure, the reader may be cheated of vicarious experience, but he emerges enriched by his own linguistic and imaginative experience. A serious prose art capable of constituting the national voice is paradoxically demonstrated through this joke: "The Nose" triumphantly proclaims its existence *as pure instrumentality*.[45]

A COMPARABLE mastery, this time in a minor key, informs "The Carriage," written in 1835 (as Gogol was beginning *Dead Souls*). This is the shortest of all Gogol's finished stories, and in reputation the slightest, perhaps because it stands alone outside the three major cycles and so is deprived of that weight by association that accrues to the anecdotes of the Ukrainian and Petersburg Tales, and to the episodes of *Dead Souls*. Nonetheless this story, which Tolstoy was tempted to call Gogol's best work and which he hailed as "the peak of perfection in its kind,"[46] represents a crucial link in his evolution. It is his first fictional foray into provincial Russia, to which he had no ties at all, either of emotional attachment, experience, or observation—and it employs the narrative method he had been perfecting to body forth inanity in a nearly pure form. A note for *Dead Souls* identifies "the idea of [its provincial] town" as "Inanity* (*Pustota*) carried to the highest degree" (VI, 692)—but, as Aksakov notes, Gogol's discovery of the symbolic possibilities of that idea was gradual; beginning with "a curious and amusing anecdote," he came to realize only later, in his own words, "to what powerful thoughts and profound phenom-

* Webster: "Inane: Without contents; empty, esp. void of sense or significance, pointless . . . As noun: that which is inane; esp., the void of space."

ena an insignificant subject might lead."[47] "The Carriage" relates to the first stage of that process.

The basic anecdote is straightforward and minimal, just sufficient to sustain his narrative embroideries. A retired officer, as self-satisfied as Lieutenant Pirogov, as well-married as Major Kovalyov aspires to be, and as boastful as Khlestakov, hyperbolizes on the theme of an incomparable carriage he has bought; invites an incredulous visiting general to dine with him and inspect the carriage on the following day; oversleeps, and, reminded of his invitation when the guests are already arriving, pretends not to be at home, only to be discovered curled up in his quite ordinary carriage by the officers who have decided to have a look at it anyway. That is all there is by way of story: an innocent blowhard is discomfited—in the interests not of poetic justice but of simple exhibition. "Ah, you are here!" says the general at the end, and that, in the terms of Gogol's artistic strategy, is the point.

But the point involves the setting too, for setting explains character and vice versa. If the Ukraine of the Dikanka stories was the locus of a romantic folk poetry, the Ukraine of Mirgorod the home of intimate dreams and unnatural Petersburg the locus of absurdity, then the eventless Russian provinces add a new theme: they are the locus of boredom. Gogol emphasizes this invidiously, by making his language eventful as his material is not. A single monstrous paragraph, constituting almost a third of the text, introduces the town of B., and the central character, Pifagor (Pythagoras) Pifagorovich Chertokutsky. The narration here is, by unmotivated turns, objective, subjective, summary, and specific, which is not to say that the narrator is nowhere reliable—that, after all, would amount to a kind of consistency—but rather that he compels constant wariness in the reader. The somewhat awkward process of interpolated comment may illuminate Gogol's rhetorical fabric in the opening lines with the least damage:

The town of B. became very lively when the * * * cavalry regiment was quartered there. [*As Setchkarev notes, a Pushkinian beginning; but Gogol's statement, though incontestable, is also ironically misleading, for the whole of the story will make clear how radically we must adjust our notion of what it can mean to grow "very lively."*] Up to then it was incredibly dull. [*The same concision, but in a conversational key, so that the objectivity of the opening is abruptly called into question: Whose view is this?*] It used to be that when you drove through it [*motif of the road and the visit, reminiscent of the beginning of "Old-*

World Landowners" and the ending of the two Ivans, and foreshadowing Dead Souls] and gazed at the dirty little one-story houses that stared at the street with an improbably sour look, you felt—but there is no expressing what you felt in your heart at such times: [*neither the familiar declaration of impossibility nor the colon suggesting clarification to come is properly "Gogolian" here; for once they can be taken at face value*] a misery, as if you had lost at cards or [*now we approach ironic ambiguity*] just uttered some inappropriate stupidity [*because of the lurking suggestion that one might utter appropriate stupidities*]; in a word [*fair, but anticlimactic in its inadequacy to what has already been expressed*], you did not feel good. The plaster on the houses had slid off with the rain, and the walls, instead of being whitened, turned motley; the roofs were largely thatched with reeds, as is the custom in our southern towns [*objective description cum generalization; the narrator is presenting his bona fides and soliciting the intelligent reader's trust*]; to improve the view [*ambiguous irony, attaching to the town or the mayor or both*], the mayor had long since ordered the gardens cut down. You never met a soul on the streets [*a pun, in view of what follows*], except perhaps[?!] if a cock strutted across the roadway [*now begins a skillful series of subtle non-sequiturs, culminating in an absurdity that will further characterize not the narrator but the mayor*], soft as a pillow from the dust that stood nearly a foot thick on it and turned into mud at the least shower, when the streets of the town of B. would fill up with those stout animals the mayor of the place calls Frenchmen. [*This is in the first place a comment on the mayor's xenophobia, but it also signals a confounding of the animal and the human, usually to the detriment of the latter, as will be seen in the description of the mare with the human name, Agrafena Ivanovna, "strong and wild as a southern beauty," and in Chertokutsky's exclamation—almost arrogant in this context— "Akh, what a horse I am!"*] Thrusting their serious snouts [*more of the same*] out of their baths, they raise such a grunting that there is nothing for a traveler but to urge his horses on the more strenuously—though it is, for all that, hard to encounter a traveller passing through the town of B. [*not only a reprise of the road motif, but a tacit assertion of the typicality of such godforsaken places.*]

It is among the chief aristocrats of such a locale that Chertokutsky is "the most remarkable of all" (III, 179).

This brief sample may stand for the way the story functions throughout; to summarize or paraphrase is to falsify, because significance is displaced from the level of "content" to that of narration. The text, as Biely observed of *Dead Souls*, appears to consist of nothing but details, which Gogol has turned into "a pearl of perfection." The strategy of exhibition, with all its subtle modulations, will go unchanged into his novel, to the enlarging accompaniment of a commentary designed to fulfill an epic ambition which his strictly narrative talent, for all its brilliance, could not.

5

Confronting a Public, I

We have already noted Gogol's early concern with the theater in light of the problem of the artist's relation to his audience. In the parallel context of his improvisation of a vocation, that concern takes on a different appearance and has its own history.

The development of his central narrative gifts is in large part the development of theatrical tendencies. "The Fair at Sorochintsy," which opens the Dikanka collection, comprises a string of scenes, most of them farcical, interlarded with lyrical descriptions, gravitating at the end to overt soliloquy. In all his subsequent fiction, dialogue and monologue are almost self-sufficient values; and his characters, who tend to be presented as witting or unwitting performers, share the reader's attention with a narrator who is himself often more nearly a performer than an anonymous *metteur-en-scène*. As for the reader, he is not infrequently the object of provocations and is treated as one member of an invisible audience.

Gogol's gifts were by no means purely comic: a bleak sadness can often be seen underlying his work. But what is theatrical is generally comic. S. T. Aksakov records a conversation of 1832 which showed that Gogol had already reflected seriously on Russian comedy and developed "his own original view." The subject was Zagoskin, a popular historical novelist and playwright:

Gogol praised him for his gaiety, but said that he did not write as he should, especially for the theater. I objected flippantly that we had nothing to write about, that in society everything was so monotonous, smooth, decorous, and empty . . . but Gogol gave me a significant look and said that that was untrue, that the comic is concealed everywhere, that living in its midst we do not see it, but that if an artist transposes it into art, [puts it] on the stage, then we would collapse with laughter at ourselves, and would marvel that we had not noticed it before.[1]

Hints of such a transposition can be seen in the second half of "Nevsky Prospect," "Diary of a Madman," and "The Nose"— but in each case the audience identification Gogol considered so important was limited by his choice of marginal heroes, and by the very odd narrative emphases that marked these works. Gogol's experiments in stage comedy deal, by contrast, with characters, situations, or drives that make audience recognition easy, at least initially: bureaucrats in authority, aspirants to matrimony, gamblers, rogues.

His gift for "divining character" on the basis of speech and gesture—essentially a talent for creative mimicry—made the theater (for which his father had written several amateur pieces) naturally attractive to him. Like Russian fiction, moreover, but to an even greater degree, Russian prose drama in these years represented a qualitative void waiting to be filled. Foreign works and crude native vaudevilles predominated. "Dramatic literature is in great decline here," the *Moscow Telegraph* observed in 1831, and two years later, greeting Griboyedov's *Woe from Wit* as something virtually unprecedented, that journal proclaimed that it was "time to resurrect the fine art of drama."[2] Here, for an uncommitted writer, was one more role a–begging.

Gogol's first response came in 1833, a year of creative crisis and indecision. Wavering between fiction and history, satisfied with neither, he looks away, characteristically, to a new area of activity. In a letter to Pogodin, dated 20 February 1833, he confesses:

Somehow the work doesn't go well these days. The pen scratches the paper, but not with the old inspired and complete pleasure. I barely begin to accomplish something on my History, and already I see my own shortcomings: either I regret that I didn't approach the matter more broadly, with vaster scope, or else an utterly new system suddenly arises and pulls down the old one . . . For the time being, to hell with the work I have sketched on paper; it will have to wait for another, more tranquil time. *I don't know why I thirst so for contemporary fame these days.* All the depths of my soul are straining outward. But I have got absolutely nothing written to date. I haven't told you: I'm wild to write a comedy . . . In the last few days even the plot was beginning to take shape, the title was already written on a thick white notebook: *Vladimir of the Third Class*—and how much malice! laughter! salt! . . . But I suddenly stopped, seeing that my pen kept knocking against things that the censor wouldn't possibly pass. And what is the point if the play won't be performed? Drama lives only on the stage. Without the stage, it is like a soul without a body . . . Nothing remains for me but to think up the most innocent plot, one that even the neighborhood policeman couldn't take offense at. But what is comedy without truth and malice! And so I can't take up the comedy. Yet when I take up History—the stage moves before me, applause thunders, mugs thrust out of the loges, the balcony, the stalls, baring their teeth, and—to hell with history. (X, 263; emphasis added)

The attraction to the stage as expressed here appears to be quite without the moral-didactic element that enters later. Nor is there any reference to serving the muse. What moves the young writer at this point is a thirst for fame, along with a desire to confront his audience directly—and, quite possibly, the hope of earning a substantial sum[3] —a set of eminently practical motives, all of which were to be realized three years hence through *The Inspector General,* with disillusioning results.

Vladimir of the Third Class survives in the form of three scenes, one of them ("The Morning of a Busy Man") published in *The Contemporary* in 1836, subtitled "Petersburg Scenes," the other two ("The Lawsuit" and "The Servants' Quarters") only in the *Collected Works* of 1842–43. The play as a whole was to center on a bureaucrat's obsessive efforts to be decorated with the Order of Vladimir, Third Class—"only so that people might see the authorities' kindness to me" (V, 107)—and was reportedly to end in frustration and madness, with the protagonist imagining that he himself is a third-class Vladimir.[4] This line clearly went into "Diary of a Madman," written the following year; ancillary intrigues involved a disputed will, a wily scoundrel, young lovers, a mother determined to marry her poor son to a rich heiress—stock items which suggest that Gogol may have done well to abandon the project. For complex plot tends to reduce characters to functions, whereas his genius—as he was discovering in these years—was best deployed in creating situations for the nuanced *exhibition* of simplified characters.

But Gogol was also trying his hand at new forms in these years. The process was one of trial and error, the materials—as in the case of the Petersburg Tales—frequently borrowed from more or less familiar sources. He already brought to the stories of this period a masterly sense of style and technique, the result of his accumulated experience in handling narrative; so the familiar was renewed and transformed. In drama the process was more halting. In 1833, abandoning *Vladimir of the Third Class,* he undertook a comedy that would be published only after nearly a decade of intermittent revision in the *Collected Works* as *Getting Married** (*Ženit'ba*); in 1835 he began *Alfred,* a historical drama about the ninth-century Anglo-Saxon king, but abandoned it less than halfway through (only after his death was the manuscript found and published);[5] and in 1836 or thereabouts he began work on *The Gamblers,* a comedy finished in Rome and published in 1842. This, together with *The Inspector General* and the dramatized essays he later appended to it—"After the Play" (1842) and "The Denouement of *The Inspector General*" (1846)—is the sum of his dramatic efforts.

The evolution of *Getting Married* is characteristic. In 1833 Gogol finished nine scenes of it. During the next two years he revised and expanded; in 1836 he announced its completion, then took the manuscript back for a reworking that was accomplished between 1838 and 1840; revised it once more before submitting it for publication—and even after that made changes in the copy he sent to the actor Shchepkin. This is more than a matter of polishing: contemporaries who had seen or heard of the work in progress referred to it variously as "The Suitors," "The Provincial Bridegroom," "The Choice of a Bridegroom," and "The Matchmaker." Changes in setting and conception parallel this confusion. Early drafts are set in the country and show the same kind of low comedy that filled *Evenings;* subsequently the action was transferred to Petersburg and the satirical element enlarged, with the merchant and bureaucratic classes as targets. Only in the later stages was the psychological theme made central, as the final and more abstract title indicates. The play thus illustrates a decade-long process of crystallization. Conceived as an instrument that might bring "contemporary fame," it emerged as the work of an artist who had turned his back on the contemporary in the belief that one should have "only posterity in view."

Two AND A HALF years after confessing his desire to take up dramaturgy, Gogol still had nothing fit for staging. The Petersburg stage

---

* Usually translated as "Marriage." Nabokov's Shavian rendering, however—which I follow—corresponds better to Gogol's emphases in the play.

was a wasteland: not a single new Russian comedy was performed in 1835; and his desire to write for the theater had not abated. What had changed was the level of his confidence—and his ambition. *Arabesques* and *Mirgorod* were in print, marking the end of a period and moving the young critic Belinsky publicly to associate Gogol's name with the ineffable symbol of his highest artistic standards. Gogol, Belinsky wrote, was now "the head of [Russian] literature, chief of the poets," "assuming the place vacated by Pushkin" (who was in fact at the peak of his powers!)[6] The association, at least, was genuine. Pushkin himself had urged Gogol to undertake a large work, worthy of his now proven talent; he had even supplied the idea, and on October 7 Gogol wrote him to report that three chapters of *Dead Souls* were already written. It promises to be "a very long novel" and "very funny," designed to show "all of Russia, at least from one side." But he has laid it aside for reflection, and turns to Pushkin once more with a plea for a subject— any kind, funny or not funny, but a purely Russian anecdote. "My hand is itching to write a comedy." He cannot afford to lose a moment; besides, he needs money. "Do me a favor, give me a plot. In a flash it will be a five-act comedy and I swear it will be funnier than hell. I beg you. My mind and stomach are both hungry."

Pushkin evidently obliged—though the transaction itself is shrouded in fog and the degree of his willingness remains unclear. He himself had planned to write something based on a provincial governor's mistaking a casual traveler for an official from the capital. Indeed, he had been personally involved in such a situation and had surely heard of others: a number of variants were in the air in the 1820s and 1830s and found expression in the work of a number of writers. The anecdote clearly had a peculiar contemporary appeal.[7] This was what he "yielded" to Gogol—not a property so much as a situation.[8] In the event, auspices and anecdote proved ideal, the former guaranteeing the "purely Russian" nature of the latter, which was pregnant with comic possibilities precisely suited to Gogol's maturing genius. The result bears this out: *The Inspector General* took form, as promised, "in a flash": within two months the play had been completed and revised for submission to a theater.

The beauty of the project lay in its possibilities for transcending conventional categories. Gogol's two earlier efforts at stage comedy had been satirical in conception, their themes resolvable into conventional terms, making character and plot largely instrumental. In *Vladimir of the Third Class* the unambiguous target is the pursuit of status and wealth; *Getting Married* is a satire of matrimonial ambitions, its comedy based on deviations from a clearly deducible norm. (Thus it originally opened with its desperate provincial ingenue sending her servant to local fairs to round up prospective husbands, and later revisions incorporating discoveries made in *The Inspector General* only lend elements of personal pathology that limit its power of generalization.) *The Inspector General* has no such simple targets; it is not a comedy of intentions but of reactions; it exposes not vices and vanities but vital being. Its instrument is an unprecedented kind of poetry, its laughter (Rabelaisian rather than Swiftian) directed not "at separate negative phenomena, but [at] the revelation of a particular aspect of the world as a whole."[9] It is precisely the breadth of brilliantly realized possibilities—psychological, social, and artistic—that makes satire so inadequate a concept in accounting for *The Inspector General,* and the difficulty of disentangling any of these strands without falling into misrepresentation is what makes the work Gogolian in the highest degree.

Gogol's earliest draft elaborated the situation, basically as a parody of Judgment Day. The mayor of an unnamed provincial town relays to his terrified officials a report that an inspector has been dispatched incognito from the capital; their panicky discussions are cut short by the news that a young man has been staying for some days at the inn, refusing to pay or to go on. The conclusion is drawn: he must be the government inspector. In fact, he is a vacuous young nonentity who has gambled away his travel money and is slowly starving at the inn. The comedy of real terror based on false assumptions is thus doubled when the mayor pays him a trembling visit; from this point on, a compounded comedy of errors moves these characters to radical self-exposure—even as they struggle to stave off an infinitely shallower one, and elaborate an increasingly shared daydream in the process.

There is genius already in Gogol's making the false inspector a naïf. Had he been conceived as a confidence man, acting deliberately, we would have had only a variation on the standard theme of the trickster tricked. Here he is a perfect partner in *folie à deux* for the mayor and his associates as together, like jugglers balancing an ever-growing column of objects, they create an edifice of wish-fulfillment that is toppled at the end by the announcement that the real inspector has arrived. Creation thus goes hand in hand with exposure, and quickly outweighs it. Two dramas coalesce in the second act and develop in tandem thereafter, their authors being, respectively, Khlestakov and the mayor—fictions within Gogol's fiction (the whole being presented as an accidental usurpation of the "real" drama anticipated in the opening lines and announced as about to begin in the closing ones). But the exposures within the play are exposed as relatively paltry matters by the play itself. The center of gravity of *The Inspector General* is poetry and celebration.*

These last are the elements Gogol strengthened in his first revision and continued to polish thereafter. In blocking out the situation, he had made use of stereotyped characters; now he delegated a portion of his creativity to them. Khlestakov becomes more than an empty young man with picaresque tendencies. He is not, Gogol explained, "a habitual liar; he himself forgets at moments that he is lying . . . He expands, he feels good, he sees that everything is going well, that he's being listened to, and for that reason alone he speaks more smoothly, unconstrainedly, from the soul . . . He lies with feeling, and his eyes express the pleasure that this gives him. This is in general the best and most poetic moment of his life —almost a kind of inspiration" (IV, 99–100). To Khlestakov's poetry of hyperbole the mayor adds poetry of another kind, hardly less remarkable—with his ominous dream about "two unusual rats . . . of unnatural size," his advice that the patients in the town hospital "shouldn't look like blacksmiths," his talent as a logician ("Alexander the Great is a hero, but why break chairs?") (IV, 11, 13, 15). The gathering momentum of the play—psychological and dreamlike—is the result of impulses being freed. And if the stage action is built on surprises, these manifest themselves, as Nemirovich-Danchenko observed, in the characters, "in the many-facetedness of the human soul, however primitive it may be."[10]

This is the aspect of the play that most challenges critical terminology, resting as it does on a disparity between subtle psychol-

---

* See Turgenev's reaction to Gogol's reading of the play in 1851: "I sat bathed in joyful emotion: this was a real feast and holiday for me." "Gogol'," in his "Literaturnye i žitejskie vospominanija." *Polnoe sobranie sočinenij i pisem v 28-i tomax*, XIV (Moscow-Leningrad, 1967), 70.

ogy and the crude (in human terms) vehicles for it, which, by a dangerous inertia, are commonly referred to as characters. Gogol's dramatis personae are beings of a quite special kind, biographically indeterminate, motiveless, given to apparent imbecility, incompletely yet somehow profoundly and recognizably human. In Sinyavsky's formulation, "all the passions and hopes that move these creatures are in general directed to manifesting themselves in human form and with human dignity—as they understand these things; [their aspiration is], so to speak, to rise to a human degree."[11] From the disparity between impulse and its verbal expression comes a sort of nuanced psychological primitivism— and a large share of the comedy. Khlestakov's letter to his friend— which, intercepted and read by the town officials in the last act, disabuses them of their belief in his exalted rank—describes the mayor as being "stupid as an old gray mare," the postmaster as "most likely a scoundrel [who] drinks like a fish," and so on. Here are the stereotyped terms of satire, and their insufficiency is by now plain. They cannot touch either the common human impulses or the poetic lunacies in which those impulses eventuate under the influence of this carnival atmosphere. "How happy I am," Khlestakov declares on being presented to the mayor's wife, "that I have pleasure of a kind in seeing you" (IV, 47).[12] Interrupted by the latter in his courtship of the mayor's daughter ("Your eyes are better than important matters"; "Your lips are better than any weather"), he turns his amorous artillery on the wife: "My life hangs on a thread. If you do not crown my constant love, then I am unworthy of an earthly existence. With a flame in my breast I ask for your hand"—to which she can only reply that she is "in a certain sense . . . married" (IV, 73, 74, 76). In such cases, the comedy comes from the qualification; intended as a polite filler, it functions as nonsense and yet contains the ironic ghost of an unintended truth—*the last perceptible only to the audience,* since the speakers have been deprived of the capacity to recognize nonsense at any level, their own or others'. Banalities, clichés, malapropisms (such as the welfare commissioner's proud report that the local hospital patients are "recovering like flies"), non-sequiturs—all are transformed into agents of self-assertion. Always the nature of the desire is clear, be it the desire to please, impress, assert authority, or merely to be what one seems (compare Sinyavsky's observation that the dramatis personae "represent something midway between a character and a parody of the post he occupies in the town.")[13] A minor but characteristic example is provided by the mayor's wife in her exchange with her daughter at the beginning of act 3:

Maria. Oh, mama, mama! Somebody's coming, down the end of the street.

Anna. Where is somebody coming? You're always having some kind of fantasies. Hmm, yes, there is somebody. Who is it? Rather short . . . dressed like a gentleman . . . Who is it? Eh? But this is annoying! Whoever might it be?

Maria. It's Dobchinsky, mama!

Anna. What Dobchinsky? You're always imagining things . . . It's not Dobchinsky at all— (*Waves her handerkerchief.*) Hey, you! Come over here! Quickly!

Maria. It really is Dobchinsky, mama.

Anna. You only say that to argue. I tell you it's not Dobchinsky.

Maria. What did I say? What did I say, mama? Now you see it is Dobchinsky.

Anna. Well, yes, it is Dobchinsky, I see it is now—what do you want to argue about? (IV, 40–41)

Here, alongside the revelation of near-sightedness, is the assertion of parental authority. All authority in this play seems similarly to exist in inverse proportion to real identity.

Gogol's intuition involved the generalizing potential of such a situation. More than a decade later, he declared that he had sought in *The Inspector General* "to collect into one heap all that I knew to be bad in Russia" and to expose it to laughter (VIII, 440). At the time of writing the locus of the negative had been identified in his work as Petersburg, the capital of illusion. And *The Inspector General* clearly emerges from the Petersburg cycle which it extends, continues, and crowns ("The Overcoat" comes later and makes its distinctive contribution by building on the discoveries of this comedy.) But it is no longer the denizens of Petersburg that interest Gogol; it is the appeal of the idea of Petersburg, whose potency is here demonstrated even in the remote heart of provincial Russia, in a town (as the mayor says) from which "you could gallop three years and not reach any [other] country" (IV, 12).

Like so much else in the play, Petersburg is double. At the opening and again in the final line, it figures as the seat of authority, the ground of judgment—but this role remains ideal and potential. What is shown is Petersburg as dream symbol of a banal glory: this is the image to which all in the play pay homage. It ap-

pears first in the monologue of Khlestakov's servant, Osip, as he
lounges on the master's bed at the opening of act 2. He has praised,
momentarily, the vegetative joys of village life:

Well, and who'd argue? When it comes down to the truth, life in Petersburg is best of all. So long as there's money, life is refined and polític:
theeyaters, dogs dance for you, anything you like. Everybody talks fine
and sensitive, almost like your nobleman. You go to Shchukin's, the
merchants shout "Sir!" at you; in the ferryboat you sit down right next
to a government clerk; if you want company—go to a shop: There a cav-
alier will talk about life in camp and announce what every star in the sky
means, so you see it just like in the palm of your own hand. An old officer's wife will wander in, sometimes a housemaid will look in—and one
who . . . ai–ai–ai! (*Smirks and shakes his head.*) Fancy manners, damn it!
You never hear an impolite word, everybody calls you mister. Get tired
of walking, you hail a cab and sit there like a lord; and if you don't want
to pay, that's all right: Every house has a back gate, too, and you can skip
through so not even the devil will find you. (IV, 26–27)

Khlestakov himself soliloquizes in the same vein soon after, indicating what Petersburg means for him. Starving, he has considered
selling his trousers:

No, better to go hungry a bit and arrive home in my Petersburg suit.
Too bad Iokhim wouldn't rent me a carriage; it would have been fine,
dammit, to come home in a carriage, drive up like some fancy devil to a
neighboring landowner's porch, with lanterns and Osip mounted behind
in livery. I can imagine the fuss everybody would make: "Who is it?
What is it?" And the footman—gold livery—goes in (*drawing himself up
and acting the footman*): "Ivan Aleksandrovich Khlestakov from Petersburg, is he to be received?" And they, the bumpkins, don't even know
what "Is he to be received?" means. (IV, 30)

The bumpkins, however, do know what Petersburg means. It
is the idea that brings them to life—at least to that privileged intensity of life which they display until its withdrawal in the dumb
scene leaves them like relics of Pompeii. This idea is anterior even
to that of the inspector; it is what gives him his authority; more,
his awe-inspiring magnificence. In Khlestakov's drunken monologue, the details (thirty-five thousand couriers looking for him, a
melon costing seven hundred rubles on the table) impose because
their hyperbolic scale corresponds to the magnificence of the idea.
Under the influence of what Sinyavsky justly calls Khlestakov's
siren song, each of his hearers surrenders to his own unrestrained
dreams. The mayor, once related to Khlestakov by marriage, will
be a general and command universal deference; his wife will have

"the best house in the capital," and a room "so fragrant that you won't be able to enter it." Bobchinsky, more modest, desires only to have his existence authenticated by association:

Bobchinsky. I humbly beg you, when you go back to Petersburg, tell all the various nobles there, senators and admirals: Do you know, your Excellency or Highness, in such and such a town there lives one Pyotr Ivanovich Bobchinsky. Just say that: there lives one Pyotr Ivanovich Bobchinsky.

Khlestakov. Very well.

Bobchinsky. And if you happen to be with the sovereign, then tell the sovereign, too: Do you know, your Imperial Majesty, in such and such a town lives one Pyotr Ivanovich Bobchinsky.

Khlestakov. Very well. (IV, 67)

Petersburg is a conferring power. Khlestakov's "soul thirsts for civilization"; in his fantasy-Petersburg, accordingly, he hobnobs with Pushkin: "It used to be I'd ask him often, 'Well, what do you say, friend Pushkin?', and he'd answer, '*You* know, friend; everything's somehow—*you* know' . . . A real character" (IV, 48). Power for the mayor, *la vie en rose* for his wife, existential significance for Bobchinsky: the idea of Petersburg, genie-like, confers all.[14]

Functioning as a powerful absence in the play, as a magical, intensifying power, Petersburg is an ideal still awaiting realization —an unharnessed and undefined power, much as Russia will appear in the final troika image of *Dead Souls*. The irradiation of banal desires turns banality incandescent, producing an unlikely poetry and a brilliantly original comedy. Gogol's symbolic presentation, however, pointedly leaves open the possibility that worthier values, if attached to the national symbol, might produce a real magnificence.

Perhaps the subtlest feature of the play is its implicit power of generalization. In its originality *The Inspector General* challenges all our assumptions and forces us to reconstrue most of our categories —psychological," "social"—even, as Nabokov points out, comedy itself, since the play is something more: "poetry in action," with poetry understood as "the mysteries of the irrational as perceived through rational words."[15] Nabokov's formula errs only in dismissing the semblances generated by this process—semblances of comment on Russian character and society that are no less present and effective in the text for being pre-propositional. The world of *The Inspector General* may be a closed one, but it is (as Arnold Kettle observed of the world of *Oliver Twist*) one that is "strikingly, appallingly relevant" to the real one.[16]

The social aspect is a case in point. The inclusiveness of Gogol's picture is important to remark. He does show justice (Lyapkin-Tyapkin), education (Khlopov), health care (Gibnerf/ Hübner), the post office (Shpekin), welfare institutions (Zemlyanika), the police, the merchants, and so on*; and this may indeed call to mind an image from his article "On the Teaching of World History," where he writes that "one cannot come to know a town completely by tramping all its streets: for that one must ascend to an elevated place, from which the whole may be seen as in the palm of one's hand" (VIII, 30). But to suggest that he does so principally in order to say something about the social microcosm on the stage is to mistake the way his art functions.[17] If he sought to present a social microcosm on the stage, it was for the sake of juxtaposing it with the social microcosm constituted by the audience in the theater in a way that might justify his epigraph: "Don't blame the mirror if your mug is crooked." What is social is less the text than the theatrical event.

Vyacheslav Ivanov seems to have been the first to see this when, in 1925, he identified the nameless setting as being essentially "the comedic town (whether Athens or Cloud–Cuckooland) of old Aristophanes," and the strategy of the play as "intrinsically and Aristophanically comic." Crucial to this interpretation is the fact that the action of *The Inspector General* "is not limited to a circle of personal relationships, but, rather, presents these relationships as components of a collective life and embraces a whole social microcosm, self-contained and self-sufficient, which stands symbolically for any social confederation, and of course reflects, as in a [distorting] mirror, just that social confederation to whose entertainment and edification the comic action is directed."[18] It was part of Gogol's hermeneutic design that this play about the power of Petersburg should have its premiere in Petersburg. What is idea

---

* In David MacDonald's production for the Glasgow Citizens' Theatre, Lyapkin-Tyapkin is ingeniously Englished as Smashkin-Grabkin, Postmaster Shpekin as Myopik, School Superintendent Khlopov as Teachin, Welfare Commissioner Zemlyanika as Semolina, Constable Derzhimorda as Fistikuff, and Tryapichkin as Satirikov. (I am indebted to Laurence Senelick for this information.)

in the text becomes palpable actuality in the theater, and the ending brilliantly blurs the dividing line of the proscenium, culminating in the dumb scene, a final exhibition of the characters, frozen in terror at the announcement that the "real" inspector has arrived. At this point, the great director Nemirovich-Danchenko writes, "the audience also freezes in voiceless contemplation" and "the indissoluble connection between the stage and the hall reaches an ideal force."*

The effect may have been part of Gogol's plan—it was certainly implicit in the text of 1836—but it found full expression only in the revision that followed the first performances, so that the failure of early audiences to take the point in part at least reflected the author's own failure to develop it sufficiently. In the initial stage version the mayor reacts with helpless rage at learning that he has been duped, and as the assembled company turns on Dobchinsky and Bobchinsky, blaming them for the whole catastrophic mistake, the gendarme appears with his summons to report to the newly arrived official from Petersburg. The characters freeze in astonishment, and the curtain falls.

Already in this version Gogol's intention to avoid any resolution on stage is plain. And that intention is crucial, since if justice were to be done or the fates of the dramatis personae sealed in any way, the audience might settle back complacently as uninvolved spectators of a completed experience. The relative weakness of the original ending, however, lies in the ease with which it could be mistaken for something more conventional. What the revisions do is make clear that the play is not the representation but the agent of significant experience. In so doing, they cap a tendency that is evident from the beginning, for *The Inspector General* is punctuated

---

* Though Gogol's stage direction indicates that this scene should last "almost a minute and a half," Nemirovich-Danchenko notes that, to the best of his knowledge, it never lasted longer than fifty-two seconds: "And when I asked the prompter, who has to signal the curtain, how he decided, he answered, 'I call for the curtain when I feel that one more second and my heart will burst.'" At one performance, he adds, a woman sitting in the orchestra, "who had laughed goodheartedly at the mayor all evening, exclaimed with terror, trying not to break the silence after only fifteen seconds of the dumb scene, 'My God! he's going to have a heart attack.' Spontaneously and naively, she had herself felt the beating of the mayor's heart" ("Sceniceskoe obajanie *Revizora* Gogolja," *Ežegodnik imperatorskix teatrov,* no. 2, 1909, 34).

with statements that assume a fuller meaning on the other side of the footlights:

Ammos Fedorovich: Yes, this sort of situation is—unusual, simply unusual. There must be some reason for it. (IV, 12)
Khlestakov [to the Mayor's terrified stuttering]: I can make nothing of it. It's all nonsense. (IV, 50)
The mayor [on the brink of glory, having just been asked to consent to give his daughter to Khlestakov in marriage]: Please act as your Excellency thinks best. My head at this moment . . . I don't know what's the matter with it. I have become a greater fool than I have ever been. (IV, 78)
The mayor [to a policeman]: Announce to everyone . . . that the Mayor is marrying his daughter not to any ordinary man but to such a one as there has never yet been in the world. (IV, 82)

All this represents a particularly rich kind of dramatic irony. It is not just that the audience knows these statements to be true in a way that the speakers cannot. The "joyful astonishment" of the attentive spectator goes further, finding in them references *to the play itself, as artifice.* This reaches a particular intensity in the final scene when the postmaster, who has intercepted Khlestakov's letter to his friend Tryapichkin, shares its shattering contents with the assembled company.

Mayor. How could you dare to unseal the letter of so plenipotentiary a personage?
Postmaster. That's just it: he's not plenipotentiary and he's not a personage.
Mayor. Then what is he, according to you?
Postmaster. Not one thing or another; the devil alone knows. (IV, 90)

Early in the letter Khlestakov has urged his friend who writes for the papers (the *Library for Reading* is named in the first stage version) to make use of these provincials. In closing, he states his own intention "to take up literature, following your example. It's dreary, friend, just to go on living; finally you want some nourishment for the soul. I see one really needs to be occupied with something lofty" (IV, 90, 92).

Here the complex irony opens outward, into the hall and the larger world it represents. The Mayor carries it forward:

(*In a frenzy.*) Here, have a look, look all the world, all of Christendom, everybody look what a fool the Mayor has been made! Call him a fool—a fool!—the old bastard! Ah, you fat-nose! Took a suckling, a rag for a man of importance! . . . And he'll spread the story all over the world.

It's not enough that you'll be made a laughingstock: some hack, some scribbler will turn up who'll put you into a comedy. That's what hurts: He won't spare rank or station, and everyone will grin and clap.

The mortification of public exposure is one that Lieutenant Pirogov or Major Kovalyov might have protested, but the Mayor's next line, ostensibly addressed to the characters around him, changes the perspective, implicating and challenging the audience as well: "What are you laughing at? You're laughing at yourselves! . . . A fine lot!" Moreover, the very source of the audience's pleasure is put in question as he stamps his foot in fury and adds:

I'd take care of all those scribblers! Hacks, damned liberals! Spawn of the devil! I'd tie you all up in a bundle, grind you all into powder, and line the devil's cap with you in hell! (*Makes a thrust with his fist and stamps the floor.*)

In this Pirandello-like moment, the Mayor is thrashing in the net not of circumstance but of art. He has identified his enemies as the audience and the playwright who has called him into being; like Frankenstein's monster, he chafes at the miraculous terms of his being and threatens to cross the line into everyday life.

The announcement of the gendarme a moment later acts like a thunderclap, stunning and petrifying the group on stage; the lengthy instructions for the dumb scene describe the Mayor "in the middle, like a post, with arms outstretched and head thrown back"—*tel qu'en lui-même enfin l'éternité le change*. The dumb scene itself is a last exhibition of the artifice, drained of its comic animation and calculated to produce an uneasiness that may be food for serious reflection in the audience. Futurity at once threatens these characters in the guise of the newly arrived inspector and does not, since their creator leaves them as Pushkin did his Onegin, "at an unfortunate moment for [them] . . . for long . . . forever"— thus compelling a double contemplation of *The Inspector General* both as felt experience and as a created thing. In the latter connection Sinyavsky has likened Gogol's comedy to a multistage rocket, which

throws off one inspector-general after another, each stage, when it is exhausted, giving rise to the next and imparting momentum to the whole apparatus. The inspector-general who is awaited (in Khmykov's letter) serves as a stage for introducing into the action the false inspector-general Khlestakov, whose long sojourn on the stage supplies the stimulus for the appearance immediately after of two inspectors-general—the government official who arrives at the end and the promised comedy of Gogol, which is presaged and sketched out in [Khlestakov's] letter to Tryapichkin, driving the Mayor crazy with the prospect of universal judgment and shame. In addition, the personage who has arrived from Petersburg on express orders of the Tsar appears in the reflected light of Gogol's future comedy, and both "inspectors"—the one announced by the gendarme and the one promised by the scribbler—converge in our consciousness to form a figure of inevitable retribution. "The Inspector General" produces nothing but the "Inspector General." [19]

Such sophisticated observations represent the work of time, which allows the maturing of perspectives as it allowed the maturing of the text itself (Sinyavsky's comments pertain to the fruits of fifteen years' revision). The *Inspector General* that opened in Petersburg on 19 April 1836 was a somewhat different play, less finely tuned as text, and of a disconcerting novelty which actors and audiences tended to mistake for a cruder and more familiar thing: vaudeville, farce, satire. [20] A few critics saw aspects of the play's essential novelty (lack of "positive" characters, love intrigue, onstage resolution), but Gogol was concerned less with their judgments than with those of the public, on which he pinned his hopes. That Petersburg public, Annenkov recalls,

regarded Gogol, if not exactly with hostility, at least with suspicion and mistrust. The final blow came with the [first] performance of *The Inspector General*. The author's concern during the staging . . . seemed strange, exceeding all custom and, as some said, all propriety, but it was sadly justified by the vaudeville character imparted to the central personage of the comedy, and the note of vulgar caricature that was reflected in the others. Gogol suffered throughout the evening . . . The theater itself over the course of four hours presented the most remarkable spectacle [I] have ever seen. By the end of the first act bewilderment was written on all faces (the public was a select one in the full sense of the word*), as if no one knew what to think of the scene that had just been presented. This bewilderment grew with each act. As if finding comfort in the assumption that a farce was being presented, the majority of spectators, prevented from indulging their theatrical expectations and habits, held on to this assumption with unshakable determination. Nonetheless,

---

* See A. O. Smirnova's recollection, replete with unconscious Gogolian emphases and implications: "At the performance the Tsar was in epaulets, and the orchestra was dazzling, all wearing stars and other medals. The ministers and P. D. Kiselev [soon to be Minister of State Properties] sat in the front row. They had to applaud when the Tsar did; the latter kept both hands on the railing of his box. They laughed loudly, Kiselev louder than the rest, since he had nothing to reproach himself for." V. V. Veresaev, *Gogol' v žizni* (M-L, 1933), p. 159.

there were in this farce traits and scenes filled with such truth to life that on occasion . . . general laughter rang out. Something completely different occurred in the fourth act: laughter from time to time still rippled from one end of the hall to the other, but it was a sort of shy laughter that disappeared instantaneously. There was almost no applause; on the other hand the rapt attention, the spasmodic, intense way people followed all the nuances of the play, the occasional dead silence all showed that what was going on on the stage was engaging the emotions of the spectators. When the act was over the previous bewilderment had turned into almost universal indignation, which reached a peak with the fifth act. Many called afterwards for the author because he had written the comedy, others because they had recognized talent in certain scenes, the simple public because they had laughed; but the common judgment, heard on all sides amid the select public, was: "This is impossible—a slander and a farce." When the performance was over, Gogol showed up at N. Ya. Prokopovich's apartment in a state of irritation. The host took it into his head to present him with a copy of *The Inspector General,* just off the presses, with the words: "Have a look at your son." Gogol hurled the book to the floor, walked up to the table, and leaning on it, uttered pensively: "My God! If one or two had condemned it, well, that would be their right, but everybody, everybody."[21]

Gogol's own testimony makes clear that he regarded the performance as a catastrophe. To the actor Shchepkin he wrote:

Everybody is against me. Elderly and honored officials cry that there is nothing sacred to me if I can dare to treat government employees so. The police are against me, the merchants are against me, literary people are against me. They curse, and they go to see the play; it's impossible to get tickets for the fourth performance. Were it not for the Tsar's intercession, my play would have no chance of being seen, and there have already been people who have tried to get it banned. Now I see what it means to be a comic writer. The least shadow of truth and not one person but whole classes rise up against you . . . It is vexing for one to see people against him when he loves them, the while, with a fraternal love. (XI, 38)

That last, odd statement supplies a key. Even before the performance, Gogol regarded *The Inspector General* as a turning point in his development. Pushkin himself had stood as godfather to the enterprise, thereby investing it with a seriousness of intention never before acknowledged by the young author. Confronting his audience for the first time with a statement about the Russia they represented, Gogol, at the peak of his imaginative powers, may well have expected that audience to fall on its knees and evidence on-the-spot contrition, as Mochulsky suggests.[22] It should not be surprising, after all, that the intensity of poetic imagination which brought all these lesser creative imaginations into existence should have created as well an ideal audience—of a kind that did not and could not have existed. Indeed, the theory of laughter the author was proclaiming with such passionate seriousness posited a communication so complete as to be magical, and the values attributed to the highest kind of laughter attached in fact to the emotions and aspirations of the author who induced it. What is more, Gogol undoubtedly reinterpreted those emotions, as he did so often, after the fact. Having produced his purest comedy, one of the greatest in any literature, he chose to talk not about that but about its putative effect—and in terms both grand and vague.

What Gogol saw as the failure of his play was in fact the failure of a particular role as writer, here essayed for the first time. The success he had courted in Petersburg for seven years was at last his—a mixture of *succès d'estime* and *succès de scandale;* he had proved his quality as a writer, but found in the process that what conferred reputation at the same time trivialized it, for as his illusions fell his expectations rose. His decision to leave Russia was thus a final judgment on that literary situation in which he had sought and found a leading place. "It's saddening," he writes Pogodin on May 15, 1836, "to see the universal ignorance that moves the capital . . . It's sad when you see what a pitiable state the writer is still in in our country . . . I am not so much grieved by the bitterness against my play as concerned about my sad future . . . I am traveling to drive away my heartache, to ponder deeply my obligations as an author, and my future creations." His words clarify the nature of this turning point. The model of a professional writer is abandoned as a goal; what is embraced instead is a sense of mission, a calling. Turning away from a contemporary audience, the writer's "obligations" (how many, before Gogol, had used this word?) become more abstract, dependent upon different sanctions: collaboration, so to speak, must be sought from a different quarter. "Everything that has happened with me, all of it, has been salutary for me. All the injuries, all the unpleasantnesses have been sent me by Providence on high for my education. And now I feel that it is not an earthly will that charts my path" (XI, 45–46).

PART III

Embracing a Calling

No one suspected, dear Aleksandra Osipovna, that the young beginner who was so timid before our dear Pushkin would likewise produce his own revolution in Russian literature and would be the creator of the modern Russian novel and the modern Russian comedy in prose.

Zhukovsky to A. O. Smirnova

His historical significance utterly escapes [foreign readers]. I repeat: one has to be a Russian to understand whom we have lost.

Turgenev on Gogol's death

6

Epic Intentions

What changed with Gogol's departure from Russia in June 1836 was not so much the nature of his writing as his own attitude toward it. His letters of the period document the change. To Zhukovsky he writes of the apprentice nature of his works to date, his readiness now to "get down to business." "This is a great watershed, a great stage of my life. I know that I shall encounter much that is unpleasant, that I shall suffer want and poverty, but nothing in the world will make me return soon. Long, long, as long as possible I shall remain abroad. And although my thoughts, my name, my works will belong to Russia, I myself, the perishable part of me, will be far away" (XI, 49). To Pogodin he is more explicit and practical. Arguing against the launching of a new journal ("You don't have the charlatanism necessary for that"), he declines at the same time to participate:

I don't have a single [story], and will no longer lift my hand to write any. Let him write them who has nothing better to write. When I wrote my immature and inconclusive experiments—which I called stories only because they had to be called something—I wrote them only to try my strength and see whether my quill was properly sharpened . . . When I saw that it was not, I sharpened it again and tried again. These were pale excerpts of those phenomena which filled my head and out of which a full picture should one day be created. But one can't go on practicing forever. It is time finally to get down to business. We should have posterity in view, and not the base present . . .

The die is cast for me. Abandoning my homeland, I abandoned at the same time all contemporary desires. That pride which only poets know, which was growing with me already in the cradle, could finally bear it no longer. Oh, what a contemptible, what a base condition . . . one's hair stands on end [at the thought]. People who were born for a slap in the face, for pandering . . . and before those people . . . but pass them

145

by! I still don't have the stomach to name them . . . If I were to hear that anything of mine is being played or published, that would be only unpleasant for me and nothing else.—I see only a dread and just posterity, pursuing me with the implacable question: "Where is that work by which you can be judged?" And for the sake of preparing an answer, I am ready to condemn myself to anything—to a beggarly and wandering life, to the deep and uninterrupted isolation which, from this time forward, I carry with me everywhere . . . About Paris I have nothing to write you. The local sphere is completely political, and I have always avoided politics. It is not the poet's job to worm his way into the worldly marketplace. Like a silent monk he lives in the world without belonging to it, and his pure, unblemished soul knows only how to converse with God. (XI, 76–78)[1]

The emphases here are instructive—and fateful. They mark an intermediate stage in what he later termed the tale—saga might be a better word—of his authorship: a tactical turning away from the model of general *writer* toward that of poet as adumbrated in *Hanz Kuechelgarten* and refined in the Pushkin essay of *Arabesques*. Concern with an immediate readership recedes; the goal is now immortality, its precondition a solitude in which the poet can devote himself uncompromisingly to his task (in this case, *Dead Souls*), which is also a mission and which alone can justify him in the eyes of the God Whom he seems to have evoked chiefly for that reason.* His earlier works are valuable only as a bridge to his present position; even *The Inspector General* is relegated, logically enough, to their number. "It is terrifying," he writes his friend Prokopovich in January 1837, "for me to recall my scribblings. My soul craves oblivion, a long oblivion. And if such a moth appeared as could suddenly devour all the copies of *The Inspector General,* together with *Arabesques, Evenings,* and all that other nonsense—and if no one were to utter a word about me either aloud or in print for a long time—I would thank my stars. Only fame after death (for which, alas, I have done nothing up to now) and

---

* The letters present the progress of *Dead Souls* entirely in terms of the growing poetic ambition the novel can accommodate. "If I complete this creation in the way it needs to be completed . . . what a vast and original subject! . . . All Russia will appear in it! This will be my first decent thing, the thing that will carry my name forward . . . Enormously great is my creation, and its end will not be soon" (XI, 74–76). "The further continuation [of the book] is crystallizing in my head, purer and more majestic, and I see now that it can be something colossal . . . It is at least certain that few realize to what powerful ideas and profound phenomena an insignificant plot can lead" (XI, 322–323).

that alone is dear to the heart of an authentic poet. Contemporary fame isn't worth a farthing" (XI, 84–85).

The literal sense of that last statement should not be overlooked. Gogol's commitment to a literary vocation coincides with his discovery "that writers in our time can die of hunger" (XI, 97) —that the time had not yet come when a serious Russian writer might support himself by his pen alone. We have seen Gogol's own assessment of the situation in journalism; the book trade was, if anything, worse. "In the 1830s," one bookseller recalled, "the publication of any new novel, especially one by Zagoskin, or any other book, constituted an event. In acquiring these novelties in sufficient quantity all the booksellers, except Smirdin, were niggardly—particularly with Moscow editions. They would order ten to twenty-five copies of a book that should have been ordered in 200, and keep them under the counter for their own customers, so as not to display them on the shelf to their neighbors, and they wouldn't sell each other such books, even at retail. Thus was the whole business held back."[2] Printings, moreover, were small. *Evenings on a Farm* first appeared in the usual 1200 copies; a second edition, probably of the same size, appeared only in 1836 and was still on the market four years later, as was *Arabesques*—though *Mirgorod* and *The Inspector General* had by then sold out. *Dead Souls*, eagerly anticipated for years, was to appear in 1842 in an edition of 2400 copies, followed by a second edition only in 1846. Clearly, not much was to be hoped for from royalties, even assuming the competence and honesty of publishers.[3]

Deprived of salary, determined to submit nothing for publication until the first volume of *Dead Souls* should be completed, Gogol sought support for his sense of mission in subventions from the Tsar and loans from his Moscow friends—an arrangement justified only by his promise of future service to Russia, and one that surely contributed to turning that promise into a burden and his new feeling of freedom into one of dependence. In April 1837, pleading for Zhukovsky's intercession with the Tsar, he argues: "Were I a painter, even a bad one, I would be secure: here in Rome there are some fifteen of our artists recently sent out from the Academy, of whom some draw worse than I do: all of them receive three thousand a year. Were I to become an actor, I would be secure; actors receive 10,000 in silver and more—and you yourself know that I would not make a bad actor. But I am a writer—and therefore must die of hunger" (XI, 97). Zhukovsky, who the year before had arranged an imperial gift worth 800 rubles in return for a presentation copy of *The Inspector General,* now secured a grant of 5000, which was followed over the years by others.[4] With the aid of grants and loans, as Gogol wrote later, he lived "six years, for the most part abroad, receiving no salary from anywhere and absolutely no revenues (for six years I published nothing); these were years of wandering, years of traveling" (XII, 154).

The road at this point assumes its central place in Gogol's life —which is to say in his creative process and in his art. His career begins increasingly to resemble his fiction, to turn enigmatic through a symbolic merging that eventuates in the metaphysical entity which even now goes by his name. The writer's progress and the writings themselves are marked by process without issue or resolution; eccentric and uneven (grotesque in the literary sense), both begin to be infused with a significance as difficult to account for as it is to ignore. It should be noted that the years in question, though dominated by the project of *Dead Souls,* continue to be marked by improvisation and experiment in other forms: there is intermittent work on a drama from Cossack history (finally burned when Zhukovsky fell asleep during a reading), on the unfinished *Rome* (half historical-esthetic meditation, half *roman de moeurs*), expansion of *Taras Bulba,* revision of "The Portrait" and *Getting Married,* polishing of "The Nose" and *The Inspector General,* rewriting of "After the Play," and composition of "The Overcoat" and *The Gamblers.* As before, relatively conventional, nonproblematic words receive attention alongside fundamentally "Gogolian" ones. What has changed, however, is the level of ambition that can be seen in virtually all these projects, the will to an artistry that invokes large, value-laden questions—esthetic, moral, historical, and (especially) national.

Distance intensified the national feeling: "In Vevey," he reports in the fall of 1836, "I have become even more Russian" as a result of renewed work on *Dead Souls* (XI, 72). Distance also allowed a transfiguring perspective. Writing from Rome to a young correspondent about Germany, he confesses:

that notion of a wondrous and fantastic Germany which I carried in my mind [from reading Hoffmann] vanished when I saw Germany in fact . . . I know that land exists where all is wondrous and not as it is here; but not everybody knows the road to [it] . . . It is hard, very hard, to hold to the center, hard to drive away imagination and our beautiful, beloved dream once they exist in our heads; it is hard suddenly and completely to turn to real prose; but hardest of all is to reconcile these two disparate objects—to live at once in one world and the other (XI, 180–181).

In the same letter he goes on to confess a secret envy for his correspondent, prompted by her description of Petersburg and a train ride:

After all, I do have a Russian heart. Although at the sight—that is, at the thought—of Petersburg a chill runs through me and my skin is soaked through with dampness and the foggy atmosphere, still I did have a strong desire to take a ride on that train and hear that mixture of words and speeches of our Babylonian population in the coaches. There one could learn a great deal that cannot be learned in the ordinary course of things. There, perhaps, I would grow angry again . . . at my beloved Russia, toward which my indignant disposition is already beginning to weaken—for without anger, as you know, not much can be said: only in anger is the truth uttered.

As in most of Gogol's letters of this period, the stress is on attitudes and intentions. Like Joyce after him, he chose silence and exile (his cunning was instinctive) as the new instruments of his ambition, which was to forge in the smithy of his soul the uncreated conscience of his Rus'. For these six years in which he is preparing to confront his public again, the preoccupations are with the artist; in the years after 1842, they will broaden to include the artist's public, newly conceived as a potential alter ego. The immediate task is the reconciliation of distance with intimacy, of prosaic material with the high calling of poetry. The fundamental assumption, hinted at repeatedly to correspondents, finds summary formulation in the revised "Portrait," in the words of the monastic artist to his son:

Talent is the most precious gift of God—do not ruin it. Investigate and study everything you see . . . but learn to find the inner idea in everything, and most of all try to grasp the lofty secret of creation. Blessed is the chosen one who possesses that secret. For him there is no low object in nature. In the trivial (*ničtožnoe*) the artist–creator is as great as in the great; in the contemptible he finds nothing contemptible, for there transpires through him the beautiful soul of one who has created, and the contemptible has already received a lofty expression, for it has passed through the purgatory of his soul. (III, 135)

Much of this Gogol had claimed before; what is new is the solemn emphasis on the soul of the artist as guarantor of a quality that goes beyond mere adeptness. To be understood properly, this needs to be seen first of all in its relation to the essay in *Arabesques* where Pushkin is identified as a "unique phenomenon of the Russian spirit" even when he is describing "a quite different world" (VIII, 50–51). It is just such a quality to which—disputing Pushkin's uniqueness—Gogol himself now aspires; indeed, he considered the aspiration Pushkin's legacy to him.

MOST Russian writing on the Pushkin–Gogol relationship treats it on the biographical level, where the information is scant but the attraction enormous: How close was their acquaintance? how mutual the friendship? how intended the "gift" of the ideas for *The Inspector General* and *Dead Souls?* As a result, the larger questions— of Pushkin's image as Gogol fashioned and refined it in his text, and of the connections between Pushkin's *writing* and Gogol's— remain unexamined. Yet they are clearly the ground of the legacy.[5]

Gogol's early essays "Boris Godunov" and "A Few Words About Pushkin" show how fully and exclusively he tended from the outset to identify Pushkin with the ideal of the Russian poet.* In the circumstances, Pushkin's warm if laconic praise of the early stories, his readiness to accept the younger writer as a journalistic colleague (though that relation soon soured), and his encouragement of larger projects played a decisive role in establishing Gogol as a writer—not so much publicly as psychologically. Thus only with Pushkin's death seven months after Gogol's departure from Russia may the relationship be said to reach its apogee—within Gogol's psychic economy, where its primary value had lain all along. "All the enjoyment of my life . . . has vanished together with him," Gogol writes Pletnyov in response to the news. "I undertook nothing without his advice"—a patently false statement, which is redeemed by the likely truth of the next: "Not a single line was written without my imagining him before me. What he would say, what he would observe, what he would laugh at, what would elicit his indestructible and eternal approval—that was all that concerned me and roused my powers" (XI, 88–89). To Pogo-

---

* This view never changed. In *Selected Passages from Correspondence with Friends* (1846), Gogol writes: "Why was he given to the world, and what did his being demonstrate? Pushkin was given to the world in order to demonstrate what a poet himself is, and nothing more—what a poet is, seen not under the influence of any particular time or circumstances and not conditioned by his own character as an individual, but independently of everything . . . in his essence (VIII, 381– 382).

din he writes the same, deepening the emphasis: "My loss is greater than anyone's . . . The bright moments of my life were those in which I was creating. When I was creating I always saw only Pushkin before me. All judgments were as nothing to me; I spit on the despicable rabble that goes by the name of the public; what I prized was his eternal and indisputable word . . . Whatever of mine is good I owe entirely to him."[6]

But Pushkin's meaning for Gogol went beyond incarnating a standard and functioning as internalized, qualitative ideal. His example also licensed *a range* of poetic aspiration—from the quasi-religious notion of the poet's function in *The Prophet* and the tragic political symbolism of *The Bronze Horseman* to the virtuoso nonsense of *The Little House in Kolomna*—a range Gogol was to approximate in *Dead Souls* and one he had already marked out in his essays, *Taras Bulba,* and "The Nose." A similar license may be seen in the matter of experimental form, taking that term in the strategic rather than narrowly technical sense. "It is remarkable," Bitsilli has noted, "how many of Pushkin's things are called 'excerpts' [*otryvki*] but are nevertheless perceivable, each one, as a finished artistic whole."[7] Many instructive parallels might be drawn along these lines. For present purposes, however, it may suffice to indicate the crucial role of *Eugene Onegin,* Pushkin's novel in verse, as model for *Dead Souls,* Gogol's prose *poema.*

The crux of the matter is formulated in the penultimate stanza of *Onegin,* where Pushkin refers to his work as a "free novel" and recalls how, at the first, he dimly described his future characters through the "magic crystal" of his imagination. The freedom in question is the author's: to create a world in space and time, people it with arresting characters (as any novelist does)—and, at the same time, in a bravura performance to keep them demonstratively anchored in his text, underlining their dependence on the imagination that summoned them into being and stressing that their hold on the reader originates in their willed fictiveness, that they take their being from an improvised artifact. That artifact itself—a sustained act of poetic discourse—is a compendium of observation, commentary, confession, imagination. Its objects may be within or outside the story; its tones vary from the burlesque through the lyrical to the solemn; its explicit themes range from the humblest aspects of the daily round to the seasons of life, from particular poets to modes of literature itself. The primacy of the author as creator is continually urged, the ultimate result being to glorify not him but the art whose disconcerting power the reader has been made to feel.

This involves not only devising but dissecting literary effects, and since these have their being only in the mind of a reader, the poetic discourse that is *Onegin* includes a generous amount of attention to its reader. Pushkin by turns admonishes, cajoles, challenges, and instructs his reader—*creates* him, as an accomplice. Moreover, he moves to end the work, bypassing any narrative resolution, with a provocative dismissal of the unfinished story: "And here my hero,/ at an unfortunate minute for him,/ reader, we now shall leave/ for long . . . forever . . . After him/ sufficiently along one path/ we've roamed the world. Let us congratulate/ each other on attaining land. Hurrah!"[8]

Adapting this model to his own very different temperament and talents, Gogol was to take primarily not the horizontal, stylistic freedom but the vertical one: the freedom to move from the level of presentation to the levels of reminiscence, confession, literary and social commentary, prophecy—setting against the soulless world he depicts an image of his own soulful and passionate concerns. He may have found a precedent for his own narrative digressions in Sterne or Fielding, but the native precedent for the passages in *Dead Souls* that are traditionally called lyrical digressions could only have come from Pushkin.

Ten years after Pushkin's death and five years after the first publication of *Dead Souls,* Gogol credits Pushkin in "An Author's Confession" with having made him regard his writing more consciously and seriously: "He cited to me the example of Cervantes, who, though he had written several very good and remarkable stories, would never have occupied the place he now occupies among writers if he had not undertaken *Don Quixote*—and, in conclusion, he gave me his own subject, from which he had intended to make something in the nature of a narrative poem (*poèma*) and which, as he said, he would have given to no one else. This was the subject of *Dead Souls* . . . After *The Inspector General* I felt more than ever before the need for a large work, containing no longer simply what is deserving of laughter" (VIII, 439–440). No clarification of this phrase is offered beyond the statement that he meant to mix comic phenomena with 'touching ones." The specter of identifiable significance, he reports, arose to vex him only in the process of writing:

At each step I was stopped by questions: Why? What does this serve? What is such-and-such a character supposed to represent? What should such-and-such a phenomenon be expressing? . . . I saw clearly that I could no longer write without a clear and definite plan, that I had first to explain thoroughly to myself the aim of my work, its fundamental utility and necessity, as a result of which the author might be filled with a strong and genuine love for his labor of a kind that brings everything to life and without which work cannot go forward. In short, the author himself needed to feel, as a conviction, that in creating his creation he was fulfilling precisely that duty for which he was called to earth, for which his talents and strengths were expressly given him, and that, fulfilling it, he was at the same time rendering service to his country, just as if he were in actuality working in the government service. (VIII, 440–441)

There is a double blurring in this retrospective account. It is not clear whether the questions he cites did complicate work on the first volume of *Dead Souls* or whether Gogol is describing the impasse that led him twice to burn the manuscript of its sequel and ultimately to leave his project unfinished. In the first case, they might account for the lyrical digressions, introduced as counterweight to the negativity and apparent insignificance of the narrative matter. More important, he telescopes two distinct stages of his quest for an art of lasting significance. One involves a significance reducible to summary, the other a significance, no less consciously introduced, that permeates a work but is not so reducible. The former was his aspiration in the 1840s, and its consequences were fatal to the artist in him; the latter, quite consonant with Pushkin's urging, enters his writing from 1836 to 1842 and marks a new stage. "The Overcoat" and the first volume of *Dead Souls* are the masterpieces of this period and the vindication of a kind of artistry he was quick to forget.* Standing at the pinnacle of his narrative art, they have shown for nearly a century and a half a like resistance to analysis.

The case of "The Overcoat" is particularly instructive. By common consent Gogol's greatest performance in the short-story form, it is at the same time his last—a belated addition to the cycle of Petersburg Tales with which it was published for the first and only time during Gogol's life in Volume Three of the *Collected Works* (1843). Overshadowed in its preparation and appearance by *Dead Souls,* it seems to have been regarded by its author as almost

---

* "My friend," he writes Smirnova in 1845, "I have no love for the works I have written and published up to now, and especially *Dead Souls*"! (XII, 504).

accidental; although his intermittent work on it (1839–1841) was painstaking, he fails to refer to it even once in all his correspondence, let alone in the retrospective "Author's Confession."

"THE OVERCOAT" both draws on and transcends the best of Gogol's previous work. "In terms of plot," as one of his critics has observed, it is "the same sort of sentimental tale . . . as 'Old-World Landowners,' only with a more pronounced comic coloration."[9] (The title, however, already indicates a broader symbolic intention.) In terms of setting, theme and manner, "The Overcoat" clearly belongs to the world of the earlier Petersburg Tales.[10] It extends the ironic tone of the overture to "Nevsky Prospect," and in the image of Akaky Akakievich who sees only office texts before him, uncertain "whether he is in the middle of a sentence or the middle of a street," it develops the earlier image of bureaucrats so preoccupied with office matters that "instead of shop signs they see filing boxes, or the round face of the chief of their department" (III, 14). Like "Diary of a Madman," it deals with the privations of a petty clerk and with his pathetic rebellion; like "The Nose," it is filled with spurious logic and shot through with absurdity. Like all the stories, it deals with displacement.[11]

But there is a new depth and breadth; the story is more richly problematic than any of its predecessors—and in new ways. The complex of narrative attitudes is more devious than in "Old-World Landowners," the narrator himself more elusive. Where in that story he had voiced personal attitudes and claimed involvement in the events, here he is a disembodied voice, shifting levels bewilderingly, so that as a source of perspective he resembles the Petersburg wind he describes as blowing from all four directions at once. Like "Nevsky Prospect," "The Overcoat" is saturated with irony, but only a part of it is satirical; surveying the whole spectrum, one is struck by how much of it appears to be normless, lacking any single implied basis for judgment—which is to say any consistent rationale for the multiplicity of tones and attitudes. As in "Diary of a Madman," the motif of bureaucratic formalism dominates, enclosing the solitary protagonist. But Poprishchin suffered from frustrated ambition; the opposite is the case with Akaky Akakievich, whose very name derives from the Greek for "innocuous": he is as meekly content and as fundamentally inarticulate as Poprishchin is restless and garrulous. And where Poprishchin's progress is from a kind of normality to madness, Akaky's, heavily caricatured, is from an absolutely minimal resemblance to a human being (the critic Grigoriev saw him as existing "on the very edge of nonentity") to a simply minimal degree of the same condition—and even that progress accounts for only a portion of "The Overcoat."

The result is a text enigmatic like that of "The Nose," but differently and more fundamentally. The earlier story had involved a puffed-up officer with all-too-human desires in an absurd, surreal adventure from which he emerged unscathed and unchanged, leaving the bemused reader to ponder the question of "why authors write such stories" and what use they serve. The ultimate answer, as we have seen, is that such stories put language to luminously poetic use, making art of nonsense, playing with the reader's expectations of literature and rewarding the desirous with hints of an additional significance—satirical and psychological— which are as frosting to an already rich cake.

"The Overcoat" differs in its parable-like plot line: the reader is made to react less to the central character than to his *situation* (which, up to his death, has nothing fantastic about it). But even that reaction is unstable, because Akaky Akakievich's situation is presented now on one, now on another of three distinct levels. He is shown in the world of Petersburg, in a network of relations involving his fellow workers, his tailor, his overcoat, the Important Personage who denies him sympathy and help, his landlady, the thieves who rob him. This is the world that goes on without him "as if he had never been there," failing to perceive the disappearance of

a creature defended by none, dear to no one, of interest to no one, who failed even to attract the attention of the naturalist-observer who doesn't overlook an ordinary fly but sticks a pin through it to observe it under a microscope; a creature who humbly submitted to office jokes and went to the grave without any particular to-do—but for whom, all the same, though it happened at the very end of his life, there appeared a bright visitant in the form of an overcoat to enliven his poor life for a moment; and on whom insupportable catastrophe then descended, as it has descended on kings and the potentates of this world. (III, 169)

The corrective to such neglect, however, is offered not on the level of the neglect but on the level of a comic-grotesque narration—

and it depends for its realization on yet another level: that of the audience invited to reflect on the meaning of both the others.* As Bakhtin summarizes the situation: "The (fictitious) event which is Akaky Akakievich's life and the event which is the actual story about him merge in the distinctive unity of the historical event which is Gogol's 'Overcoat.' It is in precisely this way that 'The Overcoat' entered the historical life of Russia and proved an effective factor in it."[12] Here is one key to the elusiveness of the story: it rests on a blurring of ontological boundaries, in somewhat the way *The Inspector General* does when the Mayor's words echo as a challenge to the spectators: "What are you laughing at? You're laughing at yourselves!"

Akaky Akakievich's "life," then, is inseparable from the narrative that contains it and partakes of the radical novelty of that narrative. To call him a character is already to assume too much, just as it is to speak of the narrator as if he had a deducible "personality" or to seek the import of the story in any single perspective or stable pattern. Once more, three general discriminations can help us to grasp the special functioning of Gogol's text.

The blurring effect of assertion. This feature, which has been widely remarked, underlies the aspect of the story as comic performance. At issue in the first place are the recurrent qualifiers—the "leitmotifs of filler words," as Biely called them, that create a kind of unremovable "dotted veil" over the text: "certain," "somehow," "some," "even," "a sort of," "all the same," "it seems." To the comedy of reported events, they add the constant comedy of speech events and supply the shifts from clarity to vagueness, one of the indices of malproportion on which the grotesque effect of the story rests.[13] (They also, incidentally, establish the license for the larger shifts that give the story its capaciousness of thematic implication, by asserting the range of narrative freedom—from nonsensical chatter to lyrical pathos, from the Bashmachkin inlaws who only went around in boots to "the kings and

---

* See Gogol's draft for a "Textbook of Literature for Russian Youth," where the entry for "Tale" (*Povest'*) begins: "A tale takes as its subject events that have really occurred or might occur with any person—an event remarkable for some reason in the psychological respect, sometimes even quite without any desire to point a moral, but only to arrest the attention of the thinking man or observer." (VIII, 482).

potentates of this world."* As an example of the "grotesque sentence" typical of this story one critic has cited the following, from the protagonist's first visit to the tailor Petrovich: "The door was open, because the lady of the house, preparing *some fish or other,* had filled the kitchen with so much smoke that you couldn't see *even* the cockroaches themselves." The whole effect is undercut, he comments, if one removes the filler words.[14]

There is, however, a further dimension to this blurring on the non-comic side. At the point when, through serious deprivation, Akaky Akakievich has accumulated enough money to purchase the cloth for his new overcoat, the narrator reports: "His heart, generally quite tranquil, began to beat" (III, 155)—a hint of a literal coming to life that was not present in an earlier draft: "Akaky Akakievich's heart, which always went on almost without any beating, began to beat more strongly" (III, 533). Later, when he has been robbed of his own overcoat, the terrified and conscience-stricken Important Personage undergoes a change of his own: "He even took to saying, 'How dare you? Do you understand to whom you're speaking?' much less often to subordinates; and if he did utter these words, it was not until he had first listened long enough to grasp the point" (III, 173).

The qualification in that last clause indicates the pitfalls of paraphrase, calling into question as it does the assertion it follows (which has already been rendered shaky by the ironic "even"). More precisely, what is called into question is the *significance* of what Gogol reports; and this question—of the inferences that the narration intends or permits—is the central critical question. The ubiquitous qualifications ("even," "perhaps," "probably," "if my memory does not deceive me," "it seemed") leave unclear exactly what is being asserted; how the narrator regards it; and how the reader is meant (or allowed) to understand what he is reading.

Relativity. The import of the story is rendered elusive not only by the ambiguous assertions or shifting tones, the "orchestra of voices" that constitutes the narration; it is grounded in a deeper relativity, since even where the pattern of presentation shows a

---

* Compare Hugh Kenner's phrase about how Newman, Hopkins, and Joyce "situated minute phenomena by transcendental coordinates, along which sudden changes of scale and scope might occur momentarily." *The New Republic,* 18 June 1977, p. 26.

clear connectedness, it leaves uncertain the significance of that connectedness. This can be seen first of all in the relationship of the two principal characters, the faceless Akaky Akakievich and the nameless Important Personage (literally, "Important Face")—"the main reason for the whole disaster," as he is identified in a draft (III, 458).

Akaky Akakievich is introduced as being inherently static (even at his christening he grimaces "as if he had a foreboding that he would be an eternal titular councillor")—a creature without a self, existing timelessly in the pleasant little world of his own mechanical copying:

One director, being a good man and wishing to reward him for his long service, ordered that he be given something a little more important than ordinary copying; namely, that he be instructed to take an already prepared paper and make of it some document for another office; the job consisted only in changing the title page and changing the verbs here and there from the first person to the third. This gave him such trouble that he broke out in a sweat all over, rubbed his forehead, and finally said: "No, better let me copy something." From that time on they left him to copy forever. (III, 144–145)

It is the need to protect himself from the cold that propels him into the world of contingency; his development begins with his first exploratory visit to the tailor. Marked by a series of unprecedented events, that development is toward normality. He cries out "perhaps for the first time in his life" when told he must buy a new coat; finally reconciled to the idea, he becomes "somehow more alive." The overcoat for which he is saving is pictured as a bride-to-be, the day of its delivery "probably the most solemn day in [his] life." He goes out in the evening "for the first time in years," drinks champagne with his colleagues, feels the first stirrings of erotic attraction. After being robbed, he decides "for once in his life to show character" and demands to see the police captain; he misses work that day—"the only [such] event in his life." It is at this point that catastrophe strikes and the Important Personage is introduced—the instrument of Akaky Akakievich's only hope and so the agent of his death, which swiftly follows.*

The development thus arrested appears as a touchingly "posi-

---

* Applying for help to the Important Personage, he receives more than a refusal: "He had never before in his life received such a dressing-down by a general."

tive" one. The reader instinctively sympathizes with the increasing if derisory "fullness" of the poor clerk's life and realizes the crushing extent of his loss when the overcoat is taken from him. But though the relationship with the Important Personage is presented in moral-psychological terms, there are larger parallels that call into question this first sympathetic view, raising the suspicion that what looks like a relative liberation into selfhood may at the same time spell moral diminution. The Important Personage speaks only in formulas—a counterpart of Akaky's own tendency to stylized incoherence. He is, Gogol suggests, as much a product of position on the bureaucratic ladder as Akaky Akakievich is. Just as Akaky has drunk champagne and felt sexual desire before the catastrophe, so the Important Personage, troubled by the news that Akaky has died, seeks diversion in champagne with friends and a visit to his mistress. Just as the Important Personage appears to Akaky in his delirium, so Akaky appears to the Important Personage in his twinges of guilt. These and other parallels, in short, enforce a socially distant but unmistakable family resemblance—raising, in turn, the specter of a quite different trajectory for the poor clerk's abortive development. We have, after all, been told at the beginning that "if he had been given rewards commensurate with his zeal, [Akaky Akakievich] might even, perhaps, to his own astonishment, have found himself a State Councillor" (III, 144).

In this light, the overcoat appears as the symbol of false development, and its moral role in the story becomes a warning, in Victor Erlich's phrase, of the pitfalls of petty passions. Far from sympathizing with Akaky's development, then, the reader may be entitled to find it ultimately deplorable—and to find the predevelopmental Akaky, for all his apparent ludicrousness, more than preferable: ideal. As Charles Bernheimer observes:

In true Bergsonian manner, we laugh at the unresponsive, mechanically repetitive quality of Akaky's existence, at his self-absorbed blindness and mute hesitancy, exulting thereby in our own flexibility and freedom. But the joke is really on us. We feel superior to Akaky in our adaptability to this world, but he has found a mode of being that eschews all such degrading compromises . . . [by being] undefined as an individual.[15]

Which view of Akaky Akakievich does the narrative ultimately enforce? If we regard the question as legitimate, the answer must be neither. Both remain as presences in the text, unresolved. But the text in fact does not legitimize such a question (though it

teases the reader's traditional expectation that a story should).
Before we can speak of what it "ultimately" does, one final discrimination needs to be made. This concerns the progress of the
narrative on the most important experiential level—that of the
reader.

Dynamics: the kaleidoscope. The relativity discussed above
means that on the level of theme the same ambiguity obtains as on
the level of statement; and both are subsumed by the larger tendency of the narration to move on rather than to resolve. The unmotivated shifts of tone, like the undeveloped introduction of disparate themes, makes reading the story like looking through a
kaleidoscope. One can identify the discrete constituents of the
changing patterns but no single, dominant pattern; movement is
the crux.

Nabokov emphasizes this in his own whimsical terms: "The
story goes this way: mumble, mumble, lyrical wave, mumble,
lyrical wave, mumble, lyrical wave, mumble, fantastic climax,
mumble, mumble, and back into the chaos from which they all
had derived."[16] Alexander Slonimsky, in his brilliant monograph,
The Technique of the Comic in Gogol, spells the process out in rather
more useful terms, tracing the alternations of comic and serious to
show how "the entire story takes on a double meaning, as it
were."[17] But Slonimsky, alive to the novelty that allows two contrary views of the same matter to coexist in the work without can-
celing each other out, fails to discern the *multiplicity* of meanings
that lies beyond this doubleness.

These, as critics have remarked them over the years, fall into
four overlapping categories: the social, the ethical, the religious,
and the esthetic. The social emphasizes the pathetic side of the
story, Akaky Akakievich—the quintessential little man—as victim
of bureaucratic inhumanity and the indifferent city in general; it
sees a realistic intent behind the story and has been the dominant
view in Russia, particularly in the nineteenth century. The ethical
builds on the passage where an unnamed, transitory character is
haunted by the affirmation of human brotherhood he hears behind
Akaky's protests at office pranks that turn into persecutions (III,
144). The religious sees the main theme of the story, in Chizhevsky's words, as "the kindling of the human soul, its rebirth
under the influence of love (albeit of a very special kind)."[18] (More
recently, scholars have noted the presence of several Saints Acacius

in the Orthodox calendar, and one in particular who was a paragon of meek service; in light of these findings, "The Overcoat" becomes "a travesty of hagiography."[19]) Finally, the esthetic— which has been the main contribution of the twentieth century— sees the form of the story as at the same time the locus of value. The Formalist critic Boris Eikhenbaum identifies the work as less a story than a performance, a celebration of the artist's freedom to "violate the normal proportions of the world [and] join together what cannot be joined."[20] Building on this view the Structuralists have found still further levels of meaning in "The Overcoat." Sergei Bocharov has seen the structure of the story as resting on the fact that Akaky Akakievich "has no relation to life in the first person." Because he could not conceivably tell his own story, he is enclosed as an alien being within the word play of the narration, which dramatizes (beyond and apart from the events of the story) "his position in life and life's relation to him."[21]

What these analyses have in common is a respect for the idiosyncrasy of the form that allows full appreciation of the capaciousness of Gogol's story, its legitimate transcendence of singleness of message—the way it "triumphantly asserts literature's independence from the repressive forces of reality and gleefully demonstrates its freedom to play with the realms of matter and spirit, life and death, to which it refers but by which it is not bound."[22]

THE PURPOSE of this selective sketch is not to give a full account of Gogol's story but to suggest how it epitomizes the new stage of his artistic practice. What is new and salient in the story is, to a large extent, also found in the novel—and both have proved unusually resistant to critical definition for similar reasons. More precisely, both have shown a tendency to serve as trampolines for critical discussions which in their very pursuit of cogency run the risk of being unfaithful to texts that manifest a very low degree of cogency in thematic terms, even as they evince the highest kind of artistic cogency in the guise of a dense and constantly eventful narrative discourse (where the events are, paradoxically, *speech* events). Such discourse uses the traditional license of comedy, for comedy offers the broadest sanctions and is, of all the artistic modes, the most nearly self-justifying.[23] Thus the works in question are first of all performances, comic poems. But they are comic poems tending to transcendance: of Gogol's intention here, that alone is clear. His ambitious quest is to prove that "the high and the low can equally serve as means to the beautiful and good," that laughter can be serious because morally liberating.

Gogol's art at its most "Gogolian" does this with a tact unrivaled in Russian prose: the comic discourse never slips to mere instrumentality (hence the impossibility of paraphrase), but in its very authority turns problematic, prompting reflections in the reader that inevitably leave the text behind and that can never, no matter how often he returns to that text, find more than the original teasing cue. This process is itself encoded within the text of "The Overcoat," through the fleeting appearance of the young newcomer who witnesses the teasing of Akaky Akakievich at work: "And long afterward, amid the gayest moments, the short little clerk with the bald spot on his forehead would appear to him with his piercing words, 'Leave me alone, why do you insult me?' —and in these piercing words there rang other words: 'I am thy brother.'" (III, 144). This is not, as it has so often been taken to be, a statement of the author's position but of the reader's, at one of those points when "everything, as it were, changes before him and appears in a different guise" (III, 144). It is an example of the way "the gay can momentarily turn into the sad if only one stand contemplating it too long, and then God knows what may not wander into your head"—of the way that, in "gay and carefree moments, another, wondrous strain of thought may suddenly and spontaneously flash by" (VI, 58).

The verbs (wander, flash) themselves are significant: they suggest how the most significant themes make their tantalizing appearance in Gogol's text, with a recurrence that makes them more than fortuitous but less than primary. In the kaleidoscope's successive patterns we see images that prompt reflection; and in less arresting ones we may come to recognize their echoes, until each turn sets us to searching for another "key," and a growing familiarity with the separately meaningless shapes leads to a search for the perpetually elusive, constantly potential pattern that would fix them all in positions of analyzable beauty.

The metaphor is only approximate, but to the extent that it is valid it may suggest why those who claim "The Overcoat" is *not* about Christian charity and arbitrary authority, meekness and pride, poverty and comfort, justice, bureaucracy, city life, even literature itself—why such readers are as mistaken as those who assert that it *is* about these things. Respecting the peculiar mode of its being, it would be more accurate to say that the story is ultimately about significance and insignificance as such, in literature no less than in life. It embraces these particular instances to use them. For —as the title already indicates—the novelty of this problematic text lies in the quest it dramatizes and provokes: for serious significance, for the sense in which humble phenomena may contain it, for the criteria by which it may be identified, for the unriddling of a world. This quest is the more tantalizing because it is presented with seeming randomness, like a game of blind-man's buff, the arbitrary shifts of level and perspective in the presentation symbolizing the obstacles in that search.[24] Gogol's best art had always avoided clarity of message to pose self-regarding questions in the form of riddles. Here and in *Dead Souls* he raises the level of those riddles in line with his new conception of the comic writer as servant of the vaguest but highest ideals: ethical, moral, religious, civic, taken precisely in their ideality. "The Overcoat," in its range of tones and themes, is Gogol's amplest story, manifesting in little the qualities that inform his novel. A hermeneutic challenge, endlessly evocative, intrinsically elusive, it is his monument to the capacity of art—not to "reflect" the great realities of life but to join them.

7

***

Dead Souls:
The Mirror and the Road

Dead Souls, at once truncated and self-sufficient, is Gogol's most sustained improvisation, transcending his earlier creations, aspirations, ideas. With it he did not so much embrace the life of a writer as reconstrue his life, identifying it completely with a calling that rested in turn on the project of his novel. This was both a renunciation and an aggrandizement of self, and it led to that aggressive humility that dismayed so many in the writings that followed the first volume of his novel.[1] The first volume itself is a different story. It shows Gogol at the peak of his powers.

As with *The Inspector General* and "The Overcoat," the project begins with an anecdote, and the first draft is crude comedy, heavily satiric, in which the author seems to take a personal pleasure in humiliating his characters. ("If anyone had seen those monsters that emerged from my pen in the beginning . . . he would literally have shuddered," Gogol later recalled of this draft, which has not survived. Pushkin, he says, listened to a reading from it with growing despondency, exclaiming at the end, "God, how sad our Russia is!"—a reaction that surprised the author: "Pushkin, who knew Russia so well, had not noticed that all this was caricature and my own invention!" [VIII, 294].) Evidently Gogol for his part, had not yet seen Russia as the submerged theme of his work. Perhaps Pushkin's reaction led him to it.

In any case, the discovery was soon made as part of the reconsideration that Pushkin's reaction prompted. The surviving drafts of the next version already show it; so does a significant change of phrase—and an accompanying shift in the generic identification of his project. In October 1835, having finished three chapters, Gogol foresaw "a novel," "very long" and "very funny," in which he would show "all of Russia, though only from one side" (X, 375). By November 1836 he reports adding three pages a day "to my *poema.*" "All of Russia will appear in it"—but there is no longer any qualification of onesidedness. "Enormous and great is my creation, and its end will not be soon" (XI, 74–75). Alternatively: "The thing over which I am sitting and working now . . . is not like a tale or a novel; [it will be] very, very long, in several volumes . . . If God helps me to carry through my *poema* as it should be done, this will be my first respectable creation. All Russia will be summoned up in it" (XI, 77).

What is signaled here is the transcending of satire. Gogol later stated categorically that there was no shadow of satire in the book, adding significantly that that fact could be fully registered "only after several readings" (XII, 144). The assertion is false (all of Chapter 9 is satiric, as are scattered passages throughout); but, as Gogol's qualification suggests, the satiric element is intermittent and subsidiary to a larger esthetic aim—which is less to denounce than to create, "to illumine a picture taken from [the level of] a contemptible life and elevate it to a pearl of creation" (VI, 134).[2] Gogol's own design for the cover of *Dead Souls* makes the subtitle, *"Poema,"* more prominent than either his own title or the one the censors insisted on adding ("Chichikov's Adventures").

The word has generated no end of pilpulistic speculation. In Gogol's time it designated a long narrative poem, epic or mock-epic in the first place; Homer and Dante were the distant exemplars, Byron and Pushkin the leading contemporary adaptors. When *Dead Souls* appeared, the subtitle led enemies and friends alike into excesses worthy of the author's own creations, the townspeople of N. Senkovsky had a field day deriding the term (evidently forgetting that he had himself identified fiction as "epics [*poemy*] in prose"),[3] while Belinsky and Konstantin Aksakov engaged in a heated debate over whether Gogol was or was not to be considered a new Homer. Paradoxically, these extravagances proved that Gogol's general point had been taken: *Dead Souls* was not to be approached as an ordinary novel. (Of all Gogol's eccentric works, this is the first and only one to be thus labeled in an attempt to orient the reader.)

Once the disclaimer had been made, Gogol felt free to vary his terminology within the book itself, where it is most often called as a novel or a tale—despite his denial that either of these

ПОХОЖДЕНІЯ ЧИЧИКОВА

или

МЕРТВЫЯ ДУШИ.

ПОЭМА

Н. Гоголя

1842

Gogol's own cover design for the first edition of *Dead Souls* (1842).

terms was adequate, for reasons made clear in his posthumously published sketch of a "Textbook of Literature for Russian Youth." The section on the novel there opens with an acknowledgement that "although it is in prose, it can be a lofty poetic creation"; but the novel is likened to the drama in requiring a plot, and it is said to embrace "not a whole life, but some remarkable event in a life" (VIII, 482). The tale, by comparison ("which may receive the name of a *poema*"), is built around a single incident that "is sometimes not even worth attention and is used only to exhibit some separate picture, some lively, characteristic feature of a particular time, place or way of life, on occasion even of the poet's own fantasy" (VIII, 482). Closest of all to *Dead Souls* is his conception of "Lesser Forms of Epic":

In modern times there came into being a kind of narrative work that constitutes, as it were, a mean between the novel and the epic, whose hero, though a private and unremarkable character, is nonetheless significant in many respects for the observer of the human soul. The author traces his life through a series of adventures and changes, in order at the same time to bring to life and present a faithful picture of everything that is significant in the traits and mores of the time in question—that earthly, almost statistically caught picture of the shortcomings, abuses, vices, and everything that he has remarked in the chosen epoch . . . which might claim the attention of any observant contemporary in search of living lessons for the present in what is over and past. Such works have appeared from time to time among many peoples. Many of them, although written in prose, may nonetheless be classed as poetic creations. (VIII, 478–479)

Ariosto and Cervantes are named as examples.

Both the overlapping emphases and the distinctive features of these genres as Gogol construes them illuminate his intention in *Dead Souls;* at the same time, they make clear the degree to which he saw that work as escaping generic confines. The word *poema* in all its suggestive vagueness is a promissory note signifying an intention of originality on the highest artistic level; unspecific, it does not exclude kinship with the authors Gogol names in his draft (each of them a breaker of established convention) or with Homer. Moreover, when related to the book's striking and original title, it may carry Dantean overtones as well. These last were noted at the time, and have been since.[4] They can be seen in formal parallels (quite apart from the plan of a tripartite work following that of the *Commedia*): in the centrality of the narrator; the substitution of a progress for a story; the use of extended similes that, like those observed by Mandelstam in his "Conversation about Dante," challenge the reader to indicate "what is being compared with what, which is the main thing and which the secondary that elucidates it."[5] There is, besides, a clearly intentional openness to multitiered interpretation of the sort set forth by Dante in the *Convito*. But most of all there is the concentration on "the sorry souls of those who lived without infamy and without praise," "the sorry sect of those who are displeasing to God and to His enemies," "wretches who never were alive."[6] As Gogol recalled: "I saw that many of [their] foulnesses were not worth malice: better to show all the insignificance (*ničtožnost'*) that should forever be their lot" (VIII, 294).

"Soul" (*duša*) is one of the most frequently recurring words in Gogol's writing throughout his career. Here its Gogolian meanings reach a new plenitude—and not only because in his time it also designated an enserfed peasant (landowners were commonly said to possess so many souls). The Gogolian usage, still uncharted, covers a spectrum that runs from regarding the soul as the seat of authentic individual being, through equating it with the unconscious, to seeing it as the organ of communication with supraindividual sources of truth and beauty, not necessarily religious. Thus in the first essay of *Arabesques* painting is rated above sculpture since the latter cannot convey "those subtle, mysteriously earthly traits, regarding which you sense heaven filling your soul, and you feel the inexpressible" (VIII, 11). There is, he suggests quite without irony in that essay, a purely esthetic means to "save our poor soul" (VIII, 12). For souls in this sense are perishable (the censor had a point in objecting that Gogol's title was blasphemous); they can atrophy in life. Later, in the 1840s, he wrote that his works had been, in their succession, "the history of my own soul," a form of exorcism, bringing to expression aspects of the author's unconscious psychology. A revealing draft for Chapter 7 of *Dead Souls,* shows him looking forward, beyond these inert and repugnant characters, to presenting others of a kind "you fly to meet with love, as if they were old acquaintances . . . whom your soul once, in the years of youth, ignorant of where, in what places, during its holy absences from your body, had met on its way" (VI, 439). Such a concern with touching the inexpressible and bringing to consciousness what may be dormant in it required a symbolism more often associated with poetry than with fiction. Hence the reinforcement of his subtitle alongside the riddle of his title proper.

Today we are readier to grant that a work may pursue metaphysical ends, be eclectic, idiosyncratic, at once comically grotesque and deeply serious, and still call itself a novel without special qualification. Our concern is rather with accounting for the way texts function. And yet, when a text is as puzzling as *Dead Souls*—when the sense of its structural principle is so elusive as to make it seem nothing but a collection of details—the problem of genre definition remains central. In the case at hand, illumination is available from an unexpected quarter. I have in mind Stendhal's notoriously unproductive notion of a novel as *un miroir qu'on promène le long d'un chemin*. For *Dead Souls,* alone among the major novels of European literature, might be said to fit and validate it.

GOGOL's novel is organized and dominated by the road.* It begins with an arrival and ends with a departure; its concluding lines are a panegyric to the road. Lotman has shown how the road in *Dead Souls* involves all the varieties of "Gogolian space" as they have appeared in the earlier works—from boundlessness through fragmentation to domestic warmth[7]—thereby providing an index of the way it confers amplitude and orders the several levels on which the narrative functions. Literally the instrument of Chichikov's quest on the level of story, it leads him to planned and unplanned encounters, and so stands for experience, perspective, movement, change, life. "How much there is," Gogol writes in the last chapter, "of the strange, and the alluring, and the transporting, and the wonderful in the word: road! And how wondrous it is itself, this road" (VI, 221). For all that, the road here serves neither as pretext nor as occasion for adventures. It affords *views*—of landscapes, characters, and routines, presented through "those trivia which seem trivia only when they are put into a book" (VI, 222). The mirror moving down this road is, in the first place, Chichikov himself, the featureless hero ("neither handsome nor of displeasing exterior, neither too plump nor too thin," not exactly old "but not

---

* Appropriately enough, its earliest textual beginnings have been traced to the travel notes he made in the summer of 1835, when he journeyed from Petersburg to his Ukrainian family home. See Shenrok's "Očerk istorii teksta pervoj časti Mertvyx duš," in *Sočinenija N.V. Gogolja,* 10th ed., vol. 7 (St. Petersburg, 1896), 486–488.

any too young" [VI, 7]). Like a mirror, he is all surface: "Whatever the subject of conversation, he could always keep it going: if the talk was about stud farming, he would talk about stud farming; if it was about good dogs, here too he would contribute very weighty observations; if [the company] discoursed on the investigation carried out by the Treasury office, he showed that he was not uninformed about courtroom tricks; if there was a dissertation on billiard playing, he was up on billiards too; if the subject was virtue, he discoursed very well about virtue, even with tears in his eyes . . . He spoke neither loudly nor softly but just in the right way . . . The governor expressed the conviction that he was a reliable man; the prosecutor, that he was a sensible man; the colonel of police said that he was a learned man" (VI, 17—18). His successive encounters are less interactions than evocations of those whom he meets, and when the gallery of transitory images is complete, the mirror moves on ("Occupied exclusively with the road, he glanced only to the right and the left, and it was as if the town of N. did not exist in his memory" [VI, 222])—though not before turning opaque and becoming an object in its own right. This process begins in Chapter 9, when the town officials ask themselves "the question they should have asked in the beginning, that is, in the first chapter of our *poema*": "Who was he in fact?"—only to conclude that though "they did not know for certain what Chichikov was, nonetheless Chichikov must without fail be something" (VI, 196).

The opacity conferred at the end by giving Chichikov biographical dimensionality is meant to explain his enterprise and so prepare the next stage of his road, on which the events of this novel have been only a way station. But it has a deeper function in making clear, retrospectively, that what was presented as Chichikov's mirroring of the characters has in fact been mutual. Manilov now appears as a hyperbolic parody of Chichikov's main quality, decorum; Korobochka represents a naive variant of his suspicious canniness in bargaining; Nozdryov shows more than comparable resourcefulness in prevarication, though his is instinctive and motiveless; Sobakevich manifests the calculating side of Chichikov, with its implicit misanthropy laid bare; and Plyushkin represents the passionate side of his acquisitiveness, showing how, unchecked, it can destroy the family life to which Chichikov so eagerly looks forward. Even Petrushka, the lackey, with his indiscriminate taste for reading ("It wasn't what he read about that leased him, but more the reading itself, or, more precisely, the process of reading itself" [VI, 20]) parodies his master, who is shown in the first chapter tearing down a theatrical poster, the better to scrutinize it at leisure (he reads all the actors' names, "got down even to the price of orchestra seats and learned that the poster had been printed in the shop of the provincial administration; then he turned it over to see whether there might not be something on the other side, but finding nothing wiped his eyes, folded it neatly, and put it in his traveling box, where he had the habit of storing everything that came his way" [VI, 12]).

The portrait gallery of the book is thus a gallery of mirrors as well—to which, in the process of presentation, the narrator adds his own generalizing reflections. Only the author, whose voice emerges distinctly from that of the narrator at times, remains above this process, in the role of self-justifying commentator and ultimately of creator. Having, so to speak, gone through the looking glass to reveal Chichikov's scheme and its relation to his biography, he comments: "Had the author not looked more deeply into [Chichikov's] soul, had he not stirred at the bottom what slinks away and hides from the light, had he not revealed the most secret thoughts that one man never confides to another, but rather shown him as he appeared to the whole town . . . [readers] would be happy with him and would take him for an interesting person." But then, he adds—evincing the didactic note that separates the world of this work from that of *The Inspector General*—the reader's soul would have gone undisturbed and he might simply turn again to the card table, "the consoler of all Russia" (VI, 243).

Presentation is the work of the narrator; it embraces the projections and perceptions of the characters and offers them, embellished and in a new perspective, to be registered by the reader. The author, by contrast, appears as such, hinting at a larger enterprise of his own, as enigmatic as Chichikov's, and likening his own task to a journey. The passages where his voice dominates might collectively bear the title given Gogol's posthumous "Author's Confession," constituting as they do crucial passages in the tale of his authorship. They are all keyed to the question: why? (See Chapter 3: "But why be concerned so long with Korobochka? Whether it's Korobochka or Manilov, a thrifty life or unthrifty—let us leave them behind!" [VI, 58].) The author himself is a creature of the road; at the beginning of Chapter 6 he recalls his youthful curiosity in approaching new places; at the beginning of Chapter 7 he envies the traveler returning home and contrasts him with the writer whose mission it is to confront all the repulsive phenomena "with which our earthly, sometimes bitter and dull road seethes" (VI, 134).

Dead Souls, as Sinyavsky observes, is to a considerable extent "a book written about how it is written." The apologetic passages regularly follow the pattern of the seventh chapter, where confession breaks off: "Back to the road! to the road! Away with the wrinkle that has settled on the brow and the severe gloom on the visage! Let us plunge suddenly and wholly into life . . . and see what Chichikov is up to" (VI, 135). Into life? Yes, for in Gogol's reversible terms "the world is a living book (VI, 690) and the road he proclaims himself fated to travel "for a long time yet hand in hand with my strange hero" a means of salvation: "My God, how good you are at times, you long, long road! How often like one perishing and drowning have I clutched at you, and each time you have magnanimously delivered and saved me! And how many wondrous ideas, poetic dreams have been born, how many marvelous impressions felt while traveling you! (VI, 222). This author's voice is seldom ironic; it contains the *norms* on which the purely narrative ironies rest, thus differentiating the method of *Dead Souls* from that of "The Overcoat" and showing a new openness in articulating his fundamental themes—Gogol's vision (in the double sense) of Russia, and of himself as writer—which come together in the last chapter, in the famous lyrical passage beginning, "Russia! Russia! I see thee; from my wondrous, beautiful far-off place I see thee," and culminate in the demand: "Russia! what wouldst thou have of me? What ineffable, hidden bond unites us? Why dost thou gaze at me so, and why has everything in thee turned its eyes, full of anticipation, on me?"

This grandiloquence has few precedents in Gogol's published writing, though it appears in many letters and in such intimate fragments as "1834" and "Nights at a Villa." It is what he took to be the immediate language of his soul, and he was to offer it increasingly to his public as the conviction strengthened in him that "poetry is the pure confession of the soul and not the product of artifice or of human desiring; poetry is the truth of the soul, and therefore can be equally accessible to all" (VIII, 429). (Fortunately, *Dead Souls* as a whole displays, though for the last time, another sort of poetry, continually productive of sudden glory, the work of a language "boundless and alive as life," a language which is in and of itself already a poet" [VIII, 409].) Here was a corrective to art's liability to misinterpretation of the kind he had experienced with his play, and all the more attractive since he expected *Dead Souls* to sell "better than any other book" (XII, 49) and looked beyond the upper-class public for his readership. The authorial interpolations in *Dead Souls*—as opposed to narrative comment—are confessions and admonishments, pleas for sympathy and defiant complaints about probable misunderstanding. Testimony to a new conception of the writer's function, they parallel the programmatic revisions of "The Portrait" and "After the Play." But they remain outside the world of the novel, like the scattered fragments of an introduction the author feared his readers might otherwise pass by.[8]

THE WORLD of that novel is the weedlike culture on the Russian heartland, conceived abstractly from a distance and bodied forth in disconcerting closeups, with absences commanding the same meticulous attention as presences and thereby assuming a like status; this verbal world takes its weird consistency from such ontological mixing and implies its own relation to other worlds simply by existing as it does. The oddness of the first paragraph alone (the first seven in Bernard Guerney's translation, which also makes an even twelve chapters out of Gogol's odd eleven) has been well analyzed by Nabokov in English and by Irakly Andronikov in Russian.[9] Both see its blurring of essentials and sharp etching of irrelevancies as typical of the presented world of *Dead Souls,* semantically malproportioned to produce an effect of comic grotesquerie. Indeed this feature is recapitulated three paragraphs later in the description of Chichikov's room at the inn, which concludes: "In short, the same thing you find everywhere, with the sole difference that one of the paintings depicted a nymph with such enormous breasts as the reader, most probably, has never beheld" (VI, 9). Gogol's phrase for this is "a sport of nature (*igra prirody*)": that phrase defines the look of the town* as well as its life and has an emblematic

---

* A hatter's shop-sign announces "Vasily Fyodorov, Foreigner"; another depicts two acrobatic billiard players, with the legend, "And Behold the Establishment." "Here and there right on the street stood tables with nuts, soap, and gingerbread that looked like soap" (VI, 11).

meaning that extends throughout a narrative in which nature figures prominently.[10] Our first view of it comes in Chapter 2, as
Chichikov sets out on the first of his forays into the countryside:

Hardly had the town retreated when (quite the usual thing among us)
there unrolled on both sides of the road vistas of a wild preposterousness:
hummocks, fir groves, small, squat, sparse undergrowths of young
pines, charred stumps of old ones, wild heather, and such-like nonsensical rubbish. One came upon villages all strung out in a single line, with
huts that looked like weather-beaten woodpiles, covered over with gray
roofs, the wooden fretwork decorations underneath them resembling
hanging towels with embroidered designs. A few muzhiks in short
sheepskin jackets were, as usual, yawning as they squatted on benches
placed before the gates; countrywives, with stout faces and their breasts
caught up by shawls, were looking out of the upper windows; out of a
lower window a calf would peer, or a sow might be poking its unseeing
snout. In brief, the sights were of a thoroughly familiar nature. (VI, 21—
22; Guerney translation)

Out of this flat miscellaneousness, crystallizing into colorful incongruities, Gogol shows how each of the five landowners Chichikov
visits—solipists all—has arranged a particular landscape reflecting
his own dominant qualities. Thus the rough and solid order of Sobakevich's estate is matched by the master himself, whose very
face is described as one of those on which nature took few pains,
but simply hacked away from the shoulder with an ax, "and set
him into the world unplaned, saying: 'It lives!' " (VI, 94–95). This
technique is so artfully handled and so subtly sustained as to preclude brief citation; avoiding the allegorical consistency it threatens, Gogol manages to suggest the variety of nature through the
range of his observation and the modulation of his emphases. The
symbolic high point of all this is the long description of Plyushkin's garden in Chapter 6, singled out by Nabokov as an example
of the epoch-making novelty of Gogol's painterly rendition of
landscape.[11] The concluding lines as he translates them summarize:

In a word all was as beautiful as neither nature nor art can contrive, beautiful as it is only when these two come together, with nature giving the
final touch of her chisel to the work of man (that more often than not he
has piled up anyhow), alleviating its bulky agglomeration and suppress-
ing both its crudely obvious regularity and the miserable gaps through
which its stark background clearly showed and casting a wonderful
warmth over all that had been evolved in the bleakness of measured neat-
ness and propriety. (Nabokov, 88–89; VI, 113)

A larger point was made by Pletnyov in one of the first reviews of the book. Citing the same passage, he observed that Gogol had "with astonishing clarity set forth in these few words his whole esthetic theory . . . *His whole book is like this garden.*"[12] This corner of Plyushkin's estate is unique—"It alone lent freshness to this extensive settlement and it alone was fully picturesque in its pictorial desolation"—and it represents a norm by which to judge the eccentricities both of the presented world and of the presentation itself. No less remarkable in this respect is the companion passage in the same chapter, where narrative digression creates a scene so minute as to seem observed rather than imagined, one that similarly suggests a perspective from outside the suffocating world of the book. Chichikov is standing before Plyushkin:

And so, that's the sort of landowner who was standing before Chichikov! It must be said that the like is only rarely to be met with in Russia, where everything would rather expand than contract, and such a phenomenon is all the more striking since right next door a landowner may turn up who carouses as only the reckless Russian gentry can, burning his candle, as they say, at both ends. The unfamiliar traveler will stop in astonishment at the sight of his dwelling, wondering what sovereign prince has suddenly surfaced amid these small and insignificant proprietors: Like palaces do his white stone buildings gaze out with an infinity of chimneys, belvederes, weathervanes, and all sorts of outbuildings for the house guests. What doesn't he have there? Theatricals, balls—all night, set about with lights and lampions and live with music, his garden glows. Half the province in their best finery promenade gaily beneath the trees —no one sees anything wild or threatening in this forced illumination— when from the arboreal thickness a branch leaps out, suffused with counterfeit light, stripped of its bright verdancy, while above, darker and sterner and twenty times more dreadful for that the night sky looms and, rustling their leaves on high, disappearing deeper into the impenetrable dark, the austere treetops make their indignant protest at this tinselly glitter which has lit up their roots from below. (VI, 120)

The world of *Dead Souls* is a world of detail natural and fictive, familiar and strange—and all subtly out of joint. Even at its sharpest, this detail contributes to the general impression of indeterminacy: What time of year can it be when the peasant men sit in sheepskin coats, their women are up to their knees in a pond, Korobochka comments on a snowstorm, and the fruit trees are covered with a net to keep off the crows?[13] Thus Biely is led to conclude that "there is no plot in *Dead Souls* outside of the details," just as there is nothing except "the bare carcass of Gogol's dissertations" outside the ubiquitous nuance.[14] The people themselves become features of the landscape—Plyushkin a "rip," Sobakevich a bear, the unidentified woman in Sobakevich's house "one of those persons who exist in the world not as objects, but as foreign specks or spots on objects" (VI, 98). Korobochka is exemplary in the way, at the end of her interview with Chichikov, she fades back into the details of which she seems less the mistress than the emanation: "Reassured, [she] had already begun to examine everything that was in her yard; she stared at the housekeeper who was bringing a wooden flagon of honey out of the store-room, at the peasant who had appeared at the gate, and little by little settled back entirely into the life of her household" (VI, 58).

How these details relate to each other and cohere to fulfill a serious intention is as difficult to formulate as it is easy to feel in the reading. Paraphrase misses the sustaining magic of the language—Gogol's triumph here—and so deadens. Analysis freezes the essential movement of the text, which is not lineal, thus risking arbitrariness, not to mention endlessness. Summary supposes, fatally, that plot provides a meaningful pattern. There is no single locus or level of significance adequate to account for this text in which speech events rival human events (even *generate* them), and characters who stumble momentarily into the narrative through hearsay or are invited in to make up a simile,* share a quality of enigmatic, stubborn "thereness" with those whose presence is demanded by Chichikov's scheme or the narrator's *sententiae*. All of which doubtless accounts for the fact that in the more than a century and a quarter since *Dead Souls* was published and proclaimed a masterpiece, scarcely a single serious critical monograph has been devoted to it.[15] One looks for links and finds instead shifting fields of force; one isolates levels and discovers that their effectiveness rests on the rhythms of their discontinuity. *Dead Souls,* that strange reflection on the static and the confined, seethes with energy; even the ending is motion. The writing that indicts the mere semblance of life seems itself possessed of a disconcerting vitality. Sinyavsky explains the paradox behind this elusiveness:

The plot here is devoured by the portraits and swamped by the details.

---

* Nabokov writes spendidly of this auxiliary population, but turning from his pages to the text itself one may be nonplussed to discover that the examples he implies to be everywhere are in fact a good deal sparser, leaving vast stretches of the writing unaccounted for.

From an engaging story the accent is shifted to the characters; but in the characters (or portraits) the accent is shifted to details of setting. The novel slips into landscape—roadside or domestic; the estates with their owners are countries, islands in an ocean; each house is sketched as a self-confined ambience with its own specific local color; as is appropriate in journeys, the geographical principle comes to the fore, character being rendered primarily as a relief arising out of the environment. As interior, the interior forms a cosmos, woven out of the material of objects . . . the material of objects, blending with material of speech, produces the illusion of spatial form proper; the *poema* in Gogol's usage converges with the spatial concept of a panorama. The lyrical theme of Russia, which does not arise formally from the characters and events of the foreground, is joined with the idea of space, maximally accentuated, and is inserted not into the plot but into the purview of Gogol's prose. The formlessness and superabundance of the prose become a quality of the earth.[16]

The matter of *Dead Souls* is so difficult to handle because it is so peculiarly, materially verbal. The interpolated "Tale of Captain Kopeikin" in Chapter 10 offers an extended and crucial example. A masterpiece of *skaz* (mannered narration in which the speaker unwittingly vies with his story for attention and vivid manner overshadows ostensible matter), it consists largely of fillers, malapropisms and colorfully misdirected hyperbole. "'After the campaign of 1812, my fine gentleman'—thus the postmaster began, despite the fact that not one gentleman but a whole six were sitting in the room—'after the campaign of 1812 among those sent back with the wounded was Captain Kopeikin. Whether it was at Krasnoe or at Leipzig, anyway, just image, his arm and leg had been blown off. Well, at that time they hadn't yet made any, you know, provisions for the wounded; any sort of veterans' fund was already established, as you can imagine, so to speak, much later'" (VI, 199–200). The postmaster's purpose in telling the story is to suggest that Chichikov is really Captain Kopeikin; six pages later the police chief interrupts to point out that Chichikov has all his limbs —as indeed he could have done after the second sentence. Had the tale been meant merely to cap the absurd series of rumors about Chichikov, to demonstrate the absentmindedness of the teller or the density of the listeners, it might have been cut or summarized when the censor objected to it as politically inflammatory. Gogol, however, made a desperate plea for its necessity—in terms of form:

This is one of the best passages. And I am unable in any way to patch the

hole [which its excision would leave] visible in my *poema* . . . The piece
is essential, not for the connection of the events, but to distract the reader
for a moment . . . It has occurred to me that perhaps the censorship
took fright at [the mention of] generals. I have reworked Kopeikin and
thrown out all of that, even the minister, even the word "Excellency" . . . I have drawn the character of Kopeikin more sharply so that
it is now clear that he himself is the cause of his behavior, and not any
lack of compassion in others . . . In a word, it is all in such a form now
that even the strictest censorship, in my opinion, cannot find anything in
any wise reprehensible. (XII, 55)

The care Gogol lavished on the rhythm of his texts is a matter of
record; but there is more than distraction involved here. The
whole tale is one of those irrelevant details on which the novel
rests, and despite its irrelevance there is something in it. For one
thing, it brings the provinces into relation with Petersburg yet
again—an important element in Gogol's perspectivism. But its
uniqueness lies in the way it parodically mirrors the larger text of
which it is a part. Gogol makes this clear when, introducing it, he
quotes the postmaster's claim that if the tale be told, the result
would be "a sort of whole *poema,* and a fascinating one for some
writer" (VI, 199). The tale, in other words, exists not only to present in new focus a narration that is a performance, a colloquial
stylization replete with outlandish words, functional irrelevancies,
alternating sharpness and blur; and not only to make the largest
addition to the enormous cast of supernumerary presences. Beyond manner, it parodies the form of *Dead Souls* by ending precisely at the point where the teller announces "the beginning, one
may say, the thread, the start (*zavjazka*) of a novel" (VI,205).[17]

THE UNIVERSE of *Dead Souls* expands and contracts in the readers's
consciousness—from metaphysical intuition to densely enigmatic
vocables. That is why if we pause at any point in our reading, the
whole appears as an ontological puzzle. The smallest and so most
apparently tractable elements—the words themselves—may call
language as such into question, to such an extent can they appear
freed not only from clear referential meaning but from single specifiable relevance.[18] In this connection, the title itself is central: Biely
declared that he could write dozens of pages on the tricks of narration that arise from the ambiguity of both words.

Souls in this novel are absent, displaced, or atrophied. Sobakevich pinpoints the ambiguities when he assures Chichikov that

"some other crook would deceive you, sell you rubbish, and not souls"; his dead souls are select merchandise, each one "either a skilled workman or some healthy peasant" (VI, 102). And he gives the concept its larger extension in replying to Chichikov's objection that he is itemizing the qualities of a population that is, after all, dead:

"Yes, of course they're dead," said Sobakevich, as if reflecting and recalling that they were in fact already dead; then he added: "But for that matter you could also say what good are the people that are now numbered among the living? What sort of people are they? They're flies, and not people." (VI, 103)

The objection echoes with a stubborn plausibility despite the fact that the speaker himself gives the appearance of being a body with no soul in it—"or, if there was one, then by no means in the place where it should have been" (VI, 101). For truths issue eccentrically in this book; there is no privileged source among the characters. Sobakevich's point is borne out by Chichikov's heartfelt (*"ot duši"*; literally, from the soul) reaction to the only death in the book: "There's the public prosecutor for you! He lived and lived, then up and died! And now they'll be printing in the papers that, to the grief of his subordinates and all humanity there passed away a respected citizen, a rare father, an exemplary spouse, and all sorts of things . . . But if one were actually to look into the matter carefully . . . all there really was to you was your bushy eyebrows" (VI, 219). The narrator himself both takes and denies this view, reporting sardonically that only when the prosecutor had become a soulless corpse did those around him discover "that the deceased had in fact had a soul, though in his modesty he had never shown it. But for all that the appearance of death was as awful in a little man as it is awful in a great: he who not so long before had walked, moved, played whist, signed various papers and been seen so often among the officials with his thick eyebrows and winking eye now lay on the table; his left eye no longer winked at all, but one eyebrow was still raised with a sort of interrogative expression. What the deceased was asking about—why he had died or why he had lived—God alone knows" (VI, 210).

This is a reprise of the way the death of Akaky Akakievich had been registered, and it can produce a similar uneasiness in readers who, like Rozanov, deny Gogol the right to regard his characters as occasions for solemnity when he has already mocked

them in the very act of creating them. In the broader context of
Dead Souls, however, where the refrain of *ne to* ("not that"—not
the thing supposed or intended or required) is so constantly and
variously sounded, the prosecutor's death is as large a symbolic
event as the tale of Captain Kopeikin, and any uneasiness on the
reader's part simply proves that the point has been taken: "How
the inanity and impotent idleness of a life are replaced by a murky
death which says nothing. How this awful event is accomplished
senselessly. No one is moved. Death strikes an unmoving world.
All the more strongly thereby should the dead insensibility of life
be brought home to the reader" (Gogol's notes to Volume One;
VI, 692).

In these words the fundamental paradox of the novel is laid
bare: Living people and dead ones may be clearly distinguished in
the action, but the cumulative sense of the text denies this distinction, as it denies the autonomy of comedy. Bergson shrewdly lo-
cates the originality of a comic artist in "the special kind of life he
imparts to a mere puppet"; but when, in Vyazemsky's phrase,
Dead Souls turns into a Holbein-like dance of death, the comedy
turns painful, revealing the poles of the spectrum shown not as
death and life, but as death and death-in-life.[19] Here is a clue to the
"special kind of life" in question, and it suggests that the terms of
Gogol's presentation are not so much skewed as incomplete. Annensky explained the matter this way. In each of us there are two
persons, one of them visible and tangible, the other "enigmatic and
secret"—the carrier of an indivisible, incommunicable, primordial
selfhood. The first strives above all to be a type—that is, to assume
a social identification; the second alone creates individuality. "The
first eats, sleeps, shaves, and ceases to breathe; you can lock it in a
jail or nail it up in a coffin." But it is only the second that can be
reproached, loved, or respond to moral demands. Gogol, he finds,
"sundered the first of these two persons fused together by life
from the second, and made him so incandescently typical . . . so
stunningly corporeal, that that second person proved utterly ef-
faced. He even became outright unnecessary, so that the first, the
tangible one, now answered for both."[20]

Here is the best answer to Sobakevich's question about what
sort of people the living are in this book. The landowners Chichikov visits do not, as Biely claims, represent a progressively greater

degree of deadness; the individuating moral principle in each is *equally* absent. What they rather represent are differing degrees (and kinds) of *aliveness*—an aliveness that reaches its apogee in Sobakevich and Nozdryov, the one impressing his selfhood on everything around him and so reifying it, the other making everything a possession (or attribute) of himself and so perpetually dispersing that selfhood. Nozdryov, as Annensky, puts it epigrammatically, "is not at all a liar" but "some uncontrollable, some insane abundance," "the cheerful indifference of nature."[21] The same passionate miscellaneousness (though the ruling passions give it different contours) can be seen in Plyushkin, in Manilov—and in Chichikov himself. These figures may exist on the level of humours but, like Panurge and Falstaff, they are perfectly individuated, and profoundly nuanced in expression. To generalize the quality of any of them, one has to use his name, no common noun will do; in that sense these creations are at the same time *discoveries*.

CHICHIKOV and the landowners are the major characters of *Dead Souls,* and the major instances of Russian character; hence the narrative reminders that all have their counterparts in the capital. But they are more than exhibits. In Chapters 2 through 6, they lay the groundwork for the comedy of attribution which will turn collective in Chapters 7 through 10. Each of them, in his interview with Chichikov, can be seen projecting his peculiar fantasies onto the void of the "real" world—as if their society were a conspiracy of silence to permit this.* When in Chapter 8 Chichikov has taken possession of his ambiguous capital (consisting only of words on paper: the mortgageable lists of the dead serfs he has bought), the scene shifts back to the town, and the portraiture becomes satirical as general attention focuses on him and his putative wealth. Now it is the ladies of the town who begin investing Chichikov with new qualities. These ladies, Gogol notes, "were by no means fortune-hunters: the word 'millionaire' was to blame for it all—not

---

* Pletnyov, whose review so pleased Gogol that he copied it verbatim in his own hand, saw this, noting the absence in the book of "what we do not yet meet in our life—a serious social interest." "Chichikov ili Mertvye Duši Gogolja," reprinted in *Sočinenija i perepiska P. A. Pletneva,* I (St. Petersburg, 1885), 491.

the millionaire himself but just the word alone" (VI, 159).[22] Nor
does discovery of the truth halt this process. When Nozdryov and
after him Korobochka finally make known the nature of Chichikov's purchases, the whole town begins collectively to explain him
and his enterprise—once more by attribution. He is Napoleon,
Rinaldo Rinaldini, the devil, Captain Kopeikin. The text of
Gogol's fiction swells with internally generated fictions: the mutual mirroring now gives way to the effect of an amusement-park
hall of mirrors—from which Chichikov simply escapes, to vanish
on the last page in the last of the book's optical illusions and the
last of its changes of level.

Dead Souls exploits the narrative voices and devices worked out in
the most Gogolian of his earlier comic writings; the text abounds
with parallels, at times almost citations, from "Shponka," "Old-
World Landowners," the story of the two Ivans, "The Nose,"
"The Carriage," all five of the Petersburg Tales, *The Inspector General*. It is his last, most inclusive, and most intentional performance
in that special mode of his own devising—half monologue, half
story—by which he creates a world whose status with relation to
ordinary experience remains, like the implied personality of the
narrator, teasingly elusive. The world of *Dead Souls* differs only in
this: because it is more ample, it shows a greater consistency, the
very discontinuities suggesting a pattern, the several levels echoing
each other to signal a controlling perspective over the whole
design. Technique itself does not simply carry but becomes a part
of theme; the humblest details take on a thematic charge.
　　That theme at its broadest is the amorphousness, character-
lessness, purposelessness, senselessness, alternately ludicrous and
ominous, of life—specifically Russian life in the first place—as material for a novelist. "Well," Chichikov ruminates after the ball in a
passage reminiscent of the last scene of *The Inspector General*,
"what if some writer, say, took it into his head to describe this
whole scene as it is? Why, even there, even in a book, it would be
just as senseless as it is in nature. What kind of scene is it? Moral?
Immoral? The devil alone knows what! You'd just spit, and then
close the book" [VI, 175].) Compare Gogol's draft notes to Volume One:

The whole town with the whole whirlwind of rumors embodies the idleness* (*bezdel'nost'*) of the life of all mankind in the mass . . .
    How bring all the sorts of idleness in the world down to a resemblance
with the town's idleness? And how elevate the town's idleness to the
level of an embodiment of the world's? To manage it, include all the similarities and introduce a graduated progression. (VI, 693)

This notion of a tiered significance suggests in the first place all
those passages which insist on Petersburg variant of the same local
phenomena; but the symbolic intention, so generally expressed,
goes beyond this. Gogol's concern is with levels of interpretation,
and he might well have had in mind Dante's classic assertion that

books can be understood, and ought to be explained, in four principal
senses. One is called *literal,* and . . . goes no further than the letter, such
as the simple narration of the thing of which you treat . . . The second
is called *allegorical,* and this is the meaning hidden under the cloak of
fables, and is a truth concealed beneath a fair fiction . . . The third sense
is called *moral;* and this readers should carefully gather from all writings,
for the benefit of themselves and their descendants . . . The fourth
sense is called *anagogical* [or mystical], that is, beyond sense; and this is
when a book is spiritually expounded.[23]

I do not mean to suggest that *Dead Souls* should be tortured into
strict conformity with these medieval categories, but only that
some comparable scheme was demonstrably a part of Gogol's
intention and can in fact be fruitfully applied to this (and only this)
text of his.
    How are such levels of serious significance incorporated into a
comic novel? Some examples may make this clear, but a broad
answer can be ventured in advance. It is that Gogol found a key to
the most puzzling of his inherent tendencies when he took contemporary Russia as his theme. Even on the strategic authorial
level, that is, *Dead Souls* remains a comedy of attribution. It is a
symbolic statement of what it means to live (as Gogol claimed he
had written previously) without controlling consciousness,
without asking "why?" and "to what end?" Here was a license for
derision, or rather a serious warrant for the most ingeniously un-

---

* A letter of 1846 provides a gloss on the concept in question. "The world in
which you are now moving," Gogol writes Samarin, "is not corrupt in its root or
essence but corrupt out of depression and boredom, morbidly listless and, from
having nothing to do, vacuous and stupid" (XIII, 25).

serious presentation. No oddity, no irrelevance, no absurity but could—given the unflagging genius of the language—contribute to the painful because concrete sense of an absence.

On the first page, for example, the contextless conversation about the wheel on Chichikov's carriage is conducted by "two Russian muzhiks"—a pleonasm roughly comparable to speaking of "two American cowboys." Many Russian readers have noted this as a lapse and seen in it an unconscious reflection of Gogol's Ukrainian foreignness to Russian phenomena or a sign of his distant (Roman) perspective at the time of writing. But the very amount of attention to the single word, "Russian," proves the functional validity of the phrase, as one scholar inadvertently acknowledged in referring to this "definition which defines nothing."[24] It is a perspectival cue,* warning the reader that nothing is to be taken for granted in this examination of "everything that is every minute before our eyes but is unseen by indifferent eyes" (Chapter 6). It is, in other words, a cue to the particular kind of "making-strange" that informs the book, one element in the emphasis on *ne to*. As such it manifests in little what distinguishes such fantastic-atmospheric passages as the remarkable one that brings Chichikov back to the town of N. at the end of Chapter 6:

The twilight was already deep when they drove up to the town. Light and shadow were utterly mixed up, and it seemed that the very objects were mixed up as well. The striped toll-gate had taken on some indeterminate hue; the mustaches of the sentry on duty there seemed to be on his forehead and much higher than his eyes, while his nose was as if altogether absent . . . The streetlamps had not yet been lit; only here and there were lights beginning to appear in the windows of the houses; and in the alleys and byways scenes and conversations were taking place of a sort inseparable from this time of day in all towns where there are many soldiers, cabbies, workmen, and beings of a special sort in the guise of ladies with red shawls and shoes without stockings who dart like bats about the intersections. Chichikov did not notice them, and even failed to notice the many slender clerks with little canes who were, probably, re-

---

* See Gogol's defense of *The Inspector General* in his "After the Play": To one spectator's objection that a comedy "should be a picture and mirror of our social life . . . [and] reflect it with complete fidelity" Gogol has another respond that "this comedy is not at all a picture, but rather a frontispiece. You can see that the stage and the place of the action are ideal. Otherwise the author would not have allowed himself obvious inaccuracies and anachronisms . . . This is a composite place" (V, 150).

turning home after having taken a stroll out of town. Occasionally certain exclamations, apparently female, came to his hearing: "That's a lie, you drunkard! I never allowed him such rudeness!", or: "Don't you try to fight, you ignoramus, just come down to the station, I'll prove it to you there! . . . " In short, such words as will suddenly scald some dreaming twenty-year-old youth returning from the theater . . . He is in heaven, he has dropped in to visit Schiller—when suddenly, like thunder, the fateful words resound above him and he sees that he has come to once more on earth, and even on Haymarket Square, and even in the vicinity of a tavern, and everyday life has once more started to strut its stuff before him. (VI, 130–131)

This marvel of quiet anomaly and subtle progression would repay careful analysis; I cite it here merely as one striking instance of the way Gogol makes a scene at once specific and enigmatically general, confounds the everyday with the near-surrealistic, and fosters a sense of *huis clos* that hangs over the entire narrative.

Related to this in its functional superfluity is the introduction of Manilov in Chapter 2. The passage is remarkable in the first place for its slippery logic and its self-canceling conclusion, which make it the overwhelmingly present sign of an absence:

[With such characters] a forcible harnessing of the attention is necessary while you compel all their subtle, almost invisible traits to stand out before you, and in general even an eye already educated and disciplined in science must be forced to its uttermost penetration.

God alone might be able to say what kind of character Manilov's was. There is a class of people known as so-so, neither-this-nor-that, neither fish nor fowl, as the proverb has it. It is among them, perhaps, that Manilov should be numbered . . . During the first minute of conversation with him you couldn't help saying, "What a pleasant and kind man!" The next minute after that you wouldn't say anything at all; while the minute after that you'd say, "The devil knows what this is about!"— and you'd get as far away as possible . . . No amount of patience could get you any lively or even emphatic word out of him, of the kind you can hear from almost anybody if you touch on a subject close to his heart. Everyone has some passion of his own: the passion of one man may have turned to wolfhounds; another fancies himself a great lover of music and amazingly sensitive to all its profundities; a third is a master at valiant dining, a fourth at playing a role ever so slightly higher than the one assigned to him; a fifth, with a more limited desire, sleeps and dreams of how he might be seen strolling with an aide-de-camp for the benefit of his friends, acquaintances, and even those who don't know him at all; a sixth is already gifted with a hand preternaturally impelled to bet on some ace or deuce of diamonds, while the hand of a seventh just itches to

set things right somewhere . . . in short, everyone has something all his
own, but Manilov didn't have a thing. (VI, 24)

Reminiscent in its anticlimax of the passage in "The Overcoat" describing Akaky Akakievich's lack of recreation, this two-tiered
noncharacterization operates in still other ways. It reinforces the
sense of a closed world by the reversibility of its terms: the seven
hypothetical individuals not only assert Manilov's minimal position on the ladder of human being; they are, morally speaking,
seven sleepers, representing a range of trivial preoccupation that
will be exemplified throughout the book.

   None of this is strictly necessary, since the impression of
Manilov that emerges from his slow-motion dealings with Chichikov makes the point indelibly. But it and similar passages are absolutely necessary as contributions to the reader's complicity with
the narrator, that clever and sardonic fellow. Sharing his perspective and judgments, we are all the more likely to accept his generalizations about Russian habits, the Russian word, Russian
character—and so to credit (even when we cannot follow) his insistence that there is a sober sense to all this luminous nonsense.
The angle of vision, reinforced by overt comment, supplies a level
of consciousness which the denizens of the novel are so consistently denied.

   What are conventionally called the lyrical digressions in *Dead
Souls* thus need to be distinguished in terms of two distinct tendencies. One set enriches the presentation by growing out of it,
directly or through association; these fall within the range—an extraordinarily ample one—of what I have called the narrative voice.
The other set—the work of the authorial voice—comments on the
novel as an artifact in process of creation, emphasizing its dignity,
its uniqueness, and its difficulty. Alternately open confessions and
defiant manifestos, these are self-justifying, self-encouraging,
sometimes self-pitying excrescences in the narrowly artistic sense,
but uniquely valuable evidence of a new writerly consciousness.

   Gogol speaks of the difficulty of his task in two principal
connections. One is vis-à-vis his public. Throughout the text he
anticipates and rebuts objections: to his use of "low" colloquial
language, his taking a "scoundrel" as hero, his exclusion of love
intrigue, and so on. These amount to an attack on the conventional
novels of his time and on the expectations of their readers (whom
he treats in this respect as dangerously enfeebled if not actually

dead souls themselves). At the same time, he contrasts the happy lot of the popular writer with that of the writer

who has dared to call forth all that is constantly before our eyes but which indifferent eyes remark not—all the terrible, shocking slime of trivia that have encumbered our life, all the depth of cold, fragmented, everyday characters with which our earthly, at times bitter and dull road teems . . . The court of contemporary judgment, the hypocritically un-feeling court of contemporary judgment, which brands as low and insig-nificant the creations he has cherished, will allot him a despised corner in the ranks of writers who have insulted humanity, will attribute to him the qualities of the characters he himself has depicted, will strip him of heart and soul and the divine flame of talent. For that court of contempo-rary judgment does not recognize that equally wondrous are the lenses used for viewing suns and for revealing the movements of insects unob-servable by the naked eye; for that court of contemporary judgment does not recognize that a great deal of spiritual depth is required to illumine a picture taken from a despised stratum of life and raise it into a pearl of perfection; for that court of contemporary opinion does not recognize that lofty, rapturous laughter is worthy to stand alongside a lofty lyri-cism and that a whole gulf divides it from the affected posturing of a fair-ground entertainer. (VI, 133–134)

It is the desire for a lofty lyricism, baffled and diverted, that produces a kind of comedy which has too loosely been said to bor-der on or overlie tragedy. Thus Gogol's comedy at its most char-acteristic may stand to the world of his heart's desire as a photo-graphic negative, in which all the bright spots show up as black and only the rhythm—the mysterious, varying, perfect tact of his narrative units—gives evidence of the lyricism that he has transfig-ured not for purposes of parody but in obedience to an obscure inner prompting, a powerfully ambivalent mixture of love and contempt.

The word "love" is another red herring in traditional Russian writing on Gogol. He himself used it with some frequency, partic-ularly after 1836 when he embraced comic writing as a mission, and sympathetic critics at the time and since have recurred to the word as a way of insisting on a positive aspect often denied him. What is at issue, of course, is love not as a biographical experience but as an impulse perceptible in the text, and here the best formu-lation is, again, Annensky's when he speaks of Gogol's "ecstatic love for existence—not for life, but precisely for existence."[25] The distinction is crucial: Gogol's primary attachment is a travesty of Spinoza's *amor intellectualis,* a love that motivates the close obser-

vation of miscellaneous and insignificant things and finds its justification by transmuting them into art. As such it is parodied in the
fragment, "Semyon Semyonovich Batyushek," used in
"Shponka," confessed in "Old-World Landowners," incarnated in
Akaky Akakievich—and commented upon at the very center of
Dead Souls, in that most personal of authorial digressions which
opens Chapter 6 and introduces the theme of time into the novel.

In that passage Gogol recalls how every new place, however
drab, used to reveal "a great deal that was curious" to his "chil-
dishly curious glance": "Nothing escaped my fresh, subtle attention, and thrusting my nose out of my traveling carriage I would
gaze at the never-before-seen cut of some frock coat, and at
wooden boxes with nails, with sulphur gleaming yellow in the distance, with raisins and soap that could be glimpsed through the
doors of a vegetable shop together with jars of dried Moscow
sweets; I would gaze as well at the infantry officer walking alongside, translated from God knows what province into this local te-
dium, and at the merchant in his Siberian caftan flashing by in his
racing carriage, and I would pursue them in thought into their
paltry life." Now, however, such sights inspire only indifference,
"and what would in previous years have awakened liveliness in
my face, laughter and endless talk, now glides past and my motionless lips preserve an apathetic silence. Oh my youth! Oh my
freshness!" (VI, 110–111).

"Freshness" (*svežest'*) is a word that occurs periodically
throughout Gogol's text. It denotes a condition—openness to inspiration, creative capacity—which is exclusively reserved to the
author, the very ground of his existence as such. When the authorial digressions shift from the public's ability to understand
what he has done to his own continuing ability to do it, they signal
the only consequential drama in the book—an interlinear one.
Hence the relevance of those confessions of uncertainty which dot
the manuscripts.*

The lament over the passing of youth and freshness thus par-

---

* In Chapter 10 one of the nodal passages that connects Chichikov's progress
with Gogol's and with humanity's contained in draft the following italicized
words: "How many times, led by a sense vouchsafed from heaven, have [people]
nonetheless contrived to stumble and veer off to the side, contrived in broad day-
light to land in impassible thickets . . . [and] reach the edge of an abyss, only

ticipates simultaneously in two contexts—the drama of authorship and the antidrama of Chichikov's adventures—making its appearance doubly appropriate in the chapter that introduces Plyushkin. With Plyushkin, time enters the narrative. What we are told about the earlier lives of Manilov and Korobochka makes clear that time is not a constitutive factor there. But Plyushkin is shown to have *become* what he is, not a "dead" but a deadened soul. Gogol details the process and discusses it in monitory terms ("To such insignificance, pettiness, vileness could a man sink! could a man so change!! Does all this have verisimilitude? All this has verisimilitude, all this can befall a man"; VI, 127). A rejected draft shows even more explicitly the awareness that troubled Gogol and was intended eventually to save Chichikov: "He had forgotten that he was already at that fateful stage of life when everything turns more sluggish in a man, when he needs to be constantly roused lest he go to sleep forever." He was oblivious, Gogol notes, to the way a person beginning to age "is insensibly and almost imperceptibly taken over by the vulgar habits of society . . . which at length so encumber and envelop him that no self remains in him, but only a heap of conditionings and reflexes that belong to the world. And when you try to break through to the soul, it's no longer there" (VI, 691).

Bringing time into the novel—through Plyushkin and through the biographical sketch in the last chapter that puts Chichikov, too, on the level of becoming—brought cause for mortal apprehension in the artistic sense as well as the moral. Gogol's fateful error lay in accepting and repeating Pushkin's remark that his gift was for "divining a man" on the basis of a few observed traits. It was never that. Accuracy (as the few examples show) was never in question; the gift alluded to was for *creating* a plausible and amusing portrait, one more gratuitous item in the collection of what he came here to label as dead souls. His genius lay always in eccentric but lifelike attribution—a kind that tempts one to add "expressionist" to the other anachronistic labels (symbolist, surrealist, absurdist) that fit his work better than any current in his

---

then with horror to ask each other: 'Where is the way out? Where is the road?' *And the lofty soul becomes miserable, overcome with illness . . . and the tears are ready to gush forth"* (VI, 210–211; 833–834). A comparable note appears even more clearly in the opening lines of the first chapter of Volume Two; see below, p. 233.

own time. So long as Chichikov remained an enigmatic vehicle for this process of creation and exhibition, he served his author's genius perfectly by sharing Gogol's freedom of arbitrary movement at the expense of the static population of his book. Indeed, Chichikov's very quest for nonexistent merchandise that would, all the same, have an impact in his world parallels Gogol's quest to render an absence that would, by the force of the rendering, change the historical consciousness of his Russia. Both aim at "creation out of nothing," the literal dead souls of the title being at once a pretext and a pre-text—as were the lyrical digressions, in Gogol's view. "The full meaning of the lyrical hints," he declared, could be grasped "only when the last part comes out" (XII, 93).

It may well be, as one Russian critic cruelly observed, that Gogol's last act as a great writer was to burn the sequel to this book shortly before his death.[26] By so doing he left a monument to his own ambivalent feeling for existence—immutable, fragmentary, pregnant with an undeclared meaning, and made precious by the demonstration that "the word for a thing may be more precious than the thing itself." For, as Sinyavsky has pointed out, it is not things that Gogol makes attractive but only his redeeming and transfiguring account of them.[27] If the pleasure of the text is "value shifted to the sumptuous rank of the signifier," *Dead Souls* provides it in the fullest measure.[28] That explains Gogol's twentieth-century appeal; we are most comfortable with texts that are paradoxes and puzzles. At the same time, it explains the novel's earlier appeal and influence. As an entity at once polished and open-ended, *Dead Souls* brought together in literary form a flux of attitudes and tendencies, sights and sounds—the raw material of an unborn national self-consciousness. Fixing that flux between the covers of a book, Gogol made it an object of contemplation, and Annensky was right to see something portentous and heroic in this. "What would have become of our literature," he asks, if [Gogol] alone and for all of us had not shouldered that burden and that torment and immersed in fathomless physicality our still-so-timid language . . . ?"[29]

At this remove in time and space, we might alter the stress, noting the extent to which the deeply subjective medium that holds the pieces of this mosaic holds them fast. Ideas cannot be disengaged and discussed outside the unique form that gives them their being as literary ideas. Thus the profound truth of Gogol's claim that he never sought to be a mirror of the reality around him. In the last chapter of *Dead Souls* a view of the bleak Russian plain appears to prompt a question ("Russia! What is it you would have of me? What ineffable bond mysteriously connects us? . . . What does this boundless space prophesy?")—but the view, obeying the peculiar laws of Gogolian space ("The mighty expanse awesomely enfolds me, having been reflected with fearsome power in my very depths"), is really a vision, and at one with the question. The palpable miscellany of the book has coalesced into an abstraction, which can be questioned only rhetorically. The famous final paragraph consists almost entirely of such questions, most of them, strictly speaking, senseless: a phantom interrogation of a phantom symbol. What more fitting close to a novel that demonstrates with unprecedented brilliance the power of form without content and action without resolution—a work that finally does invite comparison with Cervantes' in the subtlety of its comedy and the depth of its symbolism, mimicking the emptiness of life no less resourcefully than the *Quixote* had mimicked life's fullness?[30]

8

Confronting a Public, II

The appearance of *Dead Souls* in mid-1842 inaugurates a new confrontation of the writer with his public, as fateful as it was complex. For six years Gogol had done nothing to appease the expectations of his admirers, who lived on rumors and hope; during his visit to Russia in 1839, as one reviewer of *Dead Souls* noted, he had disappointed those admirers by publishing nothing at all. Now he redeemed that long silence with a work that dwarfed his past performances and at the same time looked to the future for its full achievement. "There are still two large parts ahead," he had announced in the closing pages, "and that is no trifling matter." To his friends he was less restrained: the first part was "only the rather pale threshold of that great poem which is abuilding in me and will solve at last the riddle of my existence" (XII, 58). It was natural in the circumstances that *Dead Souls* should overshadow the almost simultaneous publication of his *Collected Works,* which sum up his progress to date as an artist and—though no one could have known it at the time—mark its end.

THE *Collected Works* were partly a financial enterprise, partly a revision of previously published pieces, partly a supplementary accounting for the years of silence.[1] *Evenings on a Farm* reappears unchanged, out of nostalgia. The essays of *Arabesques* are omitted, saved for a later volume on literature and art. Fragments of the youthful historical novel are marshaled to lend bulk, along with fragments from the unrealized play *Vladimir of the Third Class. Mirgorod* appears intact, save for the thoroughly rewritten and expanded *Taras Bulba,* its earlier crudities of expression (but not of conception) smoothed over, the epic narration more subtly modu-

lated (to reflect, *inter alia,* his study of the *Iliad*), and the patriotic
Ukrainian emphases changed to Russian in line with his new preoccupations.[2] "The Portrait," as noted earlier, now makes a different point, becoming an esthetic manifesto, though not much more
successful as a story; and the Petersburg cycle is rounded off with
the addition of "The Overcoat." Alongside these works the unfinished novel, *Rome,* appears. It is Gogol's tale of two cities, in which
a fragmented and superficial Paris (seen almost as a French Petersburg, secular and wholly soulless) is contrasted with a movingly
faded Rome, blessed by art and nature and so representing a value
for the "dweller of the north." Gogol's friends were ecstatic about
it. Botkin found an "extraordinary likeness between the color and
manner of Bryulov and the language and color of Gogol"; Pletnyov thought it "a wonder," which, if translated, might produce
"a high estimate of Russian literature." The technical achievement,
however, is surpassed in many of Gogol's Russian fictions, the
narrowly thematic only duplicates what is available elsewhere in
his fictional and epistolary texts, and if there is cause to remember
Rome as such, it lies in the way Gogol's image of Paris anticipates
the hostility toward modern Europe articulated by Tolstoy and
Dostoevsky two decades later.[3]

The final volume is devoted to dramatic works. It traces the
parabola of Gogol's theatrical experiments[4] and shows the extent
to which these both paralleled and were absorbed by the evolution
that culminated in *Dead Souls.* Sandwiched between *The Inspector
General* and the manifesto first drafted in response to its reception,
"After the Play," are *Getting Married* and—under the rubric of
"Dramatic Fragments and Separate Scenes, 1832–1837"—his one-
act play, *The Gamblers,* together with the surviving fragments of
Vladimir, offered now as one-act plays. These last—the first in
order of conception—point, as Gippius notes, to a kind of "intermediate genre between drama and narrative prose." They were included, presumably, to lend bulk to the volume.[5]

More substantial is *Getting Married.* Subtitled "An Utterly
Improbable Event in Two Acts (Written in 1833)," it is in fact the
realization of a project that dates from that year ("The Suitors")
but one that was written between *The Inspector General* and *Dead
Souls,* incorporating some of the experience gained from the
former and some of his plan for the latter.[6] On the one hand a brilliant exhibition of solipsistic impulses toward marriage as repre-

sented by the four enthusiastic suitors, it is on the other hand (and centrally) a disturbing comedy of reluctance, whose protagonist Podkolyosin ("Under-the-Wheels") offers a reprise and elaboration of Shponka's hesitations; to the bewilderment of spectators who thought that only a marriage could complete a comedy, Gogol's bridegroom escapes just before the last curtain by jumping out a second-story window. The psychology here is suggestive but unfocused. The prospect of matrimony, Podkolyosin insists, is strange: "I've always been an unmarried man, and now I'm suddenly to be a married one" (V, 18). It is as if he were contemplating not wedlock but suicide, a hint that remains undeveloped, leaving Podkolyosin to take his place among the typical personages that people Gogol's world whose psychic gestures are too primitive to allow motivation.[7] In any case, Gogol regarded him as "obviously less significant than Kochkaryov" (XII, 122–123), the friend who almost bullies him out of bachelorhood. The latter is a manipulator for the sake (it seems) of manipulation, an appallingly (but aimlessly) energetic liar and improvisor whose full significance was to become evident only when he appeared in the pages of Gogol's novel as Nozdryov. Here his presence threatens to overwhelm the theme announced in the play's title without quite managing to supplant it; a slight adjustment and the comedy might be no less resonantly and ironically called "Friendship." As it stands, what *Getting Married* lacks in clarity of focus it makes up for in the inspired absurdity of its near-expressionistic blur.

The Gamblers, by contrast, moves like clockwork. Completed in 1842, this foray into the world of professional cardsharps may be another byproduct of the creation of Nozdryov. Aside from the opening exchange, in which a new arrival is reassured that the hotel management "takes full responsibility" for any flea or bedbug bites (V, 65), there is none of the usual expansive absurdity here, but only a knowing economy in the depiction of what we have come to call a "sting." The action and the professional expertise on which it rests are all: among Gogol's writings, successes and failures alike, this is the least Gogolian—a perfect but impersonal piece of stage machinery about how a characterless confidence man is deftly swindled. The trick rests on false identity, but nothing here escapes the characters' own intentionality, and the suggestive doubleness so common elsewhere in Gogol's works is replaced by mere clever duplicity; there is no appeal of any kind to the spectator's emotions. Best seen as an expert but minor entertainment, it was praised as such by the most prudent of the reviewers in 1843: "If we understand a vaudeville to be not a play that is animated by a single idea but rather the presentation of a dramatic incident, then *The Gamblers* offers an exemplary (all the more exemplary, being the first) vaudeville taken from purely Russian life."[8] Gogol himself seems to have endorsed such a view when he insisted to the actor Shchepkin that this was not a comedy but simply "a comic scene" (XII, 129).

The volume collecting his dramatic works shows Gogol withdrawing his major ambition from the stage after his single, almost accidental masterpiece. Drama had first attracted him as one of the many forms in which he might prove his talent as a writer; later, when he was seeking a *role* as a writer, the theater took on a new appeal as the place where one might precipitate out of anonymity an actual micro-society. But that involved unreliable collaborators; books, he concluded, could do the same thing without mediation, and on a larger scale. "My works differ from those of others," he wrote an unknown correspondent in mid-1842, "in that everyone can judge them, all my readers without exception, because the objects are taken from the life that circulates around each one" (XII, 82). The stage, in short, helped him discover a goal which he then chose to pursue through another agency. That is why the longest piece in the last volume of the *Collected Works,* though cast in dialogue form (and often compared with Molière's "Critique de *l'École des femmes*"), was in no circumstances to be staged. It would be "indecent," Gogol said (XII, 122)—thereby acknowledging that the form was purely arbitrary. "After the Play" was meant to be read and pondered. As the concluding article not only to this volume but to the whole collection, Gogol found it particularly important and demanding painstaking work" (XII, 104). Originally sketched in 1836, it was now to be made "a bit more ideal" (XII, 84). Conceived as a catalogue of responses to his work, "After the Play" dramatizes "the position of the comic writer in society" as the author of *Dead Souls* now saw it (V, 137).

The Author, whose monologues open and close the piece, stands in the foyer of the theater where his new comedy has just opened. Fame and applause no longer move him as they would have done seven or eight years ago; it is the individual, immediate critical responses that he seeks to overhear as the crowd disperses: "I need that: I am a comic writer. All other genres and sorts of writing are subject to the judgment of a few; only the comic writer must submit to the judgment of all . . . O, how I wish that each [spectator] would point out my shortcomings and vices to me!" (V, 138). Instead, he confronts the kind of shortsighted reaction that his play had inspired in audience and actors alike (and that he anticipated with respect to his novel): complaints that the language was coarse, the depiction onesided, the observation inaccurate; that "our social sores should be concealed and not exhibited"; that there should be characters to admire, love intrigue, a real plot; that such works express negative feelings and show no evidence of having been born of "a lofty love for humanity"; that a man of letters is "the emptiest of men," "good for nothing"; that anyone could have written such a farce. Elements of what Gogol took to be a proper understanding, however, also find expression. The ideal moral orientation is shown by one Very Modestly Dressed Man, who proclaims the percipience of "the simplest eye, if it is not clouded with theories and ideals plucked out of books" (V, 146). It is he who answers the objection voiced so often to Gogol's work: "People are quick to ask the question: 'Can such people really exist?' But when was one ever seen to ask the question: 'Am I myself really free from such vices?' Never, never!" (V, 147). In his town, he adds, not all the officials are of the honest sort: "Several times already I have been on the point of quitting the service; but now, after seeing this performance, I feel refreshed"; it has given him "new strength to continue my career" (V, 143).

That is the kind of usefulness Gogol was increasingly to hope for from his writing. Here, however, the main emphasis is on asserting and elucidating the artistic value of his kind of writing. Against expectations of a conventional, private intrigue as the basis for comedy, the Second Devotee of the Arts makes Gogol's case for comedy as a "social and popular creation," citing the authority of Aristophanes (V, 143). It is time to retire the hackneyed model that has love interest as its unchanging mainspring: "Is there not more electricity nowadays in rank, financial capital, an advantageous marriage, than in love?" he asks. "The initial plot situation should embrace all the characters, and not just one or two; it should touch what agitates, to a greater or lesser degree, everyone on the stage. Each is a hero here; the course and movement of the play shakes the whole machine: not a single wheel should remain rusty, as it were, and not contributing to the action" (V, 142). Though positive and lofty feelings, love among them, may enter comedy, they are dangerous: "Everything that makes up the expressly comic side will then pale, and the significance of a social comedy will inevitably vanish" (V, 143). Does this mean, one bystander objects, that the object of comedy "must without fail be the low?" In that case, comedy must be condemned to relative triviality as a genre. The answer to this summarizes Gogol's new credo, reinforcing what he had written in Chapter 7 of *Dead Souls:*

> For the person who looks only at words, and does not concern himself with their sense, that is so. But cannot the positive and negative in fact serve the same end? Cannot comedy and tragedy express the same lofty idea? . . . Does not all this accumulation of baseness, deviations from the laws and from justice, clearly imply what is required of us by the law, by duty, and by justice? . . . In the hands of talent everything can serve as an instrument toward the beautiful, if only it is guided by the lofty idea of serving the beautiful. (V, 143–144)

To the frequent complaints that many of his works show not a single sympathetic character, Gogol now has a new spokesman explain:

> But if even one honest character were included in the comedy, and included in all his attractiveness, then the whole audience would go over to the side of that honest character and forget entirely about the ones who had just been frightening them. Then perhaps these images would not continually haunt them like living beings at the end of the performance; the spectator would not carry away a melancholy feeling and would not exclaim: Do such people actually exist? (V, 161)

The Author's own closing monologue sums up his designs on his audience and demands on his art. Praising the sharp good sense of many of the comments he has here attributed to representatives of "the clear, sound Russian mind," he nonetheless deplores the fact that no one noticed the one positive personage in his work: "That honest and noble character was—*laughter.*" The abstractness of the language here should not be allowed to pale the significance of the point being made, which is that the very instinctive ability to respond properly to Gogol's negative ideality is an earnest of awakening spiritual citizenship in that potential Russian society which Gogol himself dimly foresaw, but which existed sufficiently a few decades later for Korolenko to declare his homeland to be not so much the Ukraine or Russia but "first and foremost, Russian literature."[9] Gogol's celebrated hatred for *poshlost'* is a hatred for insensitivity, spiritual death–in–life, for which his diagnostic test was always esthetic. The links between his key concepts of Russianness, spirituality, esthetic receptivity, and comedy may seem weak in places, but he built his Weltanschauung in this period and, one may say, staked his life on the unity he thought they formed.[10] "No, a good, positive (*svetlyj*) laughter can be laughed only by a deeply good soul." The ones who can dismiss the works of a Shakespeare (or, by implication, a Gogol) as mere "entertainments" are the ones who cause him alarm—counterparts of his own creations: "My soul ached when I saw how many unresponsive, dead dwellers there were right here, in the very midst of life, awful in the unmovable cold of their souls and the barren desert of their hearts . . . 'Entertainments'! . . . But the world would doze off without such 'entertainments,' life would turn shallow, men's souls would be covered with mold and slime" (V, 170–171).

Esthetic susceptibility unites audience and writer in a higher design, at once secular and spiritual. The hyperbolic emphases of Gogol's scheme, like its arbitrary connections, are instructive:

O, may the names of those who pay sympathetic heed to such "entertainments" remain forever sacred in time to come. The wondrous hand of Providence was constantly over the heads of their creators. Even in times of trouble and persecution all that was most noble in their nations stood first of all as their defender: the crowned monarch protected them with his royal shield from the height of his inaccessible throne. (V, 171)

The simplest thing that can be said of this weird statement is perhaps also the most important: it shows the writer conscious of his loneliness, avid not for reassurance but for support. The factual parameters of that loneliness are discussed below; the point here is that the *Collected Works,* completed just after the first volume of *Dead Souls* and published at almost the same time, concludes with a document that looks forward to a new phase in the process of working out a model of the Russian writer in the nineteenth century.

THE NEW PHASE is marked by an active concern with the effect of his works in and on society. No longer simply prescriptive, the effect is seen as potentially practical; he is writing about as well as for his readers, which means that the author must take readings as he goes. He has entered into *a new relationship with his reader.* "I know in advance," Gogol writes in mid-1842, "what will be printed about me in this journal and that, but the opinions of people who are deeply practical, who know life, who have much experience and much intelligence, who have turned all these things to advantage, are more precious to me than bookish theories which I already know by heart" (XII, 82).

He was thus no longer able to practice that indifference to the contemporary which he had proclaimed as his goal some years before—as he seems to have realized, even as he resisted the realization. For the 1840s were a bewildering time, in Eikhenbaum's summary "a time of philosophic circles, the development of a new 'intelligentsia,' a time of theories and criticism . . . of people with a complicated spiritual life and even more complicated conversations about it—people with 'fates' but without 'biographies' —a time of 'reflections'; of emotional crisis.* In literature it was a time of hesitation, at least up to 1846–47" when Turgenev and Dostoevsky evinced a new flowering of Russian prose, and Gogol himself made his last, scandalous appearance in print.[11] Of all this Gogol—who had pictured Russia as a troika in full career—was aware, but he preferred to the historical notion of development the static one of deviation from a fixed norm of social health: "You look around," he wrote in the fall of 1843, "and in place of one thing you already find another: today the Hegelists, tomorrow the Schellingists, after them again some other *ists* . . . Such is the striving of society to be some kind of *ist* or other. Mankind is racing headlong, no one stands in place. Let it race, if need be. But woe to them who have been posted to stand unmoving by the fires of truth if they let themselves be carried away by the general movement—even if with the aim of bringing to their senses those who are racing along . . . Not the refutation of the transient but the affirmation of the eternal is the work of many to whom God has vouchsafed gifts out of the ordinary." The personal motivation appears in his warning that if one of the latter should "take to himself everything that is contemporary, he would lose that state of emotional tranquility, without which our self-formation is impossible" (XII, 214).

This need to work undistracted by fashion explains the violence with which he reacted to a casual statement of Annenkov's,

---

* *Nadryv*, later a favorite word of Dostoevsky's. Nabokov usefully refers to this untranslatable term as "that spasm of the soul."

to the effect that the transitional nature of the times all but pre-
cluded any activity that might affect posterity. "Only the evil
spirit could have insinuated the thought that you are living in
some transitional age," he writes. "I cannot tolerate all sorts of
opinions about our age and times, because they are all false, because they are uttered by people who are irritated with something,
or aggrieved" (XII, 298). That was in 1844; by the spring of 1848
Gogol himself was complaining that the transitional character of
the times was paralyzing his work.[12] The story of these painful
years is the story of his inability either to ignore or to embrace the
contemporary.[13]

An undercurrent of interest in the current literary scene nonetheless runs through the letters of this period, almost surrepti-
tiously. Even as he tends increasingly to write what Annenkov
calls pastoral letters to most of his friends, he remains the shrewd
professional writer in his vigorous and obscenity-laden correspondence with the poet Yazykov. "Your report on the state of current
literature," he tells him in the fall of 1844," is as true as it is, alas,
unconsoling, but in the first place it was ever thus, and in the second, who is to blame? Everybody has known for a long time that
the Petersburg writers are ****, and the Moscow ones ****" (XII,
362). "We have an older generation of writers," he writes soon
after, "masters only at depressing young people, but without the
intelligence to set them to labor and effective work. How can so
little concern have been shown up to now with investigating the
nature of man when that is the chief source of everything! . . . [Among recent university graduates] there is hardly a
single businesslike and productive talent! Even the [Slavophile
journal] *Moskvitjanin,* which has been coming out for four years
now, has failed to add a single shining star to the literary horizon!"
(XII, 444–445).

By 1846, however, he is expressing a strong interest in reading current writers, who "always have a stimulating effect on me"
(XIII, 52). He has read Nekrasov's collection *The Physiology of Petersburg* (1845) and Dostoevsky's *Poor People* in the *Petersburg Miscellany* (1846; XIII, 66). He finds a heartening number of significant, if not brilliant, prose writers on the scene (VIII, 424–425),
and seeks to acquaint himself with "the present school of writers
who aspire to portray and civilize Russia" (XIII, 211). But his
concern in all this remains focused on the reading public:

This year [1847] it will be particularly necessary for me to read almost
everything that comes out at home, especially journals and all sorts of
journalistic gossip and opinions. What has almost no value for a literary
man . . . for me has value as evidence of people's intellectual and psychic condition. I need to know with whom I am dealing; every line,
whether sham or not, reveals a part of a person's soul; I need to feel and
hear those to whom I am speaking; I need to see the public in its particularity . . . For that reason anything that bears the stamp of the contemporary Russian spirit . . . is equally needful to me; the very material
that I would previously have thrown aside with repugnance I now must
read. (XIII, 160)

The paradox is that Gogol's continuing improvisation of an
identity and role as writer should have required a reengagement
with the contemporary, even as the main action was becoming
more deeply internal and as his "capacity for any authentic (*živoj*)
literary productivity" increasingly threatened (VIII, 422). The
period after *Dead Souls* is in fact a tragicomedy of errors, dominated by the mutual expectations, illusions, and reactions of the
writer and his public.

THE FIRST practical confrontation came in the response to *Dead
Souls*. Awaited for so long, it quickly became the object of heated
discussion in both capitals, provoking the sort of "stir in literature
and among the Russian public as had not been seen for a long time
in either."[14] If it was true, as Dahl had declared a year before, that
everyone loved Gogol and there were, where he was concerned,
"no parties among readers,"[15] the fact remains that different readers loved different Gogols. Many deplored his ever having abandoned the manner of *Evenings on a Farm* and were far from ready
to sympathize with his continuing evolution. Thus his friend Prokopovich reported that "the whole younger generation is wild
about *Dead Souls,* while the old folks repeat [the opinions of] *The
Northern Bee* and Senkovsky . . . Between delight and bitter hatred . . . there is absolutely no middle ground."[16] Prokopovich
congratulated the author on that, citing the remark of one officer
—inadvertently echoing Sobakevich—that *Dead Souls* was "a
most astonishing work, albeit a terrible abomination."*

---

* The poet Yazykov's sister, a provincial lady, reacted similarly to the novel.
"Apart from vileness," she protested, there's nothing good [in it]"! *Literaturnoe
nasledstvo,* vol. 58 (Moscow, 1952), 536.

The situation in the capitals, in short, resembled that of Chapter 9, where "rumor upon rumor made the rounds and the whole town began to speak of dead souls" until that town, "which had up to then seemed to be dozing, started up like a whirlwind [and] turned out to be bustling, large, and populated in the normal way." These are the very terms of the actor Shchepkin's report from Moscow in the fall of 1842. "Yes," he writes, "talk and controversy continue to circulate around *Dead Souls*. The book has awakened Russia, which now gives the appearance of being alive. The talk about it is measureless. One could fill whole volumes if it were all put down on paper, and that gladdens me. It means: give us a good push and we'll move—and prove by so doing that we are living beings. In this awakening the idea begins to stir . . . that we together with all other peoples may not be devoid of human dignity. But it's sad that it should be so absolutely necessary to push, and that without a push we ourselves are dead souls." [17]

The book's enormous success was, as its author had hoped, an event in Russian cultural life. But it produced more than its share of eccentric reaction as readers hastened to hail the reflection of their own preoccupations in Gogol's text and sought to explain Gogol's enterprise much as the characters of the book had sought to explain Chichikov's. Those who saw only comedy dismayed the author as much as those who saw no comedy at all, for both groups missed the kaleidoscopic mixture of tones that carried the heart of his poetic message.* The most positive reviews were defenses of its artistic dignity and "truth to life"; regrettably but understandably, they had little to say about its internal problematics. Pletnyov stressed the originality of the enterprise and the "perfection of execution," but was led by his enthusiasm for the liveliness of the language to find an objectivity that allegedly made readers cease to suspect the author's "presence in places

---

* See the report of Alexandra Smirnova, who was close to the author in these years: "Why the soul expresses its feelings in one or another fashion is known to God alone. This question, of course, troubled Gogol himself. A lofty Christian at heart, he knew that our model, Christ the Savior, never laughed. So it is easy to understand what he felt when he saw that Chichikov, Sobakevich, and Nozdryov produced only laughter—mixed with revulsion . . . in people of the highest tone, and [only] in the small circle of his admirers mixed with delight at the artist." A. O. Smirnova, *Zapiski i dnevniki, vospominanija, pis'ma,* ed. M. A. Cjavlovskij (Moscow, 1929), p. 316.

where he, as narrator, is found to be present"! Pletnyov notes "the constant effect of comic beauty"—but his emphasis is largely on the noun.[18] Shevyryov, acknowledging that an esthetic critique must emphasize "not *what* the artist has chosen [as object], but *how* he has brought it into being," praises without analyzing the book's humor, irony and fantasy, to support the view that "Gogol is the only one of our writers who has remained faithful to his mission . . . firmly and steadily serving art and living only for it."[19] Belinsky, too, fell in with this tendency to see the novel in terms at once general and partial. In 1835—with the evidence of "The Nose," *The Inspector General,* and "The Overcoat" still to come— he had already perceived the essence of Gogol's work as "a comic animation, always in process of being overcome by a profound feeling of melancholy and dejection." Now, while professing equal admiration for Gogol's ability to portray reality and for his "subjectivism," he soft-pedals the latter, limiting it to the lyrical digressions, which he cites at length. "Not in a single word of the author's did we observe an intention to make the reader laugh," he writes: "everything is serious, calm, true, and profound." Predict- ably enthusiastic, he continually promised a long review that never materialized, and it remained for Chernyshevsky in the decade after his death to put Belinsky's fragments together in his *Sketches of the Gogol Period in Russian Literature.* Instead, he poured his pas- sion into polemics, first of all with Konstantin Aksakov, who had published an intemperate encomium of *Dead Souls*, taking Gogol's epic intention as accomplished fact and ranking him on that basis with Homer and Shakespeare. In the ensuing controversy, needless to say, Gogol's text figured only as pretext for a skirmish in the developing battle of Slavophiles versus Westernizers. Annenkov, who was close to both writer and critic, states the matter clearly in his memoirs:

This novel opened up to criticism the only arena in which it might take up the analysis of societal and social (*obščestvennye i bytovye*) phenomena, and Belinsky held fast to Gogol and his novel as to a godsend. He seems to have regarded it as his life's calling to treat the content of *Dead Souls* in such a way as to preclude the assumption that it contained anything other than an artistic picture, psychologically and ethnographically faithful, of contemporary Russian society . . . [His] task consisted principally in trying to drive out of the literary arena forever both the preposterous, wily, and self-serving detractors of Gogol's *poema,* and the enraptured well-wishers who failed to descry its true purport.[20]

This attitude had its variants among all those who were prepared to acknowledge the rare artistry of Gogol's novel. Talk
about realism was inevitable—and not only because of the stagger-
ing detail and the bracing colloquialism of the language. Apollon
Grigoriev later set the matter in perspective with the observation
that "Gogol's works are faithful not to reality, but to a general
sense of reality in contradistinction to the ideal."[21] For the time
being, however, Gogol had raised the question of the current state
of Russian life so forcefully that those who responded to it tended
to forget that it was a question, ignoring the terms of the presentation and, as the young Samarin observed, "arbitrarily creating for
themselves a content" that the author had been at pains to withhold.[22] In all the excited talk about the interaction of art and life,
Samarin alone seems to have understood that Gogol's real achievement lay less in getting so much Russian life into the novel than in
making his novel so central a fact of Russian life: "I think that from
the possibility of a purely artistic work's appearance in our time,
from a new fact in the world of art which cannot be denied, one
can draw a conclusion about life itself." At certain times in history,
he explains, the artist who takes his subject from the life of his
people can represent it

only as a negation of what has been, or as the absence of what will
be . . . Poetry becomes the exposure of the present . . . And if amid
this life a poet . . . reflects all the phenomena of that life, the most ridic-
ulous, trivial and obscure, and creates out of them not a satire but a *poema*
like *Dead Souls,* then we should receive it as the most obvious and incontestable earnest of life . . . The single enormous and irrefutable fact of
the elevation of this life into the world of art . . . fills the soul with
hope and strengthens us for . . . our difficult pilgrimage.[23]

This much and no more Gogol had intended to provide, evidently trusting that readers would wait patiently for the positive
indications he meant to offer in the succeeding parts of his novel.
Thus he was dismayed at the haste with which incipient ideo-
logues made bold to attribute their own views to his work. "You
are all we have," Belinsky wrote him in 1842. The "we" must have
made him wince, though the position as "sole hope for the future
of Russian literature" was one he had courted. His situation was
that of the sorcerer's apprentice: the forces he had mobilized were
threatening to exceed his control. It was not long before he added
the first part of his novel to the lengthening list of his dissatisfac-

tions, professing "no love for my works written and published up to now, and *Dead Souls* in particular." The real subject of his novel, he kept stressing, remained a secret, "and the key to it, for the time being, in the soul of the author alone" (XII, 504).

FOR SOME four years after *Dead Souls* Gogol's progress as a writer proceeds along two tensely parallel lines, to converge with explosive force in his last publications.

The first, largely internal, concerns the continuation of his novel. Annenkov reports as virtually certain the existence of Volume Two in draft at the time Volume One was published.[24] But Gogol, referring to such rumors in a letter of February 1843, reminds his friend Shevyryov that he had never told anyone how much he had ready, and estimates two more years of uninterrupted work as an absolute minimum (XII, 143). In May of 1843 he upbraids Prokopovich for demanding speed and declares that, contrary to rumors, "the second volume is not only not ready for press, it is not even written." Moreover, he suggests, the public despite its clamor may be no readier for the continuation than the author (XII, 187). In October of the same year he hints at difficulties in the writing. The new volume, he writes Pletnyov, will take a long time: "It is hard to hurry yourself "when your implacable judge has already established himself within you, demanding a strict accounting in all things and at every unconsidered impulse forward turning you back. It becomes clearer to me every minute these days how an artist can die of hunger while it seems he is in a position to make money . . . My writings are so closely tied to my own spiritual education and I need [so much of that] . . . that there is no hoping for a speedy appearance of my new works" (XII, 222). In December his words to Zhukovsky imply a fresh start (and so, perhaps, the first of the three burnings of Volume Two): "I continue to work; that is, to sketch out on paper a chaos from which the creation of *Dead Souls* must arise" (XII, 239). He had, he tells his mother in June 1844, originally intended to publish one part every three years—"but that was a human intention, and hence unreliable" (XII, 323).

These themes—testimony to an impasse that was to become chronic—recur with minor variations up to the last burning in 1852. "You ask," he writes Yazykov, whether *Dead Souls* is being written. *It is and it isn't.* The writing goes too slowly and not at all as I would wish it; the obstacles to this come frequently from illness, and even more frequently from my own self. At each step and each line such a desire to be wiser makes itself felt; moreover, the very subject and task are so tied to my own internal education, that I am absolutely unable to get ahead of myself in the writing but must wait for the self to catch up. When I move forward, the work moves, when I stop, it does. (XII, 331–332; emphasis added)

His goal was "an artless simplicity," so that every reader might call *Dead Souls* "a true mirror, and not a caricature" (XIII, 280). Then his *poema* might be "a very useful thing, because no sermon can act as effectively as a series of *living examples,* taken from the very land, the very body, of which we are part" (XIII, 263). "Many aspects of Russian life," he observed justly, "have not yet been discovered by a single writer. I should like people of all parties to say, after reading my book: 'He really does know the Russian individual. Without concealing a single fault of ours, he has sensed our worth more profoundly than anyone'" (XIV, 92).

Tormented by his ignorance of Russian actuality, daunted by the magnitude of the new role he accurately foresaw for Russian fiction, jealous of his physical isolation from the object of all his hopes, besieged by public expectations he himself had encouraged, Gogol pursued his self-education by a kind of correspondence course. He flooded his friends with letters asking them to furnish thumbnail sketches of Russian types ("The Lion from Kiev," "The Provincial *Femme incomprise,*" "The European-Type Clerk," "The Old-Believer Clerk" [XIII, 262]). Alternatively he besought them to keep diaries for his benefit—"say, in words like these: 'Today I heard such-and-such an opinion; it was expressed by such-and-such a man . . .' If he's a stranger, put down: 'I don't know about his life, but I think he's such-and-such; to look at, he's attractive and decorous (or indecorous) . . . he blows his nose this way; he sniffs tobacco thus.' In short, leaving out nothing that the eye can see, from major things to trivial" (XIII, 279–280).

And he asks for reactions, both published and unpublished, to his novel, particularly negative ones, denying that he could "go boldly ahead without looking at any criticisms" (XII, 117); he needed to gauge the public on which he now nourished grand designs. Praise, moreover, seems to have dismayed him because it represented competition over him by rival ideological camps. Annenkov reports him "horrified at the success of his novel among

Westernizers."[25] In the mid-thirties he had courted a public and suffered from the paucity of critical accounts that respected the novelty of his efforts. A scant decade later, he found himself the object of readers too impatient and critics too sympathetic for comfort. Unable to resolve the situation with the next installment of his fiction, he made his difficulties part of his text, turning directly to his readers in 1846 with a simultaneous solicitation and offering. Both grew out of what had been filling his letters to friends and acquaintances; both were astonishing and quixotic.

THE SOLICITATION came in the form of a preface to the second edition of *Dead Souls*. His friend Shevyryov had suggested a second printing as early as the beginning of 1843 but insisted that it include the second volume; hence the plan was deferred (XII, 142—143). By mid-1846 the original printing of 2400 copies had sold out, and a new one was ordered in the same quantity. It appeared at the end of the year, equipped with a preliminary address "To the Reader from the Writer," which opens:

Whoever you (*ty*) may be, my reader, in whatever place you may stand; in whatever calling you may find yourself, whether you are distinguished by high rank or are a man of the simple class, if God has given you literacy and my book has found its way into your hands, I ask you to help me.

Help is necessary because

in this book many things are described untruly, not as they are and as they really happen in the land of Russia, because I could not find out about everything . . . Moreover, through my own incapacity, immaturity and haste [!], there arose all sorts of mistakes and slips, so that there is something to correct on every page: I ask you, reader, to correct me. Do not neglect this matter. However high your level of education and life, however insignificant my book may appear in your eyes, however trivial a matter correcting and writing commentaries on it may seem to you—I ask you to do this. And you, reader of limited education and simple station, do not consider yourself such an ignoramus that you could not teach me something. (VI, 587–588)

From this point on, the fantasy proliferates:

How good it would be, for instance, if even one of those people who are rich in experience and knowledge of life and who know the circle of people I have described would make his observations on the whole book from beginning to end, not omitting a single page, undertaking to read it in no other wise than with pen in hand and a sheet of writing paper in front of him, and after reading a few pages would call to mind his whole life and all the people he had met and all the events he had witnessed and all that he had seen himself or heard from others that resembled what is depicted in my book—or that contradicts it—and described everything exactly in the way he recalls it, and sent me each sheet as it filled up with writing, until the whole book should have been read through in this way. What a vital service he would render me!

The solicitation goes beyond information and comment to embrace a kind of coauthorship:

It wouldn't be bad also if someone who is endowed with the ability to imagine or picture to himself the various situations of people and pursue them mentally in different areas of activity—if someone, in short, with the ability to immerse himself in the thought of any author he is reading, or to extend that thought, would attentively follow each character portrayed in my book and tell me how he should act in such-and-such cases, what ought to happen with him later on (judging from the beginning), what new circumstances might arise and what it might be good to add to what I have already described: All this I would like to take into account against the time when a new edition of this book, in a different and better guise, ensues. (VI, 589)

Even a certain narrative point of view is recommended to the respondent. He should, Gogol suggests, imagine he is writing to someone "incomparably lower than himself in education. It would be even better if, instead of me, he imagined some country bumpkin who has spent his whole life in the sticks, to whom every circumstance has to be explained in minute detail and with whom one must be simple in speech as with a child, taking constant care not to use expressions that are beyond his understanding" (VI, 589–590). In closing, he appeals to "journalists and literary men" —who have been useful to him in the past, "despite a certain immoderation and such enthusiasms as are common to human beings"—not to deprive him of their observations.

This bizarre document is eloquent testimony to Gogol's creative crisis, and it is not surprising that it should have fueled rumors about the shaky state of his sanity. But the psychological aspect is secondary here. The real drama is vocational and literary. A major achievement—as it had a decade before—moves the writer to attempt a new role and new forms, and the attempt now takes place in full public view; thus the rejection (perfectly consistent in view of past performance, though the public could hardly know that) of the manner of the novel he has published. Stylistic embellishment of the kind he had perfected in his best work to date would no longer suffice; his future works would reflect "that truth and simplicity which I have not had, for all the liveliness of my characters and personages" (XIII, 262). It was here, as he now began to learn, that the chief stumbling-block lay.

"I am not a master at prefaces," he acknowledged when he sent off the manuscript: "I have difficulty with that decorous language in which an author must converse with the present-day public" (XIII, 105). Only the last adjective is erroneous; his frequent protestations that he had not changed fundamentally since childhood were true in the sense that he had always had difficulty when he sought to write sincerely. In such cases, from the first, his genius produced Gogolian texts, complete with specious logic and locutions that in their subtle oddity suggested a meaning beyond the ostensible one. He was "absolutely never able," as he confessed in a letter to Shevyryov, "to speak frankly" about himself: "In my words, just as in my writings themselves, there has always existed a terrible imprecision." A middle ground between pomposity and abject humility, both unintended, consistently eluded him (XII, 394–395). In the "language of his soul," the commonest adjectives are "lofty" (*vysokij, vozvyšennyj*), "low" (*nizkij, podlyj*)—and the one that contains them both in its ambiguity: "profound" (*glubokij*).[26] These are his marked categories, the ones with which he could no more deal directly in his fiction than in his nonfiction— but which give resonance by their framing presence to his real province, that of *ne to*.

Now Gogol sought to go beyond indirection. The devil, whose domain had been *ne to*, he now saw as working prosaically, psychologically, entering souls "by the path of laziness, idleness," "so that our abilities not only fail to develop but even become dulled" (XII, 316). Shorn of his mystery, to be exposed he need only be named. So the author need no longer be clairvoyant: "For a long time now I have looked at men not as an artist . . . I look at them as brothers, and that feeling is several times more heavenly and better" (XII, 366).

RELINQUISHING as far as possible the stance of artist, it was as brothers that Gogol sought to confront his readers with the offering of *Selected Passages from Correspondence with Friends*. The subject of widespread rumors even before its appearance in the closing days of 1846, this series of sermons and essays masquerading as familiar letters was unquestionably his strangest book to date—which is only a way of saying that it shows him most radically attempting to supersede his recent achievement by developing yet another variety of authorship. Full of internal paradoxes, however, it quickly became encrusted with external ones.[27] Gogol had written it, as he thought, on the brink of death; unable to speak to or for his reader by publishing the second volume of *Dead Souls,* he would do so now by eschewing indirection and implication. The new book, moreover, would prove that he had remained active even while sick, "although in a different field [of writing]—which is, all the same, my proper field." It would be his "first practical (*del'naja*) book, needful to many in Russia" (XIII, 106). In the event, writing it proved cathartic, setting him up for a return to his novel just at the time when a storm of anger and derision broke over the book. *Selected Passages,* he acknowledged, "resounded like a slap in the face: to the public, to my friends, and, finally and most strongly of all, to myself. After it I awoke as if from a dream, feeling like some guilty schoolboy whose prank has gone farther than he intended" (XIII, 243). His characteristic mistake was to exaggerate the efficacy of intention ("what has issued from the soul cannot but be of benefit to the soul" [XIII, 106])—as if the word were already the deed and the accomplishment.

The temptation to consider *Selected Passages* primarily an expression of Gogol's psychological convolutions and convulsions, then, must be resisted. That approach has its legitimate fascination, as does the attempt to see the book chiefly as an exhibit of Russian religious thought. But both require ignoring a significant portion of the text. The alternative is to begin by recognizing with Gippius that *Selected Passages* is "a purely literary work."[28] Seen in this light, Gogol's last published book takes its place in an entirely logical continuity—in his own writing and in the story of his increasing interaction with the Russian public. Indeed it would not be too much to say that *Selected Passages* has literature as its major subject. Moreover, its fundamental strategy is a characteristic one. It is in large measure self-referential (about itself and how it is written), and the actual tendency of the writing diverges regularly and disconcertingly from the conscious intention the same text signals.

Partly this is so through inadvertence. The essentially Gogolian manner persists unbidden—in the reference to "A Farewell Tale" and often in phrasing: "I bequeathe . . . but I just remembered that I no longer have the right to dispose of this" (VIII, 222). Stylistic oddity has its larger counterpart in the ubiquitous advice on practical matters, which betrays an abiding uneasiness over unambiguous expression. "O, believe my words!" he had exclaimed in a letter, "I myself do not dare to disbelieve them" (XI, 347); here the counterpart may be represented by the closing lines of the letter on "What a Governor's Wife Is": "Just because everything in my letter is scattered and without logical order, read it through five or six times . . . It is necessary that the whole essence of the letter remain in you, that my questions become your questions and my desire your desire; that every word and letter pursue and torment you until you fulfill my request in precisely the way that I wish."[29] Such strangeness reaches its apogee in the article "To a Russian Landowner," where the gaps in logic constantly afford glimpses of the old—and now quite unintended—Gogolian irony:

Is it hard to bind a Russian to oneself? He can be so bound that afterwards you'll think of nothing but how to unbind him from yourself . . . Set about the job of a landowner properly . . . First assemble all your peasants, and explain to them what you are and what they are. That you are a landowner over them not because you wanted to give orders and be a landowner, but because you already are a landowner, were born a landowner, and because God would call you to account if you were to exchange that calling for another, because each person must serve God in his place and not in someone else's: and that by the same token they, also having been born under [your] authority, must submit to that authority . . . because there is no authority that does not come from God. And at this point show them the Gospels, that every last one of them may see all this. Then tell them that you make them labor and work not because you need money for your pleasures, and as proof burn some rubles right there in front of them, so that they may see in fact that money means nothing to you. Work zealously but a single year, and the whole thing will start working by itself, so that you won't even have to lend a hand. You'll become rich as Croesus. (VIII, 322, 327)

In a caustic review, N. F. Pavlov developed precisely this point, noting that *Selected Passages,* like Gogol's earlier works, contained "wonderful characters, scenes full of life and truth":

Oh, if only we could tear them out of your book and translate them to the sphere of art! Even the Will and Testament could be transferred to a novel or story. It might belong to a character in the full bloom of health and suffering needlessly from one ailment alone—the desire to produce an unprecedented effect! . . . And that "Woman in Society," who, taking her mentor at his word that people are waiting in every corner of the world for nothing but the dear sound of her very own voice, begins to seduce people to virtue, begging each of us with an imploring glance, wordlessly: "Please, become better" . . . Or that other who, to school herself in firmness of character, divides the money from her yearly income into seven little piles . . . —and who, once she had done this, even if you were dying in front of her, would go beg alms from someone else's pocket but absolutely refuse to take anything from one of her piles! . . . Finally, that landowner who teaches his peasants the truth of the Gospels with the thought that this is the surest path to wallowing in gold, the one who shows them the Holy Scriptures . . . and yet who says on occasion, "Ach! you unwashed snout" . . . *These are stories, novels, dramas; these are the brothers and sisters of the Manilovs, the Korobochkas, the Inspectors-General.* How much freshness and truth there might be here![30]

Though he declared that "the higher the truths, the more one must be careful with them" (VIII, 231), Gogol could not be careful enough; only a mediating irony—rejected here on principle—could make his concern with the highest truths viable. Hence the failure of his turn to metaliterature when his designs on the reader (and he believed that "half of literate Russia" would read this book) were avowedly practical. When he spoke of communication from soul to soul he had in view a kind of shared vital awareness, purposeful and patriotic, sensible and Christian.[31] But this was something he could only prepare. Tolstoy and Dostoevsky would later find expressive forms for the belief that any transformation of Russia had to begin "directly with the self, and not with any general cause" (VIII, 107)—the one embracing his conscious aims as the other did his passionate deviousness. As for Gogol's own form here, Merezhkovsky likened it to what one might expect from Chichikov if he were to go insane and turn to Christianity; Aksakov's wife compared the author of *Selected Passages* to Tartuffe.[32] The intuition in both cases is, as it were, an extension of Pavlov's: giving up the freedom of a creator, Gogol took on that of a fictitious character. One might say that in these hortatory letters he exchanged the position of Cervantes for that of Don Quixote.

The exchange, though, by no means ruled out a certain tendency to mythopoeia, the residue of his fiction-making. Contemplating Russia, he found the times out of joint, everything characterized by *ne to,* nothing functioning properly or in its proper place. Too many Russians, he wrote a correspondent in early 1846, are hard to talk with because "they still have not chosen a field of activity and are, for the time being, on the road or at a station, but not at home" (XIII, 35). In the stronger terms of *Selected Passages:* "Everything in Russia has now come unstuck and unlaced. Every individual has turned into garbage and a rag; he has made himself into a base fundament for everything and a slave of the most empty and trivial circumstances, and nowhere is there any freedom in its true sense" (VIII, 341). "Peter cleared our eyes with the purgatory of European enlightenment, put all the means and instruments for the job into our hands, and yet our expanses remain just as empty, desertlike, melancholy, and unpopulated, everything is just as shelterless and unwelcoming around us, as if we were not yet at home in our own country" (VIII, 289).[33] "The present age has fallen into a heroic sleep" (VIII, 278). "Every true Russian feeling is going to seed—and there is no one to evoke it! Our valor slumbers, our resolution and courage to act slumber, our firmness and strength slumber, our minds slumber amid the flaccid and womanish society life which empty and trivial innovations have foisted on us under the name of enlightenment" (VIII, 281). The images vary, but they have in common the sense of some fairy-tale enchantment.

In dispelling the enchantment, example—both moral and literary—can play a key role, for the task is not a process but a metamorphosis:

How can everything be returned to its place? In Europe this cannot be done: it would overflow with blood . . . In Russia there is a possibility; in Russia this can be achieved imperceptibly—not by any innovations, overturnings or reforms . . . In Russia any governor general can set this in motion in the area entrusted to his care—and how simply: just through his own life. By the patriarchal character of his life and his simple way of treating everyone he can dethrone fashion with its empty rituals and strengthen those Russian customs which are in fact good and usefully applicable to our present-day way of life. (VIII, 364)

"Be a patriarch," he had advised the Russian landowner. The assumptions here are reactionary and utopian, as they were bound to be, given a social ideal (harmony) that is fundamentally esthetic. In light of this, it is not surprising that he should find a model for his own "holy work" and "saving exploit" in "the most perfect work of all the ages," newly available and freshly influential—the *Odyssey,* as recently translated by Zhukovsky. In the essay he devotes to it, Gogol foresees an enormous influence on Russia, "*on everyone*

in general and *on each in particular*" (VIII, 238). At a time when readers have ceased "either to be enchanted or disenchanted", the appearance of "a work that is harmonious in all its parts" carries exceptional importance; superior to the original in its Russian guise,
the *Odyssey* "precisely at this time will strike [the reader] with the
majestic patriarchal nature of ancient life, with the plain uncompli-
cated working of the social order, the freshness of life, the un-
blunted childlike clarity of humanity" (VIII, 243). The *Odyssey*
will "recall much of the beauty of early life which, alas, has been
lost but which mankind must repossess as its legitimate heritage . . . In the meantime many things from those patriarchal
times—with which there is such an affinity in the Russian nature
—will spread unseen across the face of Russia. Through the fragrant mouth of poetry there is imparted to souls what can't be got
into them by any laws or any power!" (VIII, 244).

Homer's work, needless to say, has been Christianized, Gogo-
lized and moralized into a conscious social blueprint—proving, as
Shevyryov thought, that Gogol had not read the *Odyssey* clear
through (though he adds that even here one finds "sparks of excellent ideas").[34] The fact is that Gogol is seeking for the first time to
supply a basis for his criticisms of the present, an ideal by which to
justify *ne to*—the implicit charge that underlay most of his imaginative writing to date. In essence *ne to* signifies varieties of displacement: things are not what or where or as they should be; parts
usurp the function of wholes; expectations are baffled. The ideal,
therefore, must be harmony, unity, wholeness—and on a scale as
vague and hyperbolic as the attacks on its absence. This logic had
already appeared fleetingly in his texts in the ecstatic descriptions
of female beauty, the rapturous evocations of the power of art, and
the related solemn gesturing toward the inexpressible. Now it is
made central and, as it were, practical: "It seems to everyone these
days that he could do a great deal of good if he occupied the place
or post of another, and that he is only unable to do it in his own
post. This is the source of all our evils" (VIII, 225). But such simplistic reasoning can bear sustained and serious scrutiny no better
than its obverse, for both are more a matter of intuitive projection
than of cognition or judgment—primitive rationales for a certain
angle of vision and not themes as Gogol now sought to present
them.

As issues crystallized and the temper of Russian intellectual life turned increasingly ideological, many readers found Gogol's very terms repugnant. Thus a Petersburg reviewer proclaimed the book a literary auto-da-fé, and Belinsky's friend Botkin rejoiced at its widespread condemnation, which he regarded as a sign that there was a "direction in Russian literature from which a talent even stronger than Gogol's cannot deflect it; Russian literature took what it pleased from Gogol, and it has now thrown him away like the shell of an egg that has been eaten."[35] This cynical remark typifies the passions aroused by *Selected Passages,* which found their most eloquent expression in Belinsky's *Open Letter to Gogol,* full of angry disillusionment with the man he had cast in the role of one of Russia's "great leaders on the path toward consciousness, development and progress." This, paradoxically, was a role to which Gogol had not hitherto aspired; Belinsky's argument is that it was nonetheless inevitable, since "only literature, despite the Tartar censorship, shows signs of life and progressive movement" in expressing the developing forces of Russian society: "That is why the writer's calling enjoys such respect among us . . . The public . . . sees in Russian writers its only leaders, defenders and saviors."[36]

The confrontation is historically fateful. It marks the triumph of that social concern which was to dominate Russian literature for the remainder of the century. Gogol had presented his confused and patently reactionary recipes for meeting "the problems with which society is presently concerned" (VIII, 215) in the guise of a legacy; Belinsky had responded with what Herzen accurately saw as "a work of genius, and, evidently, his [own] testament."[37] Each now regarded literature in the light of its putative effect on a broad and exclusively Russian readership. Both sought immediate and practical means in the printed word toward a vaguely conceived, "authentic," and better Russia. But Belinsky—like Chernyshevsky, Dobrolyubov, Pisarev, Mikhailovsky, and so many others after him—asked of literature how it might provide ammunition for *institutional* change in Russia. Gogol—like Dostoevsky, Goncharov, Tolstoy, and Chekhov after him—looked to literature as a psychological and moral agency, an essentially personalistic instrument of what might legitimately be called consciousness raising, in the belief that a better society, being "a coalescence of individuals," would at length "take form of itself" (XIII, 443).

The times had changed radically since Gogol's last confrontation with his public five years before; cultural discourse was now politicized, and literary debates had much more than their ostensible objects in view. Belinsky's very letter to Gogol, his disciple Chernyshevsky hinted, may have represented no more than a temporary, tactical necessity.[38] Gogol, sensing the change, could only see it in rhetorical terms: "There is a certain gift of overstatement, a certain uneasiness in our time. People's heads are not in place" (XIV, 82). He sought to remain above the battle—Apollon Grigoriev observed that no one had yet approached the Slavophile-Westernizer controversy more dispassionately—but his singular eminence as literary presence would not allow this. For all their importance in Russian cultural and intellectual history, the specific points of disagreement between Gogol and the contending parties, Slavophiles and Westernizers alike, must not be allowed to obscure the larger fact: *Selected Passages* signals Gogol's exclusive commitment to writing about contemporary Russia and the spiritual state of the contemporary Russian—a task in which he saw himself, quite correctly, as without predecessors or rivals. The success of that commitment, small in any direct sense, is of less significance than the very fact that it was taken on.

Shevyryov explained the widespread anger at the book as the natural reaction of those from whom Gogol had "withdrawn the support of his name"[39]; this was undoubtedly a factor, and not only among the Westernizers. Everyone had his image of Gogol—as exposer of social abuses, as proponent of traditional Russianness, as light-hearted joker, as tutelary genius of the so-called natural school of younger writers—which is to say that Gogol as writer was increasingly being enlisted by others, for purposes quite alien to his own, in the game of cultural politics (a fate that pursued him even posthumously).[40] *Selected Passages* is, among other things, his declaration of independence. In May 1846 he had noted in a letter that Karamzin "was the first to show that the writer's calling is worth sacrificing everything for, that in Russia a writer can be entirely independent" (XIII, 61); in the book the emphasis is shifted tellingly: "Karamzin was the first to show that the writer can be entirely independent among us, and equally respected by all as the worthiest citizen in the country . . . What a lesson for us writers!" (VIII, 266–267). The independence Gogol sought was crucial to the role he coveted—and for which he felt uniquely qualified; this was nothing less than that of administering a kind of secular act of communion. Repeatedly he emphasizes the practical value of literary characters and images if only they are drawn "from our material, from our land, so that each [reader] will feel that this is something taken from his own body. Only then will he awaken, and only then can he become a different person" (XIII, 224).[41] Blocked in his effort to produce such an art, he pursues its goal through exhortation here. But he does more: he both advocates and seeks to prepare the ground for it: fully two thirds of *Selected Passages,* as it first appeared, was devoted to the theme of literature.

In these essays Gogol defends the function of the Russian writer and the uses of literature—as if responding to his own call of ten years before that writers take up criticism to educate a public and help fashion the institution of letters in their time. With respect to the public, he advocates readings from the Russian poets and defends the theater as "a pulpit from which much good can be spoken to the world" (VIII, 268); the aim is didactic only in the most general sense, the proximate emphasis being on the power of art to lift audiences out of themselves. There is more than a hint here of Tolstoy's later notion of art as a contagion of feeling, and Tolstoy was later to echo Gogol's concern with writing that might be accessible to readers of all classes. Small wonder that the sage of Yasnaya Polyana, preparing his own treatise (after having flirted with a similar renunciation), should have found that Gogol "says, and says beautifully, what literature should be," adding that he was only "trying with all my strength to say what Gogol said wonderfully about this in *Selected Passages.*"[42] The connection is all the more worth noting as a vindication of Gogol's attempt to marshall and extend a great tradition in Russian letters.

To that effort he devotes the longest and most clearsighted essay in the collection, "What Ultimately Is the Essence of Russian Poetry, and in What Its Peculiarity Consists." The subject had long preoccupied him; three times before he had attempted it, only to burn the result. Now he saw it as central, "essential to my book" (XIII, 110). Construing poetry as serious verbal art in general, he finds room in his historical tracing—perhaps the most perceptive and nuanced to date—for the prose of Pushkin (whose *Captain's Daughter* is "decidedly the best Russian narrative work") and Lermontov (whose prose he finds unequaled for "correctness, beauty and fragrance"). The aim of the essay is to characterize the distinctive features of the most noteworthy Russian artists, from the mid-eighteenth to the mid-nineteenth century, thus preparing an assessment of the relation of Russian literature to society. His appreciations are shrewd and far from tendentious, his conclusion —that a usable tradition exists, that the expressiveness of literary Russian has been progressively refined, but that it has not yet managed "either to teach society or to express it" (VIII, 403). Literature as an elite enterprise has "only gathered into a heap the innumerable shadings of our various qualities"; nowhere has it "fully expressed the Russian individual" in his ideality or in his actuality. Yet that is what he sees as the order of the day. Clear-sightedly and non-prescriptively he notes that "neither Pushkin nor anyone else should stand as a model for us: different times have already come" (VIII, 407). And he closes with a prophetic vision of a new Russia that a new literature "will draw out of our very selves and then present to us in such a way that every last one of us, whatever our differences in upbringing and opinion, will exclaim in a single voice: 'This is our Russia; we are sheltered and warm in it; we are now really at home . . . and not in a foreign land'" (VIII, 409).

The complaints about the lack of a Russian literature, so common a scant fifteen years before, are clearly outdated. Gogol now senses that its flowering is at hand, and defines with a rare prescience the qualities it would show and the role it would play. Whether he himself could participate actively in this process after having done so much to prepare it was still not clear; but *Selected Passages,* quite as much as the stalled continuation of *Dead Souls,* shows him seeking to do so. A new word is needed, and not "the soulless repetition of what is already well known" (VIII, 231). Comic writing has served its purpose; it has united an audience, revivified and democratized the literary language, broached large questions. But in the process it has led to a state where "everyone among us is laughing at everyone else, and there is within our land itself something that laughs equally at everything" (VIII, 404). Something like the Arnoldian "high seriousness" is now required; that is the burden of his essay "On the Nature of the Word," where he insists that "words must be handled honestly," being "the highest gift of God to man." "It is dangerous," he declares flatly, "for a writer to fool with words" (VIII, 231–232).

However surprising this declaration may seem from the creator of Akaky Akakievich and Captain Kopeikin, it testifies less to apostasy than to the continuing development that had consistently made him disavow each major achievement in favor of the promised one that lay ahead. (That is the sense of Grigoriev's sympathetic observation—echoed at the time even by the young Chernyshevsky—that "standing always higher than his creations, [Gogol] also stands higher than this correspondence."[43]) And it is evidenced in "Four Letters Concerning *Dead Souls*"—Gogol's first attempt to explain this development and justify his current situation *to his readers*.* His chief quality as a writer, Gogol declares there, was sensed only by Pushkin, who defined it as the gift of forcefully exhibiting all the vulgarity and vacuous triviality of life. From this gift came the achievement of *Dead Souls,*

which so intimidated and produced such a commotion within Russia— not because it revealed any . . . internal ills and not because it presented any stunning pictures of triumphant evil and suffering innocence. Nothing of the sort. My characters are by no means villains; were I to add a single good quality to any of them, the reader would be reconciled with all of them. But the vulgarity of of the whole intimidated readers. What intimidated them was the fact that each of my characters is more vulgar than the last, that there is not a single consoling phenomenon, that there is no place for the poor reader to rest for a minute and catch his breath, so that after reading the whole book it seems as if he has come out of some stuffy cellar into the fresh air . . . The Russian was intimidated more by his insignificance than by all his vices and shortcomings. A remarkable phenomenon! An excellent fear! Whoever feels such a powerful revulsion from the insignificant must surely contain everything that is opposite to the insignificant. (VIII, 293)

Here are the grounds for turning to a different manner in the succeeding volumes (but also for considering the first volume an unconventionally finished work): Gogolian comedy had rendered its national service by provoking an appetite for its opposite.

The logic is clear, but it depends on a notable omission: Gogol takes no account of the self-justifying, independently valuable functioning of his *art*. He treats it purely as a means toward an end. And this involves him in further confusion: "One must take into account," he writes apropos of his having burned the manuscript of Volume Two, "not the enjoyment of certain devotees of literature and the arts, but all the readers for whom *Dead Souls* was

---

* Such an attempt is not the least of the book's novelties; it offers a model on which Dostoevsky was to ring variations in his *Diary of a Writer,* and Tolstoy in his *Confession.*

being written . . . There are times when one must not speak about the lofty and the good without at the same time showing, clear as day, the pathways to it for each individual" (VIII, 298).

The confusion here arises from assuming that the work of art does no more than conduct a message from writer to reader. No longer an opaque thing, created by the one and recreated by the other, belonging exclusively as experience to neither, the work of art now appears to function only outside the realm of art, connecting the individual who writes with the individual who reads: a matter of concrete biographies. Such a view ignores precisely that temporary escape from biographical self which characterizes the process of writing and reading alike.[44] To dwell on its naiveté is unnecessary, and beside the point. The motive at work is a desire for simplification, of a kind that Tolstoy was later to admire and dramatize in his own more effective fashion. For Gogol at this point, the esthetic and the self-indulgent are all but equated; the gratuitous is suspect, moral consciousness alone validates or condemns.* One might well say that he was aspiring to work a "disenchantment" on himself as on his Russia—seeking to awaken from the dream of art into the practical historical world. The paradox is that Gogol had purchased his identity as a writer by foregoing, to a quite improbable extent, stable biographical identity: evasion gave him his central principle (*ne to*) and produced that free-floating irony which became his hallmark. Seeking to "awaken" from this state meant renouncing the core of his genius as he had manifested it up to now; at the same time, continuing to write meant drawing, willy-nilly, on the same unconscious sources to produce a familiar grotesquerie.

Selected Passages faithfully if unintentionally mirrors this dilemma. Where the logic is impeccable, the premises are dubious; where the premises are sound, the logic may be suspect; where both premises and logic seem reliable, their applicability to any extratextual reality may be questioned. The tangle is impossible to sort out. All the astonishing vagueness, the hyperbole, the simultaneous concealment and confession, the arbitrary assumptions in these letters on *Dead Souls* show ominous signs of solipsism and

---

* "The writer's duty is not simply to furnish pleasant exercise for minds and tastes; he will be called strictly to account if his works do not generate some benefit to the soul and if nothing remains of him by way of exhortation (*poučenie*) to people" (VIII, 221).

personal pathology. The remarkable confession that "all my recent works are the history of my own soul" (VIII, 292), the presentation of his earlier writing as a kind of exorcism or therapy, the blurring of the boundaries between himself, his readers, and the abstract Russia that unites them—all testify to a tragic confusion, even as they offer a fitful illumination of his art. Unrecognized, that confusion had served as the matrix for writing that was offered as enigmatic, with the key deferred. When he sought to eliminate it, to provide the key—to achieve self-transcendence—Gogol could only paralyze the source of his creativity.* The generally negative reaction to his new book merely compounded that paralysis by prompting a series of increasingly tortured self-justifications, in which he explained the book alternately as a provocation, a probe, a test of readers, an essay in self-awareness, a lesson to impatient admirers who kept trying to push him into premature publication. Ultimately, however, one clear truth stands out. The devil may have "inflated certain places monstrously," but the book remains, as Gogol claimed, a "legitimate and proper stage" in his evolving sense of the writer's high calling—and of the kind of art a changing Russia required.

Along with high seriousness, this art would be marked by "that fidelity and simplicity which mine has not shown, notwithstanding the liveliness of the characters" (XIII, 262); it would "lead the reader to a greater knowledge of what a Russian is" (XIV, 40); its images and characters "would serve forever as a lesson to people, though no one would call them ideal, feeling rather that they have been taken from our own body, from our own Russian nature" (XIII, 370); and it would speak to "precisely those questions that present-day society is revolving around" (XIII, 293). That, as it turned out, was to be the work of the next generation— but it is worth noting that Pletnyov (who had introduced Gogol to Pushkin only fifteen years before) was moved by *Selected Passages* to anticipate the advent of "a new literature, authentic, vitally needed, on the model of that which I descry in Gogol's letters." European annalists, he declared, would date Russian literature's appearance in the world from this book.[45] Gogol himself, in his

---

* Compare Sinyavsky: "Just at the time he becomes a caricature, the comic element deserts him" (*V teni Gogolja*, p. 286). This seems to put the cart before the horse.

reply to Belinsky's attack, betrays an interesting sense of a new age in Russia that threatens to supersede both of them: "The age at hand is one of rational consciousness . . . it weighs everything, taking all sides into consideration . . . It would have us look about with the many-sided gaze of an elder, and not show the hot impulsiveness of a knight of past times; we are children in the face of this age" (XIII, 361).

Gogol's metaphor is suggestive. The new age of realistic literature had in fact been prepared by young men (Pushkin died at thirty-nine, Lermontov at twenty-eight, Belinsky himself at thirty-seven, and Gogol at forty-two). Its actual creation, by contrast, was the work of men we are likely to think of as bearded elders: Turgenev, Dostoevsky, Tolstoy, Goncharov—all of whom lived and worked at least into their sixties and realized collectively the baffled intention which Gogol alone among the artists of his generation had formulated and proclaimed. In that sense, his faith was justified that although his last book "is not, in itself, a major work of our literature, it can give rise to many major works" (XIII, 243).

Selected Passages is the last term in the chain of improvisations that constituted Gogol's identity as a writer. With it the "riddle of his existence" is completed—not resolved, but confirmed. He did continue to write, but his efforts went increasingly into nonartistic projects, some of which were announced for publication though none was to be delivered. Of paramount interest in this connection is "An Author's Confession" (drafted as "The Tale of My Authorship"). The work is in fact a hybrid—part tale, part confession—drafted to redeem the fiasco of *Selected Passages* through clearer explanation. The tale seeks to explain the logic of his development as a writer, the confession to explain his artistic gifts and his changing attitude toward them. Neither is comprehensive, and both bear the marks of his current procrustean preoccupations.

Gogol sketches his career with amazing vagueness, placing all the emphasis on motive and intention. There are no specifics, no sense of the nature or variety of his accomplishment. He portrays his earlier works as a mixture of self-amusement and therapeutic exorcism, a kind of random, unconscious creation appropriate to "youth, a time when no questions come to mind" (VIII, 439, 454). The only works named are the ones he attributes to Pushkin's influence—*The Inspector General* and *Dead Souls*—for these alone were dignified by conscious designs. To be "responsible" in Gogol's view could only mean to be guided by such intentionality. But to be so guided was to invite paralysis; Remizov was right when he observed that in inspiring Gogol, "Pushkin poisoned him with his mind" and that "the poison took effect after Pushkin's death."[46] Gogol reports how *Dead Souls* began, characteristically, as an improvisation:

I simply thought that Chichikov's amusing scheme would lead me to a variety of persons and characters; that my own desire to laugh would, of itself, create a multitude of comic occasions, which I intended to interlard with affecting ones. But at every step I found myself stopped by questions: Why? To what end? What should be the meaning of such-and-such a character? Of what should such-and-such a phenomenon be expressive? . . ? How can one soar in imagination—assuming one has it —if at every step reason puts the question: "Why?" (VIII, 440, 453)

So Gogol found himself obliged to forswear the only kind of art at which he excelled—until such time as he might control, direct, or transcend it.* Where his earlier masterpieces had been content to leave the question open—and even, as in the ending of "The Nose," to flaunt it—he now goes on to illustrate the truth of Maurice Blanchot's dictum: "The answer is the misfortune of the question."[47]

Persisting nonetheless beneath Gogol's final attitude toward his writing is a belief in its potentially dangerous, quasi-magical power:

If even [*Selected Passages*], which consists of no more than reasoning, produces (as has been alleged) delusions and disseminates ideas that are even false; if from those letters, as has been said, entire sentences and pages remain in one's head like living pictures—what would have happened if I had come forward with the living images of a narrative composition instead of those letters? I myself sense that I am stronger in that area than in reasonings. As it is, criticism can still dispute me, but in the other case it

---

* Compare the opening lines of Volume Two of *Dead Souls:* "Why keep depicting wretchedness, and more wretchedness, all the imperfection of our life, digging up people from the sticks, from the remote corners of the realm? But what is to be done if that is the writer's nature—if he, sick with his own imperfection, is unable to depict anything except wretchedness, and more wretchedness, and all the imperfections of our life, digging up people from the sticks, from the remote corners of the realm? And so, here we are again in the sticks, in a remote corner again" (VII, 7).

would scarcely have had the power to refute me. My images have been seductive and would have stuck so fast in [readers'] heads that criticism could not have dislodged them. (VIII, 457–458)

This hypnotic merging of author and reader is more than an article of faith; it too has its developmental logic. Near the end of "An Author's Confession," Gogol exclaims, as if inadvertently: "How it happens that I should be entering into explanations of all this with the reader is something I myself cannot understand" (VIII, 463). The answer is simple enough: his designs on himself and on his reader were now inseparable. Only appropriate reader response could validate the new self. Yet readers had been reproaching him with "pride, [excessive] assurance, arrogance, ignorance of [his] audience."[48] Hence the increasing vocational doubts: "I cannot say with certainty whether the writer's calling is my calling" (VIII, 438). "In answer to those who ask reproachfully why I opened my inner storehouse to view, I can say that all the same I am not yet a monk, but a writer" (VIII, 444). Since publishing *Dead Souls*, he declares, "I have bent all my efforts toward remaining in my field and have tried to think up all sorts of means to advance my work, without even dreaming of abandoning the writer's calling" (VIII, 448–449). The very desire to publish this account bears out these words—and makes the final decision to withhold it all the more portentous. "It is probably more difficult for me than for anyone else," he notes with a candor that cannot be doubted,

to renounce being a writer, when that has constituted the sole object of all my intentions, when I have abandoned everything else, all the best enticements of life and, like a monk, have cut my ties with everything that is dear to man on earth in order to think of nothing but my work. It is not easy for me to renounce being a writer [when] some of the best moments in my life have been those in which I finally put down on paper what had long been gestating in my thoughts, when I am even now sure that there is hardly a pleasure higher than that of *creating*. But, I repeat again, as an honest man I should put down the pen, even if I felt an urge to write.

I don't know whether I would have the honesty to do this if my ability to write were not taken away, because, to speak frankly, life would suddenly lose all its value for me, and not to write would be tantamount to not living. (VIII, 458–459)*

* So, alongside continuing work on *Dead Souls*, he struggles to yoke his own self-education with that of his readership—through writing of a different kind.

Seen in this light, the final burning of his manuscript for *Dead Souls II* five years later suggests that Gogol may have chosen the most original (and the most symbolically appropriate) of all suicide weapons.

The psychological drama of his last years is intensely moving, not least because it carries a meaning that goes beyond the individual. The poignant record of the decade after *Dead Souls* is a mirror image of the previous decade. Then he had groped to become a writer, now he struggled to remain one. Gogol's has been called "the tragedy of a genre", but it is even more clearly the tragedy of a vocation.[49] Count Sollogub, a contemporary, identified it as such:

[Gogol] suffered long . . . from his impotence before the demands of the literate Russian public, which had chosen him as its idol . . . *He broke down under the weight of his calling,* which had, in his eyes, taken on enormous dimensions . . . He died from an internal struggle, while Pushkin died from an external one . . . Pushkin could not bear his fancied humiliation; Gogol could not bear his actual greatness. Pushkin could not withstand his enemies; Gogol could not withstand his admirers . . . Both tried to find around themselves a real point of support, a general sober view of the relation of art to life and of life to truth. There is not yet a place, there is not yet a broad sphere in Russian life for real artists.[50]

He drafts a "Textbook of Literature for Russian Youth"; works on a new "Dictionary of the Russian Language"; compiles notes on ethnography, on agriculture, on peasant life; plans a new collection of his theoretical essays "on literature and art and what should animate our literature," to be drawn from *Arabesques* and *Selected Passages;* and writes his "Meditations on the Divine Liturgy," which end by stressing—in terms that parallel those of his late secular aspirations—the socially unifying power of the word.

PART IV

The Surviving Presence

———

To understand an artist it is essential to see that constant which is invariably present in his creations and lies beyond "story," "plot," "manner"—behind all the forms in which his time exacts its tribute.

P. M. Bitsilli

9

The Gogolian Universe: Notes Toward a Theory

As a writer Gogol was deeply if eccentrically a man of his time. The time defined his opportunity, set its limits, and imposed a particular set of meanings on his creation in accordance with its own preoccupations. Later times, differently preoccupied, have approached that work from different angles and discovered other meanings in it. That is one of the signs of major writing, and it involves what is often called metaphorically the identification of an author's "world," whose identity can be established analytically. Usually this is a matter of transposed psychology, anthropology, and sociology, of tracing characteristic thematic patterns in a given body of writing to discover what is probable, possible, and impossible there as lived experience—and to indicate how, why, and with what effect. Two categories of experience are in question: the characters' and the reader's.

Gogol's writing, however, seems to baffle such an enterprise. It is too various, too fluid, too fragmentary. Hence it may be more appropriate to speak of a Gogolian "universe," something at once larger and more primitive than a world: an entity more susceptible of observation than of definition, a dynamic system of relations and tendencies, where things are and are not themselves (matter and energy, space and time), and where the creator's design is matter for conjecture. Such an analogy has the further advantage of compelling the investigator to realize how provisional his terms must be, how insufficient any single perspective. And its very hyperbole respects by reflecting what is a central feature of the object of study.

To fit Gogol's work, the common terms of literary criticism require qualification so extensive as to amount to reconstruction;

with many of the older ones, the effort is by now clearly excessive. "Realism," for example, is more prescriptive than descriptive in Gogol's case, despite the fact that his protagonists could hardly be more ordinary, their ambitions more mundane, their physical surroundings less conventionally poetic or more intimately a part of their being; for hyperbole swamps any realistic tendencies when simple narrative arbitrariness does not unhinge them. Strakhov saw this one hundred years ago: the main mistake of those who regarded Gogol as a realist lay in their directing all their attention to "the object of representation, and not to *the way* it is represented."[1] Still less useful is the term "romantic." Gogol's text unquestionably relates to that amorphous movement, but in ways that may be more enlightening to the investigator of romanticism than to the investigator of Gogol's achievement.[2] "Grotesque" is —or was—another story. Applied to his writing early in this century, it has proved useful by making central the idiosyncrasy of that writing. "The grotesque"—an adjective promoted with dubious legitimacy to the status of a noun—signals an interference of series: an unresolvable dualism of narrative attitude toward what is being presented, an arbitrarily shifting scale of magnitude (physical and semantic), and so a provocation to the reader. Its increasing acceptance in Gogol criticism—even in the Soviet Union—marks the welcome supersession of older labels, but "grotesque" itself may now be ready to be superseded, for it seems unable to go beyond registering a crucial difficulty in making sense of Gogol's art.

Among more generic terms, "satire" and "humor" have their obvious areas of relevance and no less obvious insufficiency. The aggression of satire is certainly prominent in much of the post-Dikanka work; and the Petersburg Tales, like *Dead Souls,* worry with unflagging derision the vices of vanity, complacency, obsession with rank, and propensity to gossip. But the aggression in question goes beyond these traditional targets. Gogol's text ridicules the great majority of the characters who appear in it—not for particular failings but for a radical cretinism ("insignificance") whose source is in the text's source and not in society or nature. The usual instrumentality is thus inverted: characters and phenomena that do not clearly merit artistic scourging nonetheless serve as pretexts for a presentation whose artistic merit is self-justifying and unquestionable. So, though identifiable satire cannot be considered the main thing in Gogol, the satirist's stance and the satirist's quasi-magical belief in the power of words, applied to vaguer ends, may be.[3]

A like qualification applies to the humor of most of the post-Dikanka works. Gogol may be playful and inventive in the manner of a humorous writer, but the sympathy of a Sterne or a Dickens vanishes after "Old-World Landowners," and his startling incongruities, like his passages of amusingly gratuitous play, serve an end about which one can say with certitude only that it involves a feeling of superiority in the reader as in the author.* The problem once more risks involving us in nominalism. By the English standards of his time, Gogol's comic writing goes well beyond humor; by the more philosophical German standards, as one of his best Russian commentators has invoked them, it constitutes a supreme example: "Humor, as the opposite of the sublime, annihilates not what is individual, but rather what is finite . . . For humor, no individual foolishness and no individual fools exist, but only foolishness as such and a nonsensical world." Humor thus appears as "the highest achievement of subjective comicality, which

---

* It is this, according to Baudelaire, that makes laughter "Satanic," and the late Gogol, confessing that he had laughed "gratuitously" in his earlier writings, seems to have half agreed with the popular Russian assumption that derision bespeaks sinfulness ("*U nas smex prinimajut za grex, sledovatel'no, vsjakij nasmešnik dolžen byt' velikij grešnik*"; Zhukovsky, letter to Smirnova, 4 January 1845).

In this connection Lotman has pointed recently to a tradition of medieval Eastern Orthodoxy which, he suggests, may well have survived as an influence on Gogol's complex comic creation. Though both the Eastern and Western churches regarded play, theatricality, masks, and disguises as signs of the devil's work, Catholicism institutionalized their use in carnival to provide a catharsis through laughter. In the Orthodox culture of medieval Eastern Europe, by contrast, "the opposite came about: The official view of carnival as a demonic ritual became internalized [so that] the permission to indulge in carnival behavior at specified intervals was connected to a belief that at such times God allowed the devil to run the world." Although carnival participants were indulging in licensed behavior, that behavior did not thereby become any less fundamentally sinful. Thus where laughter in the Western tradition cancels terror, in the Eastern tradition it *implies* terror.

Lotman does not connect Gogol empirically with this tradition, but the parallels are striking: the way Gogolian laughter is never far from fear if not horror; his presentation of the world as diabolical theater; and, most particularly, the tendency of his comic perception to be overcome by seriousness. (See Ju. M. Lotman, "Gogol' i sootnošenie 'smexovoj kul'tury's komičeskim i ser' eznym v russkoj nacional'noj tradicii," in Tartuskij gosudarstvennyj universitet, *Materialy vsesojuznogo simpoziuma po vtoričnym moderlirujuščim sistemam*, I(5), Tartu, 1974, 131–133.)

is present when the person who is manipulating comic ideas at will . . . adopts a contemplative attitude toward the world and attains to a higher cognition of life."[4] This may make Gogol out to be more of philosopher than some would admit, but its stress on his sovereign creative freedom is salutary in respecting the mystery of what that freedom created once time had turned the creation finite.

The more certain of application to Gogol's work, the broader the conventional term must be. So comedy and irony, in their different ways, can best encompass the the anomaly of his achievement. Comedy (or, more properly, the comic) is a broader term than humor—so broad indeed as to constitute a catchall for whatever kind of imaginative writing falls outside the lyric, epic, and tragic modes. As the continuing state of comic theory makes clear, it marks one of the deepest mysteries of literature, part art form and part social ritual. Essentially it represents a licensed holiday from the serious allegiances of civilized life, a vitalistic freedom to play at denying all the constraints, cultural and physical, by which we live. For artist and audience alike, it is a kind of exemption, and though Gogol's art is more than comic, its originality arises from what might be called the traditional comic sanction—a nonexclusionary counterpart to the other literary modes, whose opportunities can only be embraced along with the prohibitions that define them. The comic perspective in Gogol is constantly under threat of being subsumed and made an object of contemplation in its own right (the dumb scene at the end of *The Inspector General,* the reversal of perspective near the end of "Diary of a Madman" and at intervals in "The Overcoat" and *Dead Souls*)—but the comic sanction is primary in presenting the experience which the text may then proceed to reassess. "The playful free spirit of the artist," as Slonimsky observes, "makes comic connections . . . at will."[5]

As for irony, it is ironic that that element in Gogol should still be awaiting its investigator, for it pervades his writing from first to last and marks it on so many levels that one might see him, in Ortega's phrase, as "doomed to irony." Ranging in kind from simple declarative ("Ivan Ivanovich is a wonderful man!") through dramatic (*The Inspector General,* "Nevsky Prospect") to romantic ("The Nose," *Dead Souls*), Gogolian irony serves three broad functions. It (1) proclaims the author's creative freedom, by putting off the question of his identity in the texts (compare Fowler's definition of irony as "dissimulation"), and in so doing it (2) turns the question to the creation itself ("Why do writers write such things?"), thus (3) producing an art through which to pose the question of the possibility of art ("creation out of nothing"). In Gogol's universe of concentric ironies, even a clearly decodable instance will promptly be translated to a larger context in which it can take on—or seem to take on—a new and perplexing ironic charge. Phenomena there have blurred boundaries and shifting centers; everything falls short of or passes beyond stable identity in obedience to the universal law of *ne to* (the suggestion that a thing is not what it seems to be, not what it should be, not what you expect). Biely speaks in this regard of "irony without a clear consciousness of the aim of irony"—a phenomenon that underlies the satire *manqué* in Gogol's work (that tendency of style which suggests the aims of satire without in any clear way serving them).[6]

Here is the creating energy of the Gogolian universe, a fundamental *ne to* asserted by a nonbiographical self and made manifest in chains of energetic, eventful vocables. Sinyavsky goes so far as to invoke Gnostic myths about the creation of the world through the laughter of God, and the parallel is less farfetched than it might seem. Gogol's advice to a would-be writer ("If nothing comes to mind, write: 'Nothing comes to mind.'") seems to imply a belief, as Friedrich Schlegel put it, that "words often understand themselves better than do those who use them."[7] In Gogol's view, the verbal artifact could make reality itself seem by comparison "an artificial and caricatured thing" (VIII, 384). Many have noticed the resulting paradox in his text, whereby the complexity of expression and semantic content are inversely proportional, so that significance and even "plot" itself exist in (and not through) the very Gogolian signifiers, masking a virtual absence of the signified. Thus Victor Erlich has concluded that "in this lifeless, stagnant universe, language is the only active protagonist, the only dynamic force, both as a great impersonator of dismal reality and as a major avenue of escape from it."[8] In what sense can this be so?

Russian critics have frequently remarked the importance of sound and rhythmic value in Gogol's text. Biely, the most assiduous analyst of these, credits Gogol with bringing into prose "the whole sweep of the lyric, rendered through rhythms, making his taut lines vibrate like strings to produce the sound of assonances and alliterations."[9] Gogol himself, early and late, praised the "poetry of sounds," which he called "the poetry of poetry" (VIII, 95); he collected local names for flora and fauna precisely for their sound value. The poetic structure of many of his short pieces rests precisely on verbal and subverbal music—"A Terrible Vengeance" and "The Overcoat" might be called narrative tone poems—and key passages of many of his other works show the same feature. Little of this is likely to survive in translation; it would require the gifts of a Dickens or a Nabokov even to suggest it in English. How then account for the continuing (and even growing) appeal of Gogol in the pale English versions that are all we have?

The answer lies in style more broadly conceived[10]; first of all, in the orchestration of voices in narrative and dialogue alike. The extent to which Gogol fashioned a new kind of fictional discourse is still underrated: particular words and turns of phrase, as has long been recognized, function synecdochically, small details standing for large wholes. Recognition of this is usually confined to the referential level—the waists and mustaches that parade down Nevsky Prospect, or the sidewhiskers, three-cornered hat, and sword that make up Ivan Yakovlevich's perception of the policeman at the end of the first chapter of "The Nose." In fact, synecdoche plays a no less important role on other levels—the literary-conventional, the psycholinguistic, the sociolinguistic. When we read in the fourth paragraph of "The Nose," "Horror was depicted on the face of Ivan Yakovlevich," that innocuous phrase starts out of the page as a sharp contrast to the colloquial diction that surrounds it: the voice of a conventional short-story teller has been momentarily introduced as a foil, trailing a whole complex of associated attitudes (toward language, character, event, the reader-writer relationship). Instances of something like *erlebte Rede,* where the narrative uses the words or cadences suggestive of individual or collective ways of thought, are equally common in this text. The images in Gogol criticism of an orchestra (Vinogradov) or a mosaic (Rozanov) are attempts to identify an art of patterned implication, where discrete and disparate elements are yoked to create the illusion of a consistent whole. The power of Gogolian prose is to a large extent in this patterning or juxtaposition.

From it arises the implication—the sense of a fresh and astonishing "vision" and, beyond that, of a serious if elusive poetic message. We do not, of course, turn to Gogol's writing for information on Russia (as Belinsky thought we would), and neither do his Russian readers; what has survived the possibility of topical interpretation is what tempted nineteenth-century readers into such interpretation in the first place: a sense that this writing held some deeply enigmatic authenticity: "artistic truth," which is "the truth of a symbol to the forms of feeling—nameless forms, but recognizable when they appear in sensuous replica."[11]

UNDERSTANDING Gogol, then, must begin with understanding the function of his language. He "broke the language barrier," as Sinyavsky puts it—not by simply *using* the language that Russians speak (or spoke), but by turning to account "his inability to speak in the ordinary way," thereby illustrating the fact that "prose, like any art, presupposes a transition to an unfamiliar language and through this exotic quality assumes a parity with poetry."[12] So mimesis in his works is functionally illusory; the texts may evoke real objects, but the reality to which they testify is ultimately a verbal counter-reality. The Gogolian universe thus has its antimatter (and even its "black holes," which Nabokov was the first to signal); it also has its suggestive concentricities, like solar systems and atoms, in the macro- and micro-structures of event, which may be mimetic happening or speech event, the agencies being respectively human emotion and phonemic interplay.[13]

The peculiarities of this poetic universe, to repeat, demand attention as a corrective to the two partial views of Gogol's writing which have dominated critical accounts to date—and as the ground of their reconciliation. One view seeks the import of the work in patterns of human experience without regard to the eccentric medium in which they exist; hence, for example, the traditional complaints about Gogol's inability to present convincing women or images of love. The other, broadly formalist in orientation, catalogues Gogol's technical devices, as if Gogol's ideal reader were a student in a seminar.

In fact the Gogolian "content" is *in* the form. Such elements of content, conventionally construed, as can be seen without formalist decoding are astonishingly partial and primitive. Character is a case in point. A typical Gogolian personage (Shponka or Kovalyov, Pirogov or Khlestakov, Akaky Akakievich or Sobakevich) amounts to a centerless vehicle for a few attributes—social position, material possessions, habits without origin—filtered through a rudimentary temperament.* No significant past, no aspirations toward a future. Individual actions and reactions are a matter of psychic gesture, the counterpart of the rudimentary and stylized gestures of marionettes; those who act tend to solipsism, being as incapable of present experience as they are unmarked by experience in the past, so that dialogue is seldom meaningful exchange from the speakers' point of view. They either talk past each other or engage in a *folie à deux,* the *folie* on occasion spreading epidemically (*The Inspector General,* "The Nose," "The Overcoat," *Dead Souls*) until a whole society is behaving like a collective Gogolian personage, with rumor as the motivating and characterizing agency.[14] Patterns of relationship in Gogol thus need not and generally do not involve consciousness; they are habitual to the point of being mechanical, or superficial, or mysterious (as in "Viy"). Hence the rarity of significant experience, the characters as they exist—as they are presented—being, by and large, constitutionally incapable of it. (The few who do become entrapped in the world of experience—Khoma Brut, Poprishchin, Akaky Akakievich—end in death or madness; the meaning of that experience neither impinges on their consciousness nor enters their biographies—though, significantly, it does both for the reader.) So the Gogolian universe contains a simulacrum of life: primitive psychology, primitive experience, primitive themes, all together in their poetic self-sufficiency and semantic incompleteness raising the question of meaning in life and art alike.

These questions are raised *by* more than *within* Gogol's writing, which is to say that his creation depends for its peculiarly limited and intense life on performance in another sense than Eikhenbaum's when he speaks of "The Overcoat": the more the reader respects the idiosyncratic terms of this creation , the more fully it comes to life in him, its odd emphases and even odder lacunae producing the most unsettling responses (Lermontov's definition of a feeling as "an idea in the first stage of its development"

* Gogol described the personages of *Dead Souls* as not simply caricatures, but figures constructed *with the aid* of caricature, out of psychic parts collected from a variety of sources: "These insignificant people . . . are by no means portraits of insignificant people; on the contrary, they are collections of traits taken from those who consider themselves better than others—only, of course, reduced as it were from the rank of general to that of enlisted man" (VIII, 294).

may be particularly apropos here). The reader becomes in effect the instrument upon which the Gogolian music is performed *as well as* the audience for that music. An intense subliminal communication thus takes place between two entities for which we have no name: the shaping psyche (very different from the biographical entity that housed "the author") and the receiving psyche (no less different from the individual who takes the book from the shelf or pastes his *ex libris* in it).

These are not such truisms as they may appear. The shaping "soul" of a Tolstoy or a Chekhov, insofar as it can be discussed, is a very different thing, demonstrably anchored in temperament and cast of mind, and referrable for corrobation to the recorded facts of biography. But Gogol's biography, by his own admission, was textual; and what we can say about his texts can only be corroborated by referring to other texts of his own. His unconscious intuitions do not translate into images from the world of experience like Vronsky's horserace or the death of Ivan Ilyich, but into answering intuitions. That explains the larger-than-usual risk factor in interpretative accounts of his writing, the best of which impose by nuanced assertion rather than by comprehensive demonstration. Here we come close to the sense of the Gogolian claim that everything he had written was "remarkable only in the psychological sense" (VIII, 427). What the author as individual saw as biographical exorcism was actually a kind of expressionism *avant la lettre,* its results remarkable artistically (and not at all morally). His conviction (at the end of his career!) that he had "not yet refined" his style and language (VIII, 427) was only a complaint at the way his soul held fast to its own language and designs even as he sought to subordinate them to conscious intention.

SINCE conventional form itself is a sign of conscious intentionality, the Gogolian universe begins to be constituted only after the Dikanka stories. The writing in them does, to be sure, already show Gogolian traits, but its rationale or sanction comes ready-made from familiar genres: from romantic folk tales, theater, and legend. That is why generalizations about his "essential" writings tend to exclude these pieces or to misrepresent them; and that is why later works that depend on plot seem relatively weak (*Taras Bulba,* "The Portrait," *The Gamblers,* "Rome"), their brilliant passages notwithstanding. "A Terrible Vengeance," in the way the intensity of its symbolic pattern renders the closing explanation inadequate, shows his work beginning to break free. And "Shponka" in its provocative "incompleteness" already exists entirely within the Gogolian universe, which consists of fluid discourse. *Mirgorod* thus is a step forward into artistic maturity precisely because it shows consistent signs of accommodating a psychological regression. What makes these stories Gogol's most intimately expressive is the constant exploitation of the child's point of view, the child's needs and emotions (framed, to be sure, by a shrewdly adult awareness in much the manner of Dickens). Kindly attachment, nurturing and unquestioning, characterizes the old-world landowners, who are proof against any negative complexity much as their estate is proof against any amount of thieving and mismanagement; their virtues are childlike simplicities. The society of the Cossack encampment in *Taras Bulba* is "simply a kind of wild riot of high spirits," its terms exactly those of the "close circle of schoolmates" to which Gogol likens the warriors repeatedly and at length. "Viy" similarly deals with a pair of schoolfellows, concentrating symbolically on Khoma's first and fatal encounter with the mysteries of eroticism. The two Ivans are travestied toddlers. And the "I" whose words open and close the collection, unidentified and unidentifiable, incarnates that protean Gogolian word which establishes his universe and renders the conventionally supernatural henceforth redundant. (For the conventionally supernatural is a kind of explanation of what would be much more mysterious and unsettling without it; the authentically fantastic requires its own kind of "truth, naturalness, and probability" [VIII, 161].) "The Nose" announces the completion of the Gogolian universe and underlines the fact in its closing paragraphs.

There is a natural temptation in the circumstances to work backward, speculatively, toward the biographical sources of what is distinctive in the writing. This has been recently attempted with high intelligence by Simon Karlinsky, as it had before him by F. C. Driessen; but the supposition of a guilty homoeroticism, like the supposition of a classic Oedipus complex, has sharp limitations. Aside from unprovability and the vexed problem of what constitutes fair evidence, the chief of these is that the problem of personality tends to supplant the problematics of art. Extratextual assumptions dominate the case, leading to extratextual conclusions that may enhance admiration of particular advocacies more than of particular writings. The Gogolian universe, it seems fairer to say, models the "soul" of its creator in the radical sense of giving it its only possible perceptible form. For soul, as used here, refers ultimately to that silence out of which the writing originated, the very impulse to creation freed as far as possible from biographical contingency. So for all important purposes (and to a degree unmatched by any writer of his time) the text is Gogol and Gogol is the text, simultaneously compelling recognition and resisting definition.

What is it that we recognize? One is tempted to reply: style, the characteristic Gogolian locutions. The parodies and imitations on record, however, make it clear that this is not quite the case.[15] What we rather recognize is the unique thematic resonance his phrases take on from their participation in the characteristic workings of the larger Gogolian text. By theme here I mean something more fundamental than those recurrent objects of concern—rank, stupidity, greed, moral vacuousness, the famous *poshlost'* itself— all of which may be found in "reality" and in his writings alike. Behind them, organizing the rival reality that is Gogol's poetic universe and expressing only *its* laws, are certain pervasive entities which cannot be reduced to propositional statements. In fact, they manifest themselves textually as dynamic tendencies, modalities of concern, patterns of relationship.* Because they comprise key elements of Gogol's artistic code and because they are not to be confused with themes as usually construed, I propose to use the terms "thema" and "themata."[16]

The point can be illustrated by considering what I take to be a central cluster of such themata. Because they are not in their nature susceptible of direct expression, putting labels to them is bound to be quixotic, and those offered here should be taken as arbitrary, awkward, and provisional. Each of the themata in question forms a whole constellation of smaller themes (in the more usual sense);

---

* The relativity theory that applies to the Einsteinian universe thus has its counterpart in the Gogolian. Like time and space, energy and matter, so technique and theme—or, in more traditional terms, "form" and "content"—may turn out to be functionally indistinguishable. This is always true of literature in some degree, but it has seldom been so radically manifested in prose and never, in Russian, before Gogol. Hence the difficulties encountered by critics who approach his writing with Newtonian assumptions.

their boundaries are vague and they overlap. To the extent that they do constitute a cluster, moreover, it follows that the latter can be read in any sequence with only slightly altered effect. None of its members is clearly privileged. Each in its shifting relation to the others contributes to an implication. For present purposes they will be considered under the headings of Metamorphosis, Evasion, Identity, and Recognition.

Metamorphosis. Sudden change dominates the Gogolian fictions from first to last. In the early stories evil spirits try on forms like actors in a wardrobe room: dogs and evil stepmothers turn into cats, and the devil goes around in human shape. A typical instance shows a Cossack dancing with abandon at a celebration:

But when the captain lifted up the icons, [the Cossack's] whole face suddenly changed: his nose grew longer and twisted to one side, his mobile eyes turned from brown to green, his lips turned blue, his chin began to quiver and grew pointed like a spear, a tusk thrust out of his mouth, a hump appeared behind his head, and the Cossack turned into an old man [!] . . . Hissing and clacking his teeth like a wolf, the strange old man vanished. (I, 245; "A Terrible Vengeance")

In "Viy" an old woman is revealed as a witch, only to metamorphose into a beautiful young woman with "eyelashes as long as arrows," and finally into a blue, pursuing corpse. A minion of the devil prolongs his earthly life by taking the form of a portrait (in the story of that name), leading its possessors to ruin.

All such happenings carry a ready-made and quite sufficient explanation in the supernatural, specifically in traditional notions of Satan as man's adversary. Alternative explanations involving a kind of psychological allegory, though supererogatory, may appear, but never as more than hints or overtones (the incest motif in several of the Dikanka stories, and particularly in "A Terrible Vengeance"). As the Gogolian universe takes form, however, a transposition occurs: what was previously overtone—anxiety, obsession, the logic of dreams and fantasies—becomes dominant, and the still-prevalent metamorphoses now involve supernatural intervention only as an ambiguous, probably figurative coloration (the Mayor claiming that the devil has blinded him, the demon lighting the streetlamps along the Nevsky Prospect, Major Kovalyov's suspicions that he has been hexed). "Viy" is at the center of this shift, the demonic there being so overwhelmingly a psychological phenomenon as to render the falsely explanatory appeal to folklore an artistic mistake. Gogol would have done better to leave the events of the story entirely in the realm of the uncanny—as by a stroke of genius he did in the final version of "The Nose," that supreme fiction of metamorphosis which has been judged to be on a par with Ovid's.

Annensky, who made the judgment, suggestively identifies four distinct transformations of the nose—on the material, social, mystical, and literary levels,[17] thereby providing a rough paradigm of the status and meaning of metamorphosis in the Gogolian creation. The ontological tampering that had previously required the sanction of a devil or a dreamer now needs none. Henceforth the threat of metamorphosis in one sense or another pervades the Gogolian universe (the extended similes of *Dead Souls* show its tug), built into its very fabric by a narrator who is himself protean.

To say this of Gogol's universe is to emphasize its fluid perspectivism. Figurative metamorphosis is everywhere latent alongside the "literal" (the nature of the case requires quotation marks): what a thing is depends on when and how one looks at it, and the text controls both. "The Overcoat" offers the most dazzling example. There the question of how we are to regard Akaky Akakievich rests on the vexed question of what he is, as presented, and presentation itself is a matter of not-quite-congruent views. It has been observed that the comic element in Gogol consists in "a distinctive play of oppositions, or antitheses, between something meaningful and something meaningless," and that these antitheses alternate, "so that one particular thing—a phrase, a word, an idea—which has seemed to make sense suddenly proves to be nonsense; or vice-versa, what has seemed like nonsense proves to make good sense."[18] This observation points to the ground of the largest metamorphosis of all. For even the main thing, the comic element itself, "may turn into sadness in the twinkling of an eye if you stand too long contemplating it, and then God knows what may not wander into your head." Such a metamorphosis occurs at the end of "The Fair at Sorochintsy," the first story of his first collection, and the tendency keeps pace with the maturing of his comic talent. We find it at the conclusion of the story of the two Ivans, of *The Inspector General*, of "Diary of a Madman"; and the troika that thunders out of the last page of *Dead Souls*, which a moment before had been Chichikov's, now appears as nothing less than the awe-inspiring, spectral embodiment of Russia itself.

Metamorphosis is the ramifying expression of the creation

constantly going on in Gogol's universe. Its ultimate source is the creative impulse that brought that universe into being: "freshness," a conferring, fundamentally lyrical energy. For Gogol's best art itself operates a metamorphosis on its objects, taking the inconsequential and, without either ennobling or disguising it, making it a matter of discursive consquence. A universe so constituted, however, reveals a special kind of entropy. The engendering, lyrical-comic energy weakens over time (even the time of individual works), producing changes of status. At first glance the world of Gogol's text seems to illustrate with uncanny accuracy Santayana's characterization of existence as such: "a conjunction of things mutually irrelevant, a chapter of accidents, a medley improvised here and now for no reason, to the exlusion of the myriad other farces which, so far as their ideal structure is concerned, might have been performed just as well. This world is contingency and absurdity incarnate, the oddest of possibilities masquerading momentarily as a fact."[19] But what may be senseless in nature undergoes a radical change when translated into a universe of discourse, for the latter presupposes some context of human significance, however recondite. Enigmas exist only in conjunction with a quest for meaning. The struggle Gogol's art enacts is a struggle to justify its own existence in specifiable ways, even as it baffles the specification.* And the faith that animates it (textually, not psychologically) is directed toward the eventual possibility of such specification.

There is thus a certain logic to the course Gogol's work took in the last years as it sought a final metamorphosis of the Gogolian hero, of readers, of the author, and of his art itself. The emphasis throughout his writing on fragmentation, disjunction, disharmony implies a totalistic ideal in which every part and every relation would participate in the positive version of what it replaced, irradiated by the meaning of the whole.[20] The other themata show a correspondingly implicit tendency to the immolation of the art they organize.

Evasion (the Road). If metamorphosis is the central process in the Gogolian universe, then the road is its central image, operating

---

* From this it follows that the author's repeated references to the riddle of his existence should more properly be seen as referring to the riddle of his art (and not only his).

similarly on every level and evolving as the work evolves. Gogol's penchant for travel was a lifelong trait; were it merely biographical, it would be of no concern here. But when he declared the road to be "an absolute need," his "salvation," his "only medicine," he had his creation in view. So there is nothing paradoxical in his late declaration that he had "never had any urge or passion for foreign parts" (VIII, 450). His "creative capacity," he emphasized, was "only too connected with the sudden need to tear myself away from a place and travel"—"a need which I cannot explain to myself," but one on which his health, "spiritual and physical," depended (XII, 29). "My head is so strangely set up that at times I need suddenly to rush away some substantial distance to exchange one impression for another, to clarify my spiritual gaze and be in a position to encompass and reduce to unity what I need" (XII, 145–146). There are clues already in the stress on suddenness, impulse, and perspective. The urge to move on is always connected in one way or another with the problematics of identity, more specifically with frustrating identification from without. A basic feature of the author's life, it finds expression—sometimes direct, sometimes metaphorical—as the defining trait of the Gogolian narrative persona. "I was fleeing from myself," he explained when he first bolted abroad in 1829. But this flight from self was at the same time a flight *toward* self: his identity in the present, he never tired of repeating, was nothing, his identity in the future—a textual identity to be judged by the indices of artistic creation—everything. What mediated between the two was the road. It kept fixity, accountability, knowability itself at bay. ("I travel to be traveling.") Up to its final metamorphosis, therefore, Gogol's is not the familiar allegorical road of life, but an instrument of evasion in all the crucial Gogolian senses.

Evasion recurs in a great many of the works, both as narrative strategy and as overt theme; and it resonates in particularly striking ways where surrogate figures are concerned. Thus Hanz Kuechelgarten turns away from his "suffocating and dusty" provincial home, yearning "strongly, strongly" for "far-off, far-off parts." Thus also the famous cry of the narrator-turned-traveler at the end of the story of the two Ivans, Poprishchin's fantasy escape at the end of "Diary of a Madman," Podkolyosin's exit through a window in *Getting Married*. In *The Inspector General* Khlestakov, the instrument by which a whole society is unmasked, "a phantasmagoric figure . . . like a false, personified deception, gallops off with the troika God knows where" (IV, 118); and the rhetorical "conclusion" of *Dead Souls* is no more than a moving on. For all the variety of their meanings in context, these images have, as Sinyavsky notes, something in common: they point "away, beyond, above, past." They signify "shaking off the dust."[21]

Evasion, then, stands for movement into the unknown, freedom to become, deferral of judgment. In the major writings it is evasion that supplies the poetic energy and the implicit positive element. It does so by encoding in work after work a powerful and primitive impulse to escape that hitherto unnamed state which Gogol images as burial alive, death-in-life, mere existence where habit stifles "soul." The earliest letters are filled with this theme, which will inform the subsequent artistic text. At eighteen he envies his friend Vysotsky "the sweet assurance that your existence is not insignificant" (X, 80) and complains of being "buried in dead stillness along with creatures of base obscurity," the mere "existers"* of provincial Nezhin (X, 98). Turning thirty, he hopes that continuing childhood ties at least may still permit "lyrical heartfelt outpourings," the signs and source of creative freshness, whose "sworn enemies" are symbolized in the routine of arising in the morning already preoccupied with the thought of dinner (XI, 196). "It cannot be," he exclaims apprehensively in 1840, "that I have died completely, that everything exalted has cooled in my breast beyond recall" (XI, 274). For a writer the cardinal sin is "to bury his talent in the ground" (XII, 196); if, instead, he can "live and breathe through his works" (XI, 325), he thereby rises above routine, boredom, the death of the soul—existence unsanctified by meaning. Thus meaning or significance—a fundamental thematic concern in the Gogolian text—is for all its portentousness identifiable only negatively via the principle of *ne to,* a potential presence, the *ex post facto* reward and justification of an activity that is pro-

---

* The noun is Gogol's own coinage and points to a fundamental axiom of his creation. Existence and meaning do not naturally coincide; the second is not to be discovered in elements of the first, but must rather be conferred on them. Hence the insistent tendency in Gogol's writing to present nullities and significances separately, as it were chasing each other through his pages in a baffled quest for union. See the brilliant discussion of this problem by S. G. Bočarov, "O stile Gogolja," in AN SSSR, *Tipologija stilevogo razvitija novogo vremeni* (Moscow, 1976). pp. 439ff.

cess and movement and must be pursued in a state of freedom from conventional categorization. There is the largest ground of vicarious experience in these texts: what the reader relives most importantly is, by a characteristic displacement, the experience of the author—not Nikolai Vasilievich Gogol but that self-created, textual Gogol who must be understood to be as pervasively present in his universe as God is in ours. From this it follows that Gogol's art needs to be seen not as a way of saying something (even in the sophisticated sense in which Pushkin and Tolstoy "say" something in their works) but as a way of *doing* something: proving its own possibility, and so legitimizing that maximalist sense of further possibilities, that faith which produced the proof.

All this concerns the shaping impulse of the Gogolian universe; but the road also has discrete organizational functions in the several works, as we have seen. At first, it breaches the boundary of a closed world which symbolizes home and childhood, and where the terms for understanding are familiar and traditional. (So even when the marvelous erupts within it, the note of bewilderment—that hallmark of the post-Ukrainian works—is absent.) Seen largely from the perspective of this world, the road communicates with what is alien and menacing: "Everything there is not right, even the people are not the same" ("*Tam vse ne tak, i ljudi ne te*"; "A Terrible Vengeance"). An adolescent ambivalence toward this symbolic world provides the lyrical frame of *Mirgorod,* which opens with a nostalgic view of the road back and ends with a negative one. The Petersburg Tales, by contrast, body forth a world of adult experience, ruled by abstraction and irrelevance and as intolerably present as the earlier one was irretrievably absent, a new prison where society replaces community, temptation replaces adventure, and illusion (except in "The Portrait") replaces magic. All are victims here, the more sympathetic being those childlike souls (Piskaryov, Akaky Akakievich) who have no worldly ambition, the rest, presented with a harsher irony, enjoying various degrees of soul-deadening success. There is no way out save through dream or fantasy. The artist Piskaryov "belongs among the citizens of Petersburg to the same extent that a face we see in dreams belongs to the material world" (III, 16); the beauty that captivates him in the young prostitute he meets is compound of "everything that remains of the memories of childhood" (III, 18); and clinging to them leads inevitably to a state where "dreams became his [whole] life" (III, 28). Fantasy similarly offers the only escape for the madman Poprishchin: "Save me! Take me! Give me a troika with steeds swift as the whirlwind! Take your place, driver; ring, bell; rise up, steeds, and carry me from this world!" (III, 214).

The closed worlds of the Ukraine and Petersburg, for all their obvious differences, have in common a stressed non-Russianness. When Gogol confronts the theme of Russia—as he does in *The Inspector General*, "The Carriage," *Dead Souls*, and *Selected Passages*—the road becomes central and takes on a new range of meanings. Russia proper is amorphous and unencompassable; it *contains* the road and requires it. So Khlestakov and Chichikov, the heroes of the only works by which Gogol hoped to be remembered, are cast as travelers, surrogates for the author who was to proclaim in his last book, "It Is Necessary To Travel Throughout Russia." With this a fateful realignment takes place between the writer and his thematics. The escape to Petersburg had led to the discovery of vocation; the escape from Petersburg signified the embrace of that vocation, and with it a commitment. If *Dead Souls* seems colder in its brilliance than any of the previous writings, it is because there alone the values of childhood and free fantasy have virtually no place. An informing nostalgia for the past has yielded to an anxious concern for the future. When the road rises to conscious primacy with the commitment to that novel, it signals a new quest for direction, for a goal that will justify the journey.

This is not to say that the element of free play ceases to characterize the writing (though it does flag more often, to be replaced by an anxious rhetoric); the point is rather that it is subordinated to other values. The negative freedom of the road is no longer absolute. As before, it confers superiority to what is depicted, but a provisional one: the promised end must redeem it. "There must be a road in one's life," he told Annenkov in 1841, urging a purposeful quest.[22] Roadside views, he wrote in the same symbolic vein in a letter of 1843, are often beautiful—but they are "not yet a goal, and a road must necessarily lead somewhere" (XII, 198). Through the first volume of *Dead Souls*, the road is more than a structural principle; it constitutes a theme in its own right. A faith that the journey must yet turn into a quest informs the travels of Chichikov and his creator. "For a long time yet am I destined by some wondrous power to travel hand in hand with my strange heroes." The time is still far off when "inspiration will well up in a different key" and "men will hearken, trembling and abashed, to the majestic thunder of other words." Meanwhile: "Back to the road! to the road! Away with the furrow that has appeared on the brow and the cloud of severity on the visage!" (VI, 134–135).

"I am convinced," Gogol explained to Danilevsky, that "we will all come together on a single road. That road has only too clearly been set as the basis of our life; it is too broad and well marked for us not to find it. At the end of that road is God; and God is all truth; and truth is profound precisely in the way that it is equally comprehensible to all, to the wise man and the infant alike" (XII, 199). Thus the road is the agency of an eventual and final metamorphosis which the letter just quoted goes on to identify with "the inner life." In *Dead Souls*, Shklovsky observes, "Chichikov meets a beautiful woman on the road, and there suddenly appears the theme of another life."[23] Chichikov, Gogol, Russia itself—all are on the road; the equation is no less momentous than confused—which accounts for the extraordinary ambiguities of tone that characterize the discussions of the road in the last chapter of the novel.[24]

Once the road is conceived as finite, its enabling function in Gogol's artistic creation vanishes.[25] "The Gogolian prophet," as Lotman remarks, "is unable to proclaim a program" because, by nature, he can only "preach movement into infinity."[26] Entropy sets in. The moral goal to which he seeks to bend his genius after the first volume of *Dead Souls* occasions a kind of literary identity crisis; evasion is now suspect, and with it his own gift: "I cannot say with certainty whether or not the writer's calling is my calling" (VIII, 438). Thus as Annensky suggested, the final burning of the manuscript of the second volume, that last symbolic statement of *ne to,* may well have provided, for the last time, "the rapture of contemplation from the road" in the sense elaborated here.[27]

Identity. The problematic nature of identity is, as Karlinsky puts it, "*the* theme" in Gogol. It operates consistently in his work on a whole series of levels, from the incidental (the civil servant who is at the same time a civil servant and an oboe in "Nevsky Prospect") to the global. That very consistency is an identifying feature of Gogol's created universe—which is to say, of his own created identity—and a key to the radical peculiarity of both.

At its most explicit the theme is represented by all those

works which center on mistaken identity—first of all by the Gogolian army of impostors and impersonators who swarm out of the puppet-theater tradition and folklore through the Dikanka stories and appear, somewhat further evolved, in "Viy" and "The Portrait." In all such cases changes of identity are clearly motivated, the merely ostensible ones psychologically and the literal ones supernaturally. Many of the mature works turn similarly on mistaken identity—"Nevsky Prospect," "Diary of a Madman," "The Nose," *The Inspector General, Dead Souls*—but they put it to more complex and larger uses. Where imposture can be said to be involved, deliberate deception is virtually absent; more characteristically the false identity in question is the creation of others, a matter of misprision. The relation becomes collaborative, the effect being to extend and generalize the problem of identity, rendering it communal. *The Inspector General* and *Dead Souls* are paradigmatic here. At no point does Khlestakov claim to be an inspector; he merely falls in, half inadvertently, with a proffered role. As for Chichikov, all the hypothetical identities assigned to him in the course of *Dead Souls* are the work of the townspeople; he has set up as no more than a buyer of unlikely merchandise. In both cases we know more surely what the protagonists are *not* than what they are.

Gogol's created world, then, is populated by the misidentified and their misidentifiers; beyond the misidentification is a mystery, another negativity. Examples:

[In church Major Kovalyov confronts the Nose, who replies:]
"Excuse me, I can't make heads or tails of what you are saying . . . Explain yourself."
"How can I explain it to him?" thought Kovalyov and, screwing up his courage, began: "I, of course . . . All the same, I am a major . . . "
"I understand absolutely none of this," answered the Nose. Explain yourself more satisfactorily."
"My dear sir . . . ", said Kovalyov with a sense of his own dignity, "I do not know how to understand your words . . . The whole matter here should be quite obvious . . . Unless you want . . . I mean, you are my own nose!"
The Nose looked at the major and its brows contracted somewhat.
"You are mistaken, sir. I am my own self." (III, 56)

Mayor: How did you dare to unseal the letter of such a plenipotentiary person?
Postmaster: That's just it: he's not plenipotentiary and he's not a person!
Mayor: Then what is he, according to you?

Postmaster: Not one thing or another; the devil alone knows what. (IV, 90)

———

[The town officials] tried to broach the subject of Napoleon, but they themselves were sorry they had tried because Nozdryov began talking such rubbish as not only bore not the slightest resemblance to truth but bore not the slightest resemblance to anything, so that the officials all sighed and went away. Only the Chief of Police went on listening with the thought that there might at least be something further; but he, too, finally gave up, saying: "The devil knows what this is all about!" And they all agreed that however you struggle with a bull, you still won't get milk from him. And the officials were left in a worse position than they had been in before, and the whole thing came down to the fact that they could by no means find out what Chichikov was. (VI, 209)

As such passages make clear, Gogol's characters have an unquestionable individuality, and yet, by the inclusive standards of "normal" fiction, they are neither fully complete nor fully human —not plenipotentiary and not persons. Something is missing. They seem to lack a center of gravity, being all *disponibilité*—or else to lack all flexibility of response, appearing as blinkered monomaniacs. The individuality in either case is unaccountably stunted and, though vivid, defies empathetic understanding. Gogol lays repeated stress on the last point while remaining ostensibly unconscious of the first. Not a voice in his textual world (not even the narrator's) represents a stable norm; the very Gogolian consistency of that world arises from the careful reader's bafflement in the face of an oddly limited, though verbally lively scene populated and presented by the oddly lobotomized.

What is in question here is the peculiar nature of identity— which is to say, of character—as represented in Gogol's writing.[28] It may be approached first of all in terms of *function.* Because the Gogolian character is not the agent of a plot whose unfolding and resolution might represent value in itself, his actions have no constitutive value; they are secondary. He is first of all an exhibited consciousness, expressed primarily through speech. The consciousness rarely extends to selfhood. Poprishchin's eerie avowal, "Maybe I myself don't know who I am," is an exception in this respect, though not in respect of the broader rule as formulated by Bitsilli: "The Gogolian being refuses, as it were, any autonomous, conscious apprehension of reality—or rather, fails even to suspect its possibility."[29] In his slavery to habit as in his response to the unexpected he obeys simply the law of inertia (Afanasy Ivanovich's conversations with his wife in "Old-World Landowners," Khlestakov's monologue in act 3). He is entirely a creature of his milieu, and he shares its deliberate limitations as acknowledged by the author in "After the Play" and described by the First Comic Actor in "The Denouement of *The Inspector General*": "Take a good look at the town depicted in this play! Everyone without exception agrees that there is no such town in all Russia: it is unthinkable that the officials anywhere should be, every last one of them, such monsters; if only two or three of them were honest—but here there's not one. In short, there is no such town" (V, 130).

The word for this kind of limitation is caricature; Gogol himself uses it twice with reference to *Dead Souls* (VIII, 282, 294). The sense is a general one, for, as Gombrich and Kris point out, "a caricature reveals its true sense to us only if we can compare it with the sitter, and thus appreciate the witty play of 'like in unlike.'"[30] Since there can be no question of such comparison, the imagined norm must be fictional character as the reader expects to find it. In other words, the deviation here is not from nature but from nature as refracted by established fictional conventions—which means, in fact, from those conventions themselves (and ultimately from the usual contract between writer and reader). Gogol caricatures not people but storytelling, making it a moot question whether he writes in the first place about life or about art. The ability to "divine a person and by a few traits suddenly to exhibit him entire, as if he were alive" (VIII, 439) is thus a matter of divining how a Gogolian character once conceived as such would behave in a given situation: a matter of a preliminary simplification, a setting of extreme limits, followed by the conferring of a liveliness that those very limits must render surprising, if not downright uncanny.

The liveliness is linguistic. Many Gogolian characters show an inadvertent artistry, and a few stand apart as clear surrogates for their creator, exhibiting aspects of his own situation and gifts. Thus Khlestakov caricatures the way an improvised poetic identity dwarfs the prosaic "real" one. Abetted by the breathless expectancy of the terrified townsfolk, he rises through invention to "the most poetic moment of his life" (IV, 100), a transfigured scribbler (*ščelkoper;* XIII, 128) who orchestrates what is impossible in nature. "Diary of a Madman" similarly travesties the writer in Poprishchin, a creator of Quixotic (if not Cervantine) brilliance, who demonstrates a truly Gogolian embellishment of prosaic detail, the same energetic and verbally inventive transformation of data, the same gift for the artistic elaboration of psychological preoccupations (by inventing the dogs' correspondence), and the same lyrical gift in his closing entry.[31] Nozdryov, an older, stronger, utterly unmotivated Khlestakov, appears as an unrestrained creator of counter-realities and exemplifies the spontaneous generation of fiction as pure irresponsibility.* Chichikov, of course, is the supreme surrogate, who, his own identity masked, devises fictions, orchestrates them and inspires others to join in the creation. He even replicates the gift of "divining" a person by letting a few details exfoliate in his imagination; a crucial passage is devoted to this in Chapter 7, where he peruses the list of dead serfs he has bought and brings them stunningly to life, inventing biographies, scenes, dialogue.[32]

These characters are at once the most energetic and the most problematic in terms of identity, showing, in Sinyavsky's words, how "anything in Gogol can at any moment become anything (being basically nothing) . . . It all depends on what contents are put into the hollow body of the Gogolian marionette at a given time. And in the last analysis it will turn out to be a zero in any case."[33]

The image of marionettes—a recurrent one in Gogol criticism —suggests that the puzzling incompleteness of Gogolian characters may come from their existing on the borderline of two semiotic systems, appearing now as creatures of the one, now of the other, much as puppets depend for their effect on seeming to be both human and nonhuman.[34] Their speech—and the psychological impulses that provide its themes and energy—is individual, suggestive, and quasi-realistic in its colloquialism. But the larger individuality that would normally be signaled is absent; they are fashioned psychically in just the way (the way of caricature) that Sobakevich is said to have been fashioned physically: a few broad strokes and, without further ado, they are set in motion with the exclamation: "It lives!" For this the author is responsible, as Gogol

---

* See the long account in Chapter 10 of his "exposure" of Chichikov, where he is unable to hold his tongue even when it threatens to incriminate him: "Indeed it was difficult [to stem the tide of invention] because details so interesting that it was absolutely impossible to refrain from them appeared of their own accord" (VI, 209).

repeatedly and artfully underlines. Yet the author has taken un-usual pains to baffle any quest for a clear intentionality in his text.

His works thus do and do not exist to exhibit character, just as they do and do not make use of character to convey a message.* They are all in this sense trials of the word, exercises in poetic mas-tery whose success is to be gauged simply by the way they make readers exclaim, "It lives!" The Gogolian character takes on his pe-culiarity from his participation in the Gogolian enterprise. Like the works that contain him, he is an episode in an arrested evolution. The problem of his identity is inseparable from the problem of narrative and authorial identity (the first consistently masked, the second consistently evaded); that is why the texts insist on it. The reader's problem is to find a point of view adequate to compre-hend the sustained exhibition of creatures more than half mired in solipsism. And that problem too—of the perceiver and the per-ceived—is encoded within the text.

Recognition (Eyes). Motifs of vision play a central role in Gogol's creations from first to last, most strikingly in the early works where the supernatural and the uncanny dominate. Not only do annihilating glances seal the doom of Khoma Brut in "Viy" and of Chartkov in "The Portrait." Lightning darts regularly from the eyes of young beauties, signaling the ineffable, intolerable, and in-describable. In "Woman," the first publication to be signed with Gogol's name, it is said of Alkinoya that "the lightning of her eyes wrenched loose one's whole soul" (VIII, 147). In *Taras Bulba* the Polish girl directs a shattering glance at Andriy, so that he seems to "vanish and be lost" (II, 318). In the fragment of a Petersburg tale "the eyes, the ineffable eyes" of a young woman seen through a window, "with their abyss of soul . . . were insupportable for the student" (III, 331), prefiguring the way "a single glance" from the young prostitute turns Piskaryov's world topsy-turvy ("Nevsky Prospect"; III, 19). The late fragment *Rome* begins: "Try looking at the lightning when, parting the clouds black as coal, it quivers in a very flood of brilliance. Such are the eyes of . . . An-nunciata" (III, 217). Even Chichikov invokes the same imagery,

---

* By message here I do not mean a moral, but only some generally coherent concern roughly commensurate with the exhibition. In the absence of such, the esthetic value assumes quasi-independence, much like Major Kovalyov's nose.

ironically debased: Women's eyes, he muses, "are an endless realm; let a man venture in, and it's goodbye to him! You won't be able to drag him out with a hook or anything else. Just try, for instance, to find words for their glitter . . . [which] takes hold of your heart and plays, as though it were a violin bow, on your whole soul" (VI, 164). Explaining his own abrupt flight from Petersburg to Luebeck with embezzled money, Gogol blamed a fictional creature with "eyes that instantly pierce one's soul. Not a single man could withstand their ardent radiance that penetrates everything" (X, 147). These "scorching glances" (I, 221) threaten nothing less than incineration; thus Gogol congratulates himself on having withstood the temptation "to glance into the abyss" of love (X, 252).

In general the area of the taboo, represented in "A Terrible Vengeance" by the fact that "no one except the sun and the blue sky" dares look into the mid-Dnieper, is associated directly with women and the erotic—most powerfully in "Viy." I omit discussion of such clear and important examples because their very explicitness invites interpretation either in the too general terms of folklore and romantic convention or else in the too personal terms of speculative psychoanalysis—and because they are subsumed in a broader thematic pattern which, being less obvious, may be all the more deserving of attention for that. Just as the devil develops in Gogol's writing from a conventional figure into a feature of style,[35] so the annihilating glance—redolent of arcane knowledge and preternatural power—ceases to figure as such, only to assume a subtler and more pervasive role as organizer of the Gogolian text. A key statement from the closing pages of *Dead Souls* indicates how this is so.

You fear a penetratingly directed gaze; you yourselves are terrified to direct a penetrating gaze at anything; you like to glide over everything with unthinking eyes. (VI, 245)

In this passage the writer, his creation, and the reader are all in question—not, it should be emphasized, as individual beings but paradigmatically, as functions of the text. All are related, through the association of vision with fear, to that law of the Gogolian universe which identifies vision with power. Whether it be positive and vital, or negative and destructive (the evil eye), it is the animating principle. Most of Gogol's characters are shortsighted; so they are repeatedly likened by their creator to wooden dolls, walking coffins, dead souls. They are conceived, in other words, as inert material to which, for purposes of "exhibiting them palpably and visibly to the eyes of the world" (VI, 134), some semblance of vitality must be lent—that "strange vitality" described in "The Portrait" "which might light up the face of a dead man risen from the grave." The writer's task is "by some unnatural force to bring the object alive, so that it seems as if it were gazing out with a thousand eyes" (VIII, 373). Here is the creative process: the literal lending of the creator's own vitality to the objects of his imaginative vision in order "to light up a picture taken from a contemptible sphere of life and elevate it into a pearl of creation" (VI, 134).

The elevation is a matter of lifting the material into significance (however paradoxical and problematic). Its effect is to make the ideal reader see through the eyes of the creator (thus the complaints about the failure of readers to do so, prominent in work after work). The goal, clearly, is a complicity uniting character, author, and reader-spectator—a matter of seeing and being seen, and so of marking the existence of each, albeit on different levels and in different ways. The paradigmatic case here is *The Inspector General*, whose very title suggests discovery and whose action takes place before the eyes of an audience. The failure of the Mayor and Khlestakov to see through each other offers a sustained and triumphantly comic demonstration of myopia, and of the way naked psychological impulse can be used to confer unnatural vitality on marionettes. The final tableau exacts the price: the punishing glance that petrifies the ensemble.

This case is paradigmatic because overt: the characters are literally frozen in a dramatic change of perspective, seen suddenly *sub specie aeternitatis*. Less obvious cases, however, embody the same strategy. One may recall the transcendent words of the visiting general that make the point of "The Carriage": "Ah, you are here!" One may recall the iconic representations of Akaky Akakievich in his progress through the world of Gogol's narrative—"a being [who] disappeared and vanished," "defended by no one, dear to no one, interesting to no one"—and realize how Gogol's artistry has supplied his homunculus not only with attention but with immortality. The same might be said of Major Kovalyov, Lieutenant Pirogov, the whole gallery of characters in *Dead Souls* —in fact of all the personages in all the works that are based on exhibition rather than on plot. The twentieth-century emphasis on the centrality of narrative performance in Gogol's writing needs a complementary emphasis on the fact that these works are *literary imitations* of performances. By virtue of being written, they serve the function of permanent exhibitions.

In them as in the graphic conclusion to *The Inspector General,* then, there are certain quasi-Dantean overtones. The characters in question have reached some limit and stand condemned at best to endless repetitions of the path that has brought them to this last judgment.* All of them, seeing as they do with "unthinking eyes," achieve an unenviable immortality through a kind of seeing of which they are themselves incapable. Gogol could well have had his own works in view when he wrote of Pushkin's: "In the eyes of people who are quite intelligent but who lack poetic sensitivity, they are unfinished excerpts . . . in the eyes of people gifted with poetic sensitivity, they are full poems, thought out, complete, containing everything they need to contain" (VIII, 381). To be authentically seen is to be known, to take on status in a world of value. For the majority of Gogol's characters, that status is negative; the look is at the same time a judgment that petrifies or otherwise annihilates them.†

The threat of the identifying look, then, is ubiquitous in Gogol's poetic universe. Narration itself is responsive to that threat; hence those ingenious shifts by which the narrative voice, for all its ironic use of the pronoun "I," nonetheless eludes identification. At the origin of the Gogolian creation and pervading it is an impulse to simultaneous exhibition and concealment which may best be understood in light of Sartre's disquisition on *le regard d'autrui.* In Sartre's terms the sense of self in solitude is a sense of free possibility which is condensed and narrowed into self-con-

---

* "A Terrible Vengeance" sets the pattern: Annihilating retribution comes to the wizard as he sees the giant horseman "suddenly open his eyes . . . and begin to laugh" (I, 278). The story itself, moreover, is presented as the verbatim account of a performance and ends by underlining the power of the art that confers permanence (explicitly, that of the blind *bandora* player and implicitly, that of the reteller in prose).

† The change of status which the finished exhibition accomplishes is thus a transcending of the principal mode of exhibition (generally comic). The narrator of *Dead Souls* comments on the instability of comic perception, remarking how "the gay can, in an instant, turn into the sad if only one stand before it too long" (VI, 58), and the pattern of Gogolian endings shows how regular a tendency this is in his universe.

sciousness when it is made an object by "the look of the Other":
The Other, as perceiving glance, "transcends my transcendence."
"In order for me to be what I am, it suffices merely that the Other
look at me. My transcendence becomes for whoever makes himself a witness of it a purely established transcendence, a given-tran-
scendence; that is, it acquires a nature by the sole fact that the *Other*
confers on it an outside. To apprehend myself as seen is, in fact, to
apprehend myself as seen *in the world* and from the standpoint of
the world. Thus I, who in so far as I am my possibles, am what I
am not and am not what I am—behold now I *am* somebody." The
perceiving Other thus represents "the hidden death of my possibilities." [36]

We have seen how exclusively Gogol's pride and sustaining
faith attached precisely to his possibilities, how constantly he
expressed fear of premature identification and judgment, insisting
that his existence as a writer was a riddle whose solution lay in a
constantly receding future. The early pseudonyms, like the habitual disowning of all his work to date, give clear evidence of what
was at once a psychological complex in his life and, more importantly, a shaping principle of the creation that dwarfed it. Re-
jecting recognition of anything other than his possibilities, Gogol
was, as it were, warding off the Medusa glance that might freeze
him en route to their realization. [37] His best art does the same thing,
proclaiming a self-sufficiency that seems by turns absolute and
provisional. It is against this background that the lyrical exclamation in the closing pages of *Dead Souls* can be seen to mark the limit
of expansion of the Gogolian universe. There, to cite Gogol's own
paraphrase, he voices the feeling "that everything in [Russia], from
the animate to the inanimate, has fixed its eyes on him and is
expecting something from him" (VIII, 289). His defense of this
grandiloquence as "simply the awkward expression of a genuine
feeling" only underlines its fatefulness. Once the writer is aware of
being a cynosure, by the logic that has informed his text he and his
task must be changed. Gogol's struggle henceforth was to remain
a writer, abandoning evasion and seeking new themes. The failure
of this last metamorphosis, this forsaking of the freedom of the
road, this embracing of identity, moved him to what was an *auto-
da-fé* (Nabokov's term) only in the personal sense; for the Gogol
that concerns us here, it was a reversion to the authenticity of incompleteness, an affirmation of the finality of *ne to*.

10

Sense, Shape, End

The themata outlined here, however incomplete and subject
to revision, offer terms for fixing Gogol's elusiveness, for posing it as a problem and opening it to the possibility of explanation.
They inform action and characters, the shape of the narratives that
present them, and the artist's enterprise as a whole; in that sense
they constitute Gogol's distinctive verbal universe as ultimate context, and are manifest within it equally as manner. The Gogolian
style itself flaunts its metamorphic powers, its fluid becoming, its
resistance to stable identity, its challenge to the perceptive reader.
At the heart (center and origin) of the cluster is a single strategic
principle which in its very primitivism gives Gogol's work the in-
exhaustibility of art and makes endless the possibility of discerning
rival patterns within it.

The principle is that of *ne to*—a constant denial (as fact or as
value) of what appears in the represented reality and in the representation itself. This principle can be seen in the very first stories—
the closing melancholy that calls in question the humor of "The
Fair at Sorochintsy," the melons and cucumbers in "A Bewitched
Spot" that are not melons and cucumbers but "the devil knows
what"—and culminates in the paradox of dead souls, which are
neither one thing nor the other.[1] Nothing in Gogol's text is quite
free from the suspicion of that *ne to* which it asserts so constantly,
energetically, playfully, abundantly, and excessively.*

---

* The very tendency to hyperbole is a variety of *ne to,* most obviously when
the expression evokes the inexpressible. "Not a single person in the whole world
could have told what was going on in the sorcerer's soul; and had anyone looked
and seen, he would never have been able to sleep through the night or to laugh

257

It is this strategy that supplies the basic comic element—what Suzanne Langer terms "the comic rhythm"—to Gogolian writing: intrinsically inexhaustible, it offers through the very medium of presentation "an image of human vitality holding its own in the world," exhibits "a brainy [verbal] opportunism in face of an essentially dreadful universe," and so conveys a paradoxical version of "the pure sense of life [that] is the underlying feeling of comedy."[2] But the operation of *ne to* goes on to embrace this effect, too. The Gogolian masterpieces without exception can be read either as hilarious or horrifying, and whichever way they are read, an awareness of the alternative is always present. The refusal of single vision leaves possible only an unresolved mixture of responses, made permanent by the authority of art. That authority is the one unequivocal thing in these texts, and if we are to seek the locus of stable meaning in Gogol's writing, we must seek it there.

To say this is to move the quest for artistic meaning from matter to manner, from content to form—an area that Simmel properly identified as "one of the most relative and subjective in the entire area of thought," since "what is form in one respect is content in another": "upon closer scrutiny, the conceptual antithesis between the two dissolves into a merely gradual [opposition], having a determinateness which is between the general and the specific."[3] That last quasi-Gogolian phrase marks the relevance of the insight; if the terms in question are not separate entities, they are at least separable tendencies—one of which may constitute the "dominant" that makes the other an ancillary matter. Gogol clearly provides a case where the "dominant" is stylistic, where (as one Russian theorist put it) "style overgrows plot, subordinates the dynamics of the latter to itself and assumes, so to speak, an independent (*samocennoe*) significance."[4]

The point is by now familiar: Gogol's achievement was to demonstrate, more radically than any writer of his century, the sheer power of his chosen medium. Basically the function of this

---

again even once. It was not malice, not terror, and not fierce frustration (*dosada*). There is no word on earth for it" (I, 277). Hyperbole itself, when it is transparent, turns into a play on words that can only be perceived as such in their failed transcendence: "Limitless, infinite, the boundless love of God for man is more boundless than eternity itself" (XII, 71). On this feature of Gogol's writing see Valery Bryusov, "Burnt to Ashes," in Maguire, ed., *Gogol from the Twentieth Century;* and D. Ciževskij, "Neizvestnyj Gogol'," *Novyj Žurnal,* no. 22, 1951, esp. 153ff.

power is to supply the emphatically positive counterpart to its emphatically banal targets: freshness, vitality, surprise, freedom of action, freedom from time and place and constraint of all kinds, freedom from the ordinary logic of language itself—all embodied in a language that, once it entered public discourse, altered it, no less than it alters a reader's experience once having entered it. The experience of language is what gives these works their unprecedented allure as literature, so that one oscillates between admiration of the often baffling response they compel and the medium they seem created to glorify. Here is the fundamental *ne to:* scratch a Gogolian character and you find bare verbal tissue; examine a Gogolian phrase and you find the energy of human aspiration, human contradiction.

This ultimate paradox of literary art is Gogol's fundamental message. The rest is implication—and of the most various sorts: psychological, social, ethical, moral, religious—all encoded, demonstrably and at the same time incompletely, in the texts. One's sense, explicitly abetted by the narration, that there is "more to these works than what they are" (*ne iščerpyvajutsja soboju:* Sinyavsky's phrase about Gogol's characters) leads legitimately and inevitably to a search for allegorical meaning. But if the search be for singleness and consistency, it is doomed. Far more than most fictions, Gogol's seem to illustrate the principle of complementarity, according to which certain basic lines of interpretation are at once necessary and mutually exclusive. Moreover, because the data that sustain them are primitive and fragmentary, to trace large patterns of meaning means extrapolating beyond what can be shown as textually warranted. The interpreter is placed in a double bind: he misses the point if he ignores allegorical meaning, and errs if he confronts it.

It is curious but hardly consoling to find the author himself in his position—as when, to the embarrassment of his admirers, he tried to reduce *The Inspector General* to an allegory of the individual soul.[5] Less may not be better, but in Gogol's case, it is more accurate. So the alternative claim that the true hero of that work is Laughter has the virtue of locating the allegory in *an effect,* which amounts to saying that the play is artistically significant because it is functionally effective—a near tautology, but not a complete one. At this point one needs to recall the literary situation Gogol entered—all those laments about the absence of an original prose art that might constitute a national voice. What they posed was the question of the possibility of literature—and that, in a sense going beyond the historical, is the question to which Gogol's sustained and increasingly serious improvisations represent an answer. The terms of the question concerned not what the looked-for literature would say, but what it should do; it would be recognized by its efficacy. Gogol's genius was to devise an answer by writing about the question.

Almost all of Gogol's writing is in some important sense about literature. Overt commentary on storytelling sets off his telling of stories from first to last, the programmatic high points being the concluding lines of "The Nose" and the many key inter-polations in *Dead Souls*. Accompanying these is a no less constant, implicit treatment of the same concerns, showing "how the literary construction may express its creator's attitude toward the very act of writing."[6] Obvious examples are the last scene of *The Inspector General* and the description of Plyushkin's garden, but in fact whole works may do the same. Like a hall of mirrors, they contain the elements of surrogate fictions, comically debased: "authors" are represented by all the Gogolian prevaricators and, at another level, all the Gogolian gossipmongers—memorable stylists every one and often inadvertent aphorists. To these travesties of novelists, spinning what they take to be realistic plots out of their solipsism and retailing them as rumor, Gogol adds a travestied form of fictional motivation: some foolish hobbyhorse (*zador*) operating in the place of passion (a hobbyhorse being in fact a passion without any higher sanction).

Rather than seek to pass off his fictions as documents in the realistic manner, moreover, Gogol takes pains to emphasize their status as *made* objects—to suggest something about the nature, place, and power of literary art as such on the real-life spectrum that runs from the individual soul and individual psychology through the cultural and social . . This is more than a matter of textual hints. Gogol anticipates the ideal function of his works in society by including parodic models of that functioning within the works. We have already observed how, within the basic fiction of *The Inspector General,* other fictions are generated, each with its denouement; how the fictive reality of Khlestakov's visit to the town threatens to pass into the "different" level of a no less fictive literature to be written by Tryapichkin or Khlestakov (or the anonymous scribbler referred to by the Mayor); and how the reality that contains these—itself a literary creation—asserts its power as artifice in the closing tableau. The same thing can be observed in "The Overcoat": the Important Personage is the closest thing in the story to a conventionally presented character, one who "lives" in a network of familial and social relations and approaches a "normal" spectrum of emotions. The drama of Akaky Akakievich's development comes from his quest for a place in the clearly delimited dimension in which this personage exists—a quest that is baffled in the plot but crowned with success in the fact of the story's existence (for the latter gives Akaky Akakievich precisely the kind of sustained attention it shows him being denied). The troika at the end of *Dead Souls* only caps a constant tendency in Gogol's chief works, whereby effective conclusion is never on the level of the problem as posed. There is always an allegorical step up, so that the existence of the fiction supplies the absences it has been exhibiting.

This allegorization of the literary process necessarily includes its share of attention to the reader. Pure reading—without content —is caricatured in the habits of Akaky Akakievich, Chichikov's servant Petrushka, and Chichikov himself; moronic literary tastes help characterize the likes of Khlestakov, Lieutenant Pirogov, Poprishchin, and the officials of N. Equally prominent are the intratextual representatives of extratextual readers, such as the provincial police captain who triggers the digression after the second word of "The Overcoat," complaining of the subversive effect of "some romantic composition where a police captain appears every ten pages, at times even in an utterly intoxicated state." Through them—and through the authorial digressions of *Dead Souls,* which provide Gogol's most detailed map of misreading—these texts attack certain common reading habits in order to alert their own reader to the uncommonness of the enterprise at hand.

The bedrock allegory of Gogol's art thus concerns the miracle and meaning of its own existence. Authentic art, he insisted in "The Portrait" and elsewhere, must serve a great idea; the great idea that informs all his mature writing is the transforming and liberating power of literary creation, its ability to transcend limitation in the present. This is not a matter of assertion but of demonstration. As his fictions transform the least promising matter into occasions of delight, they open the possibility of a like transformation in the area of life. They communicate aspiration. So if the objects of his writing provoke pessimism, its dynamism, directed constantly toward an unknown future, does the opposite—as the four themata show.

When the author of *Dead Souls* confessed that his characters "never fully separated from my self, and therefore failed to assume genuine autonomy" (VIII, 295), he was pointing to the way they (and all their predecessors) are implicated in the basic subliminal aspiration that shapes the universe of his creation, embracing reader and writer too as part of its hidden theme: the large, life-enhancing potencies of literature.[7] His intentions in writing, when he tried to formulate them directly, were bound to be inadequate to that larger intentionality which permeates his texts, providing their peculiar dignity and validating his claims for a "lofty laughter" that has nothing in common with simple amusement.

The Gogolian universe, then, objectifies a faith it communicates as intuition. Arising in a void to mirror an emptiness, it gave that emptiness dimensionality and virtuality, made of it a space that might be filled. Content was to be supplied by life, and read back into texts that so conspicuously lacked it. This has been done for well over a century now, the kind of content varying with the cultural preoccupations of the times. By and large the Russian nineteenth century supplied a social content, extrapolating from Gogol's attention to social position and from the embedded fragments of physical Russian reality. When, at the turn of the century, literary thought turned metaphysical and symbolist, all the eccentricity of the Gogolian universe came in for admiring emphasis; no longer seen as mimetic, it was now an artistic statement in its own right and one impossible to make in other terms. This marked a gain in registering textual specificity, a relative liberation of Gogol's writing from time if not place (for the Symbolists, Blok and Biely chief among them, found the Gogolian text mirroring their own passionate concern with Russian destiny). In the late twentieth century, when the very possibility of literature is once more in question and the notion of semantic content has been eclipsed by an interest in pure verbal functioning (*écriture*), Gogol appears as a great and precocious examplar, his fictions offering "true artistic pleasure," the pleasure of the text. Here is the international Gogol, ancestor of Kafka and the theater of the absurd. Such a view testifies all the more impressively to the vitality of the Go-

golian art even when deprived of the language that gives so uncanny a *justesse* to so many of his eccentric *mots*. The vitality that
remains is structural, a matter of linkages and presentation. It is, at
bottom, that mysterious energy of attraction and repulsion which
unifies and holds in place this unique verbal universe, from the
molecular structure of sentences and paragraphs to the constella-
tions of finished works, constituting it as autonomous process and
allowing us to see it as something approaching an absolute: artistic
prose as such.

NOTES

INDEX

Notes

1. The Gogol Problem: Perspectives from Absence

1. N. V. Gogol', *Polnoe sobranie sočinenij* (Moscow, 14 vols., 1937–1952), X, 123. All subsequent references to Gogol's writings, unless otherwise indicated, are to this edition and are included in parentheses in the text.

2. A. S. Nikolaev and Ju. G. Oksman, eds., *Literaturnyj muzeum,* I (Petersburg, 1922), 98.

3. Quoted in Nikolaj P. Barsukov, *Žizn' i trudy M. P. Pogodina* (22 vols., St. Petersburg, 1888–1907), VIII, 521.

4. See Vasilij Gippius, *Gogol'* (Leningrad, 1924), p. 41. The art critic V. V. Stasov, recalling his schooldays, dates the younger generation's infatuation with Gogol from the appearance of the story of the two Ivans in 1833: "The delight with Gogol at that time was unparalleled. He was read everywhere with something like intoxication. The unusualness of the content and the types, the unprecedented naturalness of the language, humor of a kind previously unknown to anyone—all this acted in a simply intoxicating way. With Gogol a completely new language was established in Russia; it pleased us enormously by its simplicity, force, accuracy, astonishing liveliness, and closeness to nature. All the Gogolian expressions and turns of phrase passed quickly into general usage . . . All the young men began speaking the language of Gogol." "Učilišče Pravovedenija sorok let tomu nazad, 1836–1842 gg.," *Russkaja starina,* no. 2, 1881, 414–415.

5. "O russkoj povesti i povestjax g. Gogolja," in V. G. Belinskij, *Polnoe sobranie sočinenij* I (Moscow, 1953), 306.

6. In his letter to Gogol of 20 April 1842 Belinsky writes: "You are now *the only one* among us—and my moral existence, my love for creative work, is closely bound up with your fate; without you, it would be goodbye for me to the present and future of the artistic life of my homeland." Ibid., XII (Moscow, 1959), 109.

7. The phrase is Shevyryov's. Belinsky, he writes, "unquestionably belongs among the most remarkable figures of contemporary Russian literature," having been educated through apprenticeship on *The Moscow Telegraph, The Telescope,* and *Talk of the Town* (*Molva*), which were "his Göttingen, Jena, and Berlin." (Quoted in Barsukov, VIII, 353.)

8. Ibid.

9. For an account of the Gogol celebrations of 1909 and particularly of Bryusov's speech and reactions to the Andreyev statue, see Boris Zajcev, "Gogol' na Prečistenskom," in his *Moskva* (Munich, 1960), pp. 64–68.

10. V. V. Zelinskij's anthology of contemporary reviews, *Russkaja kritičeskaja literatura o proizvednijax N. V. Gogolja* (3 vols., Moscow, 1900), contains inexplicable omissions and no editorial apparatus; the smaller Soviet *N. V. Gogol' v russkoj kritike* (Moscow, 1953) is vitiated by the dogmatism of its inclusions and exclusions alike. In English, Paul Debreczeny's *Nikolai Gogol and His Contemporary Critics* (Transactions of the American Philosophical Society, vol. 56[n.s.], part 3 [Philadelphia, 1956]), is devoted more to summarizing than to interpreting historically the reactions to Gogol's work in his lifetime; and Robert A. Maguire's excellent *Gogol from the Twentieth Century* (Princeton, 1974) is a selection rather than a survey (though its introductory essay contains valuable insights).

11. G. A. Gukovskij, *Realizm Gogolja* (Moscow-Leningrad, 1959), p. 25.

12. G. I. Čudakov, *Otnošenie tvorčestva Gogolja k zapadno-evropejskim literaturam* (Kiev, 1908). The author provides a detailed list of what Gogol might have read, but is constantly obliged to introduce his assertions with such phrases as "one may assume." Annenkov reports flatly that "of all the names of foreign poets and novelists he was acquainted by more than guesswork or hearsay with only one—that of Walter Scott." P. V. Annenkov, *Literaturnye vospominanija* (Leningrad, 1928), p. 59.

13. Helen Muchnic, *An Introduction to Russian Literature* (New York: Dutton, 1964), pp. 97–101.

14. When on occasion he tried, the attempts were usually retrospective and highly questionable. In general, it is hard to disagree with the proposition that "there can scarcely have been a writer in world literature whose subjective self-estimate was so far from the bases of his artistic work." Kornej Čukovskij, *Sobranie sočinenij v šesti tomax,* IV (Moscow, 1966), 111.

15. Characterizing the letters in general, his great editor, Tikhonravov, puts the matter most gently when he remarks that they are "not always distinguished by frankness." The first drafts for Gogol's article "On the Development of Periodical Literature" (1836), for *Dead Souls* and "After the Play," he notes, taken together "not infrequently provide more valuable facts about the poet's inner life than his letters"—which, in their guardedness, "do not reveal a desire to initiate his friends into [his] literary activities" (*Sočinenija N. V. Gogolja,* 10th ed., I [Moscow, 1889], vii). Dolinin comments more directly on the way "*Wahrheit* and *Dichtung* get inextricably entangled" in the letters; and Veresayev elaborates the point in Gogolian accents: "One's mine boggles at the extent to which he constantly falsifies in his letters, what untrue information about himself he communicates. Often it is even quite impossible to understand what his reason for doing so may be—there is, apparently, no reason, only an irresistible tendency to mystifications and subtle diplomacy." A. S. Dolinin, "Puškin i Gogol'," in N. V. Jakovlev, ed., *Puškinskij sbornik pamjati Professora Semena Afanas'eviča Vengerova; Pušinist,* IV (Moscow-Petrograd, 1922), 182; V. Veresaev, *Gogol' v žizni* (Moscow-Leningrad, 1933), p. 5.

16. Vinogradov's phrase, which he proposes as more appropriate to Gogol's narrative style than the frequently applied *skaz,* since a Gogolian work is a free creation which functions by "sharp and intermittent verbal shifts that produce the illusion of a constant succession of storytellers, who metamorphose abruptly into

a 'literary' writer." See V. V. Vinogradov, *Poetika russkoj literatury: Izbrannye trudy* (Moscow, 1976), pp. 191, 254–255.

17. W. H. Auden, *The Dyer's Hand and Other Essays* (New York: Vintage Books, 1968), pp. 292–293.

18. Boris Ejxenbaum, *Moj vremennik* (Leningrad, 1929), pp. 89–90.

19. Belinskij, X (1956), 293.

20. Vladimir Nabokov, *Nikolai Gogol* (Norfolk: New Directions, 1944), pp. 63–74; V. V. Vinogradov, "Iz istorii russkoj literaturnoj leksiki," *Učenye zapiski Moskovskogo gosudarstvennogo pedagogičeskogo instituta imeni V. I. Lenina,* XLII (1947), 3–5. See also Ju. S. Sorokin, *Razvitie slovarnogo sostava russkogo literaturnogo jazyka; 30–90e gody XIX veka* (Moscow-Leningrad, 1935), pp. 329–330.

21. Jurij Ivask, "Literaturnye zametki," *Mosty,* no. 6, 1968, 174–175. This brief article offers a brilliant exposition of the peculiarly verbal essence of Gogol's art.

22. Quoted in V. Veresaev, *Kak rabotal Gogol',* 2nd ed. (Moscow, 1934), p. 76.

23. Andrej Belyj, *Masterstvo Gogolja* (Moscow-Leningrad, 1934), p. 200.

24. S. A. Vengerov, *Pisatel'-graždanin. Gogol'* (St. Petersburg, 1913), p. 124.

2. The Sense of Absence: Immediate Contexts

1. Turgenev corroborates the point, writing in 1869 of the fascination that surrounded Gogol's name in his last years and commenting that "at the moment there is no one on whom general attention might focus" I. S. Turgenev, "Gogol'," in his "Literaturnye i žitejskie vospominanija," *Polnoe sobranie sočinenij i pisem v 28-i tomax,* XIV (Moscow-Leningrad, 1967), 65.

2. See N. K. Kozmin, *N. I. Nadeždin* (St. Petersburg, 1912), pp. 37ff; and Vsevolod Setchkarev, *Gogol: His Life and Works,* trans. Robert Kramer (New York: New York University Press, 1965), p. 122.

3. Pushkin ("On the Causes . . ."): in A. S. Puškin, "O pričinax, zamed-livšix xod našej slovesnosti," *Polnoe sobranie sočinenij v desjati tomax* (Moscow), VII (1958), 18. A. Bestužev, "Vzgljad na russkuju slovesnost' v tečenie 1824 i načale 1825 godov," *Poljarnaja zvezda, izdannaja A. Bestuževym i K. Ryleevym* (Moscow-Leningrad, 1960), p. 488. Vyazemsky ("We are rich . . ."): quoted, along with Venevitinov, in Kozmin, *Nadeždin,* p. 96. Vyazemsky ("Judging by the books . . ."): "Zamečanija na Kratkoe obozrenie russkoj literatury 1822-go goda, napečatannoe v no. 5 Severnogo arxiva 1823-go goda," in *Polnoe sobranie sočinenij knjazja P. A. Vjazemskogo,* I (St. Petersburg, 1878), 103. Puškin ("Our infantile literature . . ."): "Pis'mo k izdatelju 'Moskovskogo vestnika'," *Polnoe sobranie sočinenij,* VII, 71. M. Ju. Lermontov, *Polnoe sobranie sočinenij,* IV (Leningrad, 1940), 465. Ivan Kireyevsky, "Obozrenie russkoj literatury za 1831 g.," *Evropeec,* no. 1832, p. 100. Belinsky: "Literary Reveries" ("Literaturnye mečtanija," 1834).

4. *Polnoe sobranie sočinenij,* VII, 22.

5. Letter of Prince V. F. Odoyevsky to N. A. Polevoy; quoted in N. K. Kozmin, *Očerki iz istorii russkogo romantizma* (St. Petersburg, 1903), pp. 521–522.

6. *Žurnal ministerstva narodnogo prosveščenija*, 1834, I, 5. Earlier he notes: "Among the principal attributes which our contemporaries demand from works of Literature, the idea of nationality (*narodnost'*) predominates. It is a quality necessarily involved in the idea of each people. And how many things must go to make it up! The traits which comprise the physiognomy of our soul existed previously as elements in the society that trained our passions, in the nature that enraptured our feelings, in the religion that exalted our thoughts, in the customs whose antiquity sanctifies them for us, in those prejudices from which no philosophy can save us" (p. 2). In the early 1830s Nadezhdin, dissatisfied with the state of French and Russian literature alike, sees both as "the expression of the contemporary state of society"—a point that Belinsky was soon to begin elaborating. Compare the latter's assertion that "literature should be the expression of the life of society, and it is society that gives it life rather than vice-versa." Kozmin, *N. I. Nadeždin*, p. 385.

7. Ivan Krylov (1769–1844), author of the famous *Fables*, could hardly be considered responsive to the Zeitgeist as it was making itself felt in these years. As for Nikolai Karamzin (1766–1826), he did in fact do much to liberate Russian prose by simplifying it, but Polevoy was surely right in claiming three years after Karamzin's death that the latter "can no longer be a model for the Russian poet, or novelist, or even prose writer." N. Barsukov, *Žizn' i trudy M. P. Pogodina*, 22 vols. (St. Petersburg, 1888–1910), II, 332.

8. "Devjatnadcatyj vek," *Evropeec*, no 1, 1832, 12, 14.

9. "Obozrenie russkoj literatury za 1831 g.," ibid., pp. 100, 103–104.

10. Bestuzhev (Marlinsky) in the *Moscow Telegraph*, 1833; quoted in Kozmin, *Očerki iz istorii russkogo romantizma*, p. 374.

11. *Severnye cvety na 1829 g.* (St. Petersburg, 1828), pp. 83–84; quoted by V. V. Vinogradov, "Jazyk Gogolja i ego značenie v istorii russkogo jazyka," in V. V. Golubkov and A. N. Dubikov eds., *Gogol' v škole* (Moscow, 1954), p. 58.

12. "O pričinax," *Polnoe sobranie sočinenij v desjati tomax*, VII, 18.

13. Quoted in V. V. Vinogradov, *Stil' Puškina* (Moscow, 1941), p. 516; for a more circumstantial discussion of this problem see his chap. 7.

14. *Polijarnaja zvezda* (1960), pp. 488, 492.

15. Quoted in Kozmin, *N. I. Nadeždin*, p. 392.

16. *Poljarnaja zvezda* (1960), p. 493.

17. Dahl and Marlinsky quoted in Boris M. Ejxenbaum, *Lermontov* (Leningrad, 1924), pp. 134, 137.

18. See Boris M. Ejxenbaum, "Problema poetiki Puškina," in his *Skvoz' literaturu* (Leningrad, 1924), pp. 165ff; and Waclaw Lednicki, "The Prose of Pushkin," in his *Bits of Table Talk on Pushkin, Mickiewicz, Goethe, Turgenev, and Sienkiewicz* (The Hague: Martinus Nijhoff, 1956), pp. 1–32.

19. V. F. Pereverzev catalogues the imitations that followed hard on the heels of Bulgarin's novel: Bulgarin's own "Peter Vyzhigin," Gur'janov's "New Vyzhigin," Orlov's "Children of Vyzhigin," and "Vyzhigin's Death," Simonovskij's "A Russian Gil Blas." He finds that the "moral-satirical" form represented by all these fictions is, by the mid-1830s, the dominant one in Russian writing, certainly the most popular, and that its hero thus succeeds to the place formerly held by the protagonist of Byronic poems. "Puškin v bor'be s russkim

plutovskim romanom," in *Puškin, Vremennik puškinskoj kommissii,* I (Moscow-Leningrad, 1936), 172.

20. For a detailed analysis of both projects, see Pereverzev, pp. 164–188.

21. The sophistication of his experiments in the *Tales of Belkin*—overlooked to a man by contemporary reviewers—offers a striking case in point; it has been exhaustively traced through his use of epigraphy by Viktor Vinogradov in his article, "O stile Puškina," *Literaturnoe nasledstvo,* 16–18 (Moscow, 1934), 171–191. On this score see also Lednicki, note 18 above.

22. Compare the questionably phrased but widely shared opinion of Count V. A. Sollogub, a contemporary: "Pushkin was a great artist, Gogol was a genius. Pushkin subordinated everything to considerations of plasticity, esthetics, art; Gogol prepared himself for nothing, followed no rules or models, knew neither grammar nor orthography. He was unique, sui generis (*samobyten, samoroden*), and frequently sinned against esthetic taste." *Vospominanija* (Moscow-Leningrad, 1931), p. 517.

23. Belinskij, I (1953), 261–262; Kireevskij, "Devjatnadcatyj vek," p. 15.

24. *Moskovskij nabljudatel',* 1835, I, 121; quoted in M. A. Belkina, "'Svetskaja povest' 30-x godov i 'Knjaginja Ligovskaja' Lermontova," in N. L. Brodskij et al., eds., *Žizn' i tvorčestvo M. Ju. Lermontova. Sbornik pervyj. Issledovanija i materialy* (Moscow, 1941), p. 519.

25. "O knižnoj torgovle i ljubvi ko čteniju v Rossii," in N. M. Karamzin, *Izbrannye sočinenija* (Moscow-Leningrad, 1964), II, 178.

26. Quoted by Leonid Grossman in his *Etjudy o Puškine* (Moscow, 1923), p. 73.

27. For an illuminating discussion of this problem as it confronted those who essayed the longer forms of fiction in the 1830s, see Boris Ejxenbaum, *Lermontov* (Leningrad, 1924), pp. 139ff.

28. V. F. Odoevskij, "Kak pišutsja u nas romany," *Sovremennik,* no. 3, 1836, 48–51.

29. "Jurij Miloslavskij, ili Russkie v 1612 godu," *Polnoe sobranie sočinenij v desjati tomax,* VII, 102.

30. P. M. Bicilli, "Puškin i Vjazemskij (K voprosu ob istočnikax puškinskogo tvorčestva)," in Sofia Universitet, Istoriko-filologičeski fakultet, *Godišnik,* XXXV (1938–139), 3.

31. V. A. Žukovskij, *Sobranie sočinenij v 4-x tomax* (Moscow-Leningrad, 1960), IV, 393, 396. Even in the 1840s, "society" tended to be equated with "circle" (*kružok*); see M. I. Aronson and S. Rejser, eds., *Literaturnye kružki i salony* (Leningrad, 1929), p. 66.

32. S. Baluxatyj, ed., *Russkie pisateli o literature* (Leningrad, 1939), I, 201.

33. "Baratynskij," *Polnoe sobranie sočinenij v desjati tomax,* VII, 222.

34. Ibid., VI, 372–373.

35. Count V. A. Sollogub, quoted in Aronson and Rejser, pp. 77–78.

36. Mickiewicz, who frequented Russian literary circles in the late 1820s, lated recalled: "Writers in Russia form a sort of brotherhood, united by many ties. They are almost all either wealthy men or government officials: for the most part, they write to acquire fame or public significance. Talent among them has not yet become a commodity, and therefore professional competition and hostility of in-

terests are seldom found among them. At least I never saw any instance of that. Literary men consequently liked to get together, saw each other almost daily, and passed their time cheerfully amid dinners, readings, amiable conversations and disputes." Ibid., p. 70.

37. Ibid., p. 5.

38. Cf. Pushkin in 1827: "Almanacs have become the representatives of our literature." *Polnoe sobranie sočinenij v. desjati tomax,* VII, 49.

39. Quoted and discussed in Boris Ejxenbaum, "Literatura i pisatel'," *Zvezda,* no. 5, 1927, 126.

40. "Pis'mo k izdatelju 'Moskovskogo vestnika'," *Polnoe sobranie sočinenij v desjati tomax,* VII, 71.

41. "Oproverženie na kritiki," ibid., p. 184.

42. The expression is Polevoy's; quoted in Barsukov, II, 333.

43. Quoted in L. Myškovskaja, *Literaturnye problemy puškinskoj pory* (Moscow, 1934), p. 40.

44. Cf. Odoyevsky's transparent—and novel—reference to "the literary rabble (*čern'*)" in his essay "On the Hostility to Enlightenment Observable in Recent Literature" (*"O vražde k prosveščeniju zamečaemoj v novejšej literature"*), *Sovremennik,* no. 2, 1836, 206. Hitherto the word *čern'* had been used, as we have seen Pushkin doing, only of the unenlightened public; now that that public had its own vigorous spokesmen, the word was becoming applicable to them as well.

45. For a detailed account, see Barsukov, III, 10–14, 228–236.

46. Faddej Bulgarin, *Sočinenija* (St. Petersburg, 1827).

47. Barsukov, II, 167.

48. Kozmin, *Nadeždin,* p. 444.

49. I. I. Panaev, *Literaturnye vospominanija* (Leningrad, 1950), p. 88; quoted in V. Kaverin, *Baron Brambeus* (Moscow, 1966), p. 66.

50. Quoted in Kaverin, *Baron Brambeus,* pp. 66–67.

51. Barsukov, IV, 375.

52. There would be no hope for Russian literature, he declared, until such time as "we write *anyhow,* not for or about anything, simply out of boredom and for boredom's sake (*tak sebe, ni za čto, ni pro čto, skuki radi i radi skuki*)"; quoted in Kaverin, p. 43.

53. "Russkij pisatel'," *Severnaja pčela,* 1836, nos. 16 (21 January) and 17 (22 January).

54. V. K. Kjuxel'beker, "Poezija i proza," *Literaturnoe nasledstvo,* vol. 59 (Moscow, 1954), 391.

55. Belinskij, "Literaturnye mečtanija," I (1953), 98.

56. The phrase is Kaverin's, in his *Baron Brambeus,* p. 53. Bulgarin's own newspaper, *The Northern Bee,* enjoyed a circulation in 1830 of 3000, which its rivals could not come close to touching. Pushkin's *Literary Gazette,* for example, had "barely 100" subscribers the following year; Kireyevsky's *European,* Pogodin reported, "with the names and contributions of Zhukovsky, Baratynsky, Yazykov, and so on [had] only 50 subscribers" in 1832; Nadezhdin's *Telescope* was comparatively successful with 700. About a decade later, Pogodin reported that *The Muscovite* (*Moskvitjanin*) had some 100 subscribers each in Moscow, Peters-

burg and the provinces. See Barsukov, IV, 6, 14, and VI, 48; see also Kozmin, *Nadeždin*, p. 436; and André Meynieux, *Pouchkine Homme de lettres et la littérature professionnelle en Russie* (Paris, 1966), chap. 4.

57. "Russkie istoričeskie dramy," in O. I. Senkovskij, *Sobranie sočinenij* (St. Petersburg, 1858), VIII, 24–25; quoted in Louis Pedrotti, *Josef-Julian Sekowski: The Genesis of a Literary Alien* (Berkeley and Los Angeles: University of California Press, 1965), p. 142.

58. "Brambeus i junaja slovesnost', "*Biblioteka dlja čtenija*, no. 3, 1834, 36–37, 43, 51, 59–60.

3. Beginnings: Miscellaneous Writings

1. L. N. Tolstoj, "O Gogole," *Polnoe sobranie sočinenij*, vol. 38 (Moscow, 1936), 51.

2. See the editorial notes in I, 495. See also V. A. Desnickij, "Zadači izučenija žizni i tvorčestva Gogolja," in V. V. Gippius, ed., *N. V. Gogol': Materialy i issledovanija*, II (Moscow-Leningrad, 1936), 52–57; and M. P. Alekseev, "K istočnikam idillii Gogolja 'Ganc Kjuxel'garten'," Ministerstva Vysšego i Srednego Special'nogo Obrazovanija RSFSR, Mordovskij gosudarstvennyj universitet imeni N. P. Ogareva, Kafedra russkoj i zarubežnoj literatury, *Problemy poetiki i istorii literatury; sbornik statej* (Saransk, 1973), pp. 172–182.

3. See Vladimir Markov, "Stixi russkix prozaikov," in R. N. Grynberg, ed., *Vozdušnye puti; al'manax*, I (New York: R. N. Grynberg, 1960), 140–145.

4. Vladimir Nabokov, *Nikolai Gogol* (Norfolk: New Directions, 1944), p. 13.

5. "Thanking you most feelingly and inexpressibly for your priceless information about the Little Russians, I ask you most urgently not to leave off sending such letters in the future. In the tranquillity of my isolation I am preparing a reserve which I will not publish until I have polished it properly; I don't like haste, still less working superficially. I ask you also, my kind and incomparable mama, to print the proper nouns and in general the various Little Russian names for things as clearly as possible. The thing I am writing, if it ever comes out, will be in a foreign language and I will need accuracy all the more so as not to distort the essential name of the nation with false nomenclature" (X, 150).

6. The signature evidently came from the four o's in Nikolai Gogol-Yanovsky, though Nabokov may be right to find "the selection of a void and its multiplication for concealing his identity" to be "very significant on Gogol's part" (*Nikolai Gogol*, p. 27). On the other hand Nikolai Fillipovich Pavlov in 1835 signed two critical articles in the *Moscow Observer* "-o-", Karamzin had used "O.O.", V. F. Odoyevsky "O.O.O.", and Senkovsky "O.O. . . . O!"—all without inviting any such imputations of significance; see I. F. Masanov, *Slovar' psevdonimov russkix pisatelej, učenyx i obščestvennyx dejatelej*, II (Moscow, 1957), 280.

7. Hugh McLean, "Gogol and the Whirling Telescope," in Lyman H. Legters, ed., *Russia: Essays in History and Literature* (Leiden: E. J. Brill, 1972), p. 85.

8. *Gogol'* (Leningrad, 1924), p. 62.

9. S. A. Vengerov, *Pisatel'-graždanin; Gogol'* (St. Petersburg, 1913), p. 152.

10. See Ju. Oksman, "Iz razyskanij o Puškine; I. Neosuščestvlennyj zamysel istorii Ukrainy," in *Literaturnoe nasledstvo*, vol. 58 (Moscow, 1952), 211–221.

11. I. I. Ivanickij, *Otečestvennye zapiski*, 1853, no. 2, otd. VII, 120; quoted in X, 752–753.

12. I. Mixnevich, quoted in I. I. Zamotin, *Romantizm 20-x godov XIX stolecija v russkoj literature*, II (Moscow, 1911), 129n2.

13. Zamotin's phrase characterizing the doctrine introduced into Russia, *inter alia*, by an 1828 translation of a portion of Goethe's *Weissagungen des Bakis*. I. I. Zamotin, *Romantizm 20-x godov*, II (St. Petersburg, 1911), 130.

14. See Gippius, *Gogol'*, pp. 40ff; Zamotin, II, 129–139; and N. K. Kozmin, *N. K. Nadeždin* (St. Petersburg, 1912), pp. 328–347.

15. A. V. Nikitenko, *Dnevnik v trex tomax*, I (Leningrad, 1955), 168–169.

16. V. Zelinskij, comp., *Russkaja kritičeskaja literatura o proizvednijax N. V. Gogolja*, 3rd ed. (Moscow, 1903), I. 48.

17. V. V. Stasov, "Učilišče Pravovedenija sorok let tomu nazad, 1836—1842 gg.," *Russkaja starina*, no. 2, 1881, 415. Parallel testimony to Gogol's enormous significance for students in the early 1830s (including Belinsky, Stankevich, and Konstantin Aksakov) may be found in K. S. Aksakov, *Vospominanija studenčestva* (St. Petersburg, 1911).

18. VIII, 24–25. Here, as throughout, I have tried neither to conceal nor to exaggerate the oddities of the original in my translation.

19. Zelinskij, I, 47.

20. Cf. "On the Teaching of World History": "What is needed is not to collect many traits but rather those which express a great deal—the most original traits, the sharpest that the people in question possessed. To extract these traits one must have a mind strong in seizing all the shadings that go unnoticed by an ordinary eye; and one must have the patience to dig through a multitude of books, sometimes the most uninteresting ones" (VIII, 27).

21. See Jurij Ivask, "Literaturnye zametki: O Gogole, Vyxod iz odinočestva," *Mosty*, XII (1966), 171–180.

22. VIII, 149. The quotation comes from one of Gogol's earliest critical pieces, "Boris Godunov: Pushkin's Poem," written in early 1831 but unpublished in his lifetime. *Boris Godunov* serves as the merest of pretexts (it is discussed not at all) for a series of stylistic exercises in the depiction of Petersburg, its atmosphere and its inhabitants—and for a series of disquisitions on art, by turns practical and emotional. The odd lumpings and juxtapositions make this a sort of prose counterpart to *Hanz Kuechelgarten*, with the difference that its materials and attitudes anticipate rather more directly the achievements of the next few years.

23. Ibid., 150–151.

24. Gippius notes this (*Gogol'*, p. 48) and remarks in Gogol's "demands for realistic breadth" the absence, for the time being, of "their future sting": moralism. A suppressed passage from the first draft of the article, however, does express Gogol's characteristic notions of the moral effect of art: Pushkin's verses are there asserted to have "schooled readers and educated them to truly noble feelings," despite the protests of "old men and pious aunties . . . that they were sowing the seeds of freethinking—only because the forthright nobility of thought

and expression and the courageous soul that informed them stood in too direct an opposition to their own inert and dull lives, useless alike to them and to the state" (VIII, 602).

25. V. G. Belinskij, "Sočinenija Aleksandra Puškina, Stat'ja pjataja," in his *Polnoe sobranie sočinenij*, VII (Moscow, 1955), 320. The remark occurs in a discussion of Pushkin's unprecedented appeal to a broad spectrum of Russian readers. It is striking to see how his words apply equally to Gogol: "Everyone—not only the educated but even simply literate people—saw in [his works] not merely new poetic productions but a completely new poetry, of which they had not only seen no example in Russian, but of which they had never even had an inkling."

26. In a letter of 10 January 1836 Pushkin reports, apropos of his plans to publish a journal: "Smirdin is already offering me 15,000 to back off from my enterprise and become a contributor again to his *Library*. But though that would be profitable, I can't agree to it. Senkovsky is such a rogue and Smirdin such an ass that it is impossible to be connected with them." (A. S. Puškin, *Polnoe sobranie sočinenij v desjati tomax*, 2nd ed. X (Moscow, 1958), 560. Smirdin, moreover, offered up to a thousand rubles to authors for permission to list their names on the title page of his journal as contributors of forthcoming articles; see Aleksandr V. Zapadov, ed., *Istorija russkoj žurnalistiki XVIII–XIX vekov*, 3rd ed. (Moscow, 1973), p. 162.

27. Nadezhdin's phrase, quoted in Kozmin, *Nadeždin*, p. 453.

28. *Biblioteka dlja čtenija*, II, sec. 5, p. 13; ibid.

29. The review was written by Shevyryov. See N. I. Mordovčenko, "Gogol' i žurnalistika 1835–1836 gg.," in Gippius, ed., *N. V. Gogol': Materialy i issledovanija*, II, 121–122; and Paul Debreczeny, *Nikolai Gogol and His Contemporary Critics*, Transactions of the American Philosophical Society, vol. 56 (n.s.), part 3 (Philadelphia, 1966), pp. 8–9.

30. Personal politics played a large and complex role in Gogol's association with both journals. Details may be found in Mordovčenko (see preceding note); E. Ryskin, "O stat'e N. V. Gogolja 'O dviženii žurnal'noj literatury v 1834 i 1835 godu' (černovaja i žurnal'naja redakcija stat'i Gogolja)," *Russkaja literatura*, no. 1, 1965, 134–143; V. G. Berezina, "Novye dannye o stat'e Gogolja 'O dviženii žurnal'noj literature v 1834 i 1835 godu'," in M. P. Alekseev et al., eds., *Gogol', Stat'i i materialy* (Leningrad, 1954), pp. 70–85.

31. V. V. Gippius, *Ot Puškina do Bloka* (Moscow-Leningrad, 1966), p. 113.

32. Pushkin's editorial policy here and in general was marked by caution and an apparently deliberate obfuscation. Gippius threads his way through the complexities of the situation in masterly fashion in his article, "Literaturnoe obščenie Gogolja s Puškinym," *Učenye zapiski Permskogo gos. universiteta*, II, 1931, 102–124.

33. "Gogol's *Inspector General* and the Comedy of Aristophanes," in Robert A. Maguire, ed., *Gogol from the Twentieth Century* (Princeton: Princeton University Press, 1974).

34. Panayeva notes in her memoirs: "When *The Inspector General* was staged, all the actors involved in it were somehow shaken. They sensed that the types Gogol had traced in the play were new for them, and that it was wrong to play them in the way they were accustomed to act their roles in the Russified French vaudevilles then prevalent" (quoted in V. V. Veresaev, comp., *Gogol' v žizni*

[Moscow-Leningrad, 1933], p. 156). P. A. Karatygin, a leading writer and performer of vaudevilles, reports the puzzled reaction of these actors to Gogol's own reading: "'What's this all about?' they whispered to each other when Gogol had finished. 'Can this be called a comedy? He reads well enough, but what kind of language is that? The servant speaks an ordinary servant's language, and the locksmith's wife Poshlyopkina sounds like any ordinary woman (baba) off Haymarket Square. What's our Sosnitsky [who played the mayor] so excited about here?' And what do Zhukovsky and Pushkin find so good in it?'" Karatygin himself was one who criticized it in such terms. "A pupil of the old classic school," his son explains, "he was still unable to disavow the classical traditions. Both the actors and a good many writers could not bring themselves to remove the powdered wigs from their heads and the French cloaks from their shoulders in order to put on Russian dress—the Siberian jacket of the merchant Abdulin or the worn and greasy coat of [Khlestakov's servant] Osip" (ibid., p. 158).

4. Beginnings: Fiction

1. See Viktor Vinogradov, Etjudy o stile Gogolja (Leningrad, 1926), p. 92.

2. Severnaja pčela, 1831, no. 220; quoted in Vinogradov, p. 218n 109.

3. Vasilij Gippius, Gogol' (Leningrad, 1924), p. 26.

4. Gogol knew and prized the Ukrainian language all his life, but he is known to have written in it only one epigram and one letter. See Gippius, p. 11.

5. Puškin-Kritik (Moscow-Leningrad, 1934), p. 295. Reference is to the stories of volume one, which appeared in September 1831; volume two followed only in March 1832.

6. Victor Erlich, Gogol (New Haven: Yale University Press, 1969), p. 30.

7. Gippius notes how the power of this creative intuition, "which Gogol himself later called 'clairvoyance,' brings into being a whole world so lively and well put together that his hypnotized contemporaries—even comparatively knowledgeable ones— . . . believed in its real existence" (Gogol', p. 28). The same effect was later observable in his writing about the Russian provinces, and for the same reasons.

8. Gippius, p. 3.

9. M. M. Baxtin, "Iskusstvo slova i narodnaja smexovaja kul'tura (Rable i Gogol')," in Kontekst: 1972 (Moscow, 1973), p. 249. Gogol himself offers some support for this theory when he refers in a draft of After the Play to "lofty holiday laughter" (V, 389).

10. See James M. Holquist, "The Devil in Mufti: The Märchenwelt in Gogol's Short Stories" Publications of the Modern Language Association, 82, (October 1967), esp. 352–355. See also Erlich, Gogol, pp. 30ff.

11. Cf. F. C. Driessen, Gogol as a Short-Story Writer (The Hague: Mouton, 1965), p. 86.

12. Andrej Belyj, Masterstvo Gogolja (Moscow-Leningrad, 1934), pp. 13–14. Biely's text has Gogol "muttering out and tapping out his rhymes (rifmy)"; the context, however, suggests that this is a misprint for ritmy ("rhythms"), and I have so construed it.

13. In Chapter 5, Danilo tells Katerina, "You do not know even a tenth part of what your soul knows" (I, 260). Biely (pp. 54–71) and Driessen (pp. 92–109) both offer lengthy interpretations of the story in psychological terms, relating it ultimately to Gogol's own psyche.

14. This attitude was to remain constant over the years. The first volume of the *Collected Works* (1842) carries a preface in which Gogol notes the immaturity of many of these stories and declares that "the whole first part should have been excluded," these being "apprentice essays, unworthy of the reader's strict attention. [But they occasioned] the first sweet minutes of youthful inspiration, and it grieved me to exclude them, as it grieves one to wrench out of memory the first games of irretrievable youth. The indulgent reader may pass over the first volume and begin his reading with the second" (I, 318). Ten years later, already near death, Gogol was ready to omit *Evenings* entirely from a planned new edition of his works; see Nikolai Barsukov, *Žizn' i trudy M. P. Pogodina* (22 vols., St. Petersburg, 1888–1910), XI, 524–525.

15. P. M—skij (Jurkevič), *Severnaja pčela,* no. 115, 1835; reprinted in V. Zelinskij, comp., *Russkaja kritičeskaja literatura o proizvedenijax N. V. Gogolja,* 3rd ed. (Moscow, 1903), I, 58.

16. Driessen, p. 116.

17. As such, it is particularly inviting to psychoanalytic interpretation. See, in this respect, Hugh McLean, "Gogol's Retreat from Love: Toward an Interpretation of *Mirgorod,*" in *American Contributions to the Fourth International Congress of Slavists* (The Hague: Mouton, 1958), pp. 225–245; and Driessen, pp. 117–181.

18. This preface, apparently written in pique over Gogol's earlier trials with the censorship, was itself most probably prohibited by the censor of *Mirgorod;* it survives in only one contemporary copy of the book and was first noticed only in this century. See II, 750–753; Driessen summarizes the facts on p. 168 of his book.

19. Though it is certainly that: the association of erotic attraction (and esthetic sensibility in general) with treason to some dominant allegiance is one of those motifs that recur with noteworthy frequency in Gogol's work. On the second of these elements, see Belyj, *Masterstvo Gogolja,* pp. 50–54 and passim.

20. Gippius, who quotes this passage (*Gogol'*, p. 70), conjectures that Gogol had read and preserved it in his unconscious memory; he might just as well have been familiar with the examples cited in the article in question.

21. Zelinskij, I, 58.

22. Simon Karlinsky has recently suggested, with high ingenuity, a provenance for the gnomes and for the story's puzzling title. See *The Sexual Labyrinth of Nikolai Gogol* (Cambridge: Harvard University Press, 1976), pp. 97–103.

23. See V. V. Ivanov, "Ob odnoj paralleli k gogolevskomu Viju," *Učenye zapiski Tartuskogo gosudarstvennogo universiteta,* no. 284, 1971, 133–142: and his "Kategorija 'vidimogo' i 'nevidimogo' v tekste: Ešče rax o vostočnoslavjanskix fol'klornyx paralleljax k gogolevskomu 'Viju',", in Jan van der Eng and Mojmir Grygar, eds., *Structure of Texts and Semiotics of Culture* (The Hague: Mouton, 1973), pp. 151–176. See also Driessen, 138–139 for his citation and discussion of parallels in Russian folklore.

24. Abram Terc [Andrej Sinjavskij], *V teni Gogolja* (London: Collins, 1975), p. 546.

25. Howard Phillips Lovecraft, *Supernatural Horror in Literature* (New York: Ben Abramson, 1945), p. 15.

26. Vladimir Nabokov, *Nikolai Gogol* (Norfolk: New Directions, 1944), p. 157; L. N. Tolstoj, *Polnoe sobranie sočinenij,* vol. 66 (Moscow, 1953), 67.

27. Terc, p. 496.

28. Zelinskij, I, 58.

29. N. A. Nekrasov, *Polnoe sobranie sočinenij,* IX (Moscow, 1950), 341.

30. V. G. Kjuxel'beker, *Dnevnik,* ed. V. N. Orlov and S. I. Xmel'nickij (Leningrad, 1929). p. 69; this diary entry (12 August 1832), it should be noted, does not refer to Gogol's work.

31. E. g., by Victor Erlich, whose terms these are; see his *Gogol,* p. 73.

32. This passage, along with the second one cited, comes from the revised version of *Taras Bulba,* published in 1842. Though they did not appear in the original *Mirgorod* text, they only give pointed expression to motifs which abound there.

33. In Chapter 4 of *Dostoevsky and Romantic Realism* (Cambridge: Harvard University Press, 1965) I have tried to indicate the contribution of this cycle to the evolving myth of Petersburg in Russian literature; here the question rather concerns the evolutionary place of these stories in their author's larger text.

34. See Nils Åke Nilsson, *Gogol et Pétersbourg* (Stockholm: Almqvist and Wiksell, 1954).

35. The editorial notes to the Academy edition of Gogol's works cite analogues and probable sources in Wackenroder, Hoffmann, Maturin, and Balzac (III, 671–672); Gippius adds the names of Washington Irving, Spinello, and Pushkin as author of "The Queen of Spades" (*Gogol',* pp. 55–56). But of course the theme of demonic intervention, like the themes of art and the artist, was in full vogue when Gogol wrote his story. In 1833 Nadezhdin had declared in *The Telescope* that for art "the material fidelity of a representation alone is not sufficient; it should breathe the life of reality and illumine the gloomy chaos of events with a single [guiding] idea. And only so can it find justification for its sovereign freedom in dealing with reality, reordering and changing events so that they may more clearly and fully express a predetermined idea." The realism dominant in France, Nadezhdin found, was "of a particular kind, an extremely dangerous realism"; were it to prevail entirely, "it would be impossible to believe either in God or in the dignity of the soul, for the world which this poetry develops before our eyes is a world without Providence or freedom." *Teleskop,* nos. 3 and 4, 1833; quoted in Kozmin, *N. K. Nadeždin,* pp. 389–390.

36. Here is the central passage in all its cumbersome opacity:

> " 'What is this?' he thought to himself: 'art, or some supernatural sorcery which has eluded the laws of nature? What a strange, what an incomprehensible thing to do! Or is there for man some boundary to which higher cognition leads and which, once he has crossed it, he is already stealing something uncreatable by the labor of man, tearing something alive out of the life that animates the original. Why is it that this crossing of the boundary set as a limit for the imagination is so horrible? Or is it that beyond imagination, beyond creative afflatus, reality at length follows—that horrible reality, into which imagination

springs from its axis in consequence of some accidental push, that horrible reality which appears to him who thirsts for it when, desiring to comprehend the beauty of man, he arms himself with an anatomist's scapel, lays bare the interior and beholds the repulsiveness of man. Incomprehensible! Such an astonishing, horrible animation! Or is excessively close imitation of nature just as cloying as a dish that has an excessively sweet taste?'" (III, 405–406)

This first version of the story (from *Arabesques*) seems to condemn realism from the point of view of romantic aspiration; the revised version of 1842 seems rather to condemn mere copying in favor of a "higher" realism. Gogol claimed to have "entirely reworked" the story in Rome (XII, 45); for an unusually interesting discussion of the sense of this reworking, see A. L. Volynskij [A. L. Flekser], *Bor'ba za idealizm* (St. Petersburg, 1900), pp. 259–267.

37. These and other items from *The Northern Bee* are quoted by Igor Zolotussky in his article, "'Dairy of a Madman' and the 'Severnaya Pchela'," *Soviet Literature,* no. 10 (331), 1975, 41, 48–50 ff. For a tracing of some topical references in this story, see also Laurie Ash, "The Censorship of Nikolai Gogol's 'Diary of a Madman'," *Russian Literature Triquarterly,* no. 14 (Winter 1976), 20–35.

38. Andrew MacAndrew's translation, *The Diary of a Madman and Other Stories* (New York: New American Library, 1960) has, for some inexplicable reason, only 19; moreover, MacAndrew contrives to omit the two mentions in the text of the protagonist's name (entries of 4 October and "25th Date").

39. On Poprishchin as ideal reader of these popular journalists, see Zolotussky.

40. A. S. Nikolaev and Ju. G. Oksman, eds., *Literaturnyj muzeum* (Petersburg, 1922), I, 96.

41. See, for example, Innokentij Annenskij, *Kniga otraženij* (St. Petersburg, 1906), I, 26–27; I. Ermakov, *Očerki po analizu tvorčestva N. V. Gogolja* (Moscow-Leningrad, 1924), pp. 167–216 (an edited translation may be found in Maguire, *Gogol from the Twentieth Century,* pp. 156–198); Nicholas I. Oulianoff, "Arabesque or Apocalypse? On the Fundamental Idea of Gogol's Story *The Nose,*" *Canadian Slavic Studies,* I, no. 2 (Summer 1967), 158–171; Jean-Paul Weber, "Les transpositions du nez dans l'oeuvre de Gogol," *Nouvelle revue française,* July, 1959, pp. 108–120.

42. V. V. Vinogradov, "Naturalističeskij grotesk (Sjužet i komozicija povesti Gogolja 'Nos')," *Evoljucija russkogo naturalizma* (Leningrad, 1929); reprinted in his *Poetika russkoj literatury: Izbrannye trudy* (Moscow, 1976), pp. 5–44. See also Vsevolod Setchkarev, *Gogol: His Life and Works* (New York: New York University Press, 1965), pp. 156, 161–162; Vasilij Gippius, "Zametki o Gogole," *Učenye zapiski Leningradskogo gosudarstvennogo universiteta,* Serija filologičeskix nauk, no. 11, 1941, 12–16; and Innokentij Annenskij, "O formax fantastičeskogo u Gogolja," *Russkaja škola,* II, 1890, bk. 10.

43. Setchkarev. p. 156.

44. Roland Barthes, *Critique et vérité* (Paris: Editions du Seuil, 1966), pp. 74–75. This remark as if glosses Roman Jakobson's observation of 1921: "The realized oxymoron betrays its essentially verbal nature; though it has meaning, it does not have anything which could be called . . . a *proper object* (as, for exam-

ple, a 'squared circle'). The character Kovalev in Gogol's short story *The Nose* recognizes the nose as such even though it shrugs its shoulders, is in full uniform, and so forth." "Modern Russian Poetry," in Edward J. Brown, ed., *Major Soviet Writers: Essays in Criticism* (New York: Oxford University Press, 1973), p. 67.

45. There is confirmation of this in Gogol's letter of 28 November 1836 to Pogodin. There he refers to those "immature and undefinitive experiments, which I only called stories because it was necessary to give them some kind of designation" as having been written "only to try my strength." "These were pale fragments of those phenomena which filled my head—out of which a full picture would eventually be created" (XI, 77).

46. L. N. Tolstoj, "O Gogole," *Polnoe sobranie sočinenij,* vol. 38 (Moscow, 1936), 50.

47. S. T. Aksakov, *Istorija moego znakomstva s Gogolem* (Moscow, 1960), p. 49; the first phrase is Aksakov's, the second Gogol's, from a letter of 28 December 1840 (XI, 322–323).

5. Confronting a Public, I

1. S. T. Aksakov, *Istorija moego znakomstva s Gogolem* (Moscow, 1960), pp. 11–12. Aksakov uses quotation marks but goes on to observe that the words cited may not have been Gogol's, though "the idea was precisely that"; in the translated passage I have made Gogol's remarks an indirect quotation.

2. Vasilij Gippius, "Problematika kompozicija *Revizora,*" in V. V. Gippius, ed., *N. V. Gogol': Materialy i issledovanija,* II (Moscow-Leningrad, 1936), 154; an edited version of this article appears as *"The Inspector General:* Structure and Problems," in Robert A. Maguire, ed., *Gogol from the Twentieth Century* (Princeton: Princeton University Press, 1974), pp. 216–265.

3. Cf. Gogol's letter to Pogodin of 8 May 1833, in which he confesses that his only hope of breaking free from his present situation is through making a substantial amount of money. "And this," he adds, "cannot be done except by writing a weighty thing" (X, 268).

4. This account derives ultimately from Gogol's friend, the great contemporary actor M. S. Shchepkin; see V, 578–579. For a sympathetic critical account of these scenes, see Simon Karlinsky, *The Sexual Labyrinth of Nikolai Gogol* (Cambridge: Harvard University Press, 1976), pp. 153–157.

5. The project evidently arose from his work in universal history. A Soviet scholar has traced its sources and analogues in detail, and conjectured that Gogol may have envisaged it as a masked commentary on the state of Russian society. See M. P. Alekseev, "Drama Gogolja iz anglo-saksonskoj istorii," in Gippius, ed., *Gogol',* II, 242–285.

6. "O russkoj povesti i povestjax g. Gogolja," in V. G. Belinskij, *Polnoe sobranie sočinenij,* I (Moscow, 1953), 306.

7. See notes in IV, 524ff; and A. A. Nozdev, "Neskol'ko dokumental'nyx dannyx k istorii sjužeta *Revizora,* in *Literaturnyj arxiv,* IV, ed. M. P. Alekseev (Moscow-Leningrad, 1953), 31–37. The most sensible interpretation of this material is in A. I. Beleckij, "V masterskoj xudožnika slova," *Voprosy teorii i psixologii tvorčestva,* VII (Kharkov, 1923), 132–133; there the author notes not only vari-

ants of the prototypical anecdote but a number of literary works based on it by Kvitka, Veltman, and Dahl.

8. In October 1851 Gogol decided to arrange a reading of *The Inspector General* for a group of actors and told O. M. Bodyansky: "The first idea for [the play] came from Pushkin, who told the story of how Pavel Svinin passed himself off in Bessarabia as an important official from Petersburg, and was stopped only when he had carried it too far and was beginning to accept petitions from the convicts there," Nikolaj Barsukov, *Žizn' i trudy M. P. Pogodina,* 22 vols. (St. Petersburg, 1888–1910), XI (1897), 522.

9. M. M. Baxtin, "Iskusstvo slova i narodnaja kul'tura (Rable i Gogol')," in *Kontekst: 1972* (Moscow, 1973), p. 256

10. V. I. Nemirovič-Dančenko, "Tajny sceničeskogo obajanija Gogolja," *Ežegodnik imperatorskix teatrov,* no. 2, 1909. 32.

11. Abram Terc [Andrej Sinjavskij], *V teni Gogolja* (London: Collins, 1975), p. 123.

12. Quotations, unless otherwise indictated, are from the final version of the play. The long process of retouching involved complexities that are fascinating but not to the present point.

13. Terc, p. 154

14. See V. Kosteljanec, "Ešče raz o *Revizore,*" *Voprosy literatury,* no. 1, 1973, pp. 195–224, to which I am indebted.

15. Vladimir Nabokov, *Nikolai Gogol* (Norfolk: New Directions, 1944), p. 55.

16. Arnold Kettle, *An Introduction to the English Novel, I, Defoe to George Eliot* (New York: Harper Torchbooks, 1960), p. 126.

17. Jurij Mann's intelligent monograph does just this, making the points here cited and observing that "never before had Russian comedy seen such a broad view of official, public (*gosudarstvennaja*) life." *Komedija Gogolja "Revizor"* (Moscow, 1966), p. 19.

18. Ivanov, "Gogol's *Inspector General* and the Comedy of Aristophanes," in Maguire, ed., *Gogol from the Twentieth Century,* p. 201. On the question of social mirroring, see also Ju. M. Lotman, "O Xlestakove," *Učenye zapiski Tartuskogo gosudarstvennogo universiteta,* no. 369, 1975, 19–53.

19. Terc, p. 160.

20. See note 34 to Chapter Three above.

21. Annenkov, "Gogol' v Rime," in his *Literaturnye vospominanija* (Leningrad, 1928), pp. 68–70.

22. K. Močul'skij, *Duxovnyj put' Gogolja* (Paris: YMCA Press, 1934), p. 43.

6. Epic Intentions

1. The image is only slightly varied two years later in a letter sympathizing with Pogodin's lonely position amid the literary philistines: "As you know, he who is armed only with a noble sword, the defender of his honor, cannot do battle with those who are armed with cudgels and staves. The field must remain in the hands of the brawlers. But we can, like the first Christians in their catacombs and cells, strive to accomplish our creations" (XI, 187).

2. N. G. Ovsjannikov, quoted in M. N. Kufaev, *Istorija russkoj knigi v XIX veke* (Leningrad, 1927), p. 105. Cf. Gogol's complaint about the stupidity of booksellers in connection with the success of *Evenings;* letter to Pogodin of 20 July 1832, X, 237–238.

3. Gogol's letter to Zhukovsky of 4[?] January 1840 sets forth figures and problems (XI, 269–271). Belinsky reports that before the second edition of *Dead Souls* appeared, copies of the first were selling for ten silver rubles instead of the original three (V. G. Belinskij, *Polnoe sobranie sočinenij,* X [Moscow, 1956], 53).

4. In December 1841 Gogol received a grant of 500 rubles from the Tsar to help him through the period of waiting for the censor's approval of *Dead Souls;* in 1843 he asked Pletnyov to present his *Collected Works* to the court, and received in response 1000 rubles from the Tsarina. In May 1844 Zhukovsky informed Gogol that the Tsarevich had agreed to his proposition that a 4000-ruble debt of Zhukovsky's should be repaid not to the Tsarevich but rather to Gogol over a four-year period (V. A. Žukovskij, *Sobranie sočinenij,* IV [Moscow-Leningrad, 1960], 529). In November 1844 Smirnova-Rosset wrote Gogol that henceforth he should borrow only from her, since she had money from the Tsar for that purpose (*Russkaja starina,* LX, no. 10, 1888, 135); and in March of the following year Zhukovsky and Smirnova procured, through the Grand Duchess and Count Uvarov, an imperial grant for Gogol of 3000 rubles in silver (10,000 in paper) to cover a period of three years (see Nikolaj Barsukov, *Žizn' i trudy M. P. Pogodina,* 22 vols. [St. Petersburg, 1888–1910], VIII, 74–75; for some curious details of the negotiation, see A. O. Smirnova-Rosset, *Avtobiografija* [Moscow, 1931], pp. 296–297).

5. Thus Gippius notes that the strictly artistic relations are "complex" and "virtually untouched by scholarship" ("Literaturnoe obščenie Gogolja s Puškinym," *Učenye zapiski Permskogo gosudarstvennogo universiteta,* II, 1931, 61). Nearly half a century later the statement remains true, though a great many scattered observations of textual parallels are to be found in the scholarly literature. My purpose here is only to indicate some major lines of filiation.

6. The letter continues: "And my current work [*Dead Souls*] is his creation. He made me swear that I would write it, and not a line but has been written with him before my eyes. I consoled myself with the thought of how pleased he would be, I sensed what would please him, and that was my highest and best reward" (XI, 91).

7. P. Bicilli, "Putešestvie v Arzrum," in *Belgradskij sbornik* (Belgrade, 1937), p. 259. Indeed, Gogol himself makes the point in *Selected Passages:* "In the eyes of people who are quite intelligent but without poetic flair, many of Pushkin's compositions appear to be incomplete (*nedoskazannye*) excerpts," whereas more sensitive readers can perceive the same works as "complete poems, thought through, finished, containing everything they need to contain" (VIII, 381).

8. *Eugene Onegin,* VIII, xlviii; the translation cited is Nabokov's.

9. A. L. Slonimskij, *Texnika komičeskogo u Gogolja* (Petersburg, 1923), p. 15 (in English as Alexander Slonimsky, "The Technique of the Comic in Gogol," in Robert A. Maguire, ed., *Gogol from the Twentieth Century* [Princeton: Princeton University Press, 1974], p. 331).

10. For a fuller discussion of its place in this cycle, see Donald Fanger, *Dos-*

toevsky and Romantic Realism (Cambridge: Harvard University Press, 1965), pp. 106–124.

11. For a suggestive sketch of how each of the stories rings variations on this theme, see Ju. M. Lotman, "Problema xudožestvennogo prostranstva v proze Gogolja," *Učenye zapiski Tartuskogo gosudarstvennogo universiteta,* no. 209, 1968, 38–45. In "The Overcoat," Akaky Akakievich's growing attachment to his future overcoat is the cardinal example of misplaced affect, and *the narrative itself* keeps raising the question of appropriate perspective implicitly, as a question of appropriate tone.

12. M. M. Bakhtin, writing under the name of P. N. Medvedev, *Formal'nyj metod v literaturovedenii* (Leningrad, 1928), p. 173; quoted by S. G. Bočarov in his brilliant article, "Puškin i Gogol' ('Stancionnyj smotritel' i 'Šinel')," in *Problemy tipologii russkogo realizma* (Moscow, 1969), p. 225. In attributing authorship to Bakhtin, I follow the assertion of Vycheslav Ivanov (*Učenye zapiski Tartuskogo gosudarstvennogo universiteta,* no. 308, 44n101); the matter, however, remains a cloudy one.

13. On malproportion as a key element in the story, see Boris Eichenbaum, "How Gogol's 'Overcoat' Is Made," in Maguire, pp. 288ff.

14. Bočarov, p. 226.

15. "Cloaking the Self: The Literary Space of Gogol's 'Overcoat,'" *PMLA,* 90 (January 1975), 57. Bernheimer's essay, too subtle to summarize here, brings structuralist insights to bear on Gogol's story in an exceptionally illuminating way.

16. Vladimir Nabokov, *Nikolai Gogol* (Norfolk: New Directions, 1944), p. 149.

17. In Maguire, pp. 334–335.

18. Dmitry Chizhevsky, "About Gogol's 'Overcoat,'" in Maguire, p. 315. Alternatively, Chizhevsky suggests, the theme might be seen as Satan's seduction of a human soul by focussing its aspirations on an unworthy material object instead of a transcendent spiritual value.

19. See F. C. Driessen, *Gogol as a Short-Story Writer* (The Hague: Mouton, 1965), p. 194; John Schillinger, "Gogol's 'The Overcoat' as a Travesty of Hagiography," *Slavic and East European Journal.,* 16 (Spring 1972), 36–41; and Anthony Hippisley, "Gogol's 'The Overcoat': A Further Interpretation," ibid., 20 (Summer 1976), 121–129.

20. "How Gogol's 'Overcoat' Is Made," in Maguire, p. 228.

21. Bočarov, p. 230.

22. Bernheimer, p. 59.

23. Hence Gogol's constant tendency to discuss laughter—which confirms successful comic communication and amounts to a bond of complicity between author and reader—rather than comedy itself. See Chapter Nine below.

24. Bernheimer alludes to this symbolism when he observes that the narrator at the very end of the story "has dropped all pretense to authority, whether reliable or unreliable, *and fused with the world he is describing.* He is no longer ignorant or forgetful of it: *the world itself is forgetful, mad, fantastic, discontinuous*" (p. 59; my italics). This refusal of narrative authority leaves readers free to interpret the story variously, but it does impose certain broad constraints which themselves

suggest an overarching theme: the moral dilemma in one's reaction to intellectually, psychologically and culturally "insignificant" people when neither fellow feeling nor indifference is quite tenable.

7. Dead Souls: The Mirror and the Road

1. Annenkov, who was particularly close to Gogol in these years, explains the increasingly inflated solemnity in his texts, epistolary and artistic, not as psychological aberration but as the direct product of his feeling of accomplishment as a writer. See P. V. Annenkov, "Gogol' v Rime letom 1841 goda," in his *Literaturnye vospominanija*, ed. B. M. Ejxenbaum (Leningrad, 1928), pp. 118–133.

2. Cf. his fears that readers of the first German translation would misinterpret the book (XIII, 30), and his comment on the German translator's preface which emphasized "merciless satire": "That is the best view a foreigner can have of these matters" (XIII, 61).

3. Senkovsky reviewed *Dead Souls* along with ten other books—among them *Cold Water as an Everyday Remedy*, *General Anatomy*, *On the Indentification and Cure of Aneurisms*, and *Practical Exercises in Physics*—greeting each in turn as "a poema"; see V. V. Gippius, ed., *N. V. Gogol': Materialy i issledovanija*, I (Moscow-Leningrad, 1936), 245–246. Senkovsky's own reference to "Epics (*Poemy*) in prose, that is, Novels, Tales, Stories, satirical and descriptive works of all sorts," is in his "Brambeus i junaja slovesnost'," *Biblioteka dlja čtenija*, no. 3, 1834, 37.

4. Shevyryov compared Gogol's similes with those of Dante in his review of *Dead Souls*, reprinted in V. Zelinskij, comp., *Russkaja kritičeskaja literatura o proizvedenijax N. V. Gogolja*, 2nd ed., II (Moscow, 1902); see esp. pp. 14–18. Herzen perceived a more general parallel; see the diary entry for 29 July 1842 in his *Sobranie sočinenij v 30-i tomax*, II (Moscow, 1954), 200. See also A. N. Veselovskij, "Mertvye duši," in his *Etjudy i xarakteristiki*, 3rd ed., (Moscow, 1907), pp. 675–676. Jurij Mann summarizes and comments on this material in his article, "O žanre *Mertvyx duš*," *Izvestija Akademii Nauk SSSR, Serija literatury i jazyka*, vol. 31, no. 1, 1972, 12–16, adding the Mandelstam reference (see next note).

5. "Razgovor o Dante," in Osip Mandel'štam, *Sobranie sočinenij v dvux tomax*, ed. G. P. Struve and B. A. Filippov, II (New York: Inter-Language Literary Associates, 1966), 426.

6. Dante Alighieri, *The Divine Comedy*, trans. Charles S. Singleton, *Inferno* (Princeton: Princeton University Press, 1970), canto III, pp. 27, 29.

7. See Ju. M. Lotman, "Problema xudožestvennogo prostranstva v proze Gogolja," *Učenye zapiski Tartuskogo gosudarstvennogo universiteta*, no. 209, 1968, 47.

8. Nabokov suggests a formal function for the "lyrical outbursts [which are not] really parts of the solid pattern of the book": they represent, he says, "those natural interspaces without which the pattern would not be what it is." *Nikolai Gogol* (Norfolk: New Directions, 1944), p. 107.

9. Ibid., pp. 75–77. Cf. Iraklij Andronikov, "Odna stranica," in his *Ja xoču rasskazat' vam . . .* (Moscow, 1962), pp. 291–298.

10. Jurij Mann makes somewhat different use of the phrase; see his article, "O poetike *Mertvyx duš*," in D. Ustjužanin, comp., *Russkaja klassičeskaja literatura: Razbory i analizy* (Moscow, 1969), pp. 195ff.

11. See Nabokov's comments and translation in his *Gogol,* pp. 86–89.

12. "Čičikov ili Mervye Duši Gogolja," 1842; reprinted in *Sočinenija i perepiska P. A. Pletneva,* I (St. Petersburg, 1885), 493; my italics.

13. On these seasonal anomalies see Jurij Mann, "O poetike *Mertvyx duš,*" pp. 190–191; and Andrej Belyj, *Masterstvo Gogolja* (Moscow-Leningrad, 1934), pp. 83ff.

14. Belyj, p. 103.

15. In such works as M. B. Xrapčenko, *"Mertvye duši" Gogolja* (Moscow, 1952) and E. S. Smirnova-Čikina, *Poema N. V. Gogolja "Mertvye duši": Literaturnyj kommentarij* (Moscow, 1964) literary curiosity is strait-jacketed by ideology. This is somewhat less true of A. A. Elistratova, *Gogol' i problemy zapadnoevropejskogo romana* (Moscow, 1972), but the author's efforts to situate Gogol's novel in continental literature prevent her from dwelling sufficiently on its unique qualities. James B. Woodward's *Gogol's Dead Souls* (Princeton: Princeton University Press, 1978) became available too late to be taken into account here.

16. Abram Terc [Andrej Sinjavskij], *V teni Gogolja* (London: Collins, 1975), pp. 378–379.

17. Jurij Mann comes to similar general conclusions, though he follows Gippius (*Gogol',* pp. 150–151) in giving primary emphasis to the politically dissident elements in the story. His account is interesting in this connection for noting the germ of the tale in Derzhavin's poem, *Vel'moža,* and for citing one of the folk songs about the brigand Kopeikin. See his *Smelost' izobretenija: Čerty xudožestvennogo mira Gogolja* (Moscow, 1975), chap. 7. esp. pp. 101–102 and 108ff.

18. Cf. A. De Jonge, "Gogol," in John Fennell, ed., *Nineteenth-Century Russian Literature; Studies of Ten Russian Writers* (London: Faber & Faber, 1973), pp. 124–125.

19. Henri Bergson, "Laughter," in *Comedy,* ed. Wylie Sypher (Garden City: Doubleday Anchor Books, 1956), p. 80; "Jazykov i Gogol'," in *Polnoe sobranie sočinenij knjazja P. A. Vjazemskogo,* II (St. Petersburg, 1879), 315.

20. Innokentij Annenskij, "Estetika *Mertvyx duš* i ee nasled'e," *Apollon,* no. 8, 1911, 51–52. An English version of this article, entitled "The Aesthetics of Gogol's *Dead Souls* and Its Legacy," may be found in *Twentieth-Century Russian Literary Criticism,* ed. Victor Erlich (New Haven and London: Yale University Press, 1975).

21. Ibid.

22. The independent life of words as such in this book has been examined in English by Nabokov and, more broadly, by Simon Karlinsky, whose observation this is; see the latter's "Portrait of Gogol as a Word Glutton, with Rabelais, Sterne and Gertrude Stein as Background Figures," *California Slavic Studies,* no. 5, 1970, 169–186. Karlinsky marshals the evidence so well that I have not sought to go over the same ground here. His emphasis, however, is more on Gogol's verbal "appetite" than on questions of rationale and function.

23. "Letter to Can Grande della Scala," in George Rice Carpenter, ed., *A Translation of Dante's Eleven Letters . . . by Charles Sterrett Latham* (Boston and New York: Houghton-Miflin, 1891), p. 194 n1.

24. S. A. Vengerov, *Pisatel'-graždanin. Gogol'* (St. Petersburg, 1913), p. 139. On this phrase see also Jurij Mann, "O poetike *Mertvyx duš,*" pp. 187ff; and Belyj,

Masterstvo Gogolja, p. 82. Smirnova mentioned criticism of the phrase by the poet Tiutchev and others to Gogol in a letter of 3 November 1844 (*Russkaja starina,* vol. 60, no. 10 [1888], 133), but he ignored the matter in his reply, noting only: "I myself don't know what kind of soul I have, Ukrainian (*xoxlackaja*) or Russian" (XII, 419).

25. Annenskij, "Estetika *Mertvyx duš,*" p. 51.

26. N. M. Pavlov, "Gogol' i slavjanofily," *Russkij arxiv,* no. 1, 1890, 145.

27. See Terc, *V teni Gogolja,* p. 129.

28. Roland Barthes, *The Pleasure of the Text,* trans. Richard Miller (New York: Hill and Wang, 1975), p. 65.

29. Annenskij, "Estetika *Mertvyx duš,*" p. 53.

30. See Americo Castro's seminal essay, "Incarnation in *Don Quixote,*" with its argument that "the basic theme of *Don Quixote* is life as a process creative of itself," in Stephen Gilman and Edmund King, eds., *An Idea of History: Selected Essays of Americo Castro* (Columbus: Ohio State University Press, 1977). Castro's work contains invaluable material for the serious comparative study of the two books that still remains to be written.

8. Confronting a Public, II

1. Gogol explained the publication differently, as a kind of training for the continuation of his novel. See his letter to Shevyryov of 28 February 1843 (XII, 143).

2. On the Homeric element, see Carl R. Proffer, *The Simile and Gogol's 'Dead Souls'* (The Hague: Mouton, 1967). On the revision in general see the interesting arguments of L. K. Dolgopolov, who treats the second version as part of Gogol's preparation for continuing *Dead Souls.* Dolgopolov emphasizes particularly Gogol's search for "the ideal of the free man," the ideal Russian community, and the role of faith in such a community; "Gogol' v načale 1840x godov ('Portret' i 'Taras Bul'ba': Vtorye redakcii v svjazi s načalom duxovnogo krizisa)," *Russkaja literatura,* no. 2, 1969, 82–104.

3. Botkin: letter to Kraeyvsky, 16 March 1842, quoted in V. F. Egorov, "V. P. Botkin—literator i kritik," *Učenye zapiski Tartuskogo gosudarstvennogo universiteta,* no. 139, 1963, 45; Pletnyov: letter to Grot, 1 April 1842, in *Perepiska Ja. K. Grota s P. A. Pletnevym* (St. Petersburg, 1896), I, 512. See also Vasilij Gippius, *Gogol'* (Leningrad, 1924), pp. 115–119; Lucy·Vogel, "Gogol's *Rome,*" *Slavic and East European Journal,* 11, no. 2 (1967), 145–158; and Sigrid Richter, *Rom und Gogol': Gogol's Romerlebnis und sein Fragment "Rim"* (Hamburg, 1964). In a later article Gippius stresses the syncretic significance of the work, noting how "*Rome* opened no new creative avenues, [rather] comprising a not always organic combination of heterogeneous elements characteristic of the various periods of Gogol's writing" (*Ot Puškina do Bloka* [Moscow-Leningrad, 1966], p. 157). For a more sympathetic view of *Rome,* see G. M. Fridlender, "O povesti N. V. Gogolja 'Rim'," in *Ot "Slova o polku Igoreve" do "Tixogo Dona"* (Leningrad, 1969), pp. 334–342. For Gogol's own—highly dubious—explanation of the basic idea in *Rome,* see his letter to Shevyryov of 1 September 1843 (XII, 211).

4. Not quite fully, however; he made no effort to salvage the attempts, over

nearly a decade, to produce a serious drama untinged by comedy. In 1832–33 he had begun some sort of melodrama evidently paralleling his fictional homage to the *école frénétique* (V, 446), and in 1835 he undertook *Alfred,* a drama from Anglo-Saxon history. A drama based on Ukrainian history, completed in 1839–40, was destroyed after Zhukovsky fell asleep during a reading.

5. V. V. Gippius, "Dramaturgija Gogolja," in *Klassiki russkoj dramy* (Moscow-Leningrad, 1940), p. 135: Gippius claims that one of the fragments, "The Servants' Quarters" (*Lakejskaja*), furnished the germ for Tolstoy's comedy, *The Fruits of Enlightenment* (p. 136). For an interesting discussion of the fragments, see Simon Karlinsky, *The Sexual Labyrinth of Nikolai Gogol* (Cambridge: Harvard University Press, 1976), pp. 153–158.

6. On the evolution of this project, see A. L. Slonimskij, "Istorija sozdanija *Ženit'by* Gogolja," in *Russkie klassiki i teatr* (Moscow, 1947), pp. 307–334.

7. Apollon Grigoriev seized on precisely this primitivism to interpret Podkolyosin as a travestied and trivialized Hamlet, one Gogolian exhibit among many serving to attack the inflated self-image of the contemporary Russian—as if to say, "You are not a Hamlet, you are a Podkolyosin." "Gogol' i škola sentimental'nogo naturalizma," in V. F. Sadovnik, ed., *Sobranie sočinenij Apollona Grigor'eva,* no. 7 (Moscow, 1915), 62.

8. *Repertuar i panteon,* no. 6, 1843, "Kritika," 96–101; quoted in V, 475.

9. V. G. Korolenko, *Istorija moego sovremennika,* bk. 1, ch. 27, in *Sobranie sočinenij v desjati tomax,* V (Moscow, 1954), 277.

10. Henceforth the bulk of his writing was devoted to seeking these links. In addition to *Selected Passages,* one might cite as example his dramatized tract, "The Denouement of *The Inspector General*" (*Razvjazka Revizora*).

11. B. Ejxenbaum, "Literatura i pisatel'," *Zvezda,* no. 5, 1927, 131.

12. The incident is reported, with illuminating commentary, in chap. 23 of P. V. Annenkov, "Zamečatel'noe desjatiletie," in his *Literaturnye vospominanija,* ed. B. M. Ejxenbaum (Leningrad, 1928); this work is available in English as *The Extraordinary Decade,* ed. Arthur P. Mendel (Ann Arbor: University of Michigan Press, 1968).

13. This vacillation can be seen throughout his revealing article, "O Sovremennike" (1846), VIII, 421–431. The end result, as formulated by Annenkov, was that "the idea of society begins to be hidden from the man who first discovered it and felt it in himself—and this disastrous isolation Gogol takes for lofty success, growth in stature, a great moral superiority. Then of its own accord the need appears to solve problems and literary tasks by means of specters and phantoms." P. V. Annenkov, "Gogol' v Rime letom 1841 goda," in his *Literaturnye vospominanija,* p. 147.

14. Anonymous review in *Vedomosti S.-Peterburgskoj gorodskoj policii,* nos. 48, 50, and 51 (16, 23, 27 June 1842). The quotation is from no. 48; depending on a copy kindly handwritten out for me by Sergei Belov, I am unable to cite page numbers.

15. Nikolaj P. Barsukov, *Žizn' i trudy M. P. Pogodina,* 22 vols. (St. Petersburg, 1888–1910), VI, 228–229.

16. Letter of 21 October 1842; in V. I. Šenrok, *Materialy dlja biografii N. V. Gogolja,* 4 vols. (Moscow, 1892–1898), IV, 54–55. *The Northern Bee* persisted in

seeing Gogol as a simple joker and concluded that the book presented "a special world of scoundrels which never existed or could have existed." Moreover, it found "the whole *poema* written in an astonishingly tasteless language and in a regrettable tone." (V. Zelinskij, comp., *Russkaja kritičeskaja literature o proizvedeni-jax N. V. Gogolja,* 3rd ed., II [Moscow, 1903], 34). Senkovsky, whose jibes at Gogol's subtitle have already been cited, echoed Bulgarin with many exclamation points and found a fitting analogue in the work of Paul de Kock. Polevoy, still attached to the Gogol of the Ukrainian stories, saw *Dead Souls* as "a slander on man and on Russia." "How much filth there is in the poem!" he writes, concluding that Gogol is related to Paul de Kock and Dickens, but even worse than they (ibid., I, 195, 204). And Professor Grot, a distinguished philologist, wrote his friend Pletnyov in July 1844: "For the displeasure at the reading of Chichikov, you yourself are at fault. You should not have tried to read it in a salon, in the presence of ladies. There's no end of talent in it, but it's a bit on the dirty side (*grjaznen'ko*)" (*Perepiska Ja. K. Grota s P. A. Pletnevym* [St. Petersburg, 1896], I, 566).

17. Letter of 24 October 1842; in *M. S. Ščepkin. Zapiski. Pis'ma. Sovremen-niki o M. S. Ščepkine,* comp. A. P. Klinčin (Moscow, 1952), p. 190.

18. "Čičikov ili Mertvye Duši Gogolja," *Sočinenija i perepiska P. A. Pletneva,* I (St. Petersburg, 1885), 480–481, 483.

19. Zelinskij, II, 2, 14.

20. Annenkov (1928), pp. 368–369. See, for more detail, chap. 22 of *The Re-markable Decade.*

21. Quoted in Gippius, *Gogol',* p. 155.

22. For an interpretative survey of such reactions, see D. N. Ovsjaniko-Kuli-kovskij, "Ljudi 40-x godov i Gogol'," in his *Istorija russkoj intelligencii,* I (Moscow, 1908), 205–233.

23. Samarin's letter to K. S. Aksakov (1842): *Russkij arxiv,* no. 2, 1880, 300–302. In this sense there is justice in Trotsky's remark that after Gogol's work "reality began to live a second life in Russia, in both the realistic novel and comedy." "Gogol: An Anniversary Tribute" (1902), in Irving Howe, ed., *The Basic Writings of Trotsky* New York: Random House, 1963), p. 318.

24. Annenkov (1928), pp. 140–141.

25. Ibid., p. 380.

26. See Freud's essay "On the Antithetical Sense of Primal Words" (1910), in Sigmund Freud, *Collected Papers,* IV (London, 1948), 189ff.

27. The censor Nikitenko seems to have shared the manuscript freely, with the result that rumors proliferated about Gogol's alleged madness, his having become a Jesuit, and so on; the speculation about Chichikov that seized the town of N. in *Dead Souls,* Shevyryov wrote, now had its counterpart in life. For details, see his letter to Pletnyov of 6 November 1846 in *Perepiska Ja. K. Grota s P. A. Pletnevym,* II, 962ff. On 18 January 1847 Pletnyov reported that the book had sold out in two weeks, not from any improvement in public taste, "but from curiosity and conflicting rumors" (ibid., III, 9).

28. Gippius, *Gogol',* p. 170.

29. VIII, 321; this article was prohibited by the censor in the first edition, along with "On the Need to Love Russia," "On the Need To Travel about Rus-

sia," "Terrors and Horrors of Russia," and "To One Who Occupies an Important Position." Gogol's full text, however, circulated widely in manuscript and seems to have been known to most of those who commented on the book.

30. "Pis'ma Nikolaja Filipoviča Pavlova k Nikolaju Vasil'eviču Gogolju," reprinted from *Moskovskie Vedomosti*, 1847, in *Russkij arxiv*, no. 1, 1890, 287–288; my italics.

31. This needs to be understood, as M. Gershenzon has pointed out, in light of Gogol's tendency to see Christ as subtle psychologist and expounder of the laws of spiritual life—which for Gogol were also the laws of social existence; see his *Istoričeskie zapiski (O russkom obščestve)* (Moscow, 1910), p. 100.

32. D. Merežkovskij, *Gogol'. Tvorčestvo, žizn' i religija* (St. Petersburg, 1909), p. 168; quoted in F. Ja. Prijma, "Bolee čem spornaja sxema," *Russkaja literatura*, 1969, no. 2, 112. O. S. Aksakova, quoted in S. T. Aksakov, *Istorija moego znakomstva s Gogolem* (Moscow, 1960), p. 166.

33. Cf. Chaadayev's "First Philosophical Letter," published in *The Telescope* in 1836: "Look around you. Does it not seem that we are all unable to stay in our places? We all have the look of travellers. No one has a defined sphere of existence; proper habits have not been worked out for anything; there are rules for nothing; there is not even a domestic hearth; there is nothing which might serve as attachment or awaken sympathy or love in you, nothing lasting, nothing constant; everything flows on, everything passes, leaving no trace either without or within. We are as if billeted in our own houses; with our families we have the air of being foreigners; in our cities we seem nomads—and even more so than those nomads who pasture their flocks on our steppes, for they are more strongly attached to their wilderness than we are to our cities." M. Geršenzon, *P. Ja. Čaadaev. Žizn' i myšlenie* (St. Petersburg, 1908), p. 208.

34. Letter to Pletnyov, 20 March 1847, in *Perepiska Ja. K. Grota s P. A. Pletnevym*, III, 9. Gogol's view is singular but not unique. The young Dostoevsky in a letter of 1840 had found Homer "parallel to Christ": "In the Iliad, after all, Homer gave the whole ancient world an organization for both spiritual and earthly life with absolutely the same force as Christ did for the new." F. M. Dostoevskij, *Pis'ma*, I (Moscow, 1928), 58.

35. "Auto-da-fé": from *Sanktpeterburgskie vedomosti*, quoted by Apollon Grigoriev, *Sobranie Sočinenij Apollona Grigor'eva*, ed. V. F. Sadovnikov, "Gogol' i ego 'Perepiska s druz'jami'" no. 8 (Moscow, 1910), 5. Botkin: letter to Annenkov, 28 February 1847, quoted in Barsukov, VIII, 579.

36. V. G. Belinskij, "Pis'mo k N. V. Gogolju," *Polnoe sobranie sočinenij*, X (Moscow, 1956), 212, 217.

37. Annenkov (1928), p. 582.

38. G. O. Berliner, "Černyševskij i Gogol'," in V. V. Gippius, ed., *N. V. Gogol': Materialy i issledovanija* (Moscow-Leningrad, 1936), II, 488.

39. S. Ševyrev, "Vybrannye mesta iz perepiski s druz'jami N. Gogolja," *Moskvitjanin*, no. 1, 1848, "Kritika," 29.

40. Cf. Gogol's own testimony on this point, in a letter to Smirnova of 28 December 1844: "When I returned to Russia [my Moscow friends] welcomed me with open arms. Every one of them, engaged in literary work . . . awaited me . . . in the certainty that I would share his thoughts and ideas, would sup-

port and defend him against the others, considering this the first condition and act of friendship, and quite unaware . . . that these demands, apart from their absurdity, were even inhuman . . . Moreover, each of them was so sure of the rightness and truth of his ideas that he considered anyone who disagreed with him as nothing less than a backslider from truth. I leave it to you to judge what my position was among people of that sort! . . . I will only note that among my literary friends something like jealousy began to appear: each of them began to be suspicious that I had let another take his place, and, hearing from afar about my new acquaintances and how people they did not know had begun to praise me, they increased their demands still further, citing as reason the length of our acquaintance" (XII, 435–436).

41. The imagery recurs constantly in the writing of this period; see, e.g., XIII, 263, 370. Compare his remark to Smirnova in Rome that no one had written history as it should be written, with the exception of Muratori, who "alone understood how to describe a people"; the others, Gogol said, "fail to find any connection of man with that land on which he has been set . . . I have always wanted to write a geography; in that geography one would be able to see how to write history." A. O. Smirnova, *Zapiski, dnevniki, vospominanija, pis'ma,* ed. M. A. Cjavlovskij (Moscow, 1929), p. 321.

42. L. N. Tolstoj, "O Gogole," *Polnoe sobranie sočinenij,* XXVI (Moscow, 1936), 874.

43. *Sobranie sočinenij Apollona Grigor'eva,* no. 8, p. 15.

44. See Roland Barthes, "The Death of the Author," in Sally Sears and Georgiana W. Lord, eds., *The Discontinuous Universe: Selected Writings in Contemporary Consciousness* (New York: Basic Books, 1972), pp. 7–12; and Georges Poulet, "Phenomenology of Reading," *New Literary History,* I (October 1969), 54–55.

45. Letter to Grot, 27 November 1846, in *Perepiska Ja. K. Grota s P. A. Pletnevym,* II, 860.

46. Aleksej Remizov, *Ogon' veščej: Sny i predson'e* (Paris: Oplešnik, 1954), p. 32.

47. "La Question la plus profonde (I)," *Nouvelle revue française,* 96 (December 1960), 1084.

48. Letter of A. O. Smirnova to Gogol, 10 December 1846; *Russkaja starina,* vol. 67, no. 8 (1890), 281–282. Her remarks here concern reactions to Gogol's moral-symbolic reinterpretation of *The Inspector General* in his "Denouement of *The Inspector General,*" but they apply equally to *Selected Passages.*

49. "The tragedy of a genre": see M. M. Baxtin, *Voprosy literatury i estetiki* (Moscow, 1975), p. 471. Compare Maurice Blanchot: "L'idée d'une vocation (d'une fidélité) est la plus perverse qui puisse troubler un libre artiste. Même et surtout en dehors de toute conviction idéaliste (où cette idée s'apprivoise alors plus facilement), nous la sentons près de chaque écrivain comme son ombre qui le précède et qu'il fuit, qu'il poursuit, déserteur de lui-même, s'imitant lui-même ou, pis, imitant l'idée inimitable de l'Artiste ou de l'Homme qu'il veut spectaculairement donner." *Le Livre à venir* (Paris: Gallimard, 1959), p. 126.

50. V. A. Sollogub, *Vospominanija* (Moscow-Leningrad, 1931), p. 380; my italics.

9. The Goglian Universe: Notes Toward a Theory

1. N. N. Straxov, "Ob ironii v russkoj literature," in his *Zametki o Puškine i drugix poetax* (Kiev, 1897), p. 180.

2. The best recent work on the subject constitutes a partial exception; see, for example, Ju. Lotman, "Istoki 'tolstovskogo napravlenija' v russkoj literature 1830-x godov," *Učenye zapiski Tartuskogo gosudarstvennogo universiteta,* no. 119, 1962, 47ff.

3. On this last point, see Robert C. Elliott, *The Power of Satire: Magic, Ritual, Art* (Princeton: Princeton University Press, 1966). To Elliott's view of satire as magical aggression, Matthew Hodgart offers a crucial, if speculative, qualification: "But this only raises the question: why is the word considered to be magical? The answer may be simply that the word is magical *because of* its satirical, that is, its literary power. A curse, like all other literary forms, is effective just as far as it is well composed, in compelling rhythms, skilful rhetoric, relevant argument and true content—which are among the normal criteria for all good literature . . . In this view, written word *precedes* magic in history: the proven power of the word to cause acute shame and demoralisation led to the attribution of magic powers to the word." *Satire* (London: Weidenfeld and Nicolson, 1969), pp. 17–18.

4. Alexander Slonimsky, citing Jean-Paul Richter and summarizing the views of Volkelt, in his *Texnika komičeskogo u Gogolja* (Petrograd, 1923), pp. 7–8. I have followed Robert Maguire's excellent translation ("The Technique of the Comic in Gogol," in *Gogol from the Twentieth Century,* pp. 324–325), substituting only "ideas" for his "concepts" (*predstavlenija*): Slonimsky's monograph is perhaps the best treatment of its subject in any language. On English humor see Harry Levin's "Introduction" to *Veins of Humor* (Cambridge: Harvard University Press, 1972); and Stuart M. Tave, *The Amiable Humorist* (Chicago: University of Chicago Press, 1960).

5. In Maguire, p. 336. Lotman strengthens the point when he notes that "gaiety for Gogol is something much more significant than what is usually understood by that word; it is a creative state of the soul" ("Istoki 'tolstovskogo napravlenija', p. 56).

6. Andrej Belyj, *Masterstvo Gogolja* (Moscow-Leningrad, 1934), p. 16.

7. Sinyavsky on Gnostic myths: Abram Terc, *V teni Gogolja* (London: Collins, 1975), p. 136. Gogol's advice: see above, p. 89. Friedrich Schlegel: "On Incomprehensibility," in *Lucinde and the Fragments,* trans. Peter Firchow (Minneapolis: University of Minnesota Press, 1971), p. 260.

8. *Gogol* (New Haven and London: Yale University Press, 1969), p. 221. See also the remarkable article of S. G. Bočarov, "O stile Gogolja," in Ja. E. El'sberg, ed., *Tipologija stilevogo razvitija novogo vremeni* (Moscow, 1976), pp. 409–445.

9. *Masterstvo Gogolja,* p. 5; see also pp. 218–235 and passim.

10. Compare Vasily Rozanov: "There is style as language. But there is as well the style of a human soul and, corresponding to that, the style of a complete body of work that issues from that soul. What is style? A level (*plan*) or spirit embracing all details and subordinating them to itself . . . The style of an author is a particular molding of language or the character of the subjects he has chosen for incarnation; finally, it is the manner of treating those subjects, connected with

the spirit of the author and fully expressing that spirit." "Gogol'," *Mir iskusstva*, no. 12, 1902, 337.

11. The phrase is Suzanne Langer's and the philosophical argument too complex to summarize here. One paragraph, however, may illuminate the matter at hand:

An artistic symbol—which may be a product of human craftsmanship, or (on a purely personal level) something in nature seen as "significant form"—has more than discursive or presentational meaning: its form as such, as a sensory phenomenon, has what I have called "implicit" meaning, like rite and myth, but of a more catholic sort. It has what L. A. Reid called "tertiary subject-matter," beyond the reach of "primary imagination" (as Coleridge would say) and even the "secondary imagination" that sees metaphorically. "Tertiary subject-matter is subject-matter imaginatively experienced *in* the work of art . . . something which cannot be apprehended apart from the work, though theoretically distinguishable from its expressiveness" (*Philosophy in a New Key* [New York: New American Library, 1948], p. 213). Pasternak appears to make the same point through the ruminations of Yuri Zhivago: "I have long thought that art is not the name for a category or a realm covering numberless concepts and exfoliating phenomena, but on the contrary, that it is something discrete and concentrated, the designation of a principle that is present in every work of art, the name for a power brought to bear or a truth worked out in it in each case. And I have never seen art as an object or aspect of form, but rather as a mysterious and hidden part of content" (*Doktor Živago* [Ann Arbor: University of Michigan Press, 1959?], pp. 290–291).

12. *V teni Gogolja*, p. 323.

13. See Donald Fanger, "Dickens and Gogol: Energies of the Word," in Harry Levin, ed., *Veins of Humor* (Cambridge: Harvard University Press, 1972), esp. pp. 141–145.

14. See Innokentij Annenskij, "O formax fantastičeskogo u Gogolja," *Russkaja škola*, 1890, II, bk. 10, p. 100.

15. See V. V. Vinogradov, *Etjudy o stile Gogolja* (Leningrad, 1926); reprinted in his *Izbrannye trudy: Poetika russkoj literatury* (Moscow, 1976), esp. pp. 230–268.

16. I have borrowed these terms from Gerald Holton's *Thematic Origins of Scientific Thought: Kepler to Einstein* (Cambridge: Harvard University Press, 1973). Holton speaks of themata as "fundamental preconceptions of a stable and widely diffused kind" (p. 24), and refers to "an a priori commitment that deserves to be called thematic" (p. 25). Though he is concerned with scientific rather than literary creation and analysis, the parallels are frequently striking, as in his observation that "both nature and our pool of imaginative tools are characterized by a remarkable parsimony at the fundamental level, joined by fruitfulness and flexibility in actual practice" (p. 29).

17. Innokentij Annenskij, "Nos (K povesti Gogolja)," in his *Kniga otraženij*, I (St. Petersburg, 1906), 3–14.

18. Dmitry Chizhevsky, "About Gogol's 'Overcoat,'" in Maguire, p. 302.

19. George Sańtayana, "Carnival," in his *Soliloquies in England and Later Soliloquies* (New York: Charles Scribner's Sons, 1923), p. 142.

20. See Bočarov, "O stile Gogolja," esp. pp. 440–445, for a discussion of the

disparity between the hierarchies of meaning in Gogol's words on the one hand, and the world to which they relate on the other. There is, as Bočarov notes, more than simple play at work here; the disparity itself carries the main thematic charge, suggesting by its stressed recurrence the utopian restoration of the lost harmony embracing words and things, utterance and meaning.

21. *V teni Gogolja*, p. 179.

22. P. V. Annenkov, *Literaturnye vospominanija* (Leningrad, 1928), p. 117.

23. V. Šklovskij, "Žanry i razrešenie konfliktov," *Voprosy literatury*, no. 8, 1965, 96.

24. These are particularly striking in the notebooks for the last chapter, where Gogol addresses the Russian plain as "my fathomless depth and breadth," and asks: "Is there anywhere god or man who can tell me what I feel when I fasten my gaze on these motionless and immovable seas, these steppes that have lost their limits? . . . Ooh, with what awesome power does [the road] embrace the majestic space! What broad strength and sweep has entered into me (*Kakaja širokaja sila i zamaška zaključilas' vo mne*)! How the mighty thoughts carry me! Holy power! to what distant regions! to what glittering, wondrous, far-off place, unknown to earth? What is happening to me? Am I human? . . . And how wondrously strange is the road itself!" V. I. Šenrok, "Očerk istorii teksta pervoj časti *Mertvyx duš*," *Sočinenija N. V. Gogolja*, 10th ed., N. Tixonravov (vols. 1–5) and V. I. Šenrok (vols. 6–7) eds., vol. 7 (St. Petersburg, 1896), 563–564.

25. The same point is made by Lotman at the conclusion of his detailed analysis of "artistic space" in Gogol's prose. "The second volume of *Dead Souls*," he writes, "presents a completely different and essentially non-Gogolian scheme of spatial relations, markedly distinct from all the previous prose." Ju. M. Lotman, "Problema xudožestvennogo prostranstva v proze Gogolja," *Učenye zapiski Tartuskogo gosudarstvennogo universiteta*, no. 209, 1968, 50.

26. Ibid.

27. A free rendering of Annensky's phrase, "*vostorg dorožnyx sozercanij*"; see his "Estetika *Mertvyx duš* i ee nasled'e," *Apollon*, no. 8, 1911, 50. Gogol's mother seems to confirm such a suggestion when she asks in a letter to Shevyryov "whether [Gogol] didn't imagine that the same thing might happen that happened in Rome when, at death's door, he burned the work of five years and by God's will recovered and wrote it all, as he thought, in a better form; he must surely have thought that this time, too, the same could happen." *Literaturnoe nasledstvo*, vol. 58 (Moscow, 1952), 763.

28. Surprisingly little attention has been paid to this problem, though an impressive body of misreading, based on the assumption that his personages can be spoken of in conventional biographical and psychological terms, exists to underline the need. An outstanding exception is the article of Petr Bicilli, "Problema čeloveka u Gogolja," *Godišnik na Sofijskija Universitet*, Istoriko-filologičeski Fakultet, XLIV, 4 (1947–48), 3–31.

29. Ibid., p. 6.

30. E. H. Gombrich and E. Kris, *Caricature* (Hammondsworth: Penguin, 1940), p. 13.

31. The poet Blok finds Poprishchin's cry, "Save me! Take me up!", to be "the cry of Gogol himself in the grip of creative torment." "Ditja Gogolja," in

Aleksandr Blok, *Sobranie sočinenij v vos'mi tomax,* V (Moscow-Leningrad, 1962), 377.

32. See especially his account of one Popov, a former house serf of Plyushkin's, as brilliantly rendered by Nabokov in his *Nikolai Gogol* (Norfolk: New Directions, 1944), pp. 102–103.

33. *V teni Gogolja,* p. 526.

34. See P. G. Bogatyrev, "O vzaimosvjazi dvux blizkix semiotičeskix sistem (Kukol'nyj teatr i teatr živyx akterov)," *Učenye zapiski Tartuskogo gosudarstvennogo universiteta,* no. 308, 1973, 306–329. Bogatyrev does not discuss Gogol, but his remarks about the doubleness of perception in the puppet theater can easily be applied to Gogol's personages, who are apprehensible at once as verbal caricatures and as semblances of real people. One must not be too categorical about this—Khlestakov, Chichikov, and the other surrogate figures clearly are based on other principles—but the analogy does cover the the characters surrounding them, allowing these to be seen not as mimetic representations of monomaniacs or solipsists, but as figures who are limited by the very design of their construction.

35. The point is made by Jurij Mann, "O poetike *Mertvyx duš*," in D. Ustjužanin, comp., *Russkaja klassičeskaja literatura: Razbory i analizy* (Moscow, 1969), p. 199; Mann's word is "fantasticality," but he uses it in a sense that makes it synonymous with the general Gogolian conception of the devil and his work.

36. This compound passage, with ellipses omitted, is assembled from Jean-Paul Sartre, *Being and Nothingness: An Essay in Phenomenological Ontology,* trans. Hazel E. Barnes (New York: Citadel Press, 1965), pp. 238–240. The use to which this formulation is put within Sartre's larger philosophical argument has no bearing on my own. Sartre's translator discusses it elsewhere as an illustration of what she calls "the Medusa complex," summarizing in rather less arcane language: "The Medusa complex represents the extreme fear of the Other's Look. It is my dread of being made helplessly and permanently an object, of being judged, of being labeled and categorized, of being reduced solely to the role which I play in a world for others, of being made a thing—in short, of being petrified. The usual way of fighting back, of course, is to try to make the Other into an object." Hazel E. Barnes, "Greek Mythical Figures as Contemporary Images," *The Key Reporter,* 41 (Summer 1976), 3.

37. A letter to Pletnyov of December 1844 employs this imagery: "God knows what goes on in the depths of a person. The situation may at times be so strange that he is like one in the grip of a lethargic sleep, who sees and hears that all, including the doctors themselves, have pronounced him dead and are preparing to bury him alive in the ground—while he, seeing and hearing all this, has not the strength to move a single muscle." He cites such failure to understand a person as frequently producing a mistaken because premature confidence that in fact he is known through and through. Better, Gogol says, to leave such questions to time, which alone can clarify and resolve them (XII, 387).

10. Sense, Shape, End

1. Alex de Jonge makes the point, citing these examples among others ("Gogol," in John Fennell, ed., *Nineteenth-Century Russian Literature: Studies of Ten*

Russian Writers [London: Faber & Faber, 1973]). His article is noteworthy for being the first, so far as I know, to give prominence to the term, though he applies it rather more narrowly than I have done here.

2. See Suzanne Langer's chapter on "The Comic Rhythm" in her *Feeling and Form* (New York: Charles Scribner's Sons, 1953), pp. 326–350. Her argument for the comic as a form of symbolic vitalism is broadly applicable to Gogol's writing, offering support and extension to Bakhtin's arguments for a Rabelaisian analogy.

3. Georg Simmel, quoted in Kurt H. Wolff, ed., *Georg Simmel, 1858–1918* (Columbus: Ohio State University Press, 1959), p. 34.

4. M. Gofman, "Fol'klornyj stil' Dalja," in B. Ejxenbaum and Ju. Tynjanov, eds., *Russkaja proza* (Leningrad, 1926), p. 232. In such cases, Gofman explains, "the center of gravity is shifted to the way the narration is registered *as such*. The semantic weight of individual words and combinations of words grows and becomes complex; intonational and phonetic factors acquire an unlooked-for importance; the syntactical aspect becomes unusually prominent, etc. *A prose arises in which the style is the main thing.*"

5. In *Razvjazka Revizora* (The Denouement of *The Inspector General*), IV, 121–132.

6. Charles C. Bernheimer, "Cloaking the Self: The Literary Space of Gogol's 'Overcoat,'" *PMLA*, 90, no. 1 (1975), 53.

7. See, for example, his statement in "An Author's Confession": It is necessary that the Russian reader really feel that the character presented to him has been taken precisely from that very body from which he himself has been created [*sic!*], that it is a living thing and his own body" (VIII, 453). Here the separateness of fictive and actual persons seems somewhat in peril; and the beginning of the next sentence ("Then only will he himself merge with his hero") further complicates the question by raising the likelihood that reader, character and writer may ultimately be one and the same in Gogol's unconscious mind.

Index

"A Few Words About Pushkin," 69–72, 150

"After the Play" (*Teatral'nyj raz"ezd*), 83, 184, 195–198

Aksakov, Ivan, on Gogol's death, 4

Aksakov, Konstantin, 165, 203

Aksakov, Sergei, 22, 122

Alfred, 72, 128

Andronikov, Irakly, 173

Annenkov, P. V., 140–141, 199–200, 203, 246, 284nl, 287n12

Annensky, Innokentii, 7, 180, 181, 187, 190, 241, 247

Arabesques, 58–72, 192, 225n

Ariosto, Ludovico, 12n, 167

Aristophanes, 82, 136, 196

Auden, W. H., 15

"Author's Confession, An," 20, 154, 222–224

Bakhtin, M. M., 90, 98, 156

Barthes, Roland, 121

Bashutsky, A. P., 112

Baudelaire, Charles, 231n

Belinsky, V. G., 5, 6, 18, 24, 71, 204; on *Dead Souls*, 165, 203; *Open Letter to Gogol*, 215–216

Bernheimer, Charles, 159

Bestuzhev, A. A. (Marlinsky), 25, 29, 30

Biely, Andrei, 7, 22, 92, 233, 262; on *Dead Souls*, 15, 124, 175, 180

Bitsilli, P. M., 151, 249, 293n28

Blanchot, Maurice, 233, 290n49

Blok, Aleksandr, 7, 262, 293n31

Bocharov, S. G., 161, 244n, 292n20

"Boris Godunov, Pushkin's Poem," 110, 274n22

Botkin, V. P., 193, 215

Bryulov, K. P., 65–67, 193

Bryusov, V., 7, 64

Bulgarin, Faddei, 30, 31, 39–40, 41–42, 87, 118

Byron, George Gordon, Lord, 99, 165

Captain's Daughter, The (Pushkin), 217

Caricature, 14, 19, 20, 236n, 250

"Carriage, The," 72, 122–124, 182

Cervantes Saavedra, Miguel de, 12n, 35, 116–117, 152, 167, 191

Chaadayev, P. Ya., 289n33

Characterization, 68, 90, 132–133, 180–181, 219, 235–236, 249–252, 254

Chekhov, A. P., 20, 23

Chernyshevsky, N. G., 203, 216

Chizhevsky, D., 160

Chudakov, G. I., 12

Collected Works, 192–198

Comedy: in Gogol's view, 81–82, 125–126; in Gogol's practice, 107–108, 161–162; function of, 187, 218–219, 232, 258. *See also* Humor; Irony; Laughter; Satire

Comic, the, *see* Comedy

Contemporary, The, 27, 30, 72, 75, 79

Dahl (Dal'), Vladimr, 30, 201

Dante Alighieri, 165, 167–168, 183

Dead Souls, 72, 76, 122–123, 146, 147, 164–191, 246; public response to, 201–204; preface to second printing, 207–209

Dead Souls, Volume Two, 192, 205–206, 209, 219, 223n

De Jonge, Alex, 294n1

Derzhavin, G. R., 78, 285n17

"Diary of a Madman," 58, 113, 115–118, 127

Dickens, Charles, 12, 231, 238, 288n16

Don Quixote (Cervantes), 152, 191

Dostoevsky, F. M., 4n, 20, 92, 200, 212, 289n34

Driessen, F. C., 94, 238

"Egyptian Nights" (Pushkin), 36

"1834," 171

Eikhenbaum, Boris, 18, 161, 199

Erlich, Victor, 89, 233

Eugene Onegin (Pushkin), 24n, 139, 151–152

Evenings on a Farm Near Dikanka, 53, 85–93, 237, 277n14

"Fair at Sorochintsy, The," 85, 88, 91–92, 125
"Farewell Tale, A," 4n
Fielding, Henry, 85
Flaubert, Gustave, 13, 21n

Gamblers, The, 128, 193, 194–195
Getting Married, 72, 128, 130, 193–194
Gippius, Vasily, 55, 87
Gogol, M. I., 293n27
Gogol, N. V.: memoirs and biographies of, 13, 17–18; life, 14–16, 47, 237, 238–239; as professional writer, 18, 47–48, 53–54, 59, 72, 83, 127, 142, 146–147, 208–209, 222–223, 225; income, 15–16, 53, 147–148, 282n4; knowledge of foreign literature, 12–13, 268n12; problem of directness, 13–14, 209, 212, 268n15; problem of classification, 4–8, 204, 229–233, 235, 262–263; on literature needed in Russia, 206, 209, 218, 221
Grigoriev, Apollon, 155, 204, 216, 287n7
Grotesque, the, 230
Guerney, Bernard, 173

Hanz Kuechelgarten, 49–52, 85
Hegel, G. W. F., 49
Hero of Our Time, A (Lermontov), 24n
Herzen, Aleksandr, 215
Hoffmann, E. T. A., 112, 114, 115, 120, 148
Holquist, James M., 90
Holton, Gerald, 292n16
Homer, 97, 165, 203, 213–214
Humor, 230–232

Inspector General, The, 72, 76, 82, 129–142, 182, 254, 259
Irony, 121, 138, 172, 232–233
"Ivan Fyodorovich Shponka and His Auntie," 93, 182, 238
Ivan Vyzhigin (Bulgarin), 31–32, 39
Ivanov, Vyacheslav, 136
Ivask, George, 21, 66

Jakobson, Roman, 279n44
Joyce, James, 149

Karamzin, N. M., 29, 32–33, 78, 216
Karlinsky, Simon, 17, 238, 247, 277n22, 285n22
Kenner, Hugh, 157n
Kireyevsky, Ivan, 26, 27–28, 32
Kock, Charles-Paul de, 288n16
Korolenko, V. G., 197
Krylov, Ivan, 38, 72, 78
Kuechelbecker, V. K., 42, 107
Kulish, P. A., 17

Langer, Suzanne, 258, 292n11
Laughter, Gogol on, 81–82, 142, 187, 197–198, 283n23
Lawrence, D. H., 15
Lermontov, M. Yu., 24n, 26, 217
LeSage, Alain-René, 31
Library for Reading, The, 43, 61, 62, 72–74, 75–77, 138
"Life," 64
Literature, Russian: forms of, 31–35; language of, 29–30, 41, 44; criticism, 26, 73, 78–79, 203; function of, 27–28, 43–44, 81, 215–216. *See also* Publishing, Russian; Reading public, Russian; Writer, Russian
Little House in Kolomna, The (Pushkin), 120
"Lost Letter, The," 85
Lotman, Yurii, 168, 231n, 247, 291n5
Lovecraft, H. P., 101

MacAndrew, Andrew, 279n38
Mandelstam, O. E., 168
Marlinsky, A. A., *see* Bestuzhev
Marriage, see Getting Married
"May Night, A," 85
McLean, Hugh, 55
"Meditations on the Divine Liturgy," 225n
Melmoth the Wanderer (Maturin), 114
Merezhkovsky, D. S., 7, 212
Mirgorod, 72, 94–110, 238, 245
Mirsky, D. S., 98
Mochulsky, K., 17, 141
Moliére, 85
Moscow Observer, The, 74, 75, 77

Nabokov, Vladimir, 17, 19, 52, 102, 135, 160; on *Dead Souls,* 173, 176
Nadezhdin, N. I., 30, 40

Narezhny, V. T., 31, 89
Nekrasov, N. A., 107
Nemirovich-Danchenko, V. I., 131, 137
Ne to, 209, 212, 214, 233, 257–259
"Nevsky Prospect," 58, 66, 111–113
"Nights at a Villa," 171
Nikitenko, A. V., 59, 288n27
Northern Bee, The, 39, 77, 94, 99–100, 104, 115
"Nose, The," 72, 74–75, 118–122, 182, 238

Odoyevsky, V. F., 26, 30, 34–35, 40, 115
Odyssey, 213–214
"Old-World Landowners," 66, 95, 96–97, 182
"On the Architecture of the Present Time," 59–60, 64
"On the Development of Periodical Literature in 1834 and 1835," 72, 75–79
"On the Middle Ages," 59, 61–62, 63
"Overcoat, The," 21, 153–163, 171

Pavlov, N. F., 30, 211–212
Pelham, or The Adventures of a Gentleman (Bulwer-Lytton), 31
Petersburg Miscellany (1846), 200
"Petersburg Notes for 1836," 80–83
Petersburg Tales, 110–122, 133, 154–155, 182, 245–246
Physiology of Petersburg (1845), 200
Pletnyov, P. A., 27, 54, 58, 86; on *Dead Souls:* 174–175, 181n, 202–203; on *Selected Passages,* 221
Pogodin, M. P., 30, 57
Polevoy, N. A., 25, 30
Poor People (Dostoevsky), 200
"Portrait, The," 58, 113–115, 149, 193
Poshlost', 19, 197
Publishing, Russian, 38–39, 41, 72, 93, 147, 272n56
Pushkin, A. S., 24n, 55, 129, 165, 218; on Gogol's writing, 5, 79, 85, 89, 120, 164; on Russian literature, 25, 26, 29, 34; prose of, 30–32, 217; as professional writer, 36–39; significance for Gogol, 12, 69–72, 141, 150–153, 255, 274n24

Reading public, Russian, 5–6, 35, 37–40, 71–72, 77, 186–187, 214–216, 225
Remizov, Aleksei, 223

Rome, 193
Rozanov, Vasily, 7, 22, 179, 234, 291n10

Samarin, Yurii, 204
Santayana, George, 242
"St. John's Eve," 85, 86–87
Sartre, Jean-Paul, 255–256
Satire, 107, 130, 140, 164–165, 230–231, 291n3
Schlegel, Friedrich, 233
"Schloezer, Mueller, and Herder," 60–61
Scott, Sir Walter, 61, 77, 78, 268n12
"Sculpture, Painting, and Music," 59
Selected Passages from Correspondence with Friends, 4, 209–222, 225n
Senkovsky, Osip, 30, 31, 43–44, 72–73, 75–76, 118, 165
Setchkarev, Vsevolod, 120
Shakespeare, William, 12n, 61, 203
Shchepkin, M. S., 202
Shenrok, V. I., 17
Shestov, Lev, 23
Shevyryov, S. P., 40, 77, 203, 207, 216
Shklovsky, Viktor, 247
Simmel, Georg, 258
Sinyavsky, Andrei (Abram Tertz), 100, 139–140, 171, 176–177, 190, 221n, 233, 244, 251, 259
Skaz, 102–103, 177
Slonimsky, A. L., 160
Smirdin, A. F., 42, 147, 275n26
Smirnova, A. O., 140n, 202n
Sollogub, V. A., 89n, 225
Soul, Goglian usage, 67–69, 168, 172, 178–179, 189
Stasov, V. V., 61–63
Stendhal, 168
Sterne, Laurence, 29, 120, 231
"Story of How Ivan Ivanovich Quarreled with Ivan Nikiforovich," 95, 102–108, 182
Strakhov, N. N., 230
Style, see Author

Taras Bulba, 66, 95, 97–100, 192–193, 237
"Terrible Vengeance, A," 66, 93, 237–238, 255n
Tertz, Abram, *see* Sinyavsky
"Textbook of Literature for Russian Youth," 156n, 166
Themata: defined, 239, 292n16; metamorphosis, 240–242; evasion, 242–247;

Themata: defined (*Continued*)
  identity, 247–252; recognition, 252–256
Tolstoy, L. N., 8, 20, 49, 102, 212, 217, 220
Turgenev, I. S., 131n

Venevitinov, D. V., 25
Veresayev, V. V., 17
Vinogradov, Viktor, 120, 234, 268n16
"Viy," 66, 95, 100–102
Vladimir of the Third Class, 72, 127
Vyazemsky, P. A., 5, 25, 36, 40, 41, 78;
  on *Dead Souls,* 180

Woe from Wit (Griboyedov), 126
"Woman," 53, 252
Writer, Russian, 35–39, 41–42, 147, 198, 200, 215, 216, 222, 271n36

Yazykov, N. M., 200

Zagoskin, M. N., 34, 125, 147
Zhukovsky, V. A., 35–36, 54, 78, 147;
  translator of *Odyssey,* 213–214; on Russian attitude to laughter, 231n